Post - Impressionists

Masterworks

Cézanne, Gauguin, Manet, Seurat, Van Gogh & Their Contemporaries

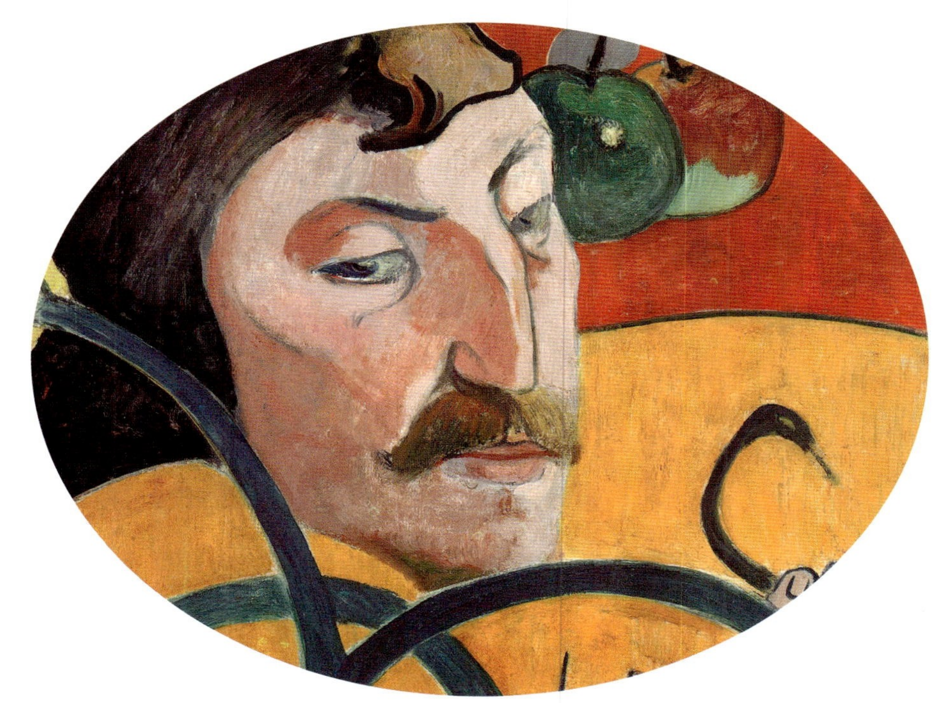

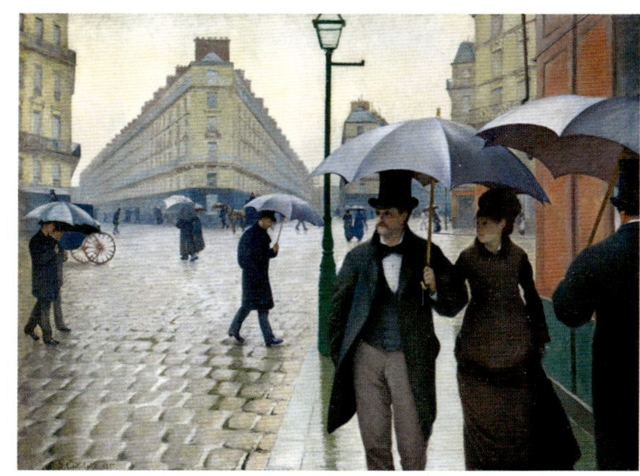

Publisher and Creative Director: Nick Wells
Commissioning & Project Editor: Victoria Marshallsay
Senior Project Editor: Catherine Taylor
Art Director: Mike Spender
Layout Design: Jane Ashley
Copy Editor: Ramona Lamport
Proofreader: Dawn Laker

FLAME TREE PUBLISHING
6 Melbray Mews
Fulham, London SW6 3NS
United Kingdom

www.flametreepublishing.com

First published 2017

17 19 21 20 18
1 3 5 7 9 10 8 6 4 2

A CIP record for this book is available from the British Library upon request.

ISBN 978-1-78664-542-5

Printed in China | Created, Developed & Produced in the United Kingdom

Post-Impressionists
Masterworks
Cézanne, Gauguin, Manet, Seurat, Van Gogh & Their Contemporaries

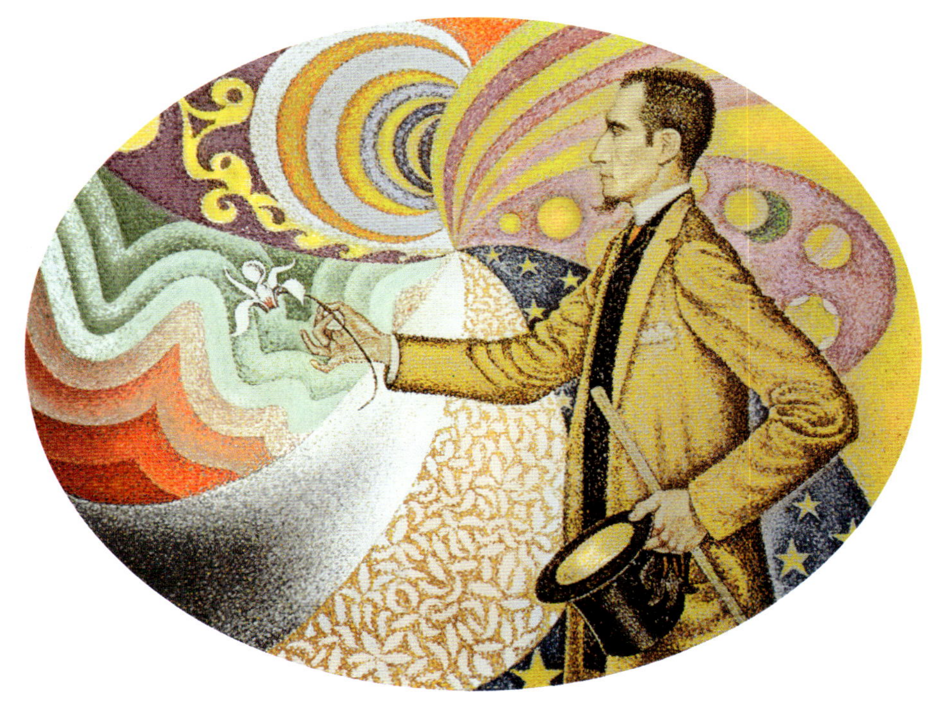

Samuel Raybone

Foreword by Dr Gavin Parkinson

FLAME TREE
PUBLISHING

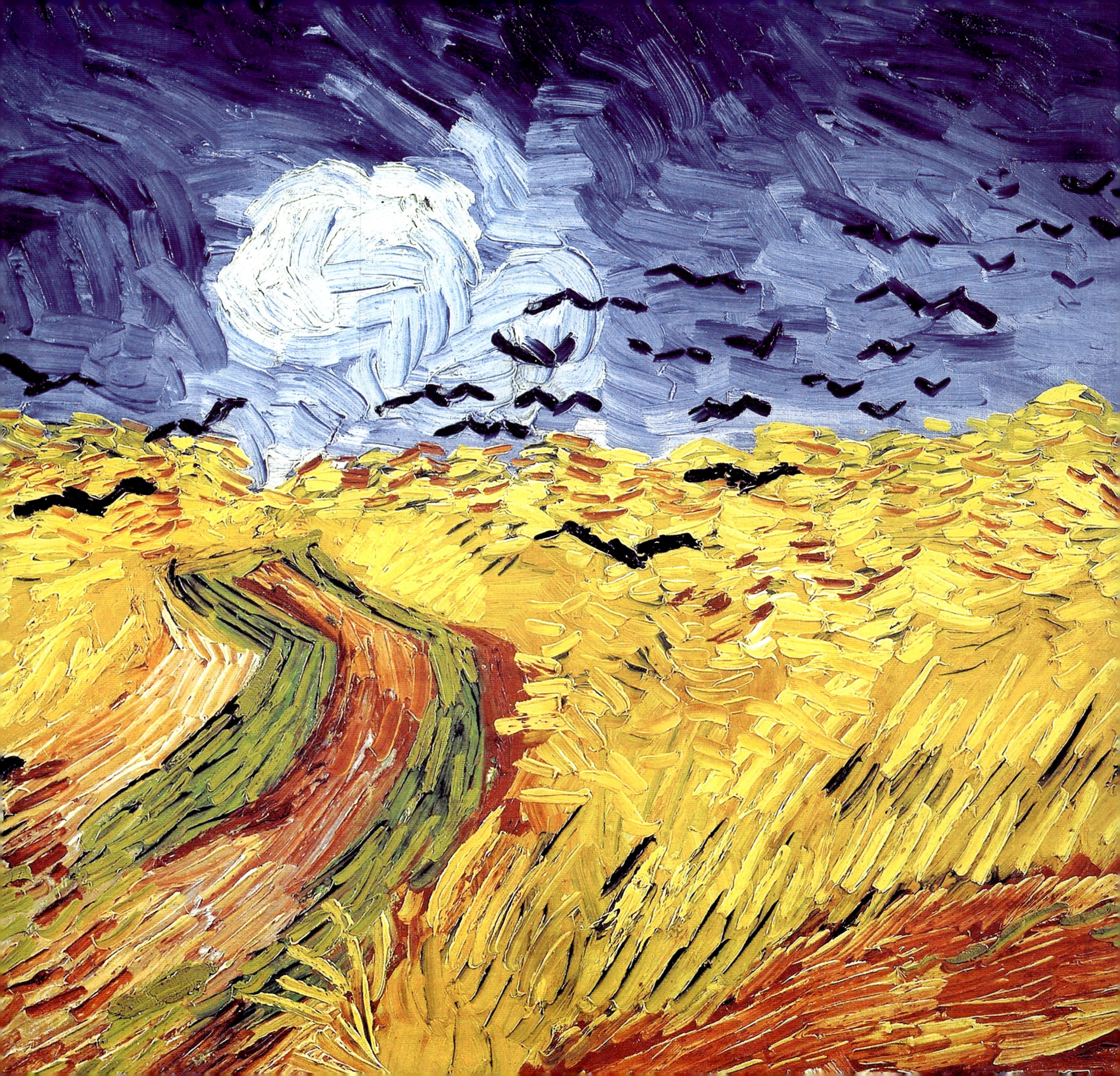

Contents

Foreword

THE TERM 'Post-Impressionism' was a retrospective one introduced reluctantly by the English painter and art critic Roger Fry in 1910 to rationalize the curatorial primacy he gave Paul Cézanne, Paul Gauguin and Vincent van Gogh in the exhibition *Manet and the Post-Impressionists* held at the Grafton Galleries in London.

Fry was seeking to characterize the artists who rejected or departed from the styles or subjects of the Impressionists, or who carried certain elements from that revolutionary movement on to new terrain, such as a preoccupation with colour theory or pictorial structure. His term was taken up in Britain and America and more rarely in France. It became especially useful in the 1920s and 1930s when Impressionism was eclipsed by 'Post-Impressionism' in the eyes of art historians as the founding moment of modern art. This historical narrative was constructed very effectively by the Museum of Modern Art in New York, which opened its programme with the extremely successful exhibition *Cézanne, Gauguin, Seurat, van Gogh* in 1929. At the time of the museum's 1936 exhibition, *Cubism and Abstract Art*, a diagram was created showing all of twentieth-century art up to then tumbling mainly out of the achievements of Cézanne, Gauguin, Seurat and Van Gogh.

After the Second World War, Impressionism underwent a reassessment, thanks partly to the global success of US Abstract Expressionism, for which paternity was sought mainly in the work of Claude Monet. Several of the Impressionists had shown together and were close friends, which helped make it seem like a coherent movement; however, this only confirmed that there had been no 'post-impressionist' movement and that the term tended to give a misleading suggestion of agreement among artists (stylistic, methodical, critical, generally intentional or other) when that was only available here and there. The art historian John Rewald demonstrated hesitancy and caution when using the term in his landmark study *Post-Impressionism: From Van Gogh to Gauguin* in 1956, where the key artists are three of the four (minus Cézanne because of his slightly later prominence among artists and dealers). Although Rewald agreed that 'Post-Impressionism' was 'not a very precise term,' he concluded that it is 'certainly a very convenient one,' while the hierarchy was so beyond dispute in Europe and America by then that Robert Goldwater could lead out his 1957 monograph on Gauguin with the apparently incontestable declaration that the artist was one of '[t]he four fathers of modern painting.' Nevertheless, as late as 1979, Alan Bowness could assert that 'no serious comprehensive history of post-impressionism has been written, and perhaps none can be written because the unity of an artistic movement is quite simply lacking.'

Both Rewald and Bowness have since been taken to task for being joint contrivers of the simplifying-by-chronologizing habits of modernist art history. However, the term 'Post-Impressionism' continues to have currency because more recent art historians such as Belinda Thomson have offered conciliatory reappraisals of the term, criticizing it for implying a unity on art after Impressionism that did not exist while maintaining the value of its signposting usage. Its tenacity and continued serviceability can be witnessed in various studies of the art of the period and exhibition titles in the twenty-first century.

One of the strengths of this book by Samuel Raybone is that it aims to show continuity and development as well as change and departure between Impressionism and what came 'after' (though it should be borne in mind that Impressionists such as Monet and Edgar Degas outlived the 'four fathers' whose achievements came later). Experimentation with colour and paint, a fascination with *Japonisme* and radical politics are all to be found among artists of both generations. On the other hand, the taste for the 'primitive,' an investigation of symbolic language, an interest in esotericism and a profound preoccupation with pictorial structure seem to mark a break with Impressionism. Raybone examines these themes deftly and insightfully in this excellent introduction to the subject.

Dr Gavin Parkinson

Senior Lecturer in 20th-century European Art, The Courtauld Institute of Art

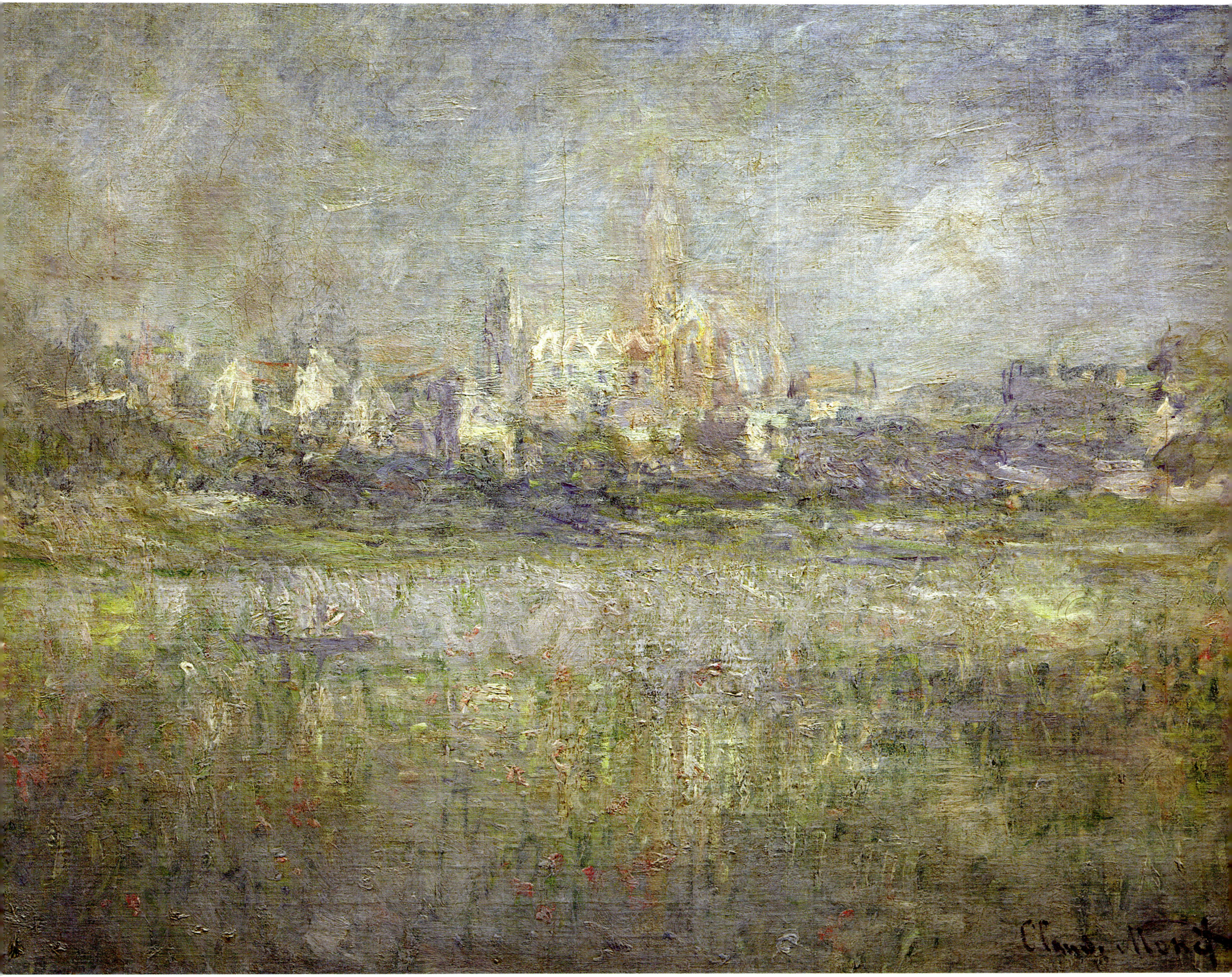

Above : *Vétheuil in the Fog*, 1879, Claude Monet (1840–1926)

Introduction

'**O**N OR ABOUT December 1910 human character changed. … All human relations have shifted – those between masters and servants, husbands and wives, parents and children. And when human relations change there is at the same time a change in religion, conduct, politics, and literature.'

Manet and the Post-Impressionists

With these words, Virginia Woolf (1882–1941) marked the arrival of Post-Impressionism in London. Between 8 November 1910 and 11 January 1911, the Grafton Galleries played host to an exhibition curated by painter and critic (and fellow Bloomsbury Group member) Roger Fry (1866–1934), entitled *Manet and the Post-Impressionists*. The major part of the show comprised over 30 works by Paul Gauguin (1848–1903), 20 by Vincent van Gogh (1853–90), 21 by Paul Cézanne (1839–1906), and eight oils and pastels by Édouard Manet (1832–83). Smaller numbers of works by the Neo-Impressionists Georges Seurat (1859–91), Paul Signac (1863–1935) and Henri Edmond-Cross (1856–1910), Symbolists Maurice Denis (1870–1943) and Paul Sérusier (1864–1927), as well as works by Pablo Picasso (1881–1973) and Henri Matisse (1869–1954) were also included.

However suspicious we might be of Woolf's celebratory hyperbole – contained within her 1924 essay on the nature of modernism, *Mr. Bennett and Mrs. Brown* – which charts a society and culture turned upside-down by the dizzying newness of modernity, she was not alone in reacting strongly to Fry's exhibition. What was, perhaps, unusual was her positivity. Where Woolf saw new forms of art that matched new forms of life, the critic of the *Pall Mall Gazette* saw 'the output of a lunatic asylum'.

Roger Ross, writing in the *Morning Post*, likewise felt that the exhibition was 'of no interest except to the student of pathology and the specialist in abnormality'. Even the superintendent of Bedlam asylum, T.B. Hyslop, was drafted in to offer his diagnosis of these maligned artists. In an essay entitled 'Post-Illusionism and the Art of the Insane' published in 1911 in the periodical *The Nineteenth Century and After*, Hyslop offered his opinion that '[c]ertain of the insane … lose … the power of giving adequate expression to what is actually perceived. Thus the pathological process underlying reversion to a primitive type of simulation of barbaric art is frequently characteristic of brain degeneration'.

Whilst such accusations made implicit, and rather hurtful, reference to the fact that Roger Fry's wife Helen Coombe was, at that moment, suffering from mental illness, the general point of contention seemed to be that the artists exhibiting under the banner of 'Post-Impressionism' lacked the observational acuity, technical aptitude and temperamental fortitude requisite for the production of great art. Unable to translate their perception of nature into art, artists like Gauguin, Van Gogh and Cézanne were accused instead of subjecting their viewers to the abnormal, barbaric and pathological vagaries of their inner minds.

'Post' Impressionism

Given the title of the exhibition, it was perhaps inevitable that Impressionism would be the yardstick against which this new generation of artists would be measured (and, as it transpired, measured rather harshly). However, the application of this moniker was itself somewhat arbitrary. As Desmond MacCarthy, the secretary of the exhibition, reported 35 years later in *The Listener*:

> *Roger and I and a young journalist who was helping us with publicity met to consider [… the title for the exhibition]. Roger first suggested various terms such as 'Expressionism', which aimed at distinguishing these artists from the Impressionists, but the journalist wouldn't have that or any of his*

alternatives. At last Roger, losing patience, said 'Oh, let's just call them Post-Impressionists. At any rate, they came after the Impressionists.'

The difficulty encountered by Roger Fry, Desmond MacCarthy and the unnamed journalist in agreeing a name perhaps points to the wide variety of the assorted painters. Indeed, there was not a coherent Post-Impressionist movement or style to draw from; unlike their Impressionist predecessors, Cézanne, Gauguin, Van Gogh, Seurat and the others had tended to work alone (or together only fleetingly), did not all share the same dealer and did not routinely exhibit together.

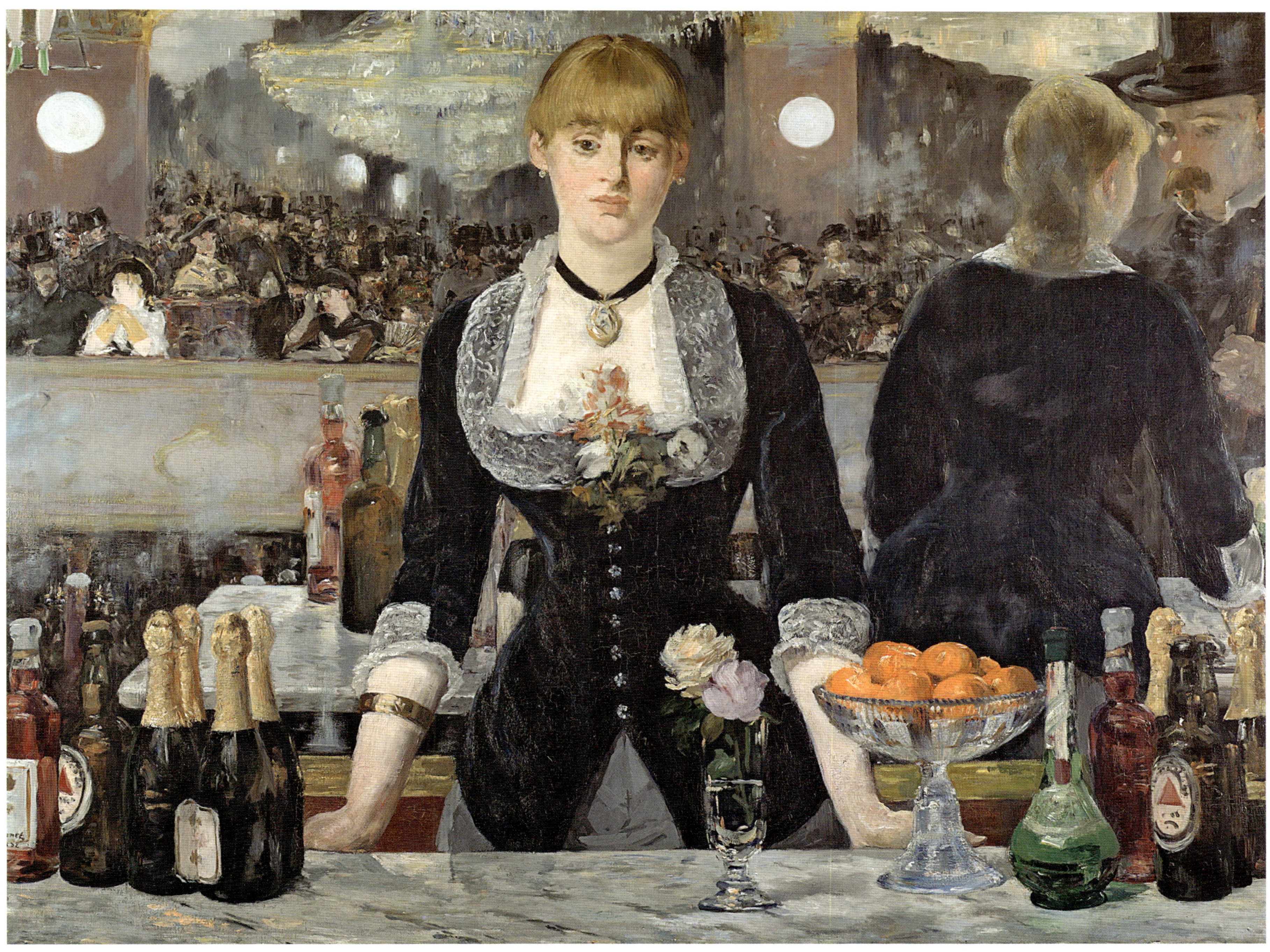

Above : *A Bar at the Folies-Bergère*, 1882, Édouard Manet (1832–83)

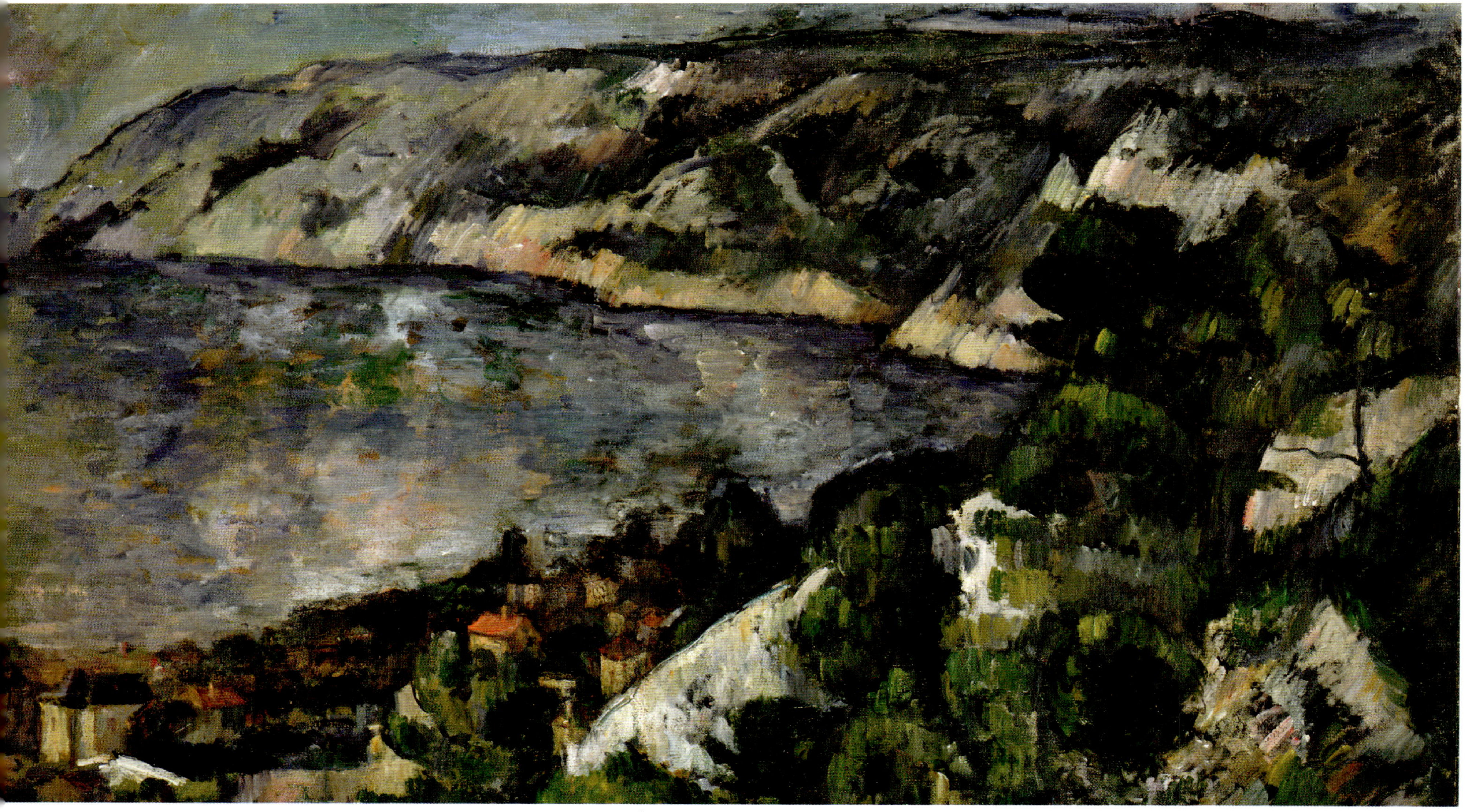

Connections

What was the through line connecting exhibited works as diverse as Manet's *A Bar at the Folies-Bergère* (1882, *see* page 9), Cézanne's *Viaduct at L'Estaque* (c. 1883, *see* page 19), Gauguin's *Breton Women Chatting* (1886) or *Spirit of the Dead Watching (Manao tupapau)* (1892, *see* page 21), Van Gogh's *Wheatfield with Crows* (1890, *see* page 23) or *La Berceuse* (1889, *see* page 22), and Seurat's *The Lighthouse at Honfleur* (1886, *see* page 19)? How could one connect Manet's spatially complex but nevertheless carefully observed scene of Parisian modernity – in which the disjuncture between the perspective of the scene and that reflected in the mirror plays off against the

naturalistic palette, accurate modelling and psychological ambiguity – with the expressive (almost violent) brushwork, pulsating palette and dense symbolism of Van Gogh's Auvers wheatfield? How could one relate Seurat's precise and systematic application of dots of pure pigment across the canvas surface – arranged according to scientific principles of colour and perception so as to most accurately describe the visual experience of the lighthouse at Honfleur – to Gauguin's exotic and strange Tahitian allegory, with its deliberately crude forms, rough texture and intense, unnaturalistic colours? Given that the rationale for their being exhibited together was a shared quality of having come 'after' the Impressionists, then perhaps examining in more detail what had come 'before' might provide the answer.

Above : *The Bay at L'Estaque*, 1879–83, Paul Cézanne (1839–1906)

Continuity and Change

Indeed, Fry himself had tried to balance the visitor's experience of continuity with, and change from, the past. In the first room of the exhibition, Fry intermingled 14 paintings by Cézanne with eight late works by Manet, meaning that nearly every canvas in the room had been produced in the 1870s and 1880s. Cézanne's quiet landscapes, such as *The Bay at L'Estaque* (1879–83, *see* left), animated by intense harmonies of green and blue, were shrewdly juxtaposed against Manet's equally colourful *A Bar at the Folies-Bergère* and *Young Woman in a Round Hat* (*c.* 1877–79, *see* right). Manet's feathered brushwork, most evident in the latter, likewise paired well with Cézanne's disconnected strokes of paint.

Each painting reads as a record of an existing place and time, be it the enticing enigma of a fashionable woman, caught at a glance as one moves through the bustling streets of the metropolis, or the more studied landscapes of Provence. While vivid, the colours of Manet and Cézanne nevertheless have a degree of realism to them; the brushwork in each relates to the experience of seeing: the blur of modernity or the slower and more introspective study of the landscapist. Each of them seemed to share a fundamental belief that painting and observation went hand-in-hand, that art was, above all, a matter of optics. It was thus reassured that the visitor proceeded into the other three rooms of the gallery, in which Cézanne's landscapes reappeared but in altogether stranger company amongst Gauguin's primitive Tahitian scenes, Seurat's regimented and prismatic dots and Van Gogh's emotionally expressive colours.

Post 'Impressionism'

The ostensibly stable ground created by the juxtaposition of Cézanne and Manet thus depended not only on certain formal similarities, but also the perception of a shared ethos on 'art': that it should, at its most basic level, be the accurate filtration of nature through the senses of the artist. In many ways, this perceived ethos was the legacy of Impressionism.

Impressionism was a movement in painting, founded in 1874 with the exhibition of a group of artists calling themselves 'the Anonymous Society of Painters, Sculptors, Printmakers, etc.', whose members included, among others, Claude Monet (1840–1926), Edgar Degas (1834–1917), Camille Pissarro (1830–1903), Berthe Morisot (1841–95) and Pierre-Auguste Renoir (1814–1919). In the seven further exhibitions that followed, the last taking place in 1886, they were joined by artists such as Gustave Caillebotte (1848–94) and Mary Cassatt (1844–1926), as well as some of the so-called Post-Impressionists, including Cézanne, Gauguin and Seurat. As with the 'Post-Impressionist' exhibition, there was no coherent or unified aesthetic programme to which every artist subscribed. Rather, they were unified by their shared rejection of the official Salon (the annual and highly prestigious government-sanctioned and juried exhibition, a painter's best opportunity for public exposure and official recognition) in favour of independent group shows, and their cultivation of private patrons rather than government commissions.

Above : *Young Woman in a Round Hat, c. 1877–79, Édouard Manet (1832–83)*

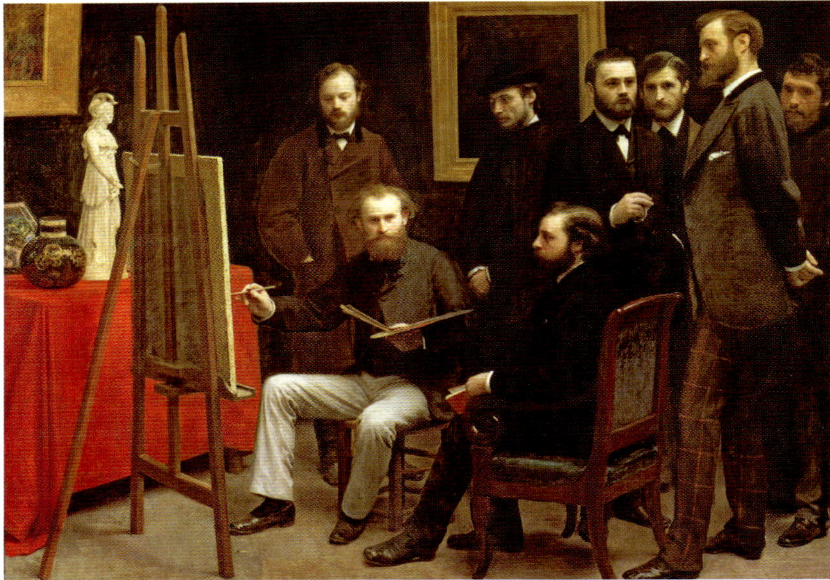

Manet and the Impressionists

Where Fry's exhibition had implicitly positioned Manet as the forefather of Post-Impressionism, his paintings had also been influential for the Impressionists. An 1870 painting by Henri Fantin-Latour (1836–1904) depicts, crowded into *A Studio in the Batignolles Quarter* (*see* above), the milieu of painters and writers who attached themselves to the person and legacy of Édouard Manet (shown at his easel). These include the Impressionist painters Renoir, Frédéric Bazille (1841–70) and Monet, the Naturalist writer Émile Zola (1840–1902), and the painter, poet and art critic Zacharie Astruc (1833–1907). This desire on the part of a younger generation of artists to align themselves with Manet rested on his status as a painter of modern life, a reputation based on his innovative and intensely controversial attempts to haul painting out of – as he saw it – the mire of staid Academic traditionalism to confront directly the changed and changing facts of modern life.

In paintings such *Music in the Tuileries Gardens* (1862, *see* above right), Manet proposed a radically new conception of what art should do in the age of modernity. The painting depicts a fashionable crowd gathered in the Tuileries Gardens near the Louvre to hear a band play. Rather than a grand

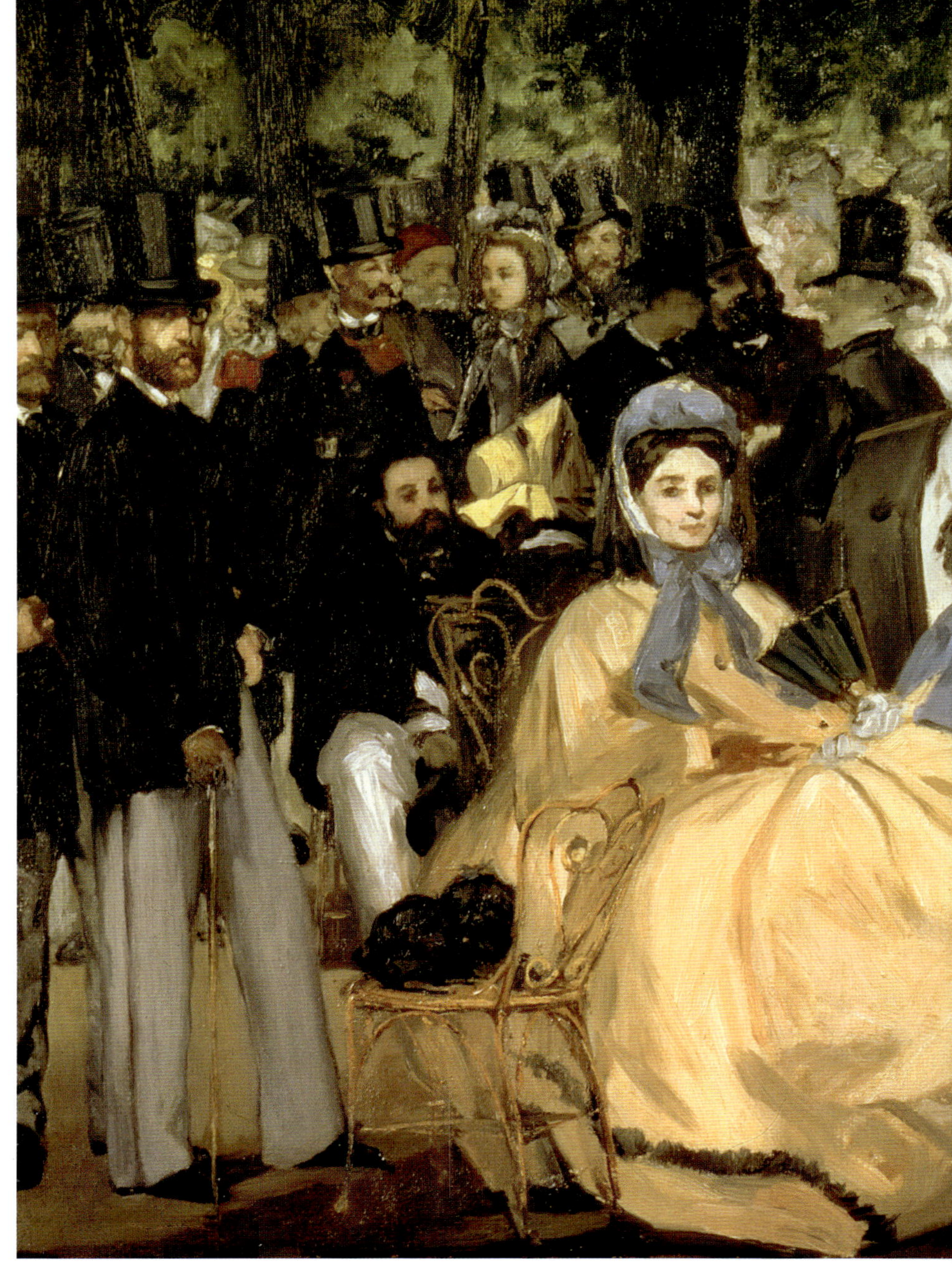

allegory or heroic historical narrative, Manet instead depicts the hubbub of modern Parisian life, of leisure and pleasure in the new city. Manet includes himself in the painting, standing on the very left edge, seemingly between the world of the painter and the world in the painting. Beside Manet stand his brother Eugène and friend Albert, Comte de Balleroy; seated nearby is Astruc, a staunch defender of Manet in the press who was to reappear in the group portrait painted by Fantin-Latour, who is himself pictured looking out at us next to the large tree in the centre of the left half of the canvas. Leaning on this tree in a brown suit is the critic Théophile Gautier (1811–72), with the

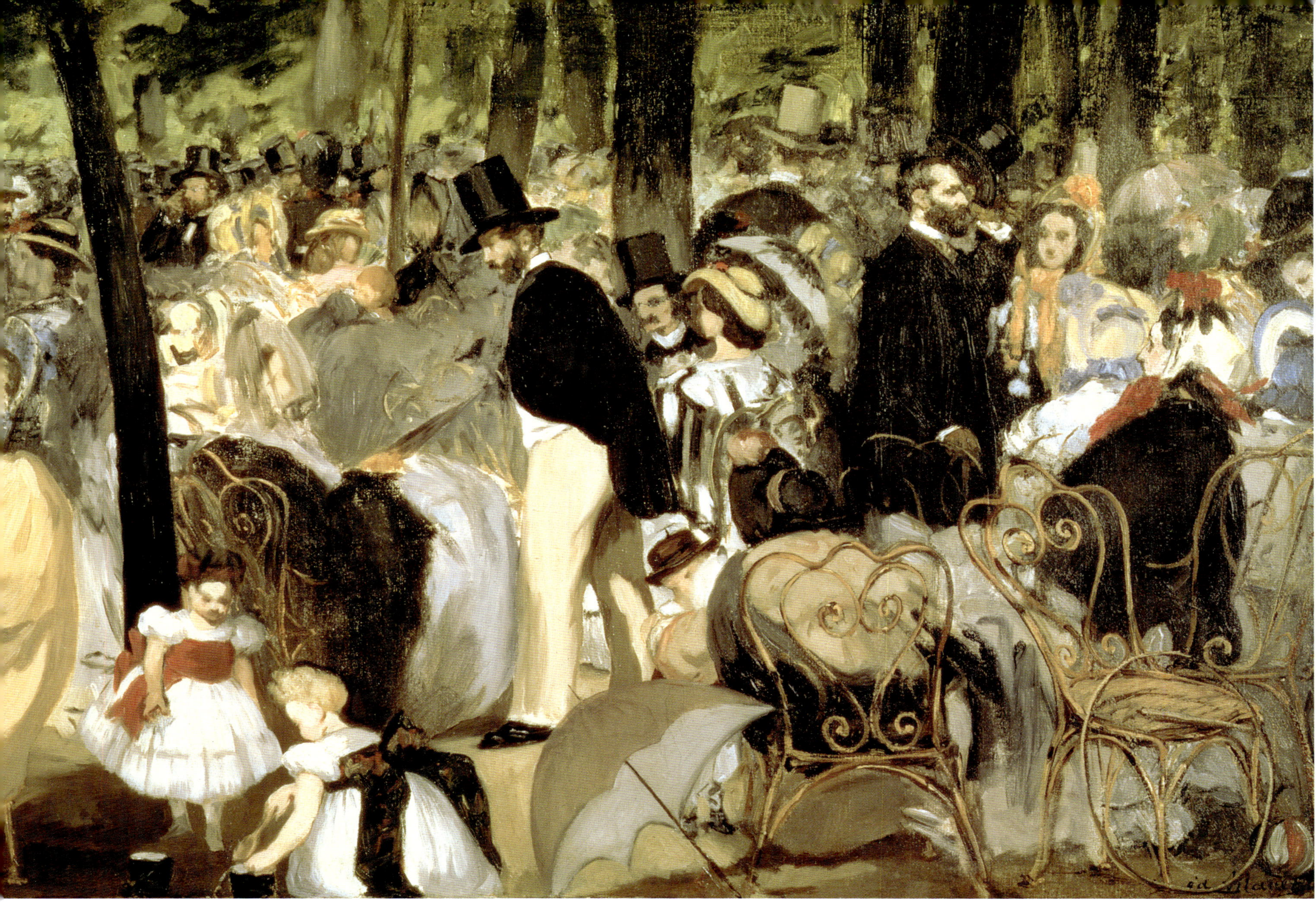

poet Charles Baudelaire (1821–67) to his left. Through a series of portraits intermixed with the crowd, Manet thus introduces us to the bourgeois artistic and literary intelligentsia of Paris in the 1860s, of which he was a part.

Haussmannization

Between 1853 and 1870, the city of Paris was radically transformed by a grand engineering project, known as Haussmannization, after its architect Baron Haussmann. Jealous of his European rivals, Emperor Napoléon III (r. 1852–70) commissioned Haussmann to thoroughly modernize Paris. Haussmann swept away the tangle of narrow, medieval streets in favour of long, wide boulevards with rows of homogenous apartment blocks. New parks, squares and fountains were created, gas lighting installed, trees planted and sewers dug.

Central Paris became the playground of the bourgeoisie, a city of uniform apartment buildings, café-concerts (such as that depicted by Manet in *A Bar at the Folies-Bergère*), restaurants and shops. These new spaces facilitated new, public

Above : *Music in the Tuileries Gardens*, 1862, Édouard Manet (1832–83)

forms of leisure: strolling, people-watching and shopping. Even, as Mary Cassatt's 1878 *In the Lodge* (*see* below) illustrates, going to the opera became a public affair, where seeing the fashionable crowd and being seen by them in turn was as much a part of the spectacle as the act itself.

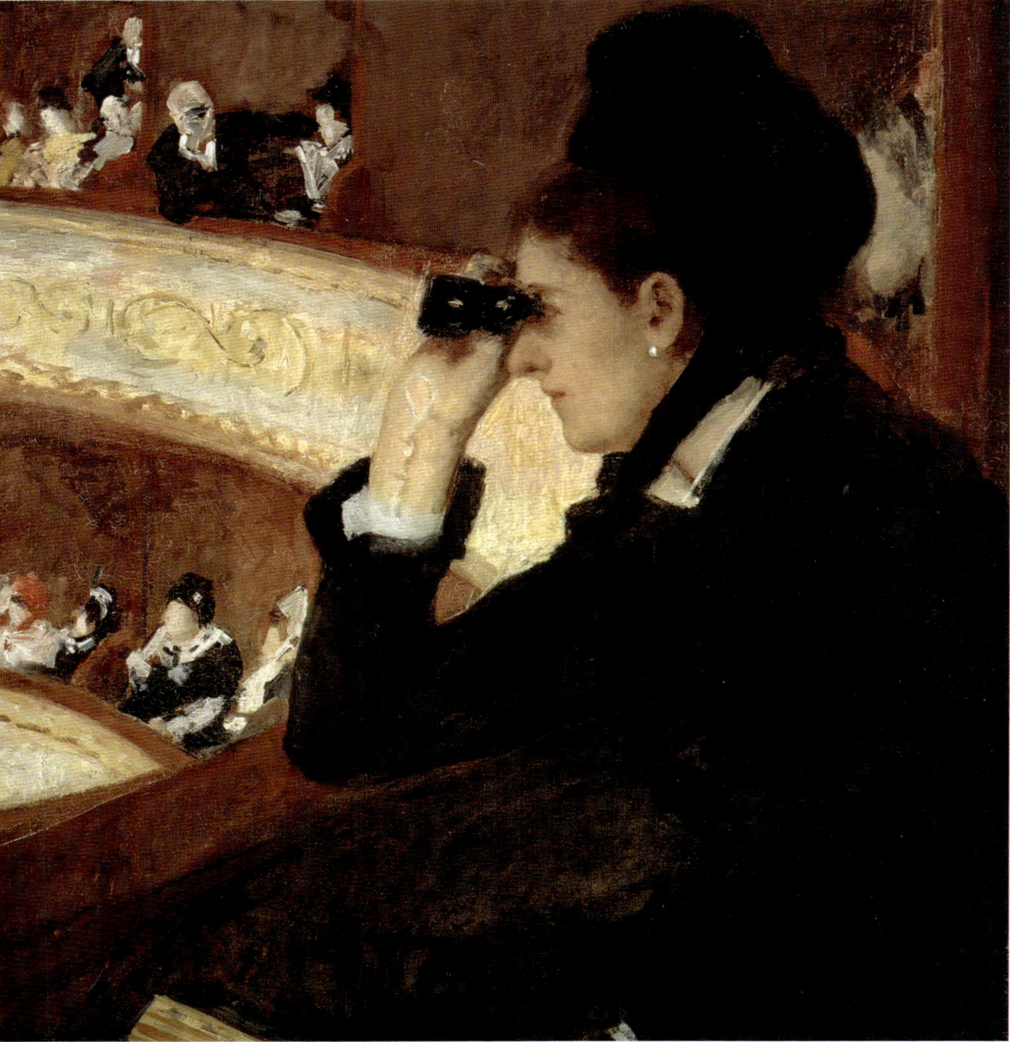

'The Painter of Modern Life'

Charles Baudelaire had very recently given literary form to the belief he shared with Manet on the virtue of painting modern life. In an 1863 essay entitled 'The Painter of Modern Life', Baudelaire argued that modern life, specifically the new spaces and leisure opportunities afforded by the transformed city, was the only

suitable subject for art. The artist must wander aimlessly but observantly through these spaces, always on the alert for a passing motif.

Baudelaire's name for the practitioner of such aimless wandering was a *flâneur*: a 'passionate spectator' who effortlessly blended in with the crowd whilst at the same time observing and recording his impressions of it:

> *The crowd is his element, as the air is that of birds and water of fishes. His passion and his profession are to become one flesh with the crowd. For the perfect flâneur, for the passionate spectator, it is an immense joy to set up house in the heart of the multitude, amid the ebb and flow of movement, in the midst of the fugitive and the infinite…. The spectator is a prince who everywhere rejoices in his incognito.*

The modern artist, as characterized and admired by Baudelaire, then, is the man in the crowd who filters through his 'acute, magical perception' visual impressions of urban life that contain suggestions of profound universal insights. That is to say, one who absorbs and critically analyses the multiplicitous sensoria of the city to produce a work of art that communicates the more profound truth hidden behind the sheen of mere perception. At the core is the physical act of walking and of looking; art is the movement between ephemeral perception and more eternal beauty or truth – between the 'fugitive and the infinite'.

Returning to *Music in the Tuileries*, we can discern the profound effect the ideas of his friend Baudelaire had on Manet's sensibility. Manet positions himself as a *flâneur*, right at the edge of the frame, half-in and half-out of the throng, observing yet immersed in a crowd enjoying that most ephemeral of the arts: music. Individual figures are picked out, yet dissolve into the crowd. Manet's looser brushwork accentuates this oscillation between detail and overall impression; his sketchy style connotes a passing glance that takes in both the 'fugitive and the infinite'. Manet's figures are strung out horizontally across a shallow picture space, as if on display as a microcosmic representation of society.

Above : *In the Lodge*, 1878, Mary Cassatt (1844–1926)

Manet's formal innovations – his unposed, frieze-like composition; his loose, sketchy brushwork, and his realistic modelling of flattened forms and abrupt transitions between light and shade – are leveraged for a singular purpose. More than simply representing a new form of modern life, Manet wanted to recreate, in the experience of our viewing the painting, the modern visual experience that went hand-in-hand with it. That is, we are invited to share the *flâneur*'s experience of quick glimpses of ephemeral phenomena, of travel between the tangible and the intangible, of new sights and experiences. It was both the unabashed celebration of modernity in Manet's subject matter, as well as his self-conscious and self-reflexive style, that the Impressionists would find so invigorating.

Monet's Impressionism

Monet's 1877 *The Gare Saint-Lazare* (*see* below), exhibited at the third Impressionist exhibition in April of that year, is characteristic of the twin goals of his early career. On the one hand, in choosing to paint inside the type of building that Théophile Gautier had described as being among the 'new cathedrals of modernity', in emphasizing the vast, superhuman scale of its interior cavity and exposed cast-iron and glass structure, Monet was identifying himself firmly as a painter of modern life. Indeed, that Manet himself had, in 1873, painted the

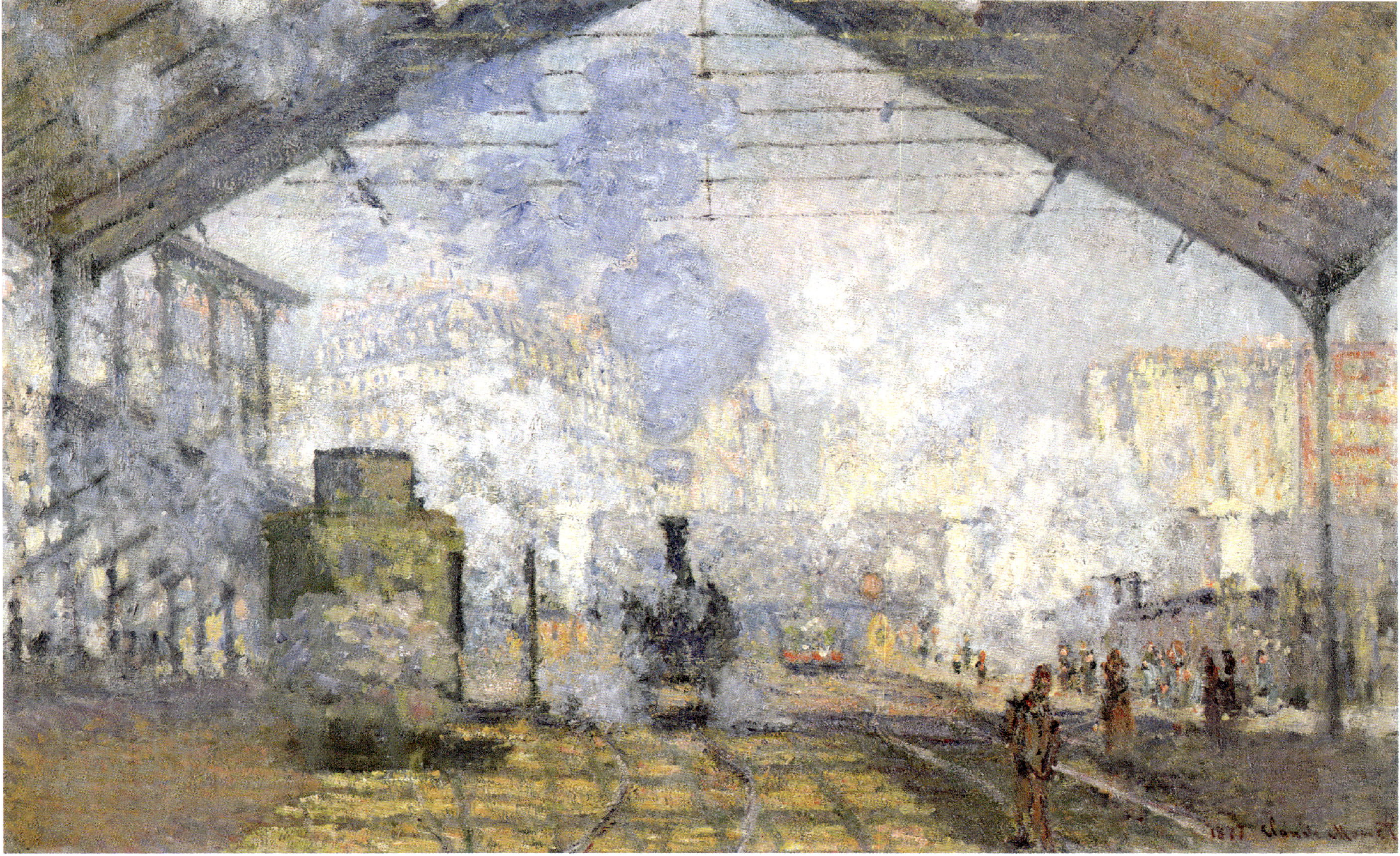

Above : *The Gare Saint-Lazare*, 1877, Claude Monet (1840–1926)

station surely figured in Monet's decision. Not only was it the rapidity of this new form of transportation that was fascinating, but also its regularity. It was only the nationwide spread of the rail network that forced each locality, which had hitherto kept its own time, on to the national (Parisian) clock. In *The Gare Saint-Lazare*, the synchronous departures and arrivals of the trains are juxtaposed with the bustle of the crowd boarding and alighting, which coalesce into a blur of black, blue and red brushstrokes. Monet was clearly interested in the visual effect of the light as it passed through the large glass windows at the top of the canvas and filtered through the haze of steam emitted by the engines.

To capture this ephemeral effect, Monet worked quickly, applying paint in individualized brushstrokes. Moreover, he painted on the spot, transcribing what he saw rather than working from memory in his studio. His keen observation of this rapidly changing scene extended to colour. Like Manet, Monet was aware that colour-relations in the real world did not match the neat divisions of conservative academic painting, with its smooth tonal gradations and neutral shadows. Such painting teaches that clouds are white, but in the context of the train station, under the blue pall of the ironwork and steam engines, Monet boldly painted the clouds of steam precisely as he saw them, in various shades of blue and grey. The spectacle of modern industry was rendered with the bravado of an acutely modern painterly vision.

In his landscapes, Monet's fascination for light's constitutional ephemerality reveals itself as well. In *Vétheuil in the Fog* (1879, *see* page 7), Monet depicted the isolated village enrobed by a thick layer of fog. Monet had recently moved to Vétheuil, which was on the same train line as Argenteuil but slightly further from Paris. Monet's rapid and sketchy approach renders indistinct the boundaries between river, land and sky, with colours and forms blending and interpenetrating. It was in the 1880s, in Vétheuil, that Monet would forcefully articulate his painterly ideology of *plein-air* naturalism – of painting rapidly outdoors so as best to transcribe on the canvas one's subjective impression of natural phenomena. For Monet, painting was a product of the traffic between nature and sensibility, between effect and impression.

Other Impressionisms

Other painters routinely categorized among the Impressionists, however, did not subscribe to Monet's ideology of art, nor his method of painting. Edgar Degas, for example, in paintings such as *The Dance Class* (1874, *see* left) shunned Monet's technique of loose and broken brushwork in favour of a tighter finish. Where Monet conveyed the motion of the commuters at the Gare Saint-Lazare by blending and blurring forms, Degas instead opted to photographically freeze his ballet dancers mid-action. Where Monet sought a gestural spontaneity before

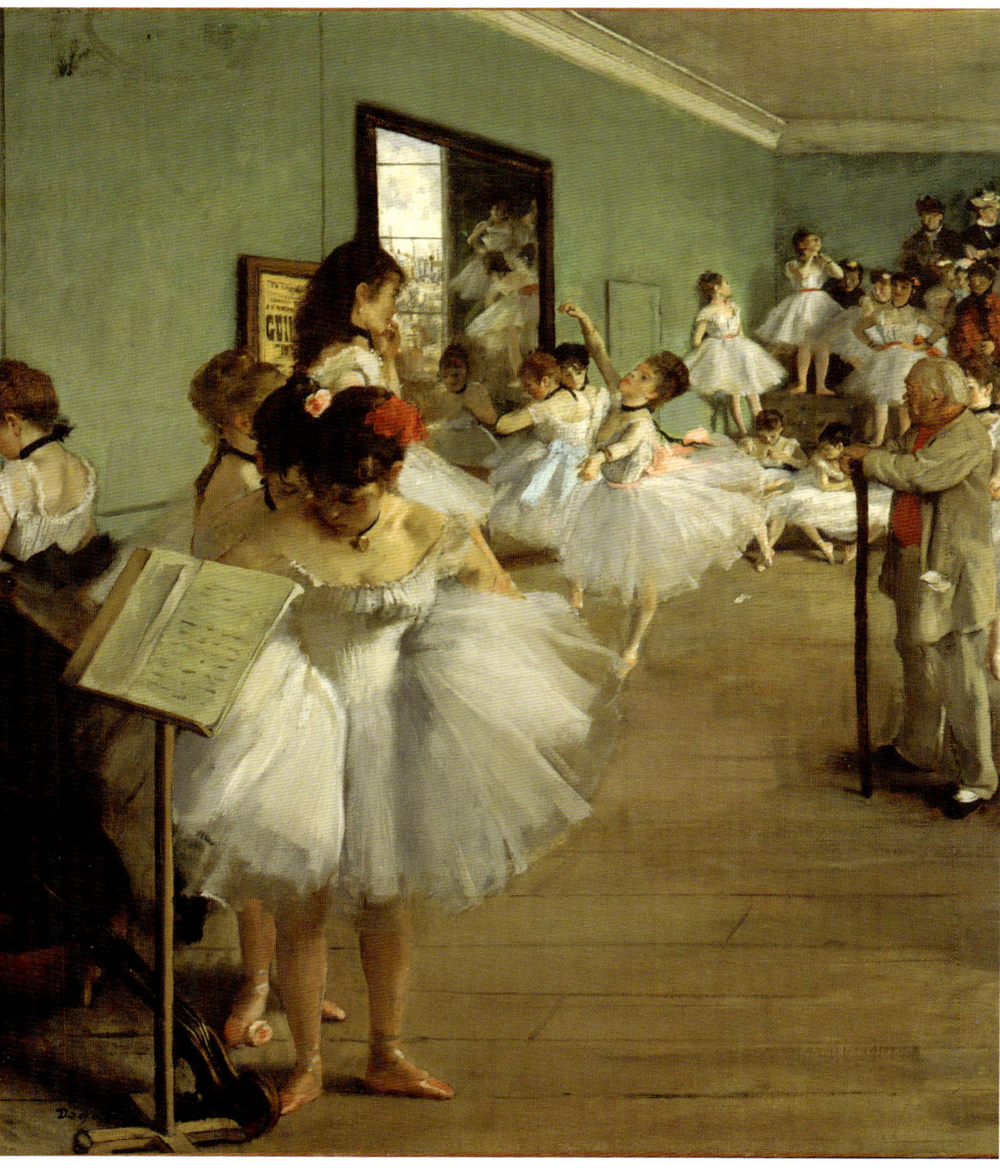

Above : *The Dance Class*, 1874, Edgar Degas (1834–1917)

nature, Degas proudly proclaimed that 'no art is less spontaneous than mine', instead prioritizing drawing and studied reflection. Degas revelled in the bold compositional devices and unusual perspectives associated with photography (which he himself practised), constraining his palette to match the supposed veracity of photographic forms.

Caillebotte, too, was more interested in the complexities of translating new urban spaces on to the flat canvas. In paintings such as *Paris Street; Rainy Day* (1877, *see* below), he combined bizarre, artificial compositional devices with the highly detailed figures and overall finish that connoted traditional standards. The plunging perspective of the streets as they diverge out from the 'Carrefour de

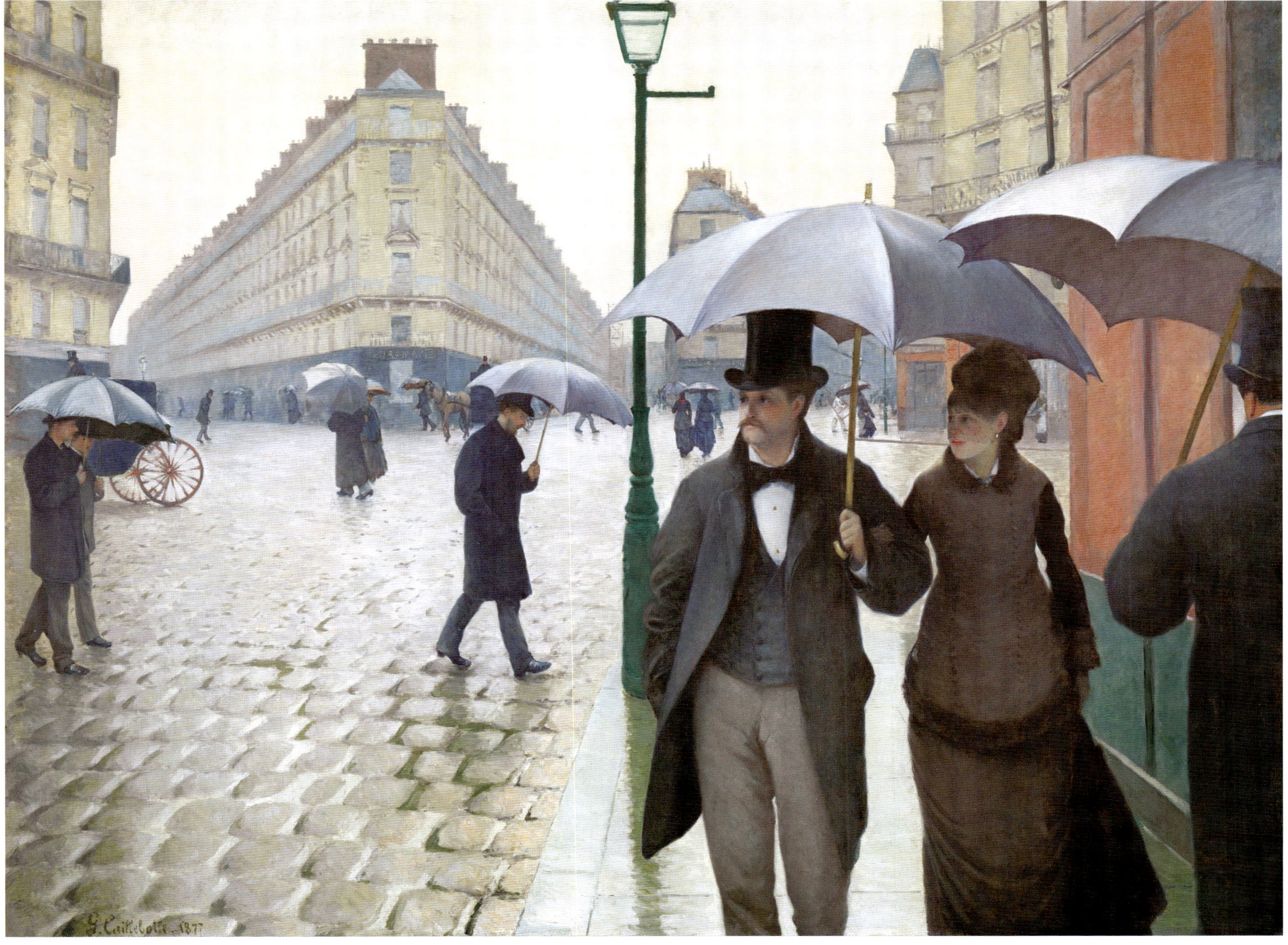

Above : *Paris Street; Rainy Day*, 1877, Gustave Caillebotte (1848–1894)

Moscou' jars with the orthogonal surface structure articulated by the intersection of the lamppost with the horizon line, which artificially divides the canvas into neat quadrisections. Figures caught awkwardly in mid-stride – as if, like Degas' ballet dancers, they have been photographed – are arranged, with the aid of the golden ratio, with calculated precision.

Camille Pissarro, whilst sharing Monet's penchant for landscapes, never adopted the rapid spontaneity of his brushwork and retained a principled fascination with the lives of the peasantry unmatched among his comrades. Auguste Renoir vacillated between the tight naturalism of Degas and a more characteristically Impressionist feathered touch. Like Monet, his early works reveal a fascination with the effects of light, but by the middle of the 1880s, as Monet had absorbed himself in capturing the transcendental 'envelope' of atmosphere that unified forms, Renoir was instead looking back to the solidarity of classicism. Taking this diversity of styles and techniques at face value, it would seem that even referring to Impressionism does not offer the key to unifying the equally divergent strands of the painters who came after it.

Positivism

However, the Impressionist legacy, to which Post-Impressionist painters were reacting, was not just a matter of technique, motif or style, but something altogether more fundamental: its ideology of naturalism. Even when Monet and Degas, who have been taken to be exemplars of the two extremes of this vector of Impressionism's heterogeneity, diverged most strongly, they were nevertheless united in their purpose to accurately describe their visual experience. Impressionist art was rooted in the beliefs of the bourgeois society pictured by Manet in the Tuileries. Not only were most Impressionist painters from bourgeois backgrounds, but it was primarily their middle-class peers who purchased their works.

The philosophical beliefs of the French middle class in the nineteenth century were influenced by the writings of thinkers such as Auguste Comte (1798–1857) and Émile Littré (1801–81). These 'Positivist' philosophers argued that reality (being) is exclusively material; if something cannot be measured, tested and verified by scientific methods, then it does not exist as such. Metaphysical speculation (thoughts, dreams, ideas, religion) was thus dismissed as being ultimately inconsequential. The reality of Impressionism was firmly rooted in the ocular perception of an existing reality, in the mechanics of vision as understood by science. The heterogeneous multiplicity of Post-Impressionism can thus be understood as consisting of two broad responses to Impressionism's naturalism. Each in their own way, the Post-Impressionists diagnosed a certain deficiency with it, or with its application, and each proposed their own solution.

Seurat

For Georges Seurat and the Neo-Impressionists he was to inspire (Neo-Impressionism being a sub-strand of Post-Impressionism), the Impressionists had paid only lip service to modern advances in the scientific study of colour perception, most importantly the ideas contained within Michel Eugène Chevreul's *De la loi du contraste simultané des couleurs* (1839). This text was the first systematic account of how colours, placed in proximity, alter the viewer's perception of each colour (a phenomenon Chevreul described as 'simultaneous contrast'), leading to the theory of complementary colours visualized by his now-ubiquitous colour wheel.

Seurat felt that the gestural spontaneity of Monet's brand of Impressionism was incompatible with his desire to accurately record his impression of colour. Instead he developed a technique known as Pointillism. In paintings such as *The Lighthouse at Honfleur*, Seurat filled the canvas with tiny, isolated dots of unmodulated, prismatic colour such that, at the appropriate distance, they would blend in the eye. Rather than imitating what the eye sees, Seurat hoped to replicate the mechanism by which it sees. Where Impressionist naturalism was one that mimicked effect, Seurat's Neo-Impressionism was one that sought

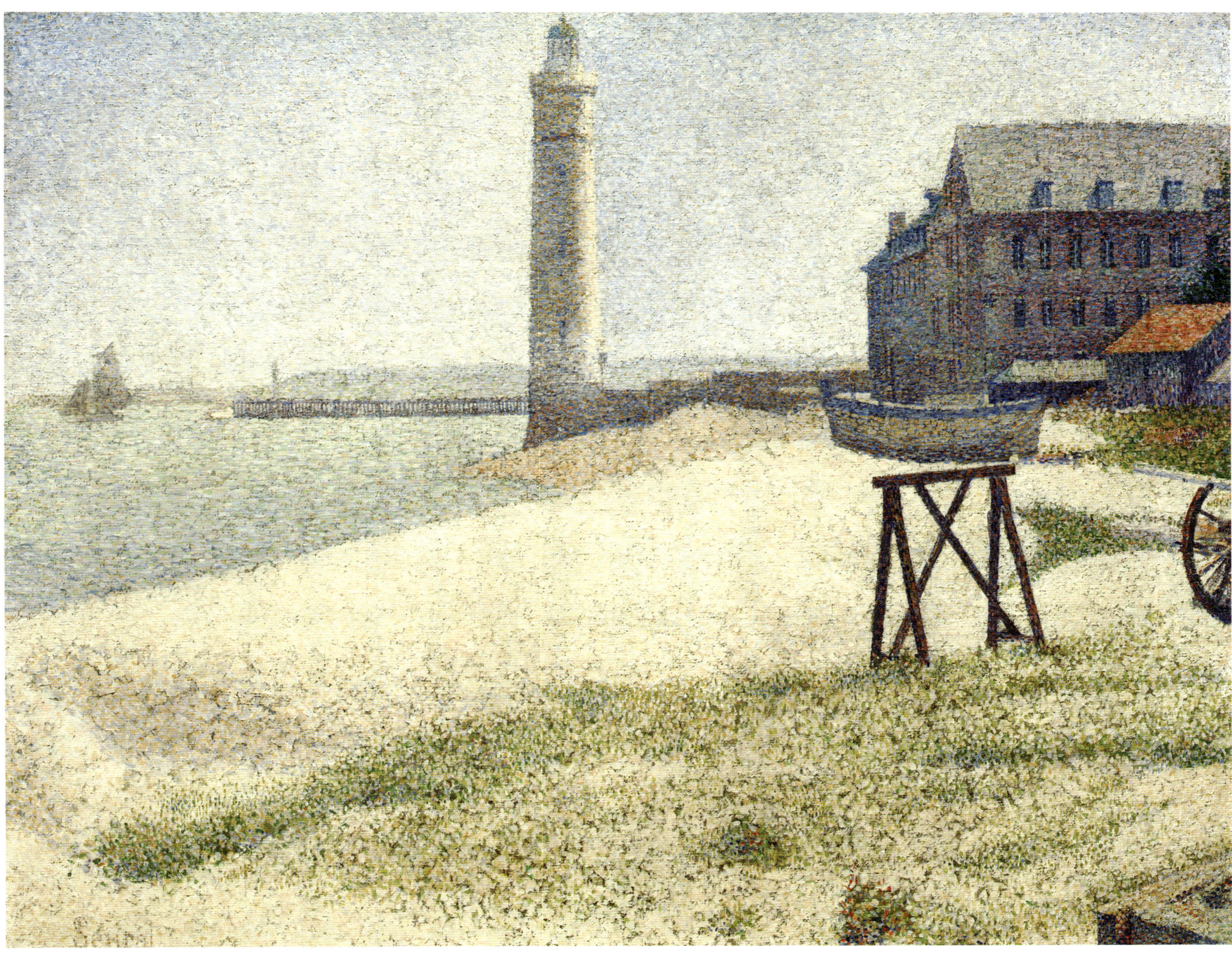

to actuate cause. Seurat believed that his meticulous methodology could be leveraged for more than mere description: he also wished to evoke a mood.

In *The Lighthouse at Honfleur* (*see* above), Seurat combined warm tones in the sand and the lighthouse with the cool blues of the sky and water within a stable, orthogonal composition, articulated through the intersection of the vertical lighthouse and horizontal jetty in order to convey the calm serenity of the seaside resort. It was in building on the advances of Impressionism – its divided brushstrokes and attention to colour relations, its honesty and firm grounding in nature – but putting them on a more rigorously scientific footing, that Seurat saw himself being post Impressionism.

Above : *The Lighthouse at Honfleur*, 1886, Georges Seurat (1859–1951)

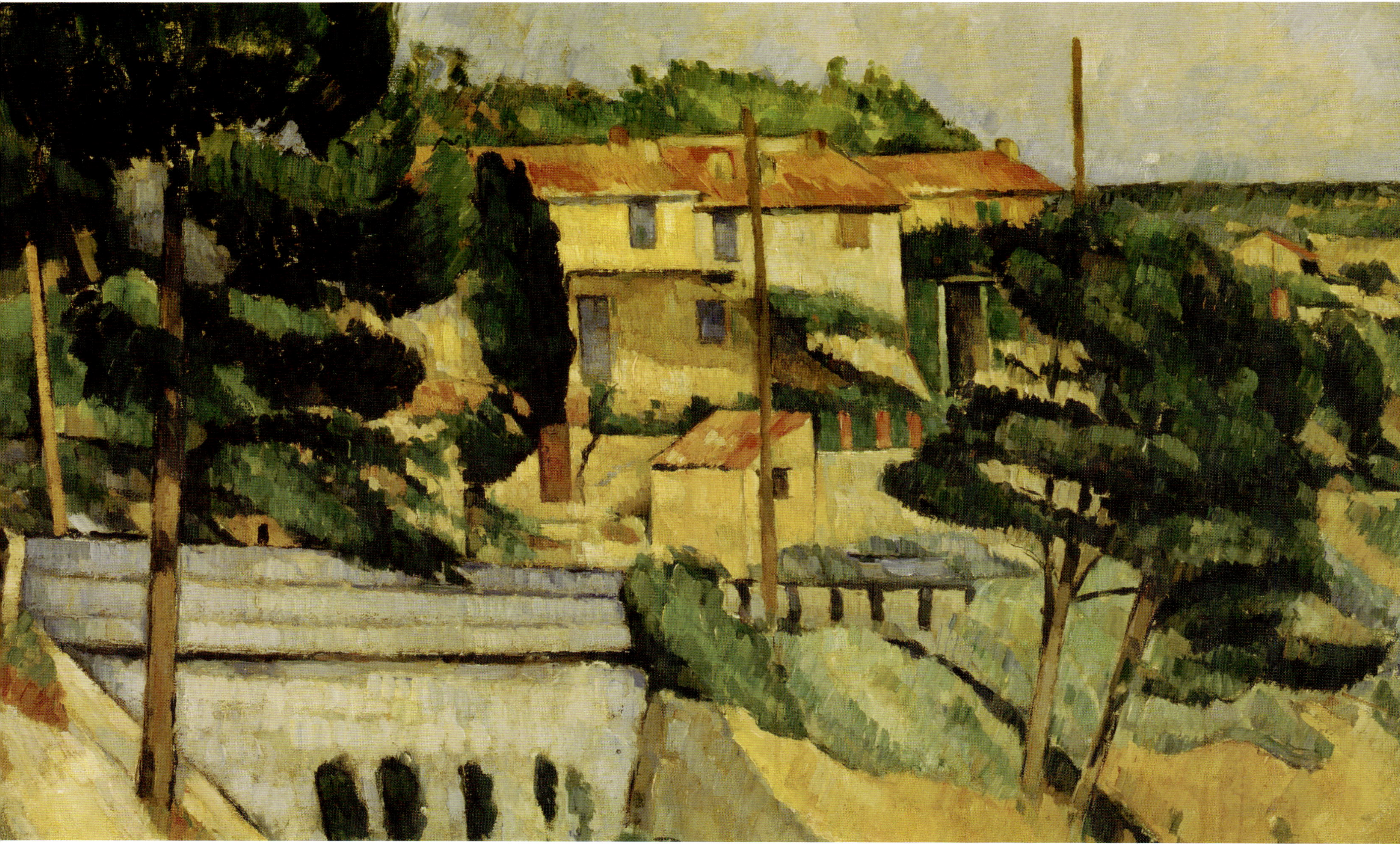

Cézanne

Like Seurat and Monet, Paul Cézanne's expressed aim was the empirical and truthful rendering of nature. However, what distinguished Cézanne was his sense of the weight and authority of tradition. Where Monet's work ostensibly signalled a radical break with the past, a rejection of tradition (understood as a lineage of artifice), Cézanne instead sought to reintegrate Impressionist breakthroughs with the formal solidity and compositional stability of the Old Masters. Referring to Nicholas Poussin (1594–1665), a Baroque painter whose work was characterized by its logical, symmetrical and ordered clarity, Cézanne spoke of his ambition to 'paint Poussin over again after nature'. Thus Cézanne felt that the instantaneity encoded in Impression's *plein-air* naturalism had engendered a neglect of the significance of form and the absence of rigorous analysis.

Above : *Viaduct at L'Estaque, c. 1883, Paul Cézanne (1839–1906)*

In paintings such as *Viaduct at L'Estaque* (*c.* 1883, *see* left), Cézanne combined a schematized and geometricized composition, flattened spaces and forms, and employed regular, broad brushstrokes. This shift in Cézanne's practice reveals his belief in the necessity of analysis. It was not enough merely to observe nature, one also had to understand it, to decompose and reconstruct it, preserving only its most essential dimensions. Impressionism, for Cézanne, was dependent upon the eye to the detriment of the brain. Referring to Monet, Cézanne famously proclaimed that 'He is nothing but an eye, yet what an eye!'

Gauguin

Paul Gauguin also felt that Impressionism was problematically ocular. However, unlike Cézanne – and indeed Seurat, Gauguin and his Symbolist comrades, who included Paul Sérusier (also present at Roger Fry's 1910 exhibition) – Gauguin sought not the ever more rigorous analysis of visible nature but the unleashing of that to which Impressionism, for all its looking, was blind: the metaphysical. '[T]he Impressionists focused their efforts around the eye,' Gauguin noted, 'not in the mysterious centre of thought, and from there they slipped into scientific reasons…. There is physics and metaphysics.'

Having originally worked in a bank, it was perhaps the hardships he endured as a consequence of the stock market crash in 1882 that soured Gauguin's view of modern European society and its bourgeois culture, a key plank of which, as we have seen, was the philosophy of Positivism. Thus Gauguin rejected both the delimitation of art within the bounds of the empirically material and urban modernity as a subject.

In mid-July 1886, the desperately poor Gauguin left Paris for a simpler and more authentic existence in Pont-Aven, Brittany. The costumes, habits and piety of the Breton peasants fascinated Gauguin, and in paintings such as *Breton Women Chatting*, he indulged in a fantasy of their exoticism, their

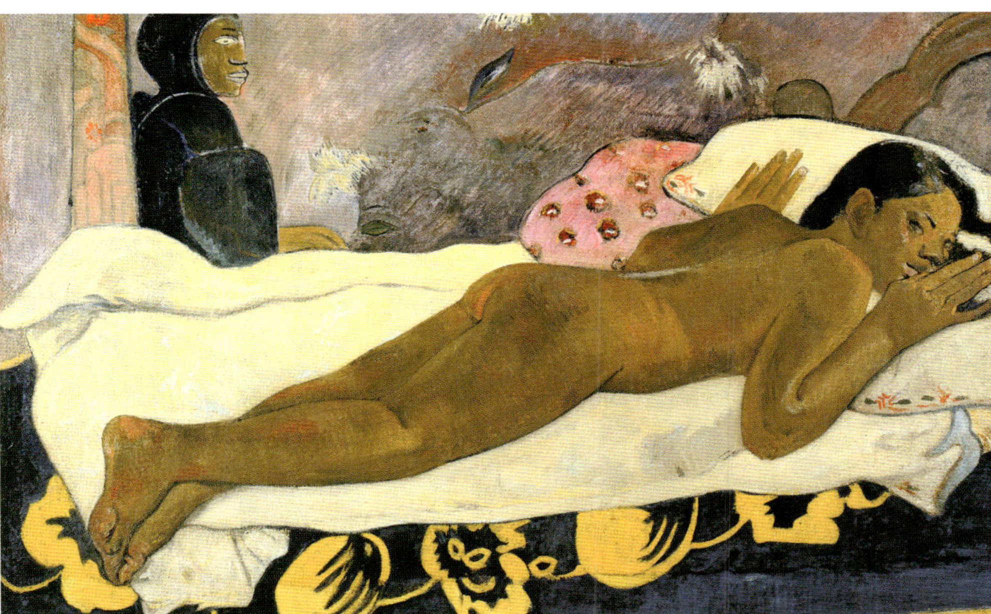

otherness with respect to the Parisian bourgeois society from which he was determined to insulate himself. On his second visit in 1888, Gauguin encountered Emile Bernard (1868–1941), whose work inspired Gauguin to make a decisive break from the Pissarro-inspired *plein-air* naturalism of his earliest works and the Cézanne-influenced style of the mid-1880s.

Cloisonnisme

Bernard had developed a style known as *cloisonnisme*, whereby the canvas surface was covered in flat patches of unnaturalistic and unmodulated colour, populated by simplified forms demarked by thick outlines (the result resembled *cloisonné* metalwork, an association which gave the style its name). Colour in these works was not supposed to accord with the ostensible look of the object, but rather to connote a realm beyond representation through its abstract, almost decorative, formal autonomy. Having met Sérusier in September 1888 and inspired him to follow his approach, Gauguin spent October and November of that year painting in Arles with Van Gogh; a fiery and incompatible relationship which reached its famously violent dénouement when Van Gogh severed his ear and threatened Gauguin with the blade.

Above : *Spirit of the Dead Watching (Manao tupapau)*, 1892, Paul Gauguin (1848–1903)

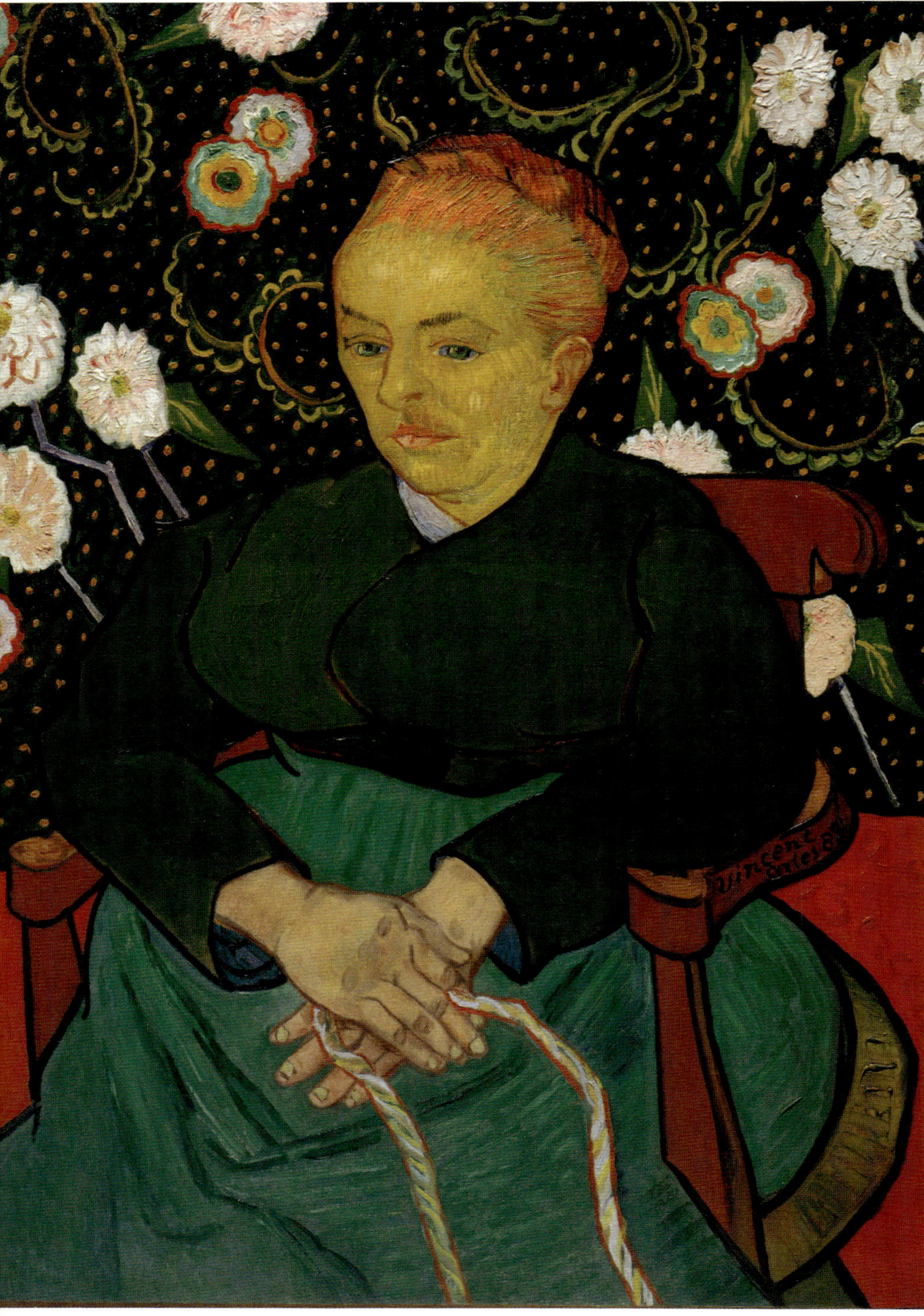

Having vacillated restlessly between Brittany and Paris for two years, in 1891 Gauguin departed for the French colony of Tahiti. It was on the Polynesian island that Gauguin developed his mature style, which, in paintings such as *Spirit of the Dead Watching (Manao tupapau)* (*see* page 21), combined on the one hand his

Above : *La Berceuse*, 1889, Vincent van Gogh (1853–90)

abstracting and simplified formal idiom of flattened planes of bold, unnaturalistic colour with, on the other, a mystical, ambiguous and erotic subject matter. Gauguin cultivated the image of himself as a kind of savage, whose distance from civilization gave him access to the profound and transcendental realm that was captivating French society at the end of the century.

Van Gogh

As Gauguin was making use of colour to signify a metaphysical reality beyond vision, Van Gogh was developing a dense, personal colour symbolism, whereby a certain colour would not only describe but also evoke a specific emotion. Van Gogh first moved to Paris in February 1886, where his brother Theo was organizing exhibitions of Impressionist painters, including Monet and Pissarro. The most decisive encounter, however, was with Seurat's Neo-Impressionism, specifically its divided brushstrokes and use of complementary colours. Unable or unwilling to submit himself to Seurat's automatic regularity, Van Gogh instead developed a more rhythmic and textural touch.

Contact with Bernard and Gauguin pushed Van Gogh in the direction of decorative abstraction, fully evident in his portrait of Augustine Roulin, wife of his friend the proletarian postmaster of Arles, entitled *La Berceuse* (*see* left). Abandoning any realistic standard of colour, Van Gogh instead made use of abstract chromatic harmonies. As he described it to Arnold Koning in 1889: 'olive green' bust, 'pale malachite green' skirt, 'quite orange' hair and 'chrome yellow' complexion, a flat patch of 'vermillion' representing 'a tiled floor or else a stone floor', paired with a 'bluish-green' wallpapered wall 'which of course I have calculated in conformity with the rest of the colours' – to create a 'lullaby in colours'. The title of the work, *La Berceuse* referred to either, as Van Gogh put it, the 'lullaby, or [the] woman rocking the cradle'. The subject is represented with a psychological and emotional richness signified almost entirely by the abstract qualities and relations of colour.

Wheatfield with Crows (*see* below), often – erroneously – claimed to be Van Gogh's final work, is dominated by powerful combinations of colour: the blue of the sky contrasts with the yellow wheat, the red path resonates with the streaks of green. Together, these colours were, in the words of Van Gogh, to express the 'sadness, extreme loneliness' of his last living days, afflicted by mental illness. This expressive use of colour is mirrored in the impasto (thickly textured), gestural brushwork, and the ominous subject matter – a path leading to nowhere and a seemingly aimless cohort of crows – a symbol of death and rebirth. Where, for Monet, the visible brushstroke was a signifier of his having worked quickly, that is, a guarantee of the objective authenticity of the painting as a true impression of nature, Van Gogh has here thus completely transformed its meaning.

Post-Impressionism

One way of resolving, therefore, the seeming incompatibility of these canonical figures of Post-Impressionism is to identify, on the one hand, a broadly shared sense of dissatisfaction with Impressionism and, on the other, a wide diversity of diagnoses and proposed solutions. Cézanne, Seurat, Gauguin and Van Gogh clearly all felt that Impressionism was a thing of the past, yet each proposed a remarkably different vision of the future. It is to each of the different facets of their work that we now turn: colour and style, subject and form, structure and order, and symbolism and expression.

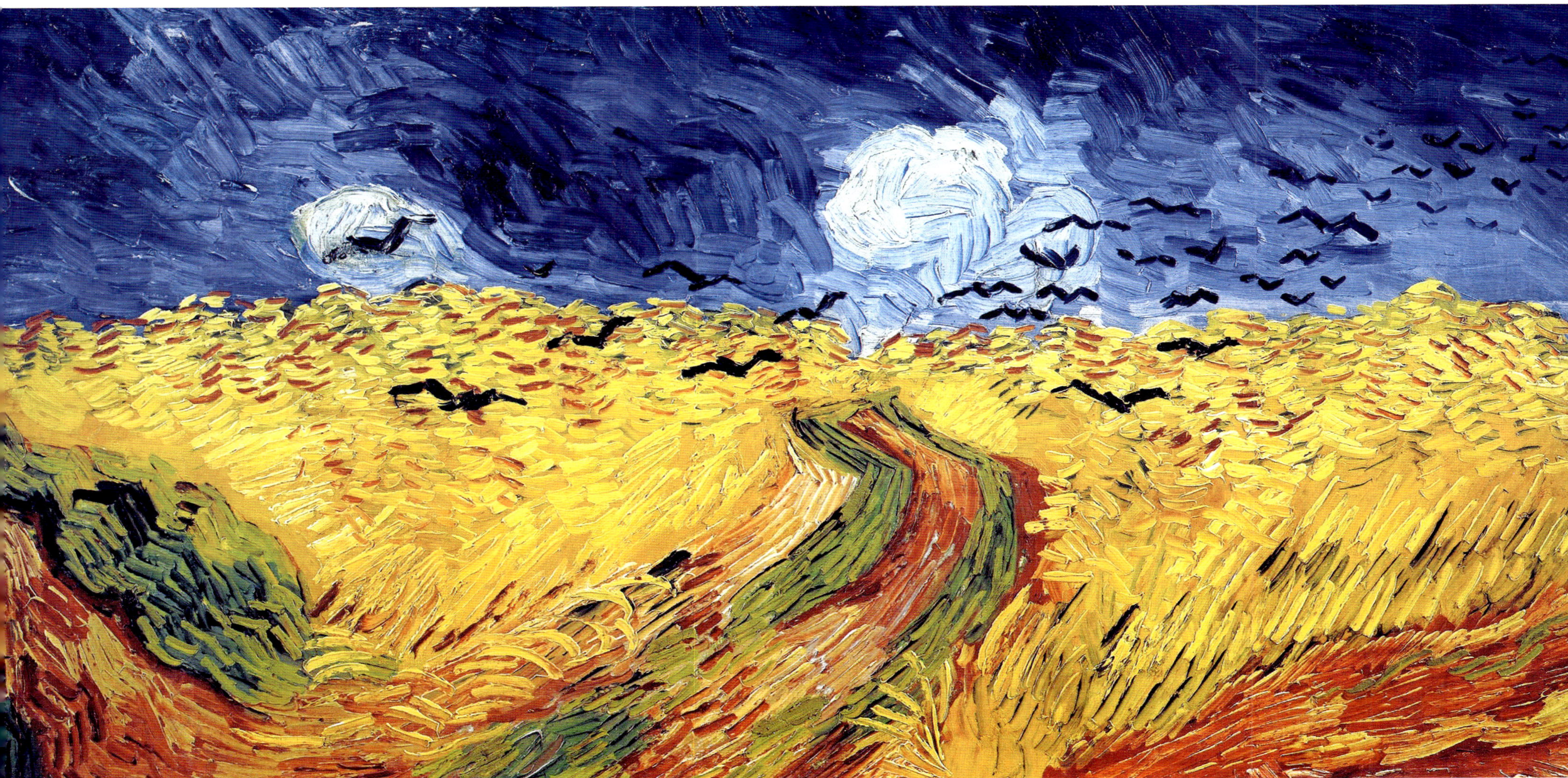

Above : *Wheatfield with Crows*, 1890, Vincent van Gogh (1853–90)

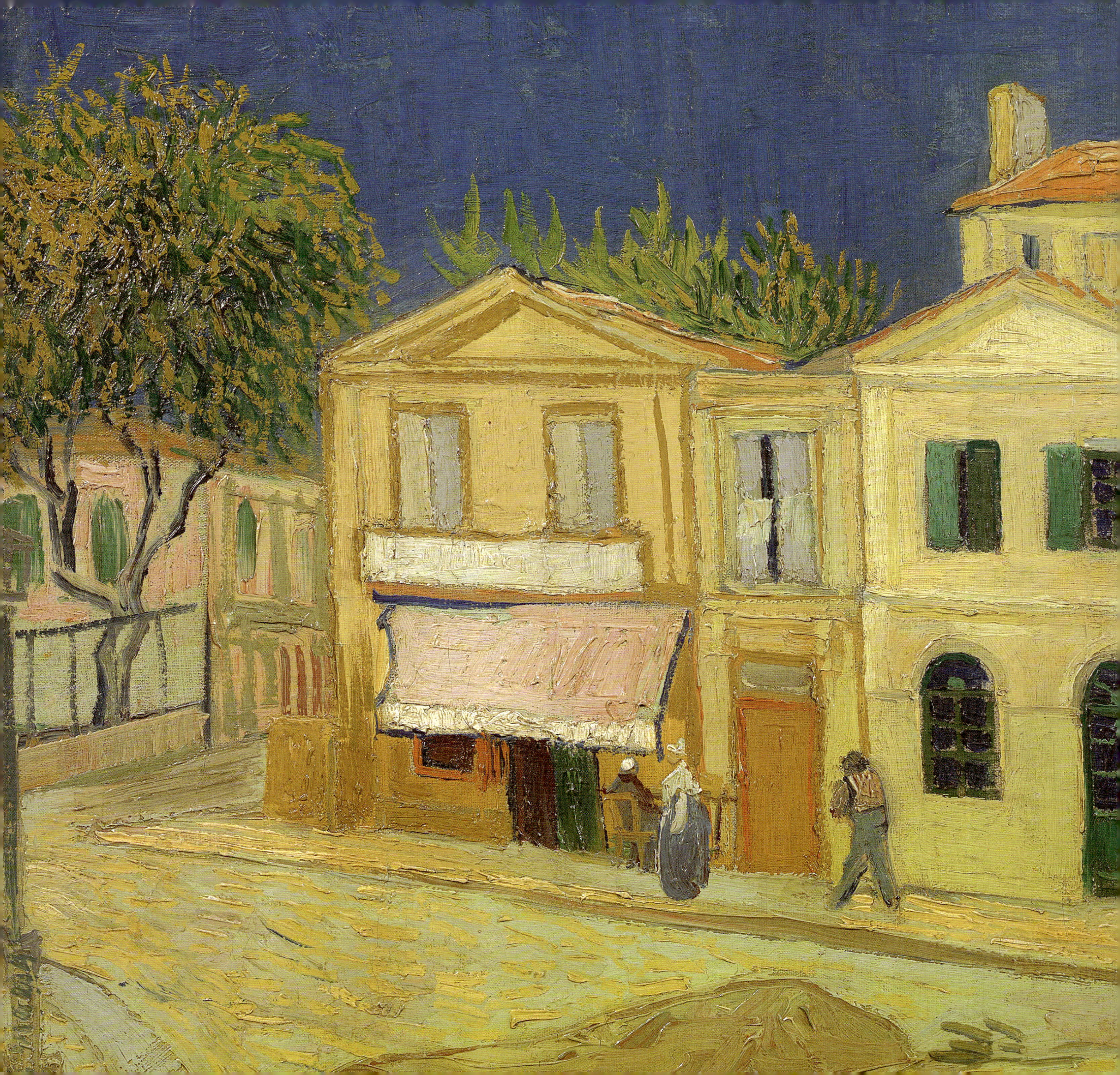

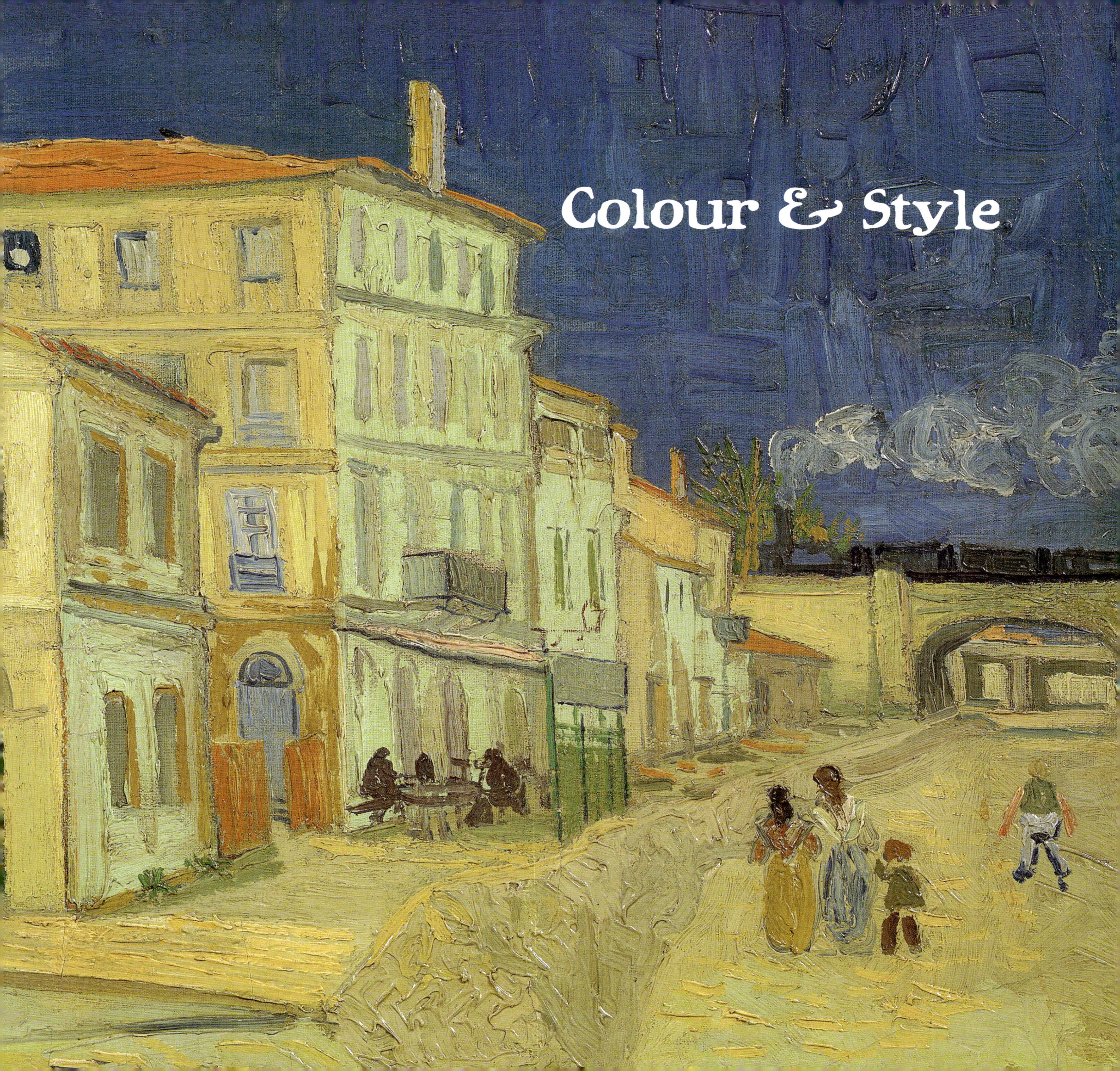
Colour & Style

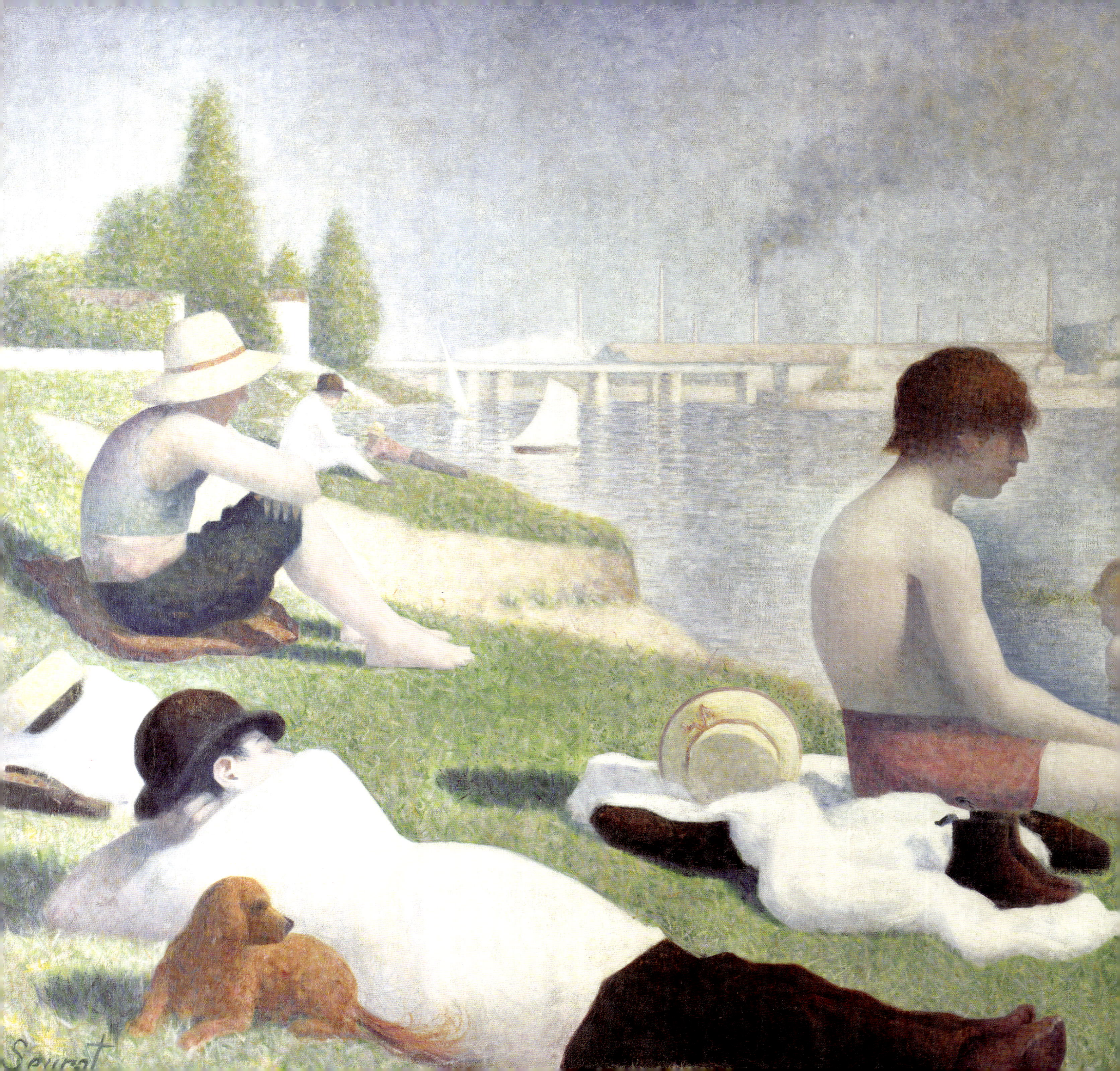
Seurat

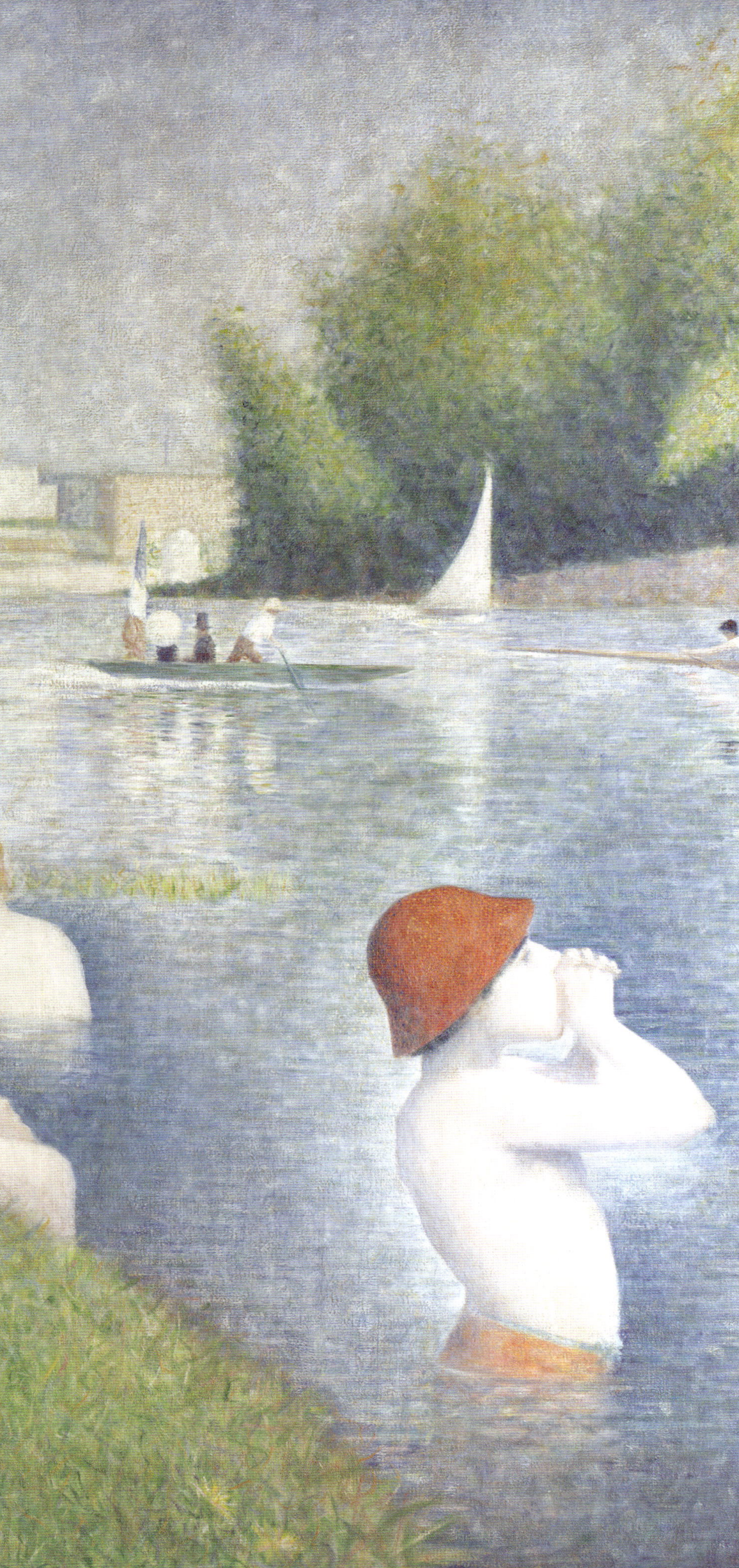

Left : *Bathers at Asnières*, 1884, Georges Seurat (1859–91)

Diversification

THERE WERE varying approaches to colour within Post-Impressionism, from Georges Seurat's science of 'optical painting' and the techniques used in the wider Neo-Impressionist movement, to the diverse styles of Paul Gauguin and his circle, and the violent harmonies of Vincent van Gogh.

A Crisis of Impressionism

Personal animosities and diverging aesthetic concerns doomed the Impressionists, who staged their final group exhibition in 1886. As early as 1879, Cézanne, Renoir and Sisley forewent the group show in favour of the Salon, with Monet following suit in 1880. In the face of what he perceived to be betrayal, Degas sought to introduce Jean-François Raffaëlli (1850–1924), Jean-Louis Forain (1852–1931) and Federico Zangdomeneghi (1841–1917), painters whose realism was in close accordance with Degas and diametrically opposed to Monet. Caillebotte dismissed these second-rate painters as 'a fighting squad in the great cause of realism !!!!' whose inclusion polluted Impressionism's social and aesthetic unity. 'Degas introduced disunity into our midst,' Caillebotte wrote to Pissarro in January 1881, 'but for three years [Degas] has been after Raffaëlli to join us [… Degas] claims that we must stick together and be able to count on each other (for God's sake!).'

However, the unity for which Caillebotte fought was already critically endangered. Disagreements about administrative, exhibitionary and commercial strategy, which came to a head in the 1880s, were being matched by an increasing diversity of aesthetics.

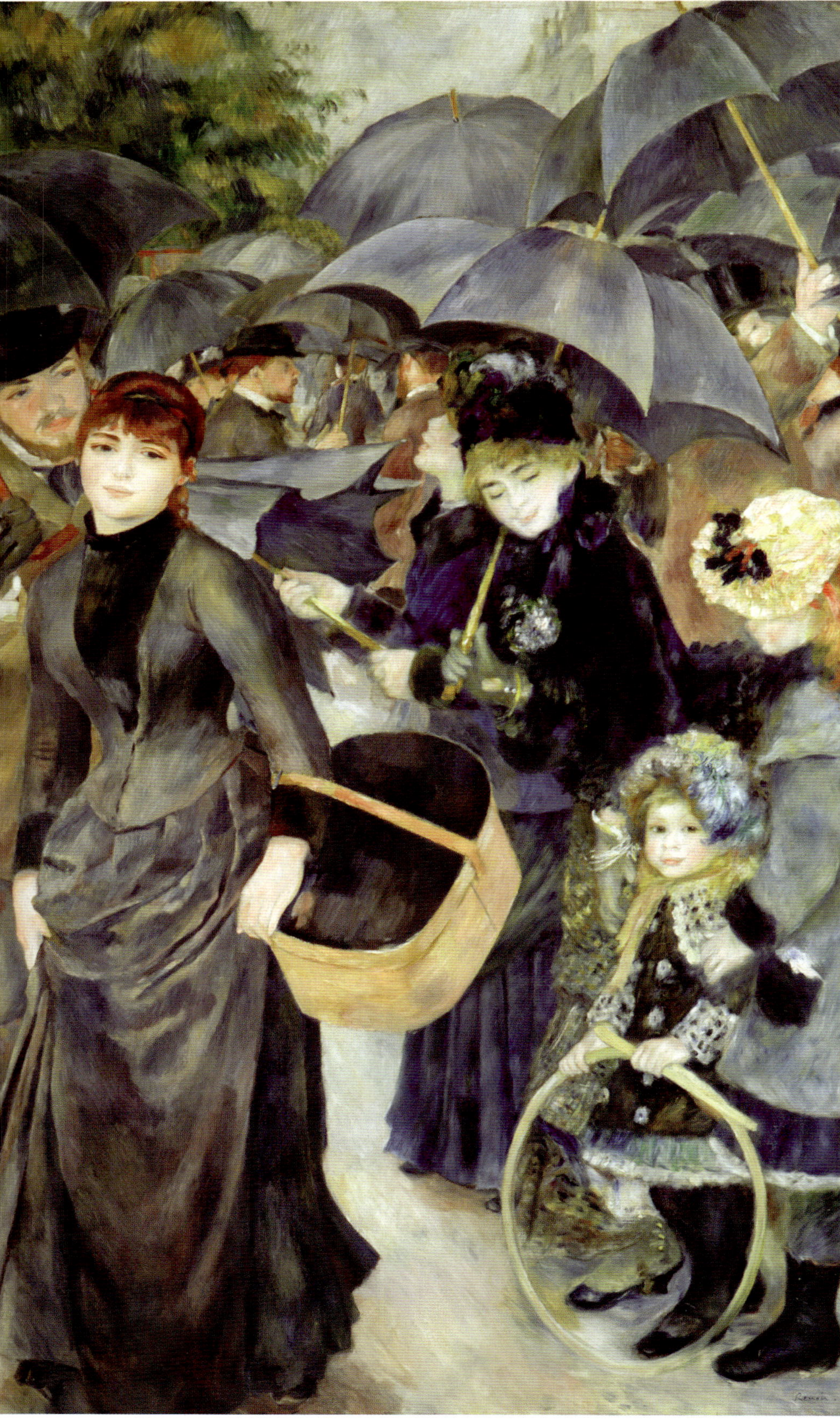

For example, in the 1880s, Renoir returned to the norms of traditional art, imbuing his paintings with a greater solidity, firmer modelling and a more conventional approach to form. In 1881, Renoir studied the Renaissance masters in Italy, including Raphael; upon his return, he reinvigorated his painting with an emphasis on draughtsmanship and modelling. 'Around 1883,' Renoir noted, 'it was as if a crack appeared in my work. I had gone as far as I could with Impressionism and had arrived at the conclusion that I did not know how to either paint or draw.'

Renoir's *The Umbrellas* (c. 1881–86, *see* left) dramatizes this deliberate return to convention. The figures furthest to the right are painted in the soft, blended style he had utilized in the 1870s. By contrast, the figures furthest to the left are sharper, modelled with drier and tighter brushwork, duller colours, and sharp, draughtsmanly edges. Renoir's later *Large Bathers* (1884–87, *see* right) is characteristic of his growing desire to hybridize the spontaneity and freedom of Impressionism with the monumentality and respectability of the Old Masters, from Ingres (1780–1867) to Raphael (1483–1520), Titian (c. 1485/90–1576) and Rubens (1577–1640). Chromatic vibrancy is combined with solid modelling, sculptural form and polished flesh. The pose and gestures of the figures, whilst active and spontaneous, nevertheless quote from Ingres' Classical paradigm.

Monet also came to search for a great monumentality in the 1880s. He travelled with Renoir to the south of France in 1883, after which his paintings of, for example, the Manneporte in Étretat reveal a search for greater formal solidity, rather than focusing on the homogenizing or unifying 'envelope' of luminous atmosphere. Pissarro, ever on the hunt for a technique or style that would soothe his persistent sense of his own mediocrity, dramatically turned to the Pointillist or Neo-Impressionist technique pioneered by Seurat. It was the contributions of the group of painters led by Seurat – including Signac, Pissarro and his son Lucien (1863–1944) – to the Impressionist exhibition in 1886 that, in their clarion and systematic critique of the Impressionist painting that had come before, finally signalled its long-presaged demise.

Above : *The Umbrellas, c. 1881–86, Auguste Renoir (1841–1919)*

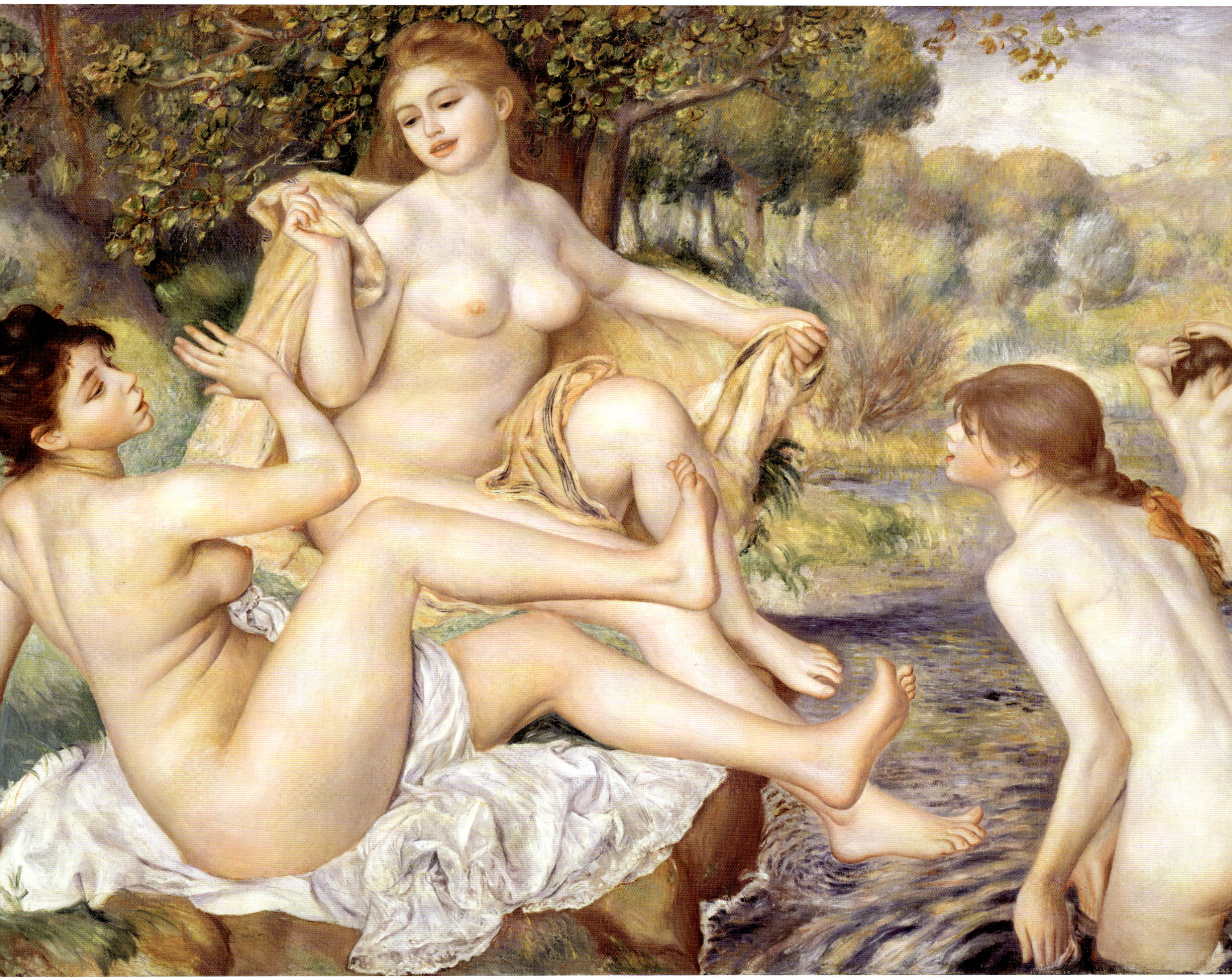

Above : *Large Bathers*, 1884–87, Auguste Renoir (1841–1919)

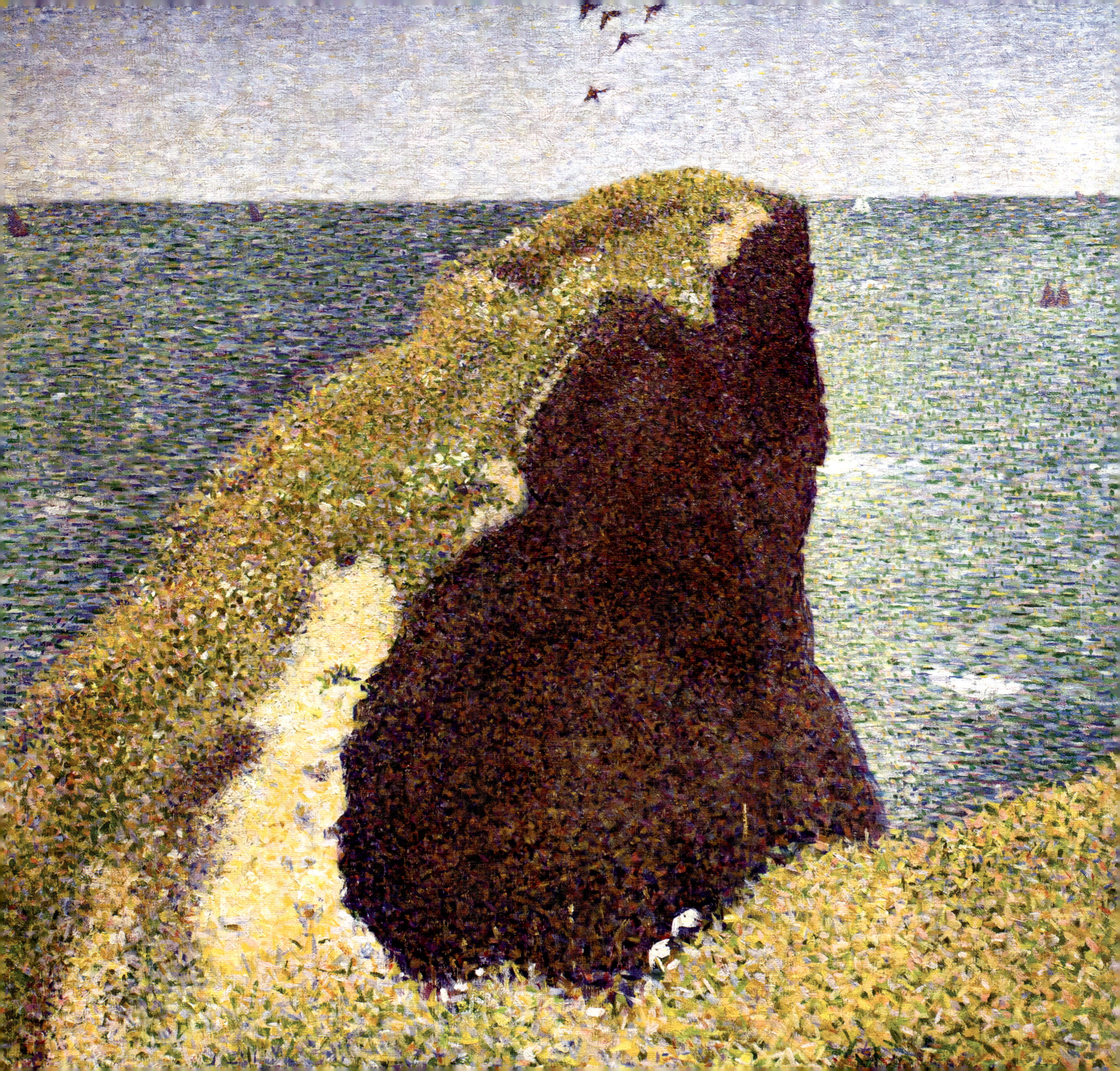

Seurat's Challenge to Impressionism

Georges Seurat was born in 1859 in Paris, the city in which he was to spend the vast majority of his short life. He studied the decorative arts at the École Municipale de Sculpture et Dessin and, after 1878, art at the École des Beaux-Arts. Influenced by his teacher Henri Lehmann (1814–82), a conservative Academician and follower of Ingres, Seurat's earliest works were monochrome conté crayon drawings that focused on the subtle relations of light and shade. However, despite his bookish and methodical personality, Seurat did not take well to Lehmann's tutelage, leaving his studio after only a year. Seurat had never submitted himself completely to his teacher's pedagogy, and in 1884, the public was first able to witness the result of his continued personal experiments.

At the first exhibition, or Salon, of the Société des Artistes Indépendants (an independent society of artists founded to bypass the strictures of the Academic Salon and exhibit 'without jury nor reward'), Seurat exhibited *Bathers at Asnières* (1884, *see* page 26). It depicts ordinary working-class Parisians bathing in the Seine and relaxing on its banks. Measuring around 2 m (6½ ft) in height and 3 m (9⅘ ft) in length, the scale of the painting certainly lived up to its Salon context (albeit a Salon in name only; Seurat's bathers were poorly hung in a canteen).

Not only in size was this a 'Salon' work. Seurat made numerous preparatory drawings, which ranged from impressionistic *plein-air* oil sketches to figure studies – for example *Seated Nude, Study for Bathers at Asnières* (1884) – a far remove from Monet's dogma of instantaneity and spontaneity, and more in line with the processes he had been taught by Lehmann. In the background, upright chimneys visibly pollute the air, revealing that we are in the industrial suburb of Asnières.

On the river itself glides a pleasure yacht and a tricolour sporting skiff; neither of the elements, new industrial suburbia and bourgeois aquatic leisure,

> *'Need we recall that even when the colours are the same, mixed pigments and mixed rays of light do not necessarily produce the same result?'*
>
> Felix Fénéon

would necessarily have been out of place at an Impressionist exhibition. Nor would, perhaps surprisingly, Seurat's solidly voluminous forms and sharply delineated edges, which would not have seemed too disjunctive had they been juxtaposed with works by Caillebotte or Renoir (for example, the latter's *Large Bathers*). Even Seurat's blue-green dominated palette bears the influence of the Impressionists. However, it was in the scientific and careful rationale by which these colours had been selected, applied and related on the canvas surface that marked Seurat's true radicalism.

A Theory of Colour

Seurat was an avid reader of art theory, and his first major discovery was Chevreul's *De la loi du contraste simultané des couleurs* of 1839. Chevreul was

Left : *Le Bec du Hoc*, 1885, Georges Seurat (1859–91)

a chemist noted for his research into animal fats; in 1824, he was appointed Director of the dyeing department at the Gobelins Manufactory, the national tapestry works. Faced with the haphazard way in which the weavers were selecting colour samples (in tapestry manufacture, because they cannot be mixed like paint, different coloured threads must be juxtaposed), one of Chevreul's first innovations was to devise a system of colour classification, a colour circle, that would allow the dyeing department and the weaving department to work from the same frame of reference.

Next, Chevreul was challenged by consistent complaints from the weavers that the black thread used for the shades of blue and violet in draperies was not black enough. Chevreul discovered that the lack of strength in the black was the result of the way humans perceive juxtaposed colours. Chevreul came to propose that '[i]n the case where the eye sees at the same time two contiguous colours, they will appear as dissimilar as possible, both in their optical composition and in the strength of their colour'.

The human brain tends to exaggerate differences, such that, were you to juxtapose two shades of grey paint, the viewer would see the lighter shade even lighter (and the darker shade even darker) than if they had been viewed in isolation. With regard to colour, he noted that:

> If we look simultaneously upon two stripes of different tones of the same colour, or upon two stripes of the same tone of different colours placed side by side … the eye perceives certain modifications which in the first place influence the intensity of colour, and in the second, the optical composition of the two juxtaposed colours respectively.

The modification perceived by the eye is again this process of exaggerating differences. In order to distinguish juxtaposed hues, the brain adds to each perceived hue a little of the complement of the other. Thus, as Chevreul's weavers bemoaned, when their black thread was being juxtaposed with blue, it would

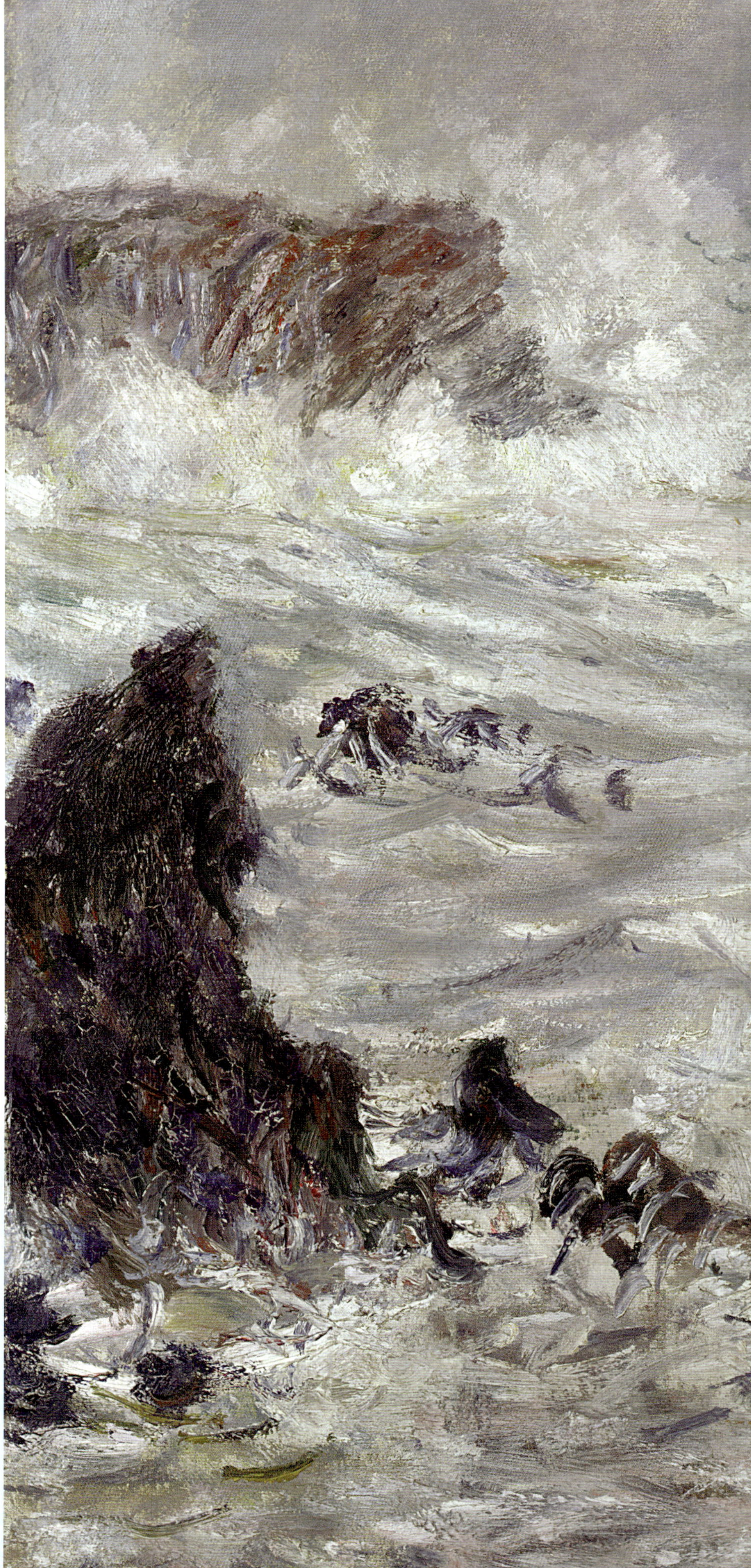

Right: *Storm, Coast of Belle-Ile*, 1886, Claude Monet (1840–1926)

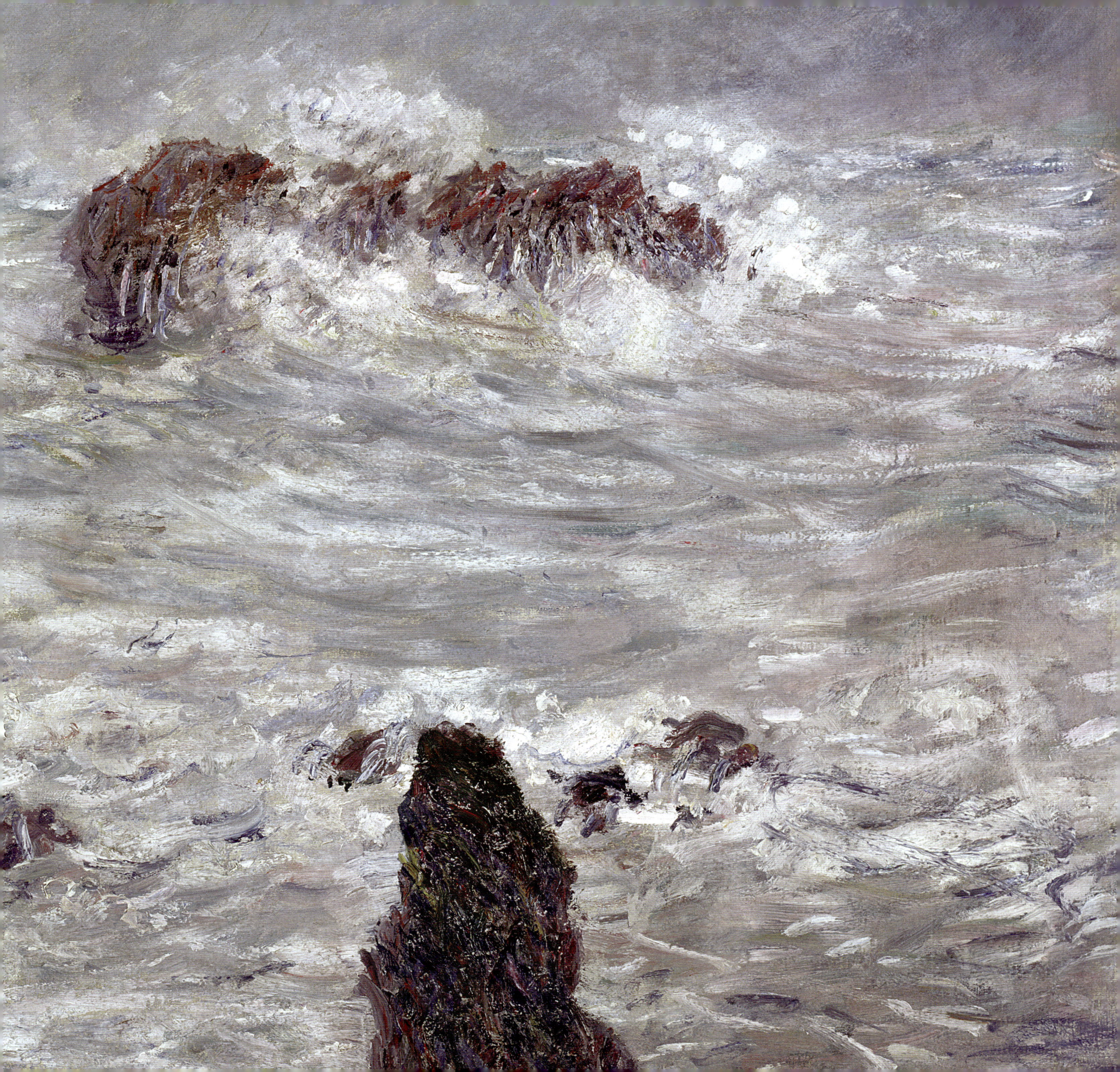

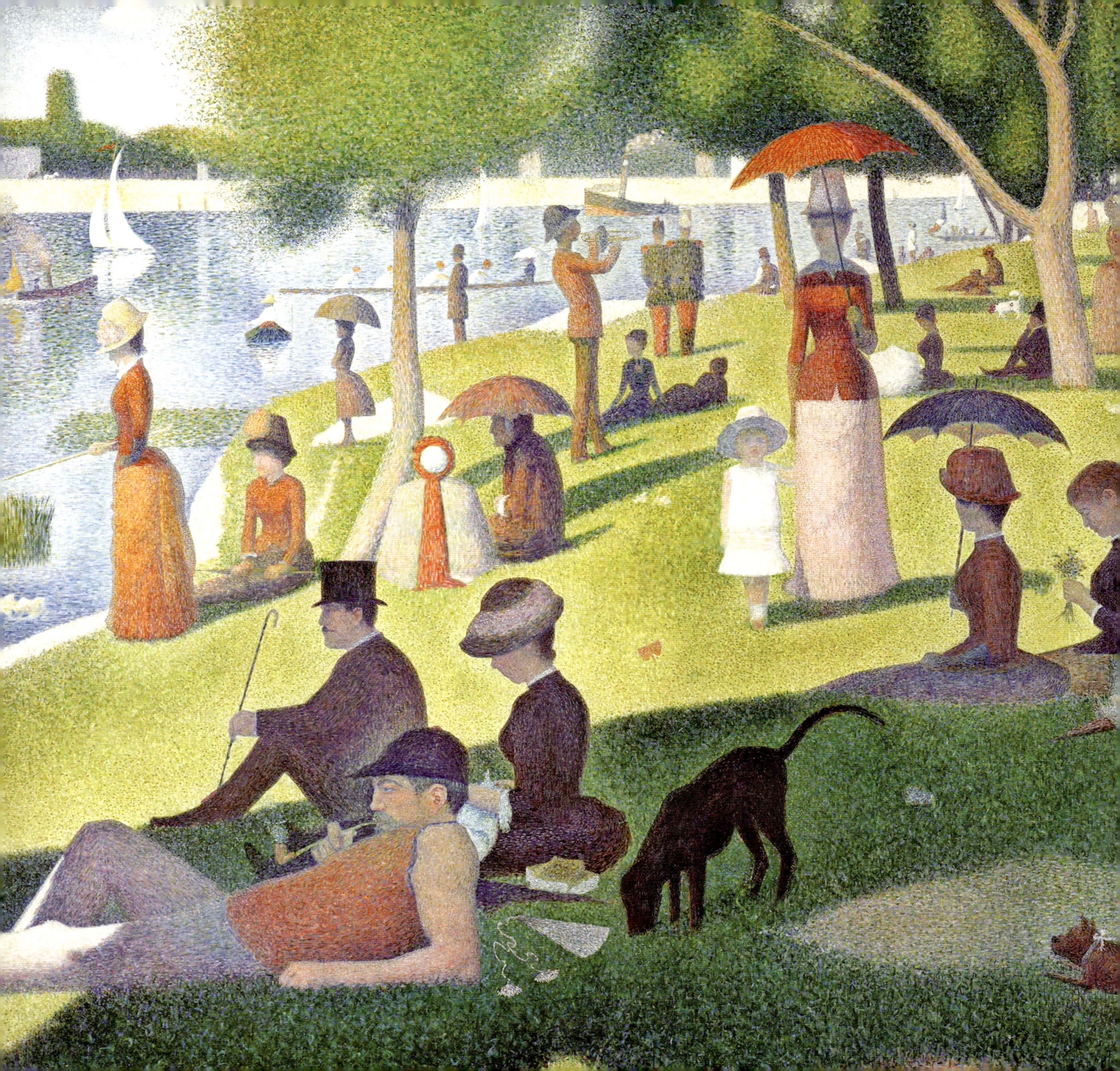

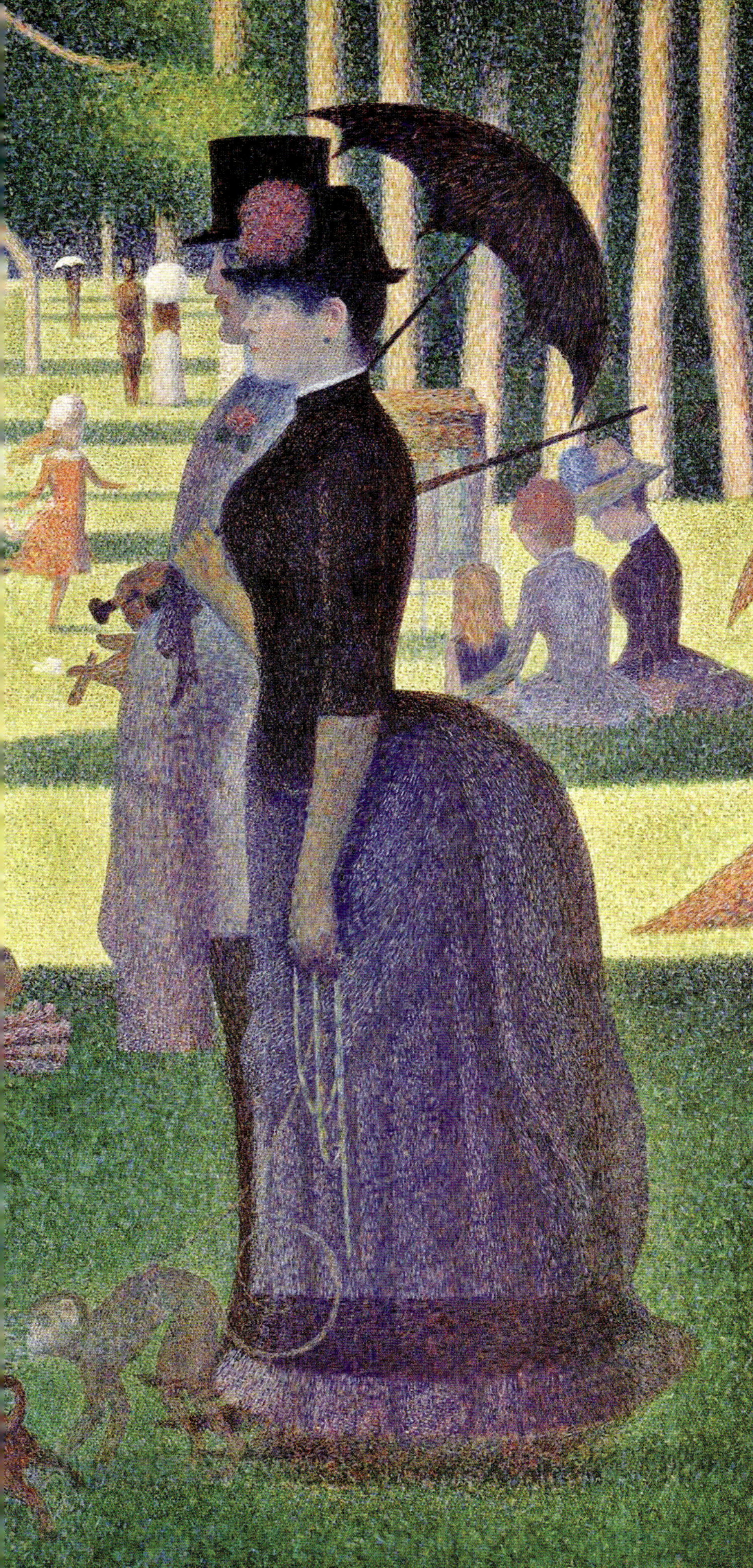

appear tinged orange (the complementary of blue), or if put next to violet, the black would take on a hint of yellow.

By the time he was painting *Bathers*, Seurat was also familiar with the more contemporary theories of the American physicist Ogden Rood (1831–1902), detailed in his 1879 book *Modern Chromatics, with Applications to Art and Industry*. Rood divided colour into purity, luminosity and hue, and emphasized the difference, already identified by the German physician and physicist Hermann von Helmholtz (1821–94), between colour as light (being additive, that is, the three primaries combine to white when mixed together) and colour as pigment (being subtractive, that is, they combine to black). Consequently, pigment could never achieve the intensity of light. One of Seurat's primary goals was thus to bridge the chasm separating paint from light, to find a formula for 'optical painting', whereby paint could achieve the seemingly impossible vibrancy of natural light.

A Formula for 'Optical Painting'

The trick, therefore, appeared to rest in the combination of two key principles. The first, the theory of optical mixture, mandated the avoidance of mixing pigments (which, being subtractive, would make them duller), and advocated instead the juxtaposition of dots of pure colours such that they fuse in the eye, thus ensuring – since the blending is of light and not pigment – its additive vibrancy. The second, the law of simultaneous contrast, stipulated the careful juxtaposition of complementary colours such that each heightened the perceived luminosity of the other. Through the dogmatic application of these scientific principles, the painter could most accurately replicate light as seen in nature on the surface of the canvas.

The depth of Seurat's understanding of the science has, however, been subject to question. It is noted, for example, that his exposure came largely second-

Left : *A Sunday Afternoon on the Island of the Grande Jatte*, 1884–86, Georges Seurat (1859–91)

hand via Charles Blanc's (1813–82) *Grammaire des arts du dessin* (1867), which had itself propagated certain misunderstandings of Chevreul's theories. Blanc erroneously understood Chevreul as advocating that painters make use of harmonic complementary colours when, in fact, it was contrasts of analogous colours that Chevreul favoured (colours with the same lightness). It was not only Seurat but also Gauguin, Signac and Van Gogh who laboured under Blanc's idiosyncratic reading of Chevreul.

Seurat's Manifesto Painting

Nevertheless, neither Seurat's commitment to the science of 'optical painting', nor indeed its ground-breaking impact, can be disputed. Both these factors achieved an early crescendo in 1886 with the exhibition of a painting Seurat considered his 'manifesto' at the final Impressionist exhibition: *A Sunday Afternoon on the Island of the Grande Jatte* (1884–86, *see* page 34). Another life-size canvas, the painting depicts the idyllic leisure of a typical Sunday, enjoyed on an island on the Seine near Asnières. Employing his method of, as he called it, 'chromo-luminarism', Seurat painted in three distinct layers. The first consisted of small rectangles of close hues of local colour, the second was a hatching of largely unmixed paint of complementary colours, and the third a covering of identically sized points or dots of complementary and adjacent colours (a refinement of the small brushstrokes of *Bathers at Asnières*, *see* page 26). The result was a

shimmering and luminous mosaic of forms, flattened to the plane of the canvas and stretched across it. The art critic Félix Fénéon (1861–1944) offered his enthusiastic praise for the 'conscious and scientific manner' in which Seurat divided tones, distinct from the 'arbitrary' manner of the earlier Impressionists. He identified that beneath the appearance of a uniform tonality Seurat had included, 'in a swirling crowd of tiny dots, all the constitutive elements of that tone'. 'These colours,' Fénéon continued:

isolated on the canvas, recombine on the retina: we have, therefore, not a mixture of material colours (pigments), but a mixture of differently coloured rays of light. Need we recall that even when the colours are the same, mixed pigments and mixed rays of light do not necessarily produce the same results? It is also generally understood that the luminosity of optical mixtures is always superior to that of material mixture, as the many equations worked out by M. Rood demonstrate.

Seurat's *Grande Jatte* was a 'complete and systematic paradigm of this new painting', more truthful for its systematic nature, since 'trickery is impossible'.

Neo-Impressionism was not simply an urban movement. In the summer of 1885, Seurat visited the Norman coast, where he painted numerous coastal scenes and seascapes, including *Le Bec du Hoc* (1885, *see* page 30), which represents the rocky coastline 15 miles east of Grandcamp. Although he made an oil study

Detail above : *Bathers at Asnières*, 1884, Georges Seurat (1859–91), *see* page 26

Right : *Gas Tanks at Clichy*, 1886, Paul Signac (1863–1935)

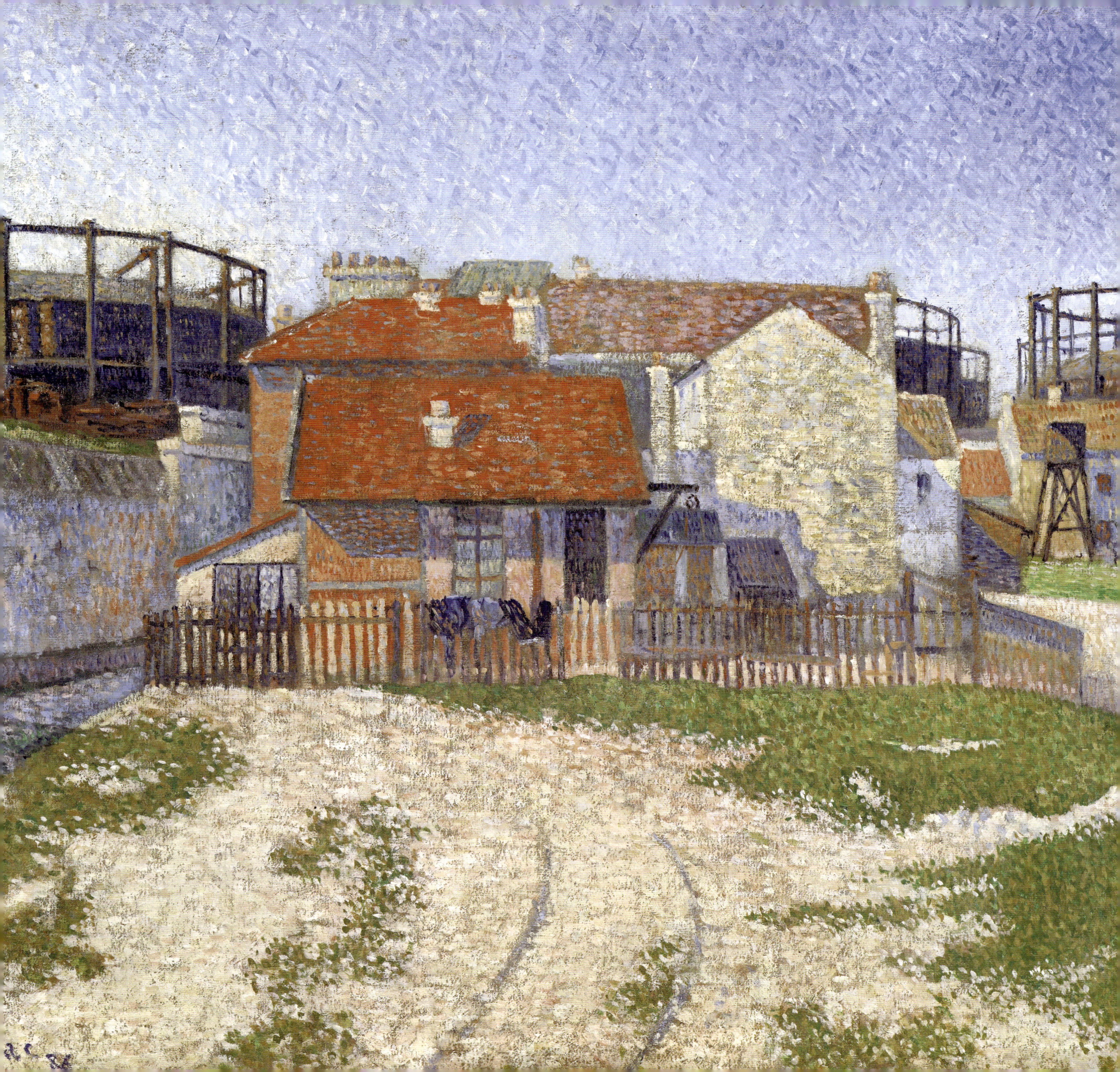

en plein-air (*Study for Le Bec du Hoc*, 1885), Seurat produced the final work in his studio. The finished work has subtly altered the viewpoint of the study; not only is the base of the cliff no longer visible, but the sky is given more space. The boat visible in the study is later joined by a flock of birds positioned above the grand sweep of the cliff, which dynamically and organically leads the eye in a kind of spiral up through the picture, balancing its effect and ensuring a careful mix of vigour and harmony. The aqua-blue and green tones of the sea – juxtaposed with the darker greens and yellows of the grass, and the blues and oranges that describe the shaded cliff edge – offer a chromatic counterpoint to the carefully crafted compositional consonance of thrusting cliff, level horizon and soaring birds.

Compare Monet's rendering of a *Storm, Coast of Belle-Ile* (1886, *see* page 33), painted a year later. Seurat produced harmony and balance by submitting himself to the unbending application of scientific principles. Monet instead conveys the changeable and chaotic drama of the weather. The visible and gestural brushstrokes connote the rapid (almost unconscious) application of paint, the bypassing of considered thought in favour of perception and description. Both Seurat and Monet sought to most accurately describe the maritime vista they each took for their subject. Their divergence is in method rather than goal.

Signac and the Essence of Painting

Exhibited alongside Seurat's monumental manifesto were works by his earliest converts, Signac and Pissarro. Signac's *Gas Tanks at Clichy* (1886, *see* page 37) demonstrates that he was drawing not only from Seurat's Pointillist method but also from his willingness to depict even the ugly, industrial side to city life (note the factory chimneys in *Bathers*). The bright red-orange of the roof is juxtaposed with its complements in the verdant grass and blue sky, and intermingled by means of a layer of pale blue and violet strokes. The shadow of the small

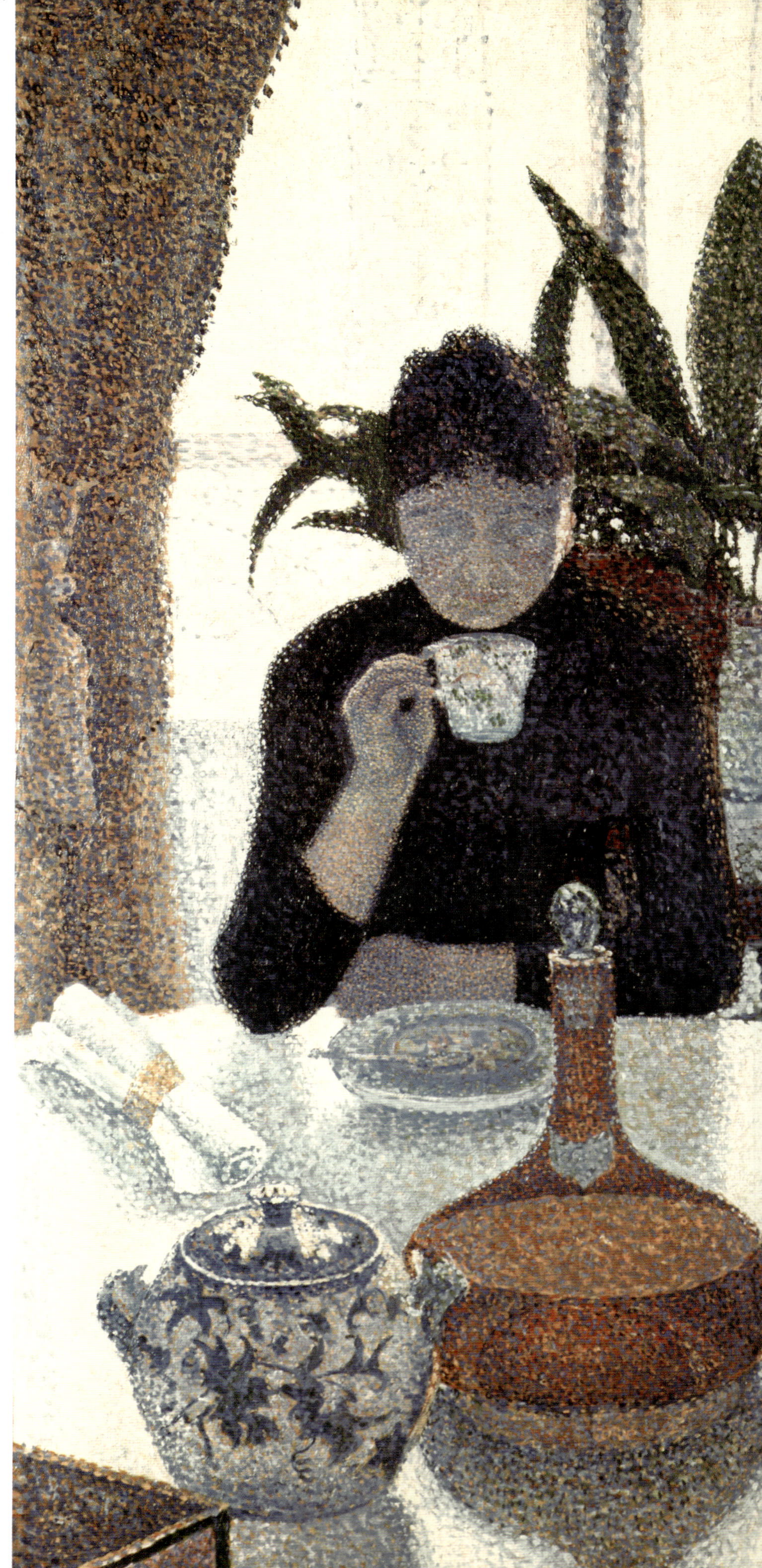

Right : *The Dining Room, Breakfast*, 1886–87, Paul Signac (1863–1935)

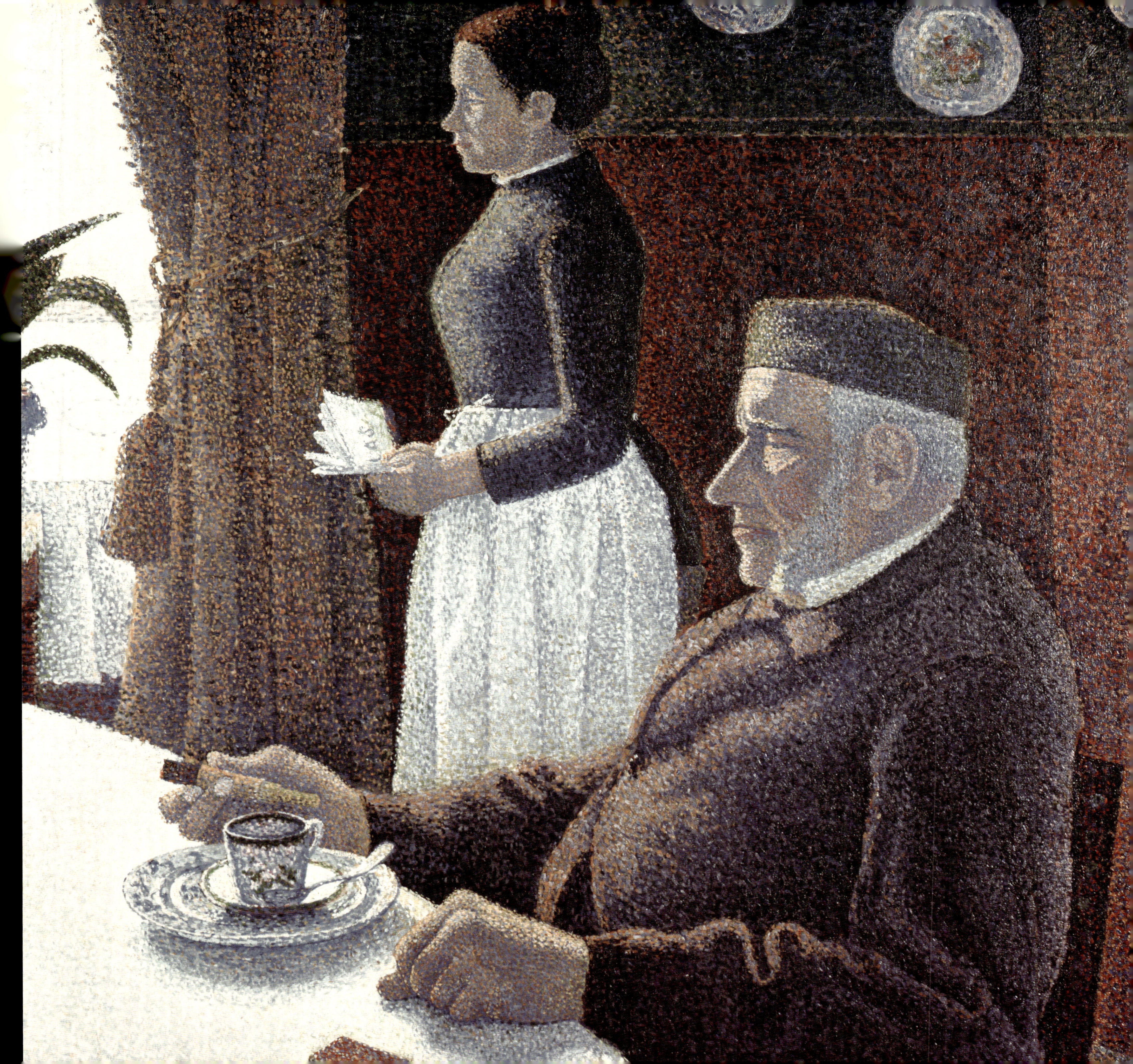

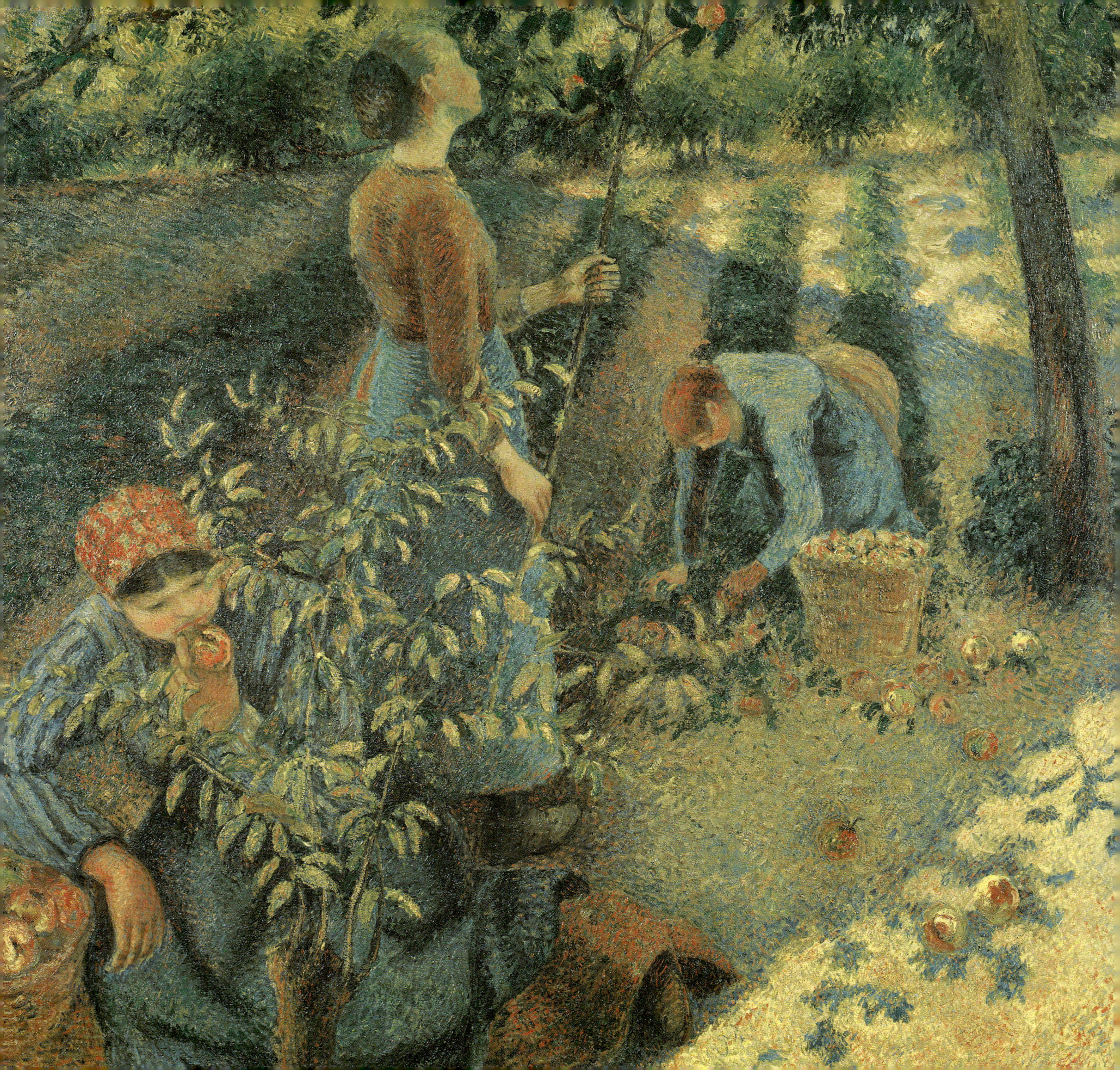

chimney is elucidated by a patch of dark blue points. The garden wall on the far left, whilst shrouded in a blue shadow, takes on the orange tint of the nearby house. Through studied attention, Signac has elevated this unassuming and overlooked patch of industrialized suburbia into a shimmering surface of light.

He would apply these principles to interiors as well as urban landscapes. *The Dining Room, Breakfast* (1886–87, *see* page 39), exhibited at the third annual exhibition of the Société des Artistes Indépendants (under whose auspices, we remember, Seurat had débuted his *Bathers*), depicts a singularly awkward and stilted breakfast scene chiefly through the juxtaposition of complementary blue and orange, and red and green, dots. In the shadow of the man's blue-and-white china teacup are dots of pale orange, and red dots in the reflection of the green-edged saucer. The orange decanter in the centre of the table is built up from a mixture of orange and blue dots; its shadow, as any reader of Chevreul would expect, features the complements red and green.

A year after praising Seurat's *Grande Jatte*, Fénéon's enthusiasm had not abated and, calling them for the first time 'Neoimpressionists', signalled that these painters had completely surpassed Impressionism's obsession with 'fugitive appearances' and the attendant temptation to 'exaggerate the features of nature in order to prove that it was a unique moment which would never be seen again'. Instead, the Neo-Impressionists sought to 'synthesize the landscape in a definitive aspect which perpetuates the sensation' it produces. Fénéon pointed out that all you had to do was 'step back a bit and all these varicoloured spots melt into undulating, luminous masses; the brushwork vanishes, so to speak; the eye is no longer solicited by anything but the essence of painting.'

Pissarro's Conversion

The significance of this challenge to Impressionism can be measured by the hostility provoked by the conversion of Camille Pissarro (a founding member of the Impressionist project) to its tenets before the 1886 Impressionist exhibition. Renoir, Degas and Eugène Manet (1883–92) – Édouard's brother, and husband of Berthe Morisot (1841–95), responsible with her for organizing the show – all wanted to exclude Seurat and this dangerous new current. In the event, Seurat and his followers were admitted but were quarantined in their own room. Alongside Seurat and Signac, Pissarro exhibited a large canvas entitled *Apple Picking* (1886, *see* left), in which he overlaid on to a traditionally Impressionist composition the Pointillist mosaic of dots.

Pissarro's first fully Neo-Impressionist canvas, however, depicted the *View from My Window in Cloudy Weather, Éragny* (1886, reworked 1888, *see* page 42). This composition adopts the geometricized simplicity of Seurat's frieze-like *Grande Jatte* and Signac's *Gas Tanks*, dividing the landscape into distinct, flattened bands, in which the buildings, animals and diminutive figure align neatly. This rational and geometric approach to composition was, as we shall examine in chapter three, as important a part of the Neo-Impressionist project as its scientific approach to luminous colour. However, the painting was originally noted more for the stridency of its colour, which the dealer Paul Durand-Ruel (1831–1922) advised Pissarro made the canvas unsalable. In 1888, Pissarro reworked it to add more foliage in the foreground and to soften the colours. This hesitant conviction presaged Pissarro's abandoning of the Neo-Impressionist manner in the early 1890s, declaring that he had found it too restrictive and impossible to reconcile with his desire to impart his individual character.

Fénéon and Gauguin

Although his 1886 review is most famous for its effusive praise of Seurat, Fénéon was not silent about the other painter exhibiting his alternative approach to colour: Paul Gauguin. It was through his friendship with Pissarro – cultivated in the 1870s when Gauguin was working in banking, collecting

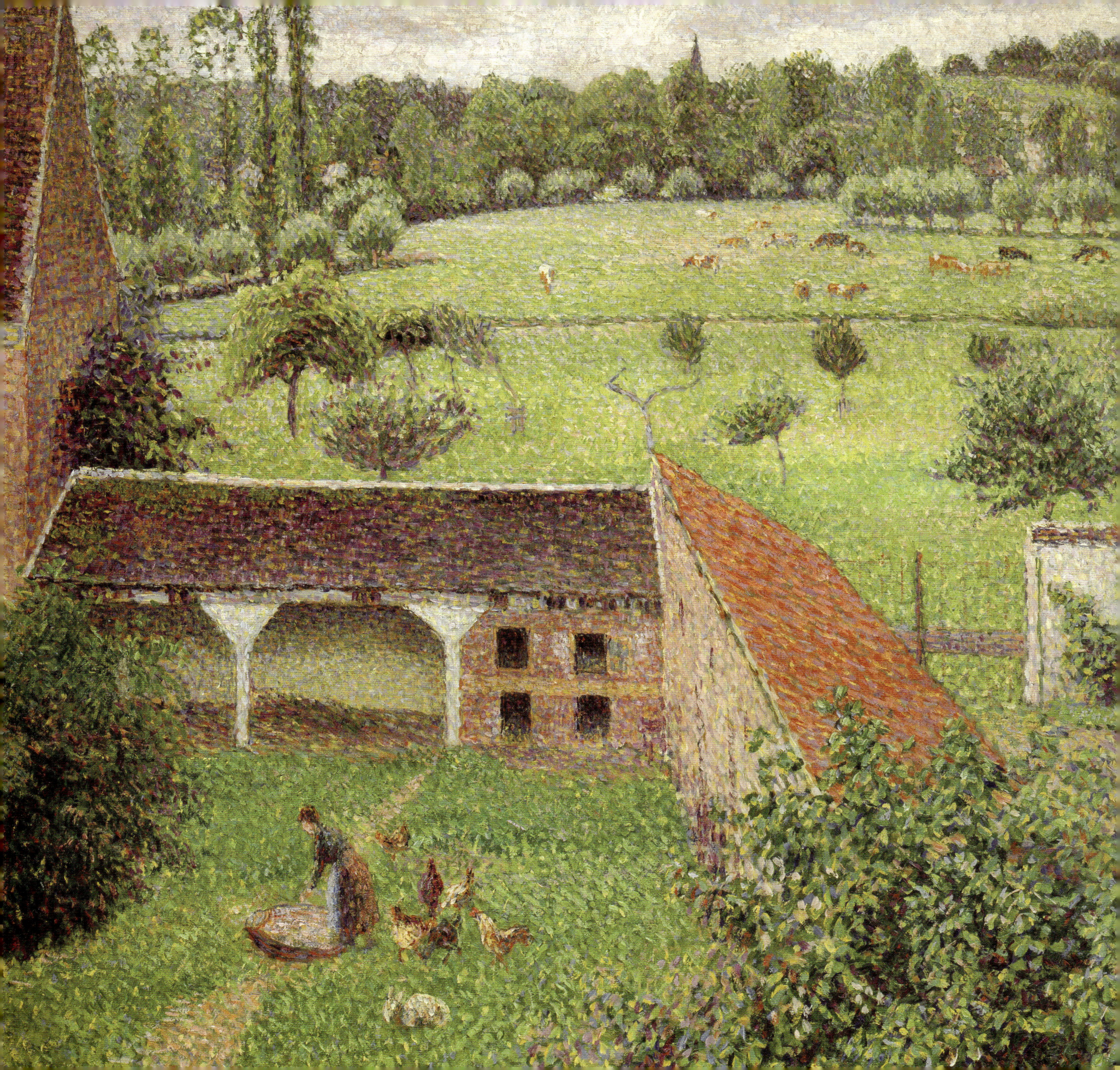

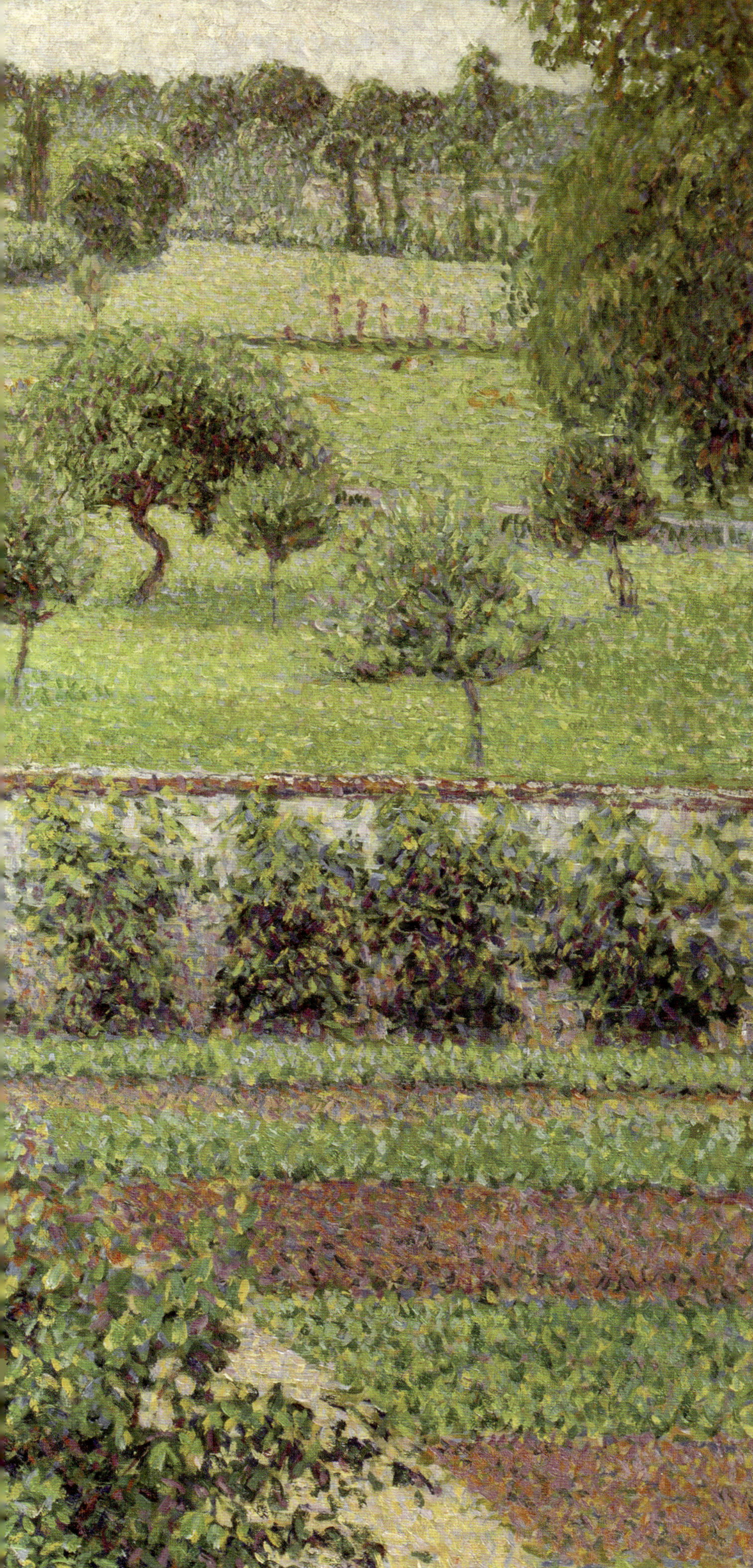

Impressionist paintings, and only painting in his spare time – that he had initially been invited to exhibit with the Impressionists in 1880. His earliest works, such as *Nude Study, Suzanne Sewing* (1880, *see page 44*) and *Snow, Rue Carcel* (1884, *see page 45*), evidence the naturalistic impulse, approach to colour and form, and choice of subject typical among the Impressionist cohort. Under the tutelage of Pissarro and Cézanne, Gauguin continued to develop more expressive colour and brushwork and, finding himself unemployed after the stock market crash of 1882, decided to devote himself to painting full time.

However, his hopes of a stable career proved ill-founded and, desperately poor, Gauguin was forced to move his family (he had married Mette-Sophie Gad, a Dane, in 1873, with whom he had had five children) to Rouen, where the cost of living was considerably lower than Paris. This solution was not to the taste of Mette, who, accompanied by the children, left for Copenhagen. In order to re-join them, Gauguin accepted a poorly paid salesman job, a short-term fix which satisfied nobody. Gauguin returned to Paris alone in 1885, saddened but now free to follow his ambition of being a painter. However, the canvases that caught Fénéon's eye in 1886 had been produced as early as 1884; speaking of works such as *Cliffs at La Bouille* (1884, *see page 46*), he wrote:

> *The muffled harmony in M. Paul Gauguin's paintings flows from the close-set tones he uses. Dense trees gush from rich, humid, lush soil, overflowing the frame, banishing the sky. A heavy air. A glimpse of bricks suggests a nearby house, hides stretch, muzzles part the brushwood – cows.*

Despite his interest in natural phenomena, for Fénéon Gauguin was thus clearly distinguished from the artists alongside whom he was exhibiting by a unique commitment to the emotional and the evocative.

Left : *View from My Window in Cloudy Weather, Éragny*, 1886 reworked 1888, Camille Pissarro (1830–1903)

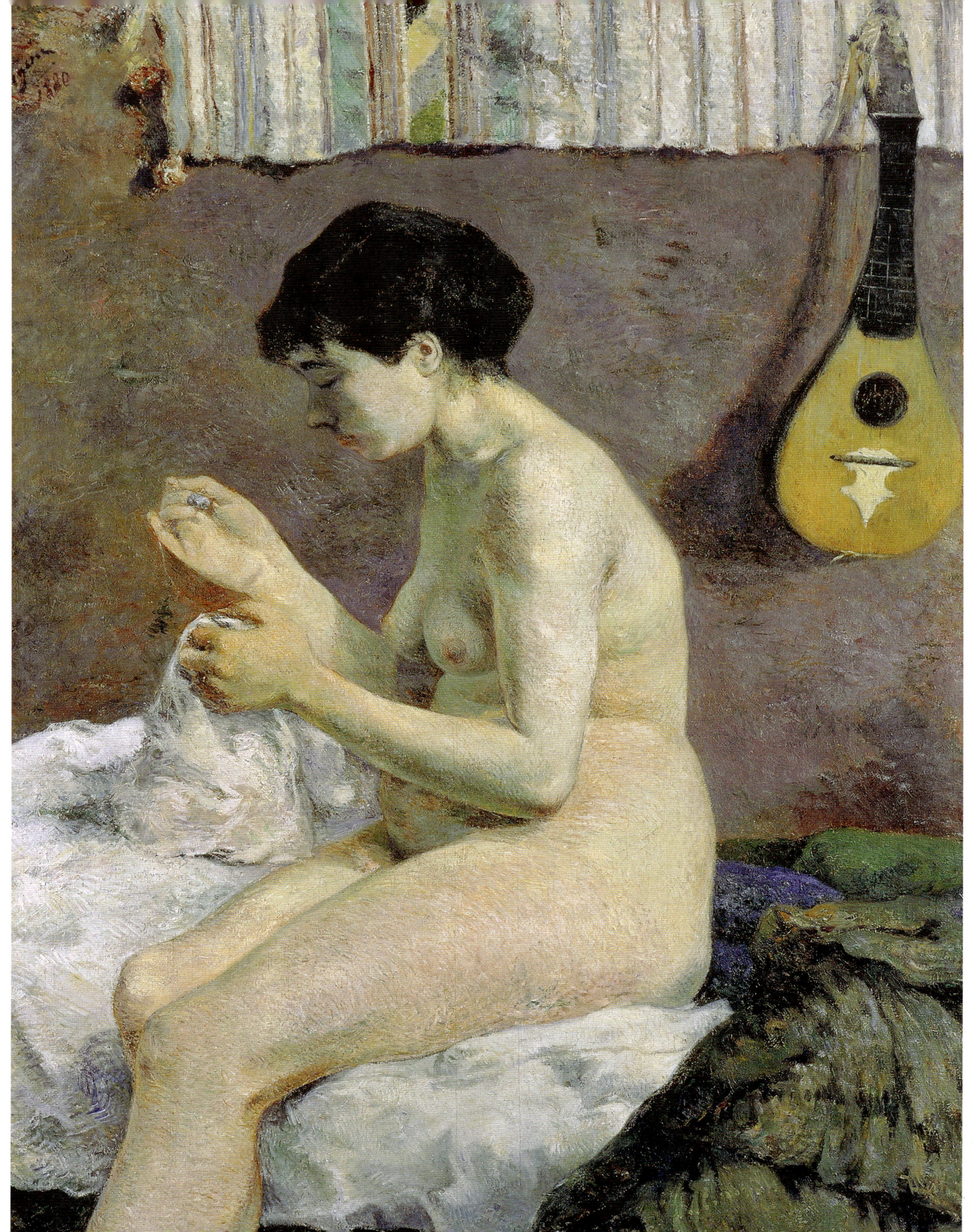

Breton Primitiveness

Gauguin further developed this desire to evoke rather than describe during his first trip to Pont-Aven in Brittany during the second half of 1886. Brittany appealed to Gauguin for its 'primitive' backwardness, characterized by the persistence of traditional customs of language, dress, religion and culture in the context of a nation being increasingly homologized along Parisian lines. It was a deliberate policy of the French government at the end of the nineteenth century to enforce political centralization (the concentration of power in Paris) and cultural homogenization. France had always been something of a patchwork of regional variations that found expression in culture and language. However, traumatized by defeat in the Franco-Prussian War (in which Prussia had besieged Paris and annexed the regions of Alsace and Lorraine, and various left-wing cities had declared their autonomy with respect to the conservative national government based in Versailles), this diversity increasingly came to be seen by those in power as a threat to national unity and, crucially, to the loyalty of provincial citizens. A crusade to eradicate non-French dialects (such as Provençale, spoken in the south) and languages (such as Breton, spoken in Brittany) went hand-in-hand with the promotion of national symbols (such as *Le Tricolore* and *La Marseillaise*) in place of regional ones. The Impressionists (in works such as Monet's *The Rue Montorgueil in Paris. Celebration of 30 June 1878*, painted in the year of the celebration) were all too happy to oblige this propagandistic mission. In this context, Gauguin's celebration of the Bretons' persistent cultural independence was a supreme expression of his disdain for metropolitan Paris, its politics and its art.

In paintings such as the 1886 *Breton Women Chatting*, Gauguin married a 'primitive' subject matter – we see four Breton peasants dressed in their traditional Catholic dress – with an ostentatiously 'primitive' painterly approach, with flattened and crudely modelled forms, rough, visible brushstrokes, clear outlines and sometimes sharply contrasting colours. Gauguin also applied this newly stylized approach to forms in his landscapes. In *Washerwomen at Pont-Aven* (1886,

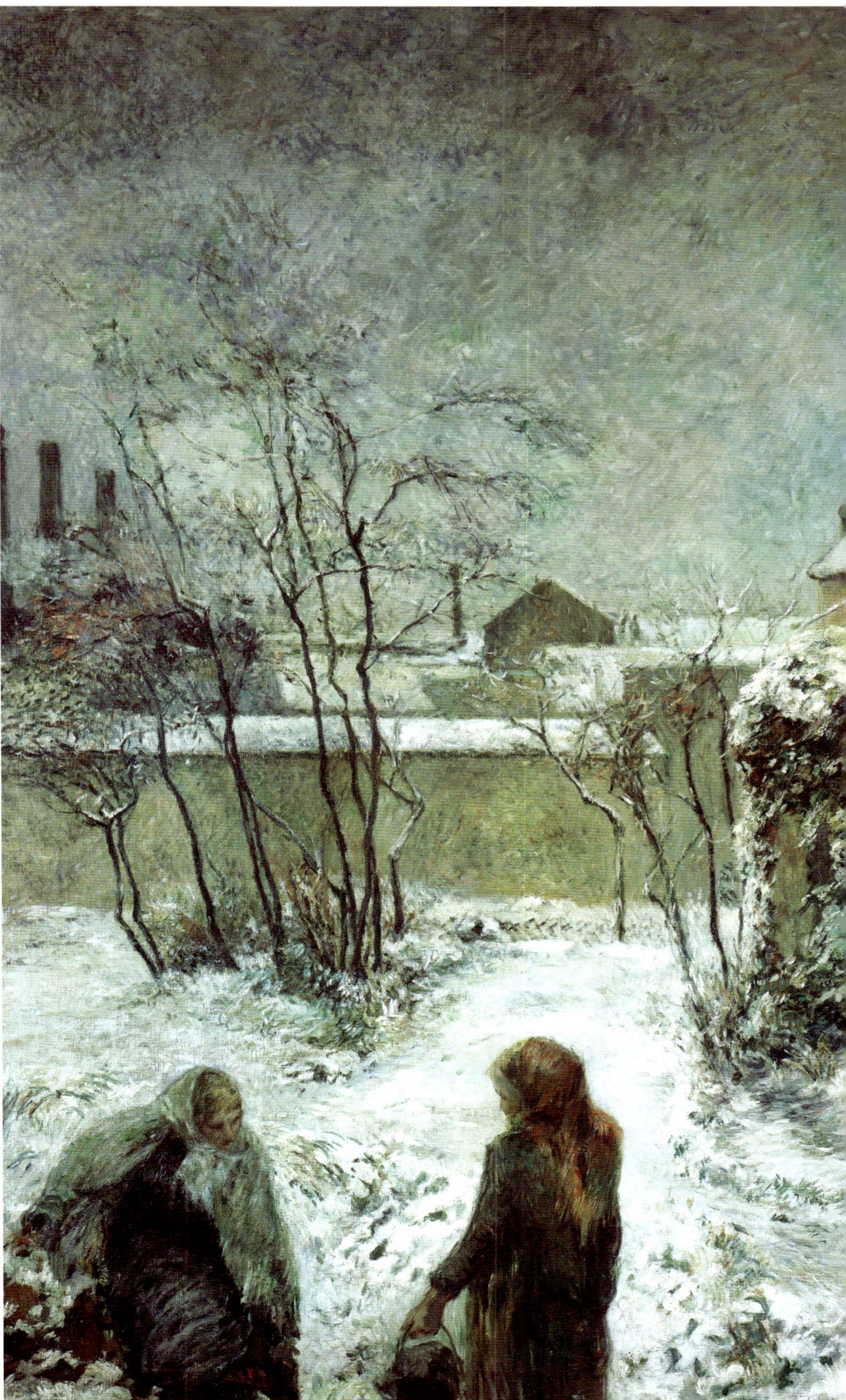

Left : *Nude Study, Suzanne Sewing*, 1880, Paul Gauguin (1848–1903)

Above : *Snow, Rue Carcel*, 1884, Paul Gauguin (1848–1903)

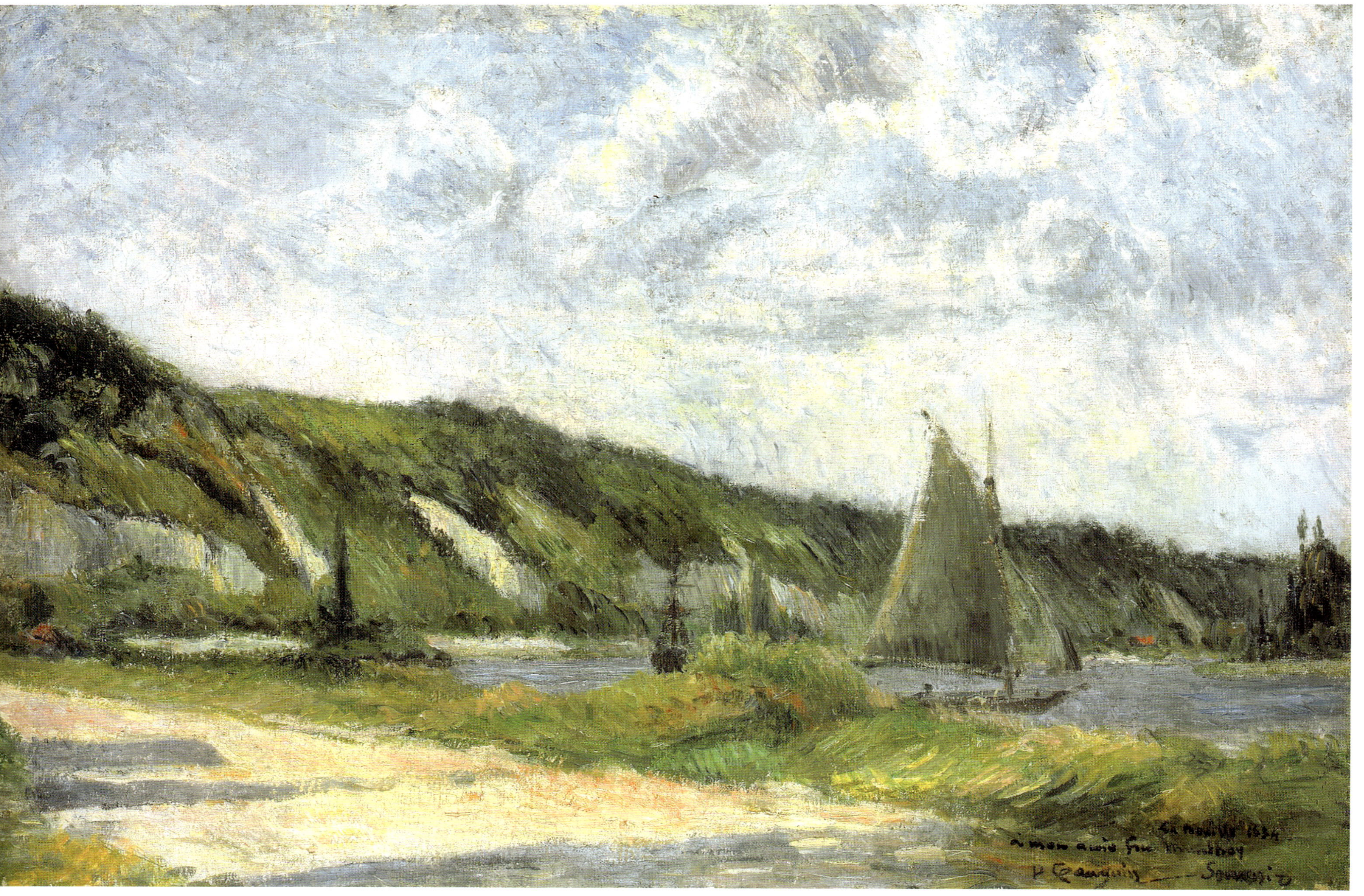

see right), Gauguin daringly organized space within a geometric schema consisting of flattened patches of colour and dynamic, if systematic, brushstrokes reminiscent of Cézanne's contemporaneous landscapes. It was during his first trip to Brittany that Gauguin connected more forcefully than ever before his progressive desire to produce new and innovative artistic forms with a concomitant commitment to retrograde and 'primitive' cultures.

Sensation

Gauguin's writing at this time stressed the antagonism between thought and sense perception, and, reversing the dominant hierarchy of nineteenth-century philosophy, argued that thought was a slave to sensory impression: 'To say that thought is spirit while the instincts, the nerves, the heart

Above : *Cliffs at La Bouille*, 1884, Paul Gauguin (1848–1903)

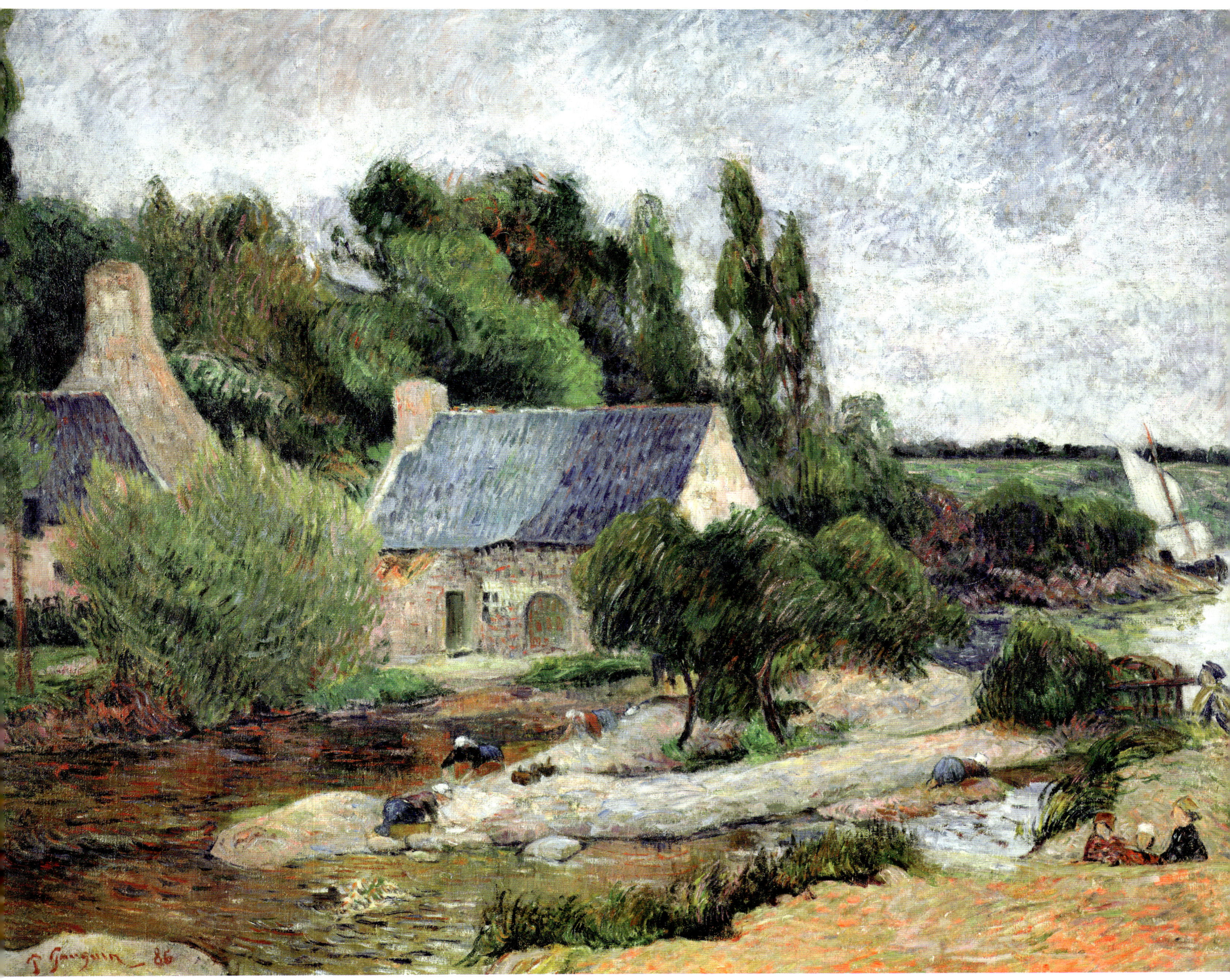

Above : *Washerwomen at Pont-Aven*, 1886, Paul Gauguin (1848–1903)

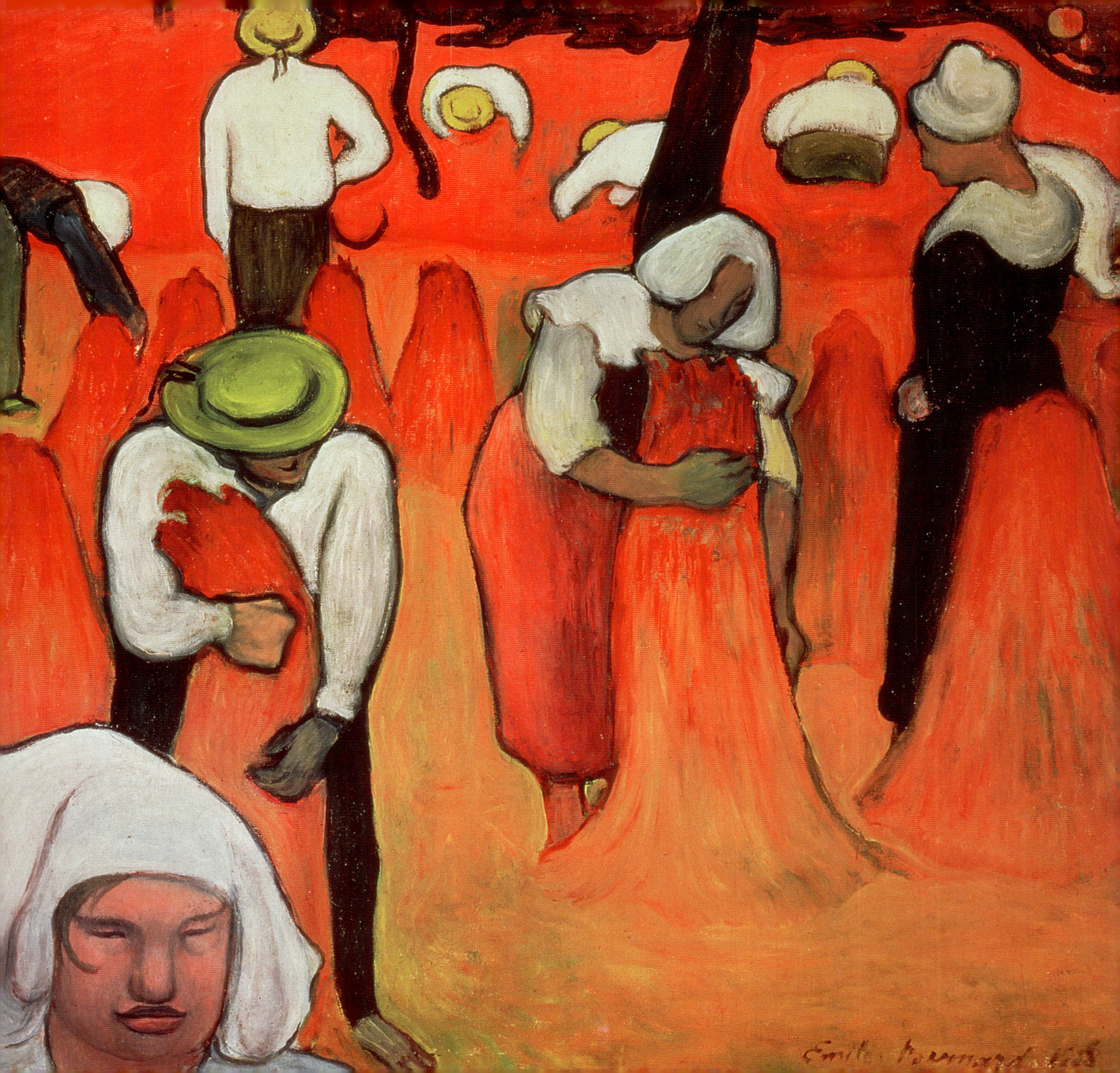

are part of matter. What irony!' At the core of Gauguin's commitment to sensation was precisely the colour science that had inspired Seurat. '… everything is contained in this word' [sensation], he wrote to his friend and fellow artist – albeit of medium talent – Émile Schuffenecker (1851–1934) in January 1885. In Gauguin's view, this science legitimized the divisionist approach (the juxtaposition of pure colours rather than their mixing) first pioneered by the Impressionists and refined by the Neo-Impressionists. However, where Seurat and the Neo-Impressionists sought to apply this knowledge in a rational, dogmatic and (ultimately) thoughtful manner, Gauguin felt that intuition and feeling, unshackled from reason, must come to the fore. Thus liberated, the very abstract and autonomous qualities of colour, line and form could stimulate in the viewer deep sensations that completely bypassed rational cognition. Nevertheless, the actual process of producing a picture was to be one not of unrestrained spontaneity but of synthesis, of recombining reference and studies from various sources.

In 1888, after a brief sojourn in Paris, Gauguin returned to Pont-Aven in Brittany, where his style underwent a radical shift, under the influence of Émile Bernard. Bernard had spent his early career painting suburban views of Asnières in Impressionist and then Neo-Impressionist styles. However, impelled by the same cultural current that saw Gauguin drift from Paris to 'primitive' Brittany, Bernard undertook a walking tour of Normandy and Brittany in 1886, during which the Gothic architecture and

medieval public sculptures made a profound impression on his sensibility. In August of that year, he met Gauguin for the first time (although the rendezvous was brief and uneventful) and, in the winter, Van Gogh. However, it was in collaboration with his friend Louis Anquetin (1861–1932), with whom he had trained in the studio of Salon artist Fernand Cormon (1845–1924), that Bernard developed a painterly style that came to be known as *cloisonnisme*, characterized by flat fields of unnaturalistic and unmodulated colour, strong outlines, simplified modelling and a decorative rather than descriptive sensibility.

Bernard's early masterpiece in the style of *cloisonnisme* was a painting of a Breton *Buckwheat Harvest* (1888, *see* opposite). The brilliant hue of red that dominates the painting is liberated completely from any descriptive function and is instead applied in largely unmodulated patches. The figures are highly stylized and simplified, again comprising flattened patches of colour bounded by thick, black contour lines. The result is a suppression of naturalistic space and detail; the harvesters and their buckwheat are pressed flat to the surface of the canvas.

Painted as its pendant, *Breton Women in a Meadow* (1888, *see* page 51) is perhaps even more crudely painted. Again, Bernard has elided realistic space in favour of a flat ground of pure colour. The Breton women are roughly painted in patches of ungraduated black, white and flesh tones and encased in the bold outline that was to inspire the critic Édouard Dujardin (1861–1949) to compare it to medieval stained glass and metalwork, coining the term '*cloisonnisme*'. Although significantly Bernard's senior (Gauguin was 40, Bernard only 20), Gauguin was nevertheless inspired to completely sever any lasting vestige of Impressionistic naturalism in his style.

Gauguin Inspired

The fruits of Gauguin's conversion were quickly evident: his *Vision of the Sermon: Jacob Wrestling with the Angel* (1888, *see* page 52) was painted in August 1888, almost immediately after his exposure to Bernard's *Buckwheat Harvest* and *Breton Women in a Meadow*. Gauguin drew from Bernard the unmodulated red ground, the simplified modelling of the Breton woman, the compression of pictorial space and the thickened contour lines. However, where Bernard strove to bring painting closer to decoration, Gauguin had a different purpose: the visual representation of immaterial thought. The Catholic piety of Breton women was a significant part of their alluring and primitive otherness. It was a signifier of their distance from mainstream French society and official government policy, which was one of *laïcité* (secularism), and open hostility to the Catholic church, which Republicans saw (quite correctly) as a bastion of conservatism and Monarchism.

Thus, Gauguin deployed the innovative formal abstraction of Bernard in order to find a way of depicting the supremely anti-positivist realm of the metaphysical: the collective religious vision of these Breton women as they exit from church. On the very right of the canvas, we see the tonsured abbé to whose sermon we presume the women have been attentively listening. Eyes closed, he leads the women in prayer as they experience a vision of Jacob wrestling with the angel. The luminous red thus symbolizes the mythical realm conjured by the religious imagination of the peasant women. The bough of an apple tree cuts across the frame, physically dividing the material from the immaterial, but also dramatizing the skewed perspective of

Right : *Breton Women in a Meadow*, 1888, Émile Bernard (1868–1941)

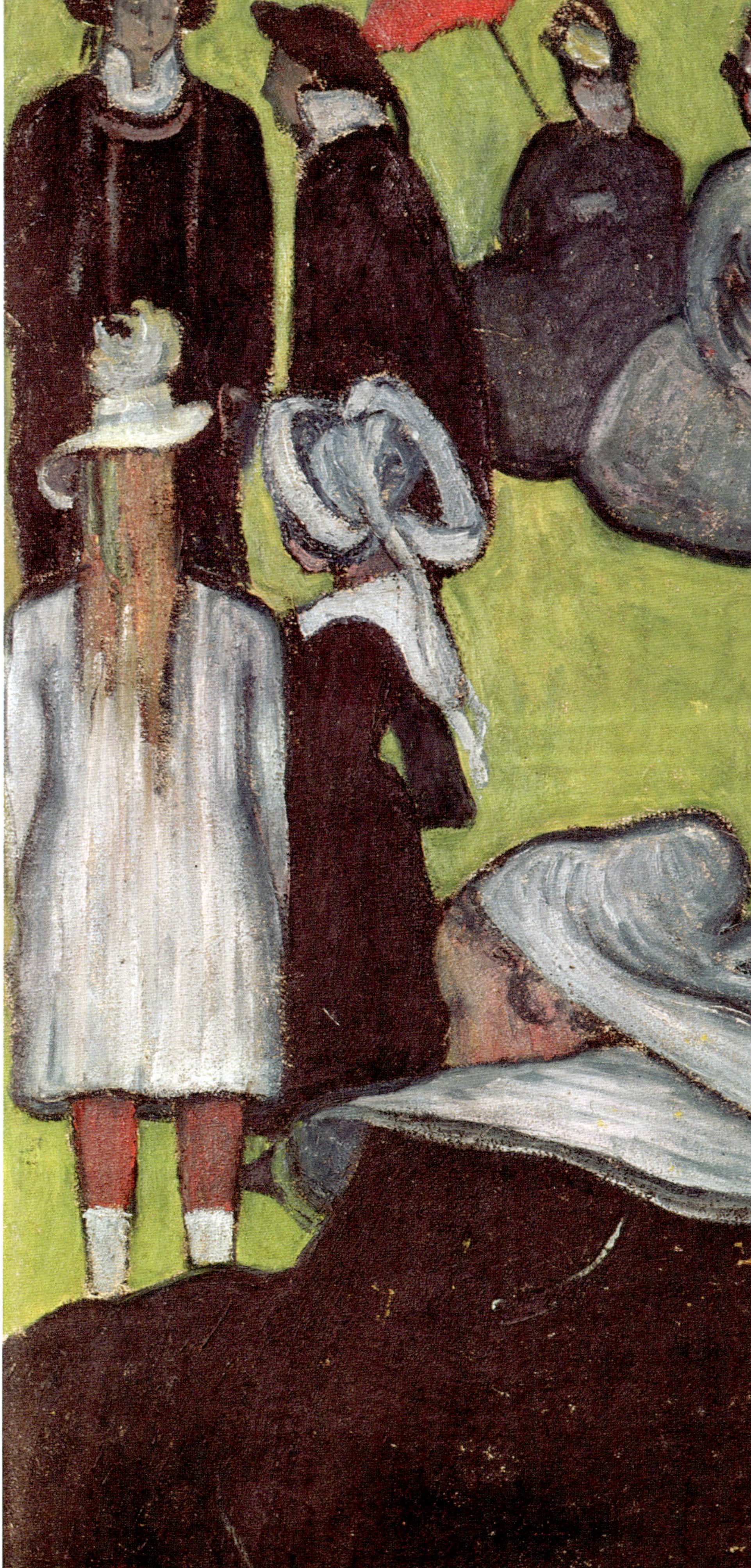

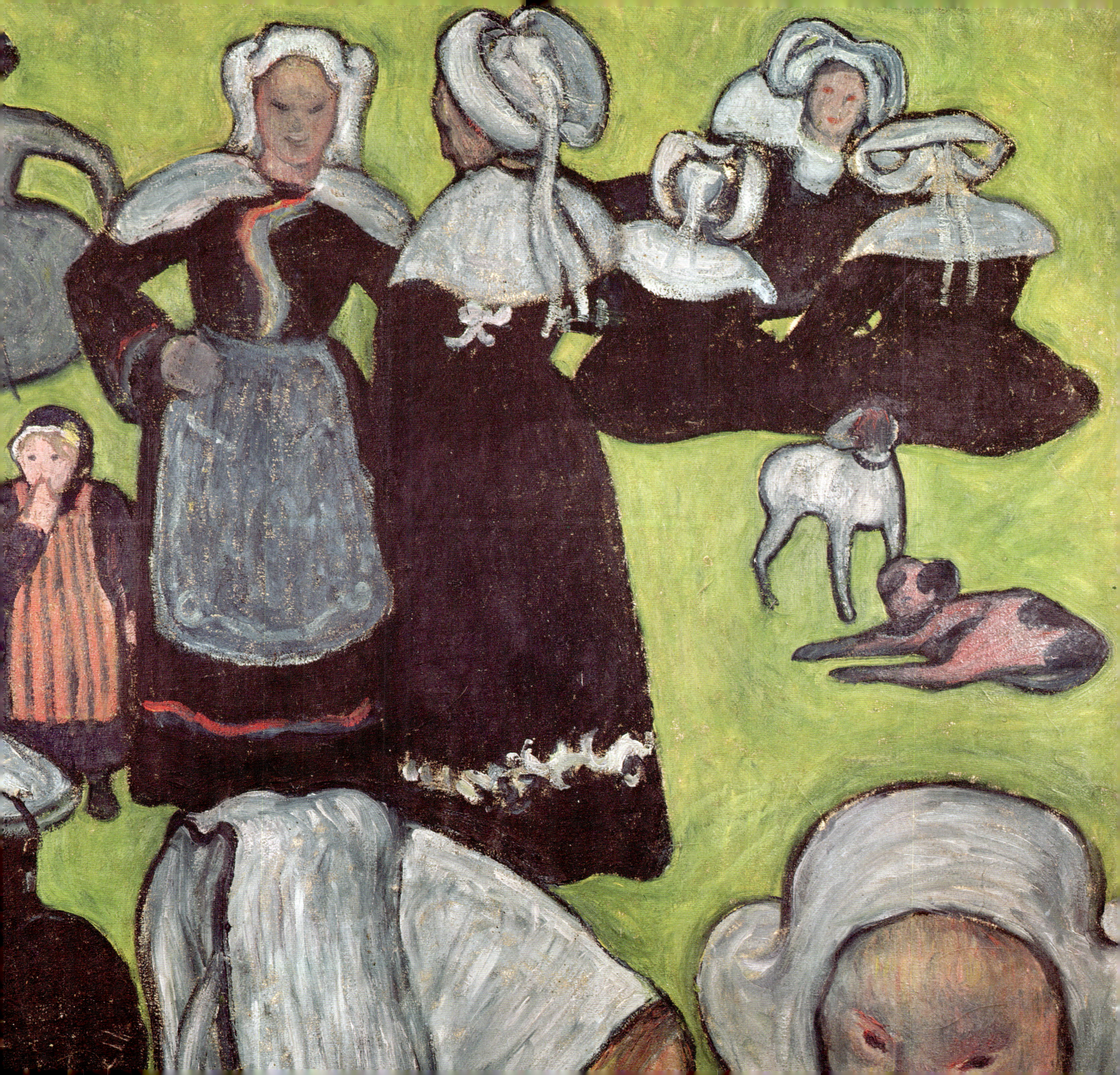

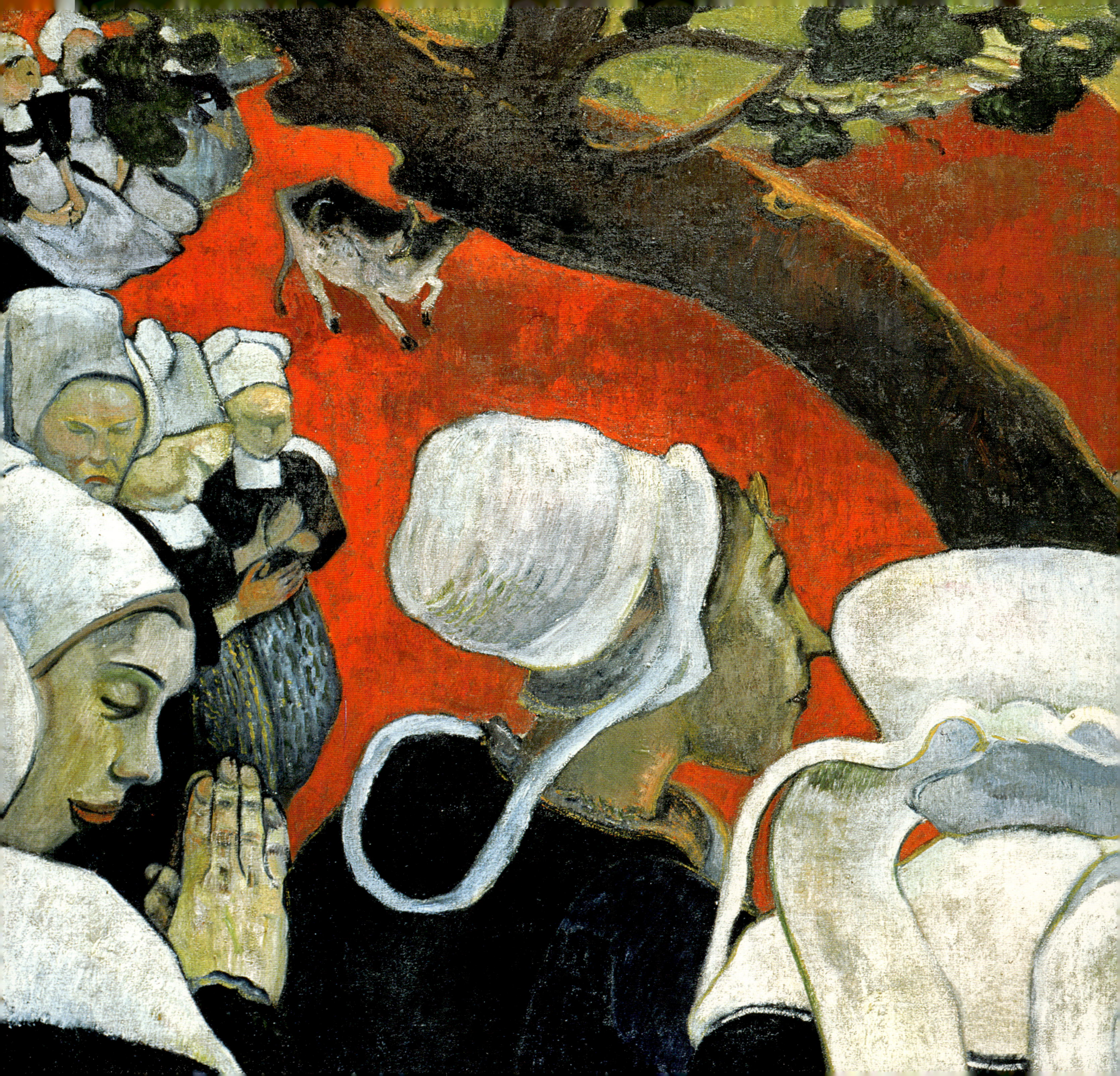

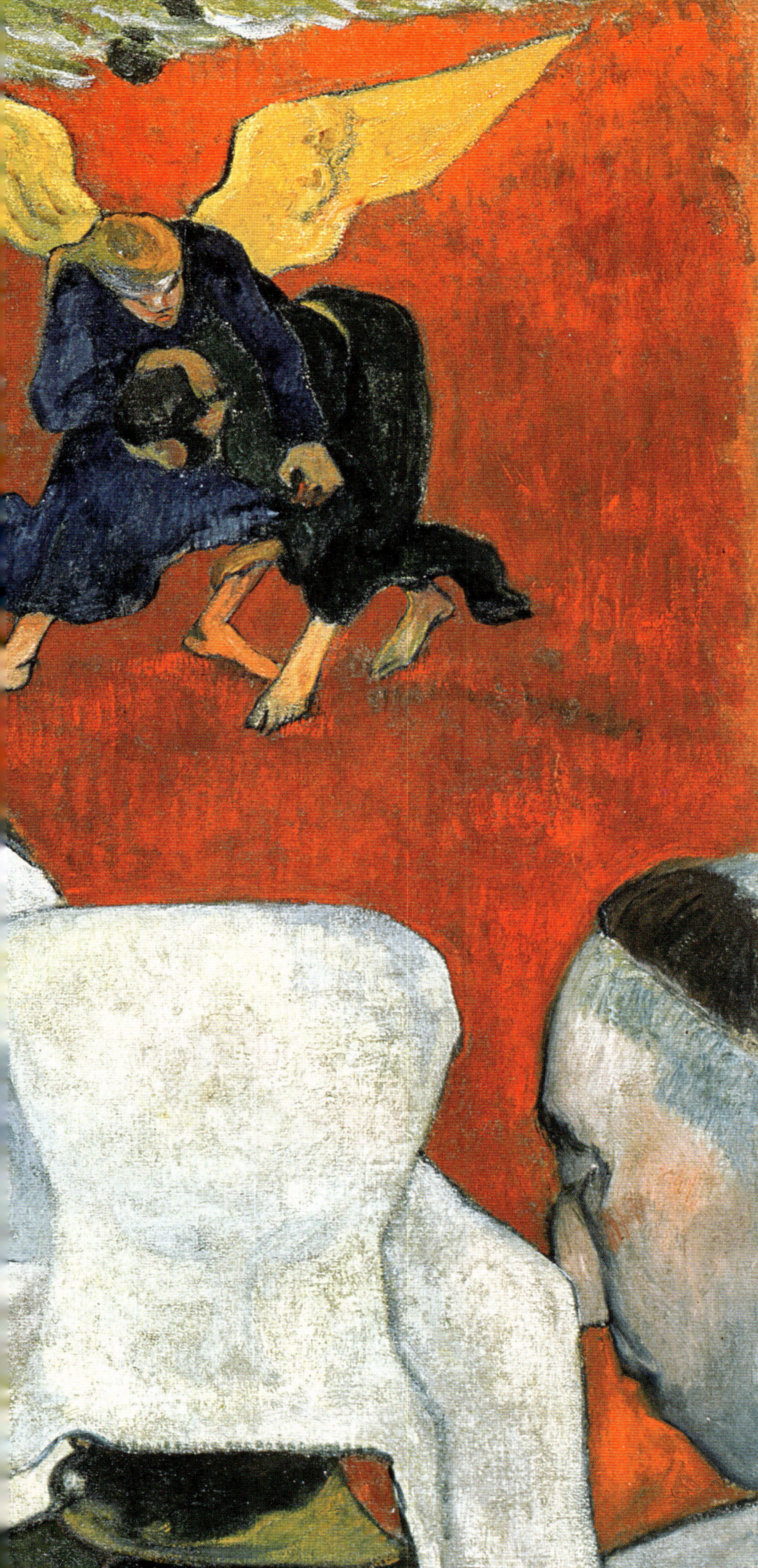

the scene. Compare the size of the cow to the Breton women ostensibly next to it. It is remarkably difficult to visualize how this tree might exist in three-dimensional space, where it begins and ends relative to the fixed viewpoint the spectator assumes.

As Gauguin himself noted, these deviations from accepted practice were designed precisely to relay this painting's synthesis of physical and metaphysical: 'For me, in this painting the landscape and the fight do not exist other than in the imagination of the people who are praying in response to the sermon – this is why there is contrast between [the] "natural" people and the fight in its "non-natural" and disproportionate landscape.'

The month after painting *Vision of the Sermon*, in September 1888, Gauguin met Paul Sérusier (1864–1927) and quickly established with him a didactic relationship, instructing him in his new-found manner of 'non-natural' landscapes. The result of this tuition was a scene of the Aven River at the Bois d'Amour that became known as *The Talisman* (1888, *see* page 54). In this painting, Sérusier managed to liberate colour from description to the greatest degree yet achieved. Flat blocks of yellow and green leaves, red soil and light blue tree trunks are doubled up by the lake's reflective surface. Barely comprehensible as a landscape, colour applied according to Gauguin's advice ('straight from the tube') exists almost entirely for its own sake.

'Les Nabis'

Sérusier returned to Paris in order to spread the word of Gauguin's discoveries to his fellow students at the Académie Julian. Enthusiastic converts included Maurice Denis, Pierre Bonnard (1867–1947), Paul Ranson (1864–1909), Ker-Xavier Roussel (1867–1944), Henri-Gabriel Ibels (1867–1936) and Édouard Vuillard (1868–1940). Thus coalescing around a common purpose, the group soon started calling themselves 'Les Nabis' (the Prophets), and

Left : *Vision of the Sermon: Jacob Wrestling with the Angel*, 1888, Paul Gauguin (1848–1903)

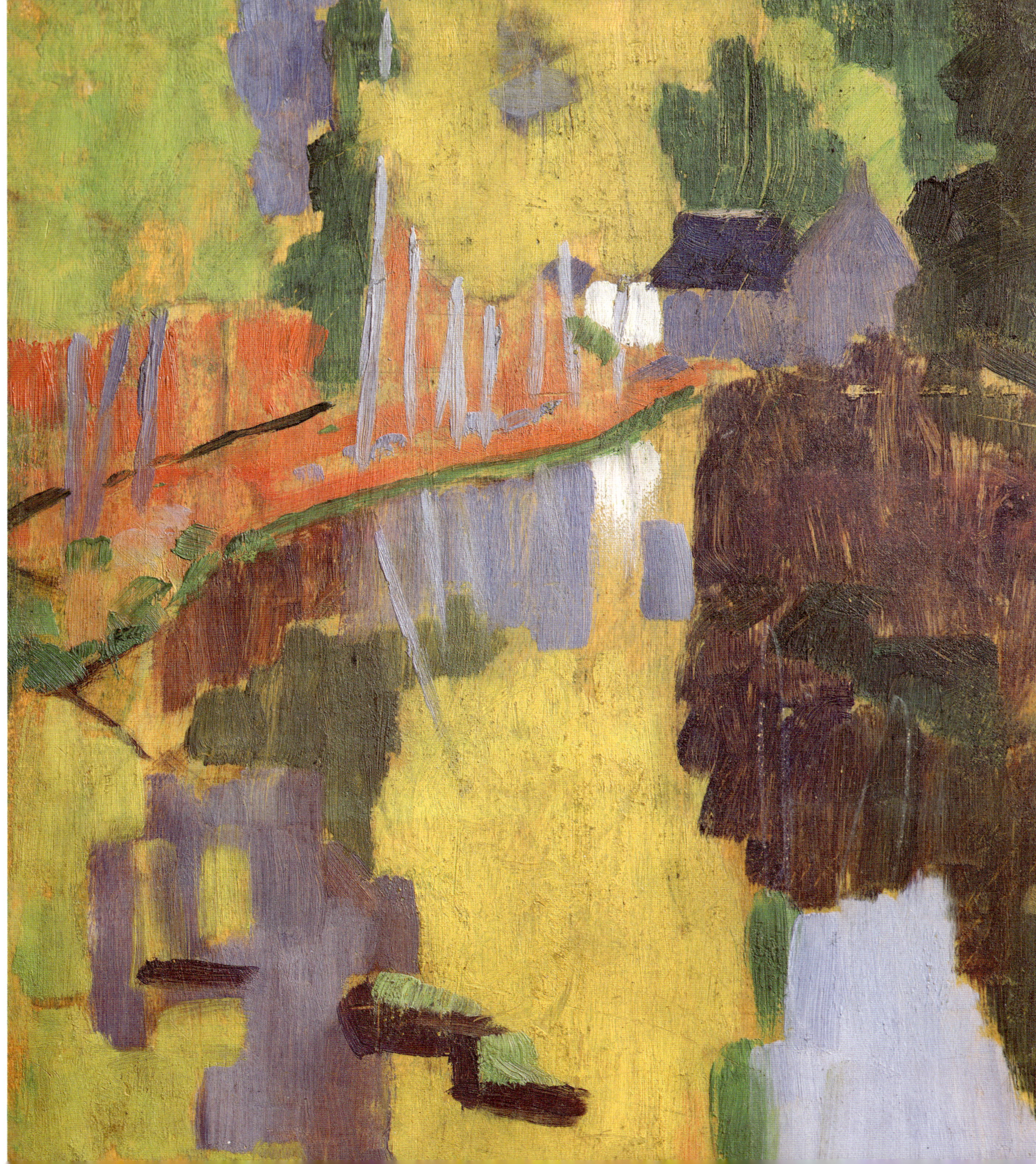

became a short-lived, quasi-religious and secret brotherhood under the guidance of Sérusier's 'dream for the future of a purified fraternity, made up only of committed artists, lovers of beauty and truth, who combine in their works and their lives that indefinable quality I translate as Nabi' (as he wrote to Denis in 1889).

Synthétisme

Leading the Nabis in Paris, Sérusier was also a member of the circle of painters around Gauguin that came to be known, because of their location, as the School of Pont-Aven, practitioners of a style called *synthétisme*, a name derived from the French verb 'to synthesize'. Their goal was to synthesize three things: firstly, the outward appearance of natural forms; secondly, the artist's subjective feelings for his subject; and thirdly, purely aesthetic considerations of colour, line and form as abstract entities. In 1889, Gauguin organized an 'Exhibition of Paintings of the Impressionist and Synthetist Group' in the Café Volpini, close to the concurrent Exposition Universelle (World's Fair). Gauguin deliberately excluded the Neo-Impressionists, instead seeking to exhibit 10 works of his own alongside others by Schuffenecker, Bernard, Armand Guillaumin (1841–1927) and Van Gogh.

In the event, Van Gogh refused to participate and so Gauguin's contribution was increased to 17 of the 93 works exhibited, and included his *Vision of the Sermon*. The credo of *synthétiste* painters was eloquently summarized by Denis in 1890 when he called for his fellow artists to remember that 'a picture before being a battle horse, a nude woman, or some anecdote, is essentially a flat surface covered with colours assembled in a certain order'. In reviewing the Volpini Exhibition, Fénéon (a rare critical voice to bother to comment on the show) noted that 'for [Gauguin] reality is but a pretext for distanced creations'.

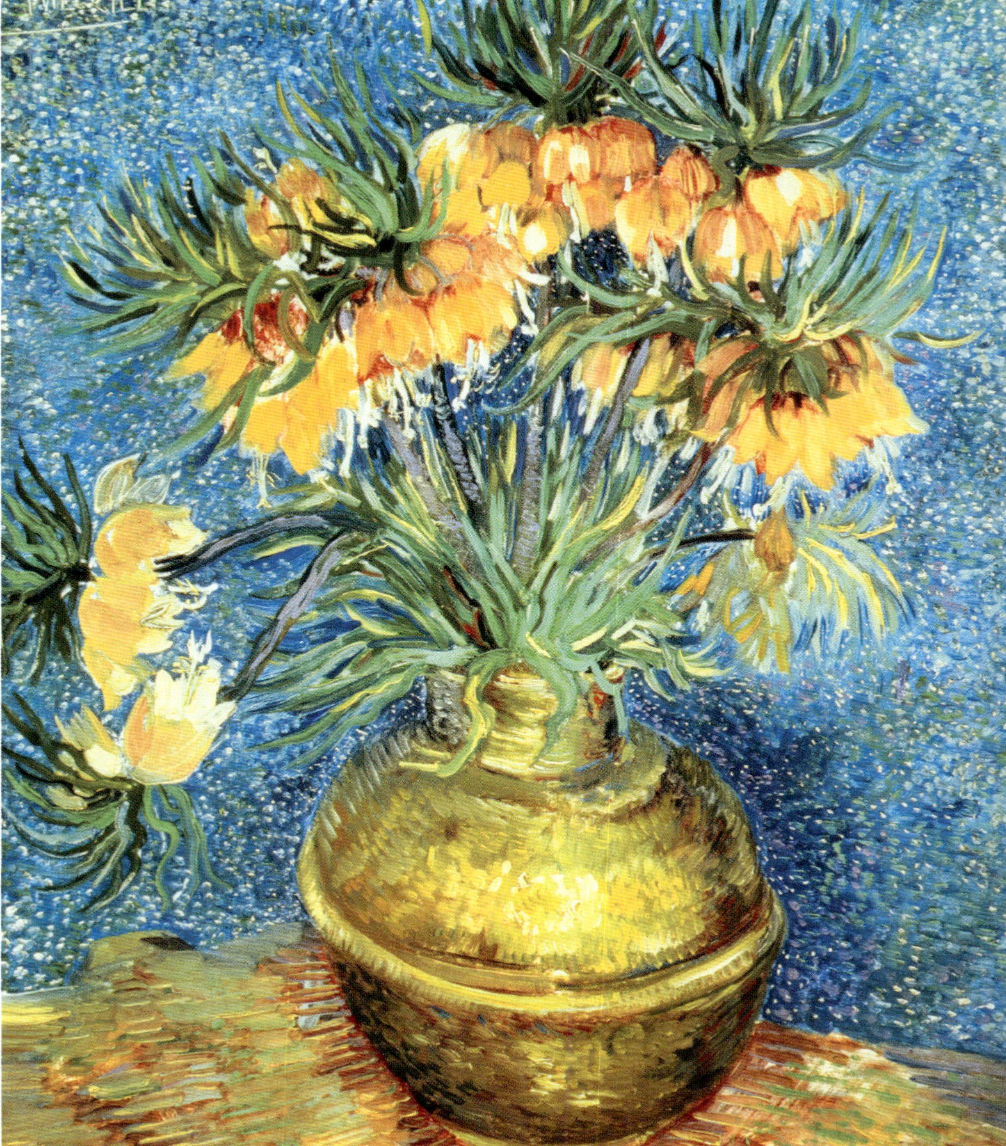

Van Gogh and Colour

For nine weeks towards the end of 1888, Gauguin visited Van Gogh in Arles, the pair working and living alongside one another in the famous Yellow House. As decisive as this moment was to be for Van Gogh, it was not the first moment that he had undertaken a deep consideration of colour in art. In 1886, Van Gogh moved to Paris and encountered for the first time the prismatic brilliance of Impressionism and Neo-Impressionism.

Left : *The Talisman*, 1888, Paul Sérusier (1864–1927)

Above : *Fritillaries in a Copper Vase*, 1887, Vincent van Gogh (1853–90)

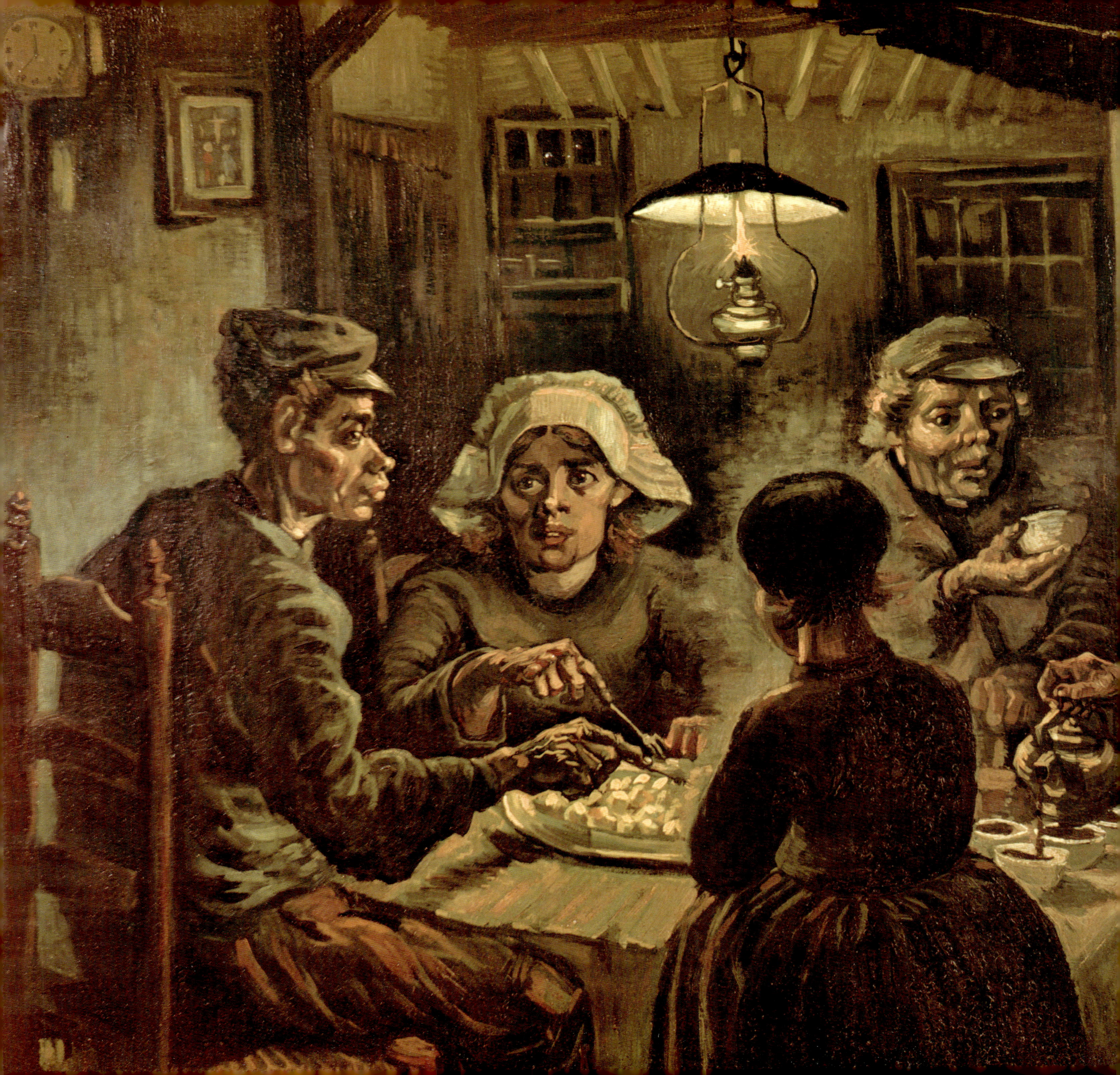

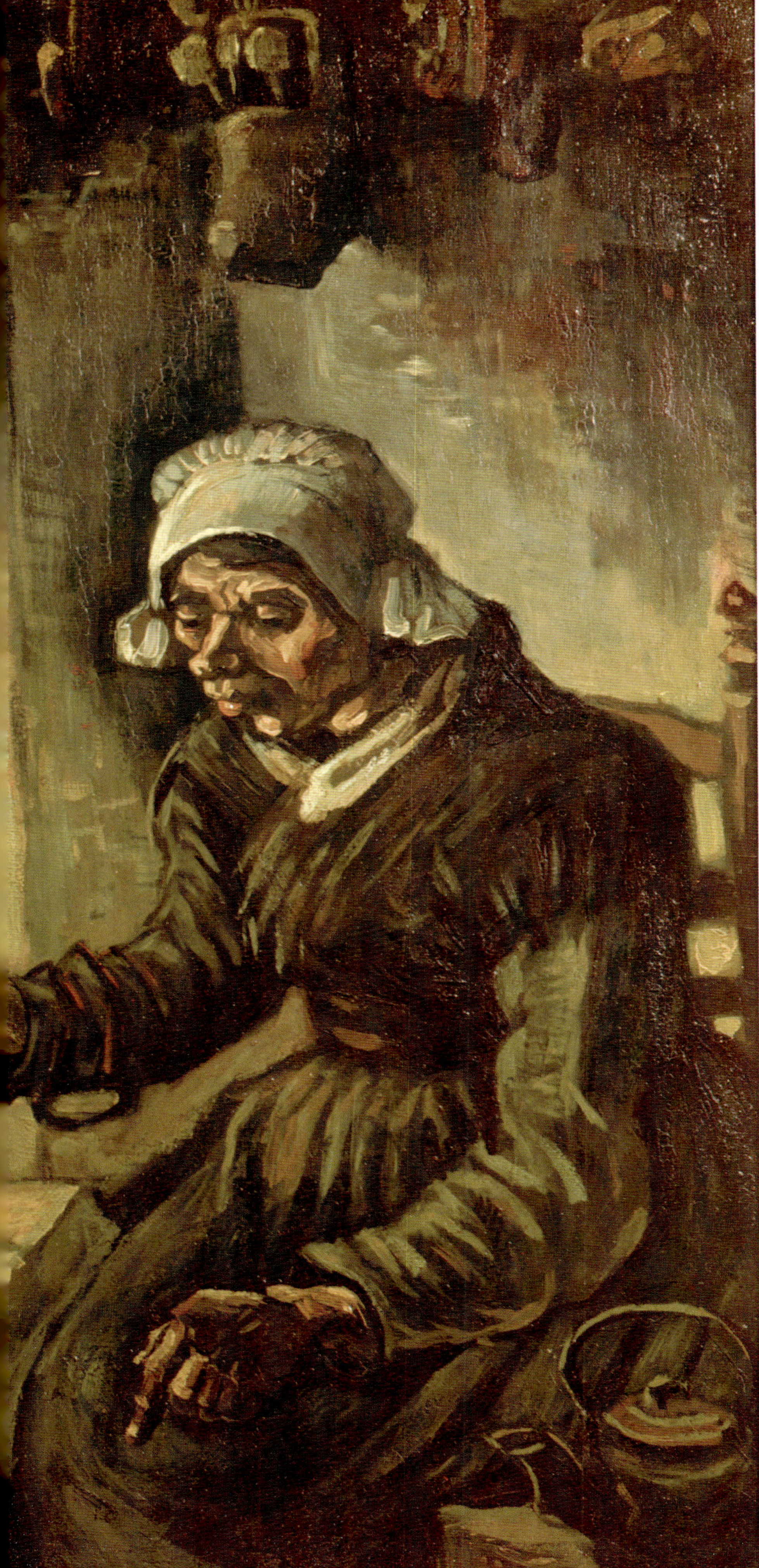

'A painter does better
to start from the colours
on his palette than from
the colours in nature.'

Van Gogh

Abandoning the sombre and heavy palette of works such as *The Potato Eaters* (1885, *see left*), Van Gogh instead submitted himself to the study of complementary colours and experiments in both Impressionist and Pointillist brushwork. His *Fritillaries in a Copper Vase* (1887, *see page 55*) is typical of this early shift in style and interest. However, even as early as 1883, Van Gogh was writing to his brother Theo that:

A painter does better to start from the colours on his palette than from the colours in nature. I mean, when one wants to paint for instance a head, and sharply observes the reality one has before one, then one may think: that head is a harmony of reddish brown, violet, yellow, all of them broken – I will put a violet, a yellow, and a reddish brown on my palette, and these will break each other.

Across three self-portraits in 1887 – two with a straw hat (*see page 59*) and one without – Van Gogh set these principles into motion. He painted a head in broken brushstrokes of reddish brown, violet and yellow (and in green and blue spots) whereby colour begets form and complementary harmonies of blue and orange, and yellow and purple (sadly, in the Van Gogh Museum version, the once-purple background has considerably faded) give the works a profoundly beautiful vibrancy.

Left : *The Potato Eaters*, 1885, Vincent van Gogh (1853–90)

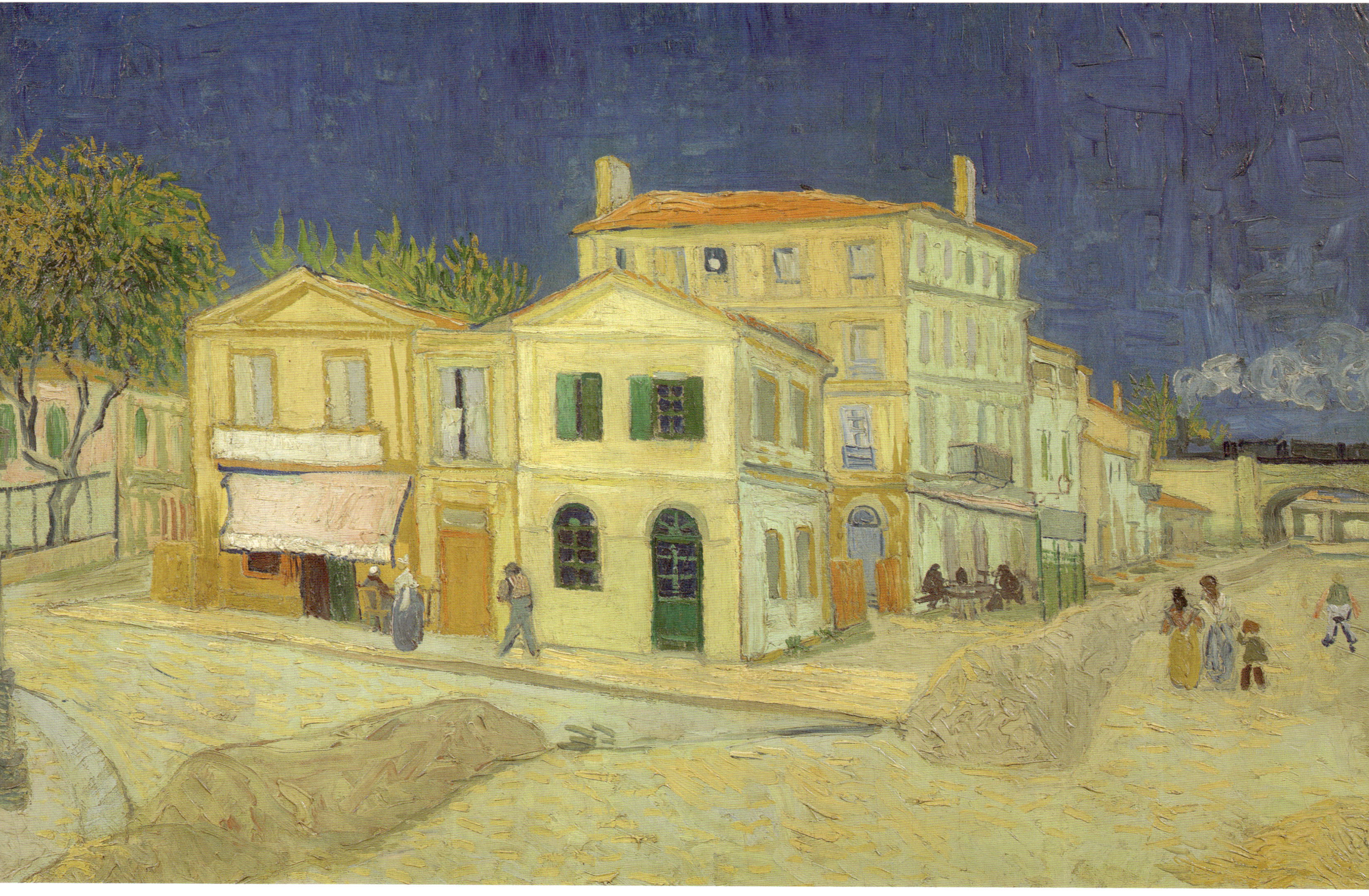

Van Gogh in Arles

Van Gogh was never completely comfortable in the city. Eventually, his yearnings for the country led him to Arles in Provence. Whilst avidly writing to, among others, Bernard and Gauguin, imploring them to join him in his self-conceived artist's utopia, Van Gogh worked with unprecedented intensity. Painting his surroundings in *The Yellow House* (*see* above), *Bedroom in Arles* (*see* page 61) and *The Night Café* (*see* page 62), all 1888, not only did Van Gogh continue to

Above : *The Yellow House*, 1888, Vincent van Gogh (1853–90)

Right : *Self-Portrait with a Straw Hat*, 1887, Vincent van Gogh (1853–90)

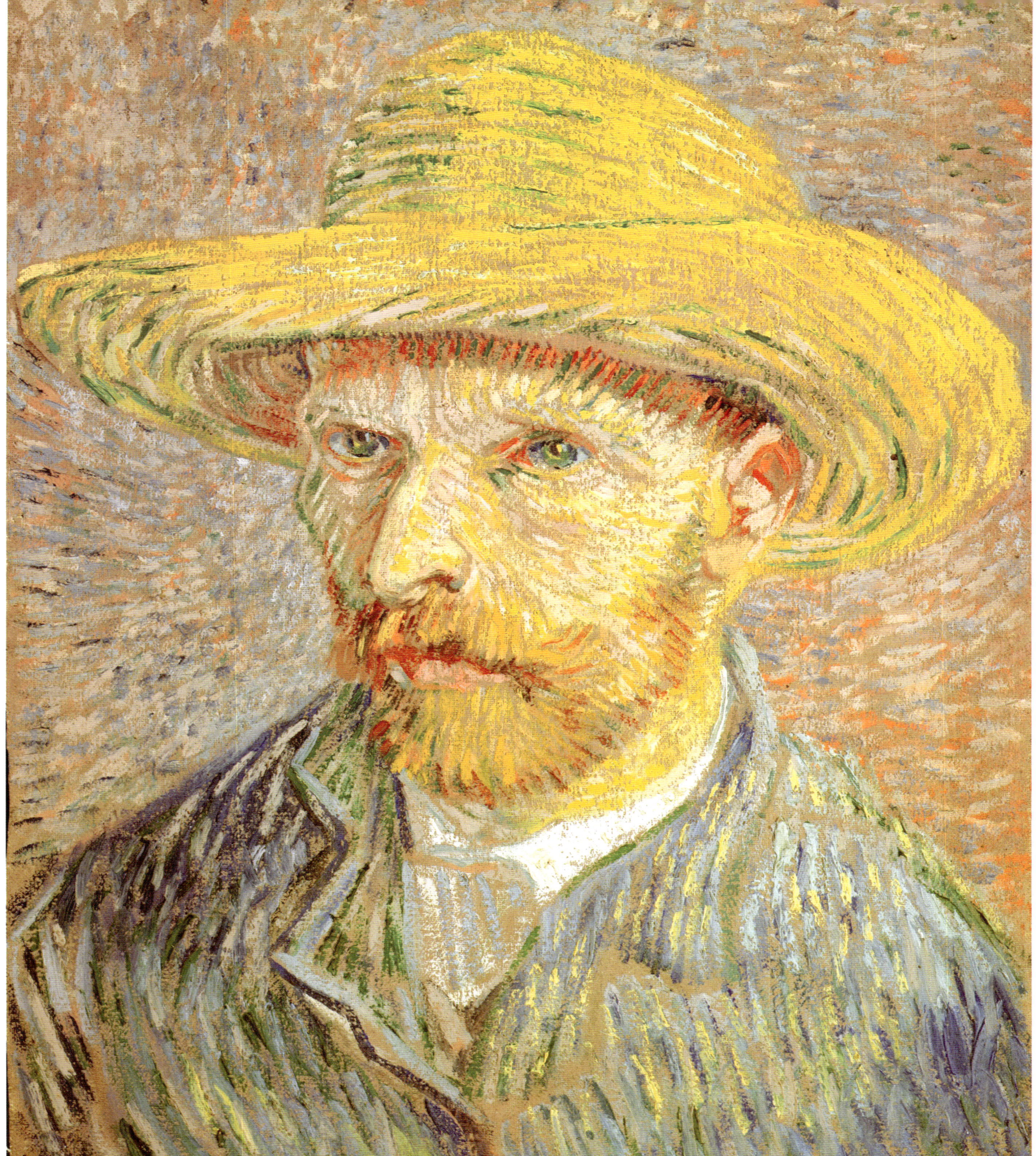

follow the development of other Post-Impressionist painters in moving away from conventional norms of perspective and modelling, but also undertook a highly original approach to colour which he used to signal both pictorial space and emotional mood.

Describing *Bedroom in Arles* to Theo, Van Gogh explained that 'here colour is to do everything', it is to 'rest the brain, or rather the imagination' as well as denote the objects within the room. Having abandoned the formulae of one-point perspective and naturalistic colour, Van Gogh instead used the abstract and equilibrious relations between colours – the 'scarlet' covers, the bed as 'yellow [as] fresh butter', the 'pale violet' walls, 'green' window, 'orange' table, 'lilac' door, and 'lemon' pillows – to literally create the feeling of 'inviolable rest' that Van Gogh himself experienced within it.

Whilst in *Bedroom in Arles* he sought a kind of beauty in colour harmony, in *The Night Café*, Van Gogh abnegated even that requirement, calling the work 'one of the ugliest things I have ever done'. Yet ugliness, borne of the clash of sickly green, vivid red and pale yellow, was precisely the point. 'I have tried to express,' he wrote to Theo,

> *the terrible passions of humanity by means of red and green. The room is blood red and dark yellow with a green billiard table in the middle; there are four lemon-yellow lamps with a glow of orange and green. Everywhere there is a clash and contrast of the most alien reds and greens, in the figures of little sleeping hooligans, in the empty dreary room, in violet and blue. The blood-red and the yellow-green of the billiard table, for instance, contrast with the soft tender Louis XV green of the counter, on which there is a rose nosegay. The white clothes of the landlord, watchful in a corner of that furnace, turn lemon-yellow, or pale luminous green.*

The historical significance of such canvases, then, lies precisely in the fact that they revealed to Van Gogh's contemporaries a powerful alternative approach

Right : *Bedroom in Arles, 1888, Vincent van Gogh (1853–90)*

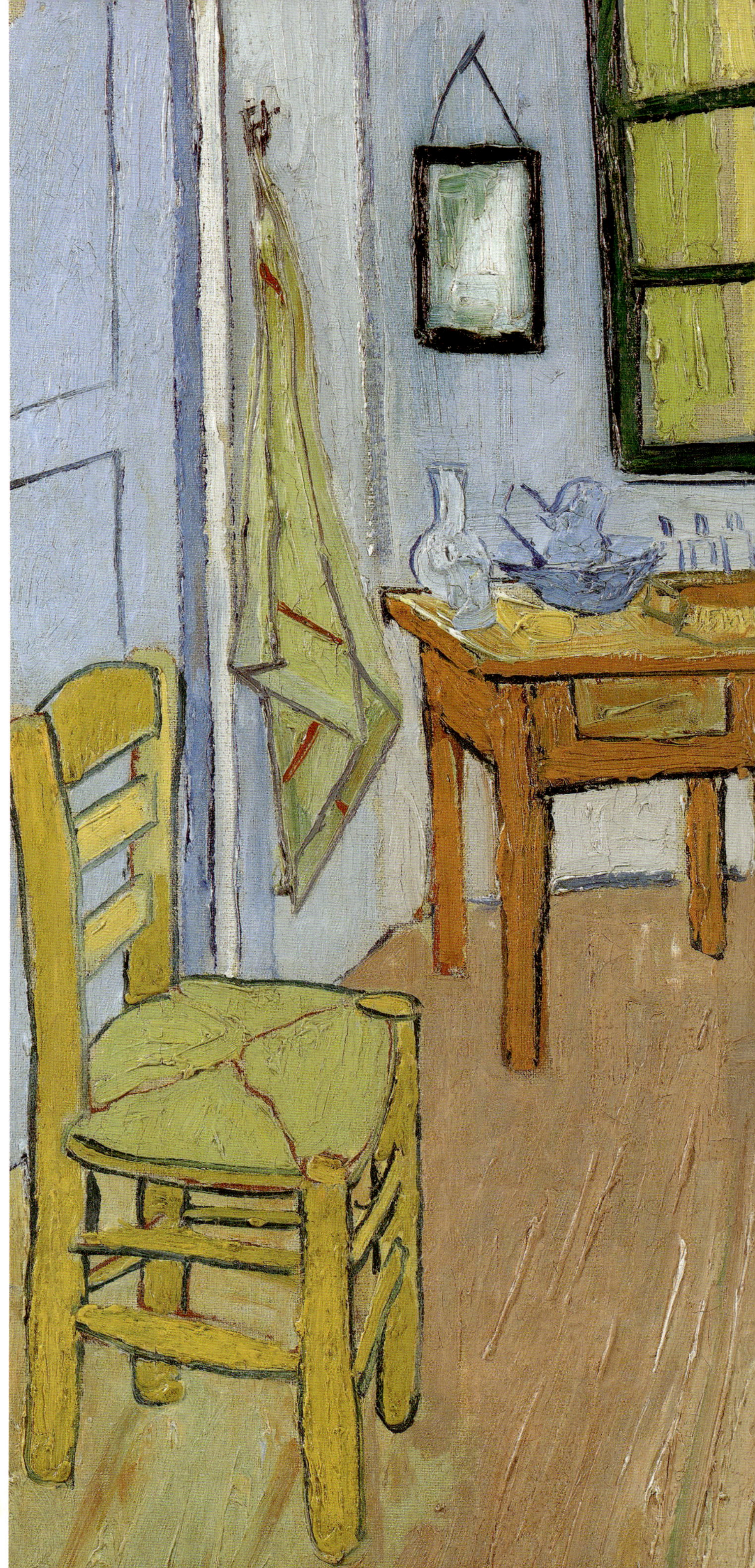

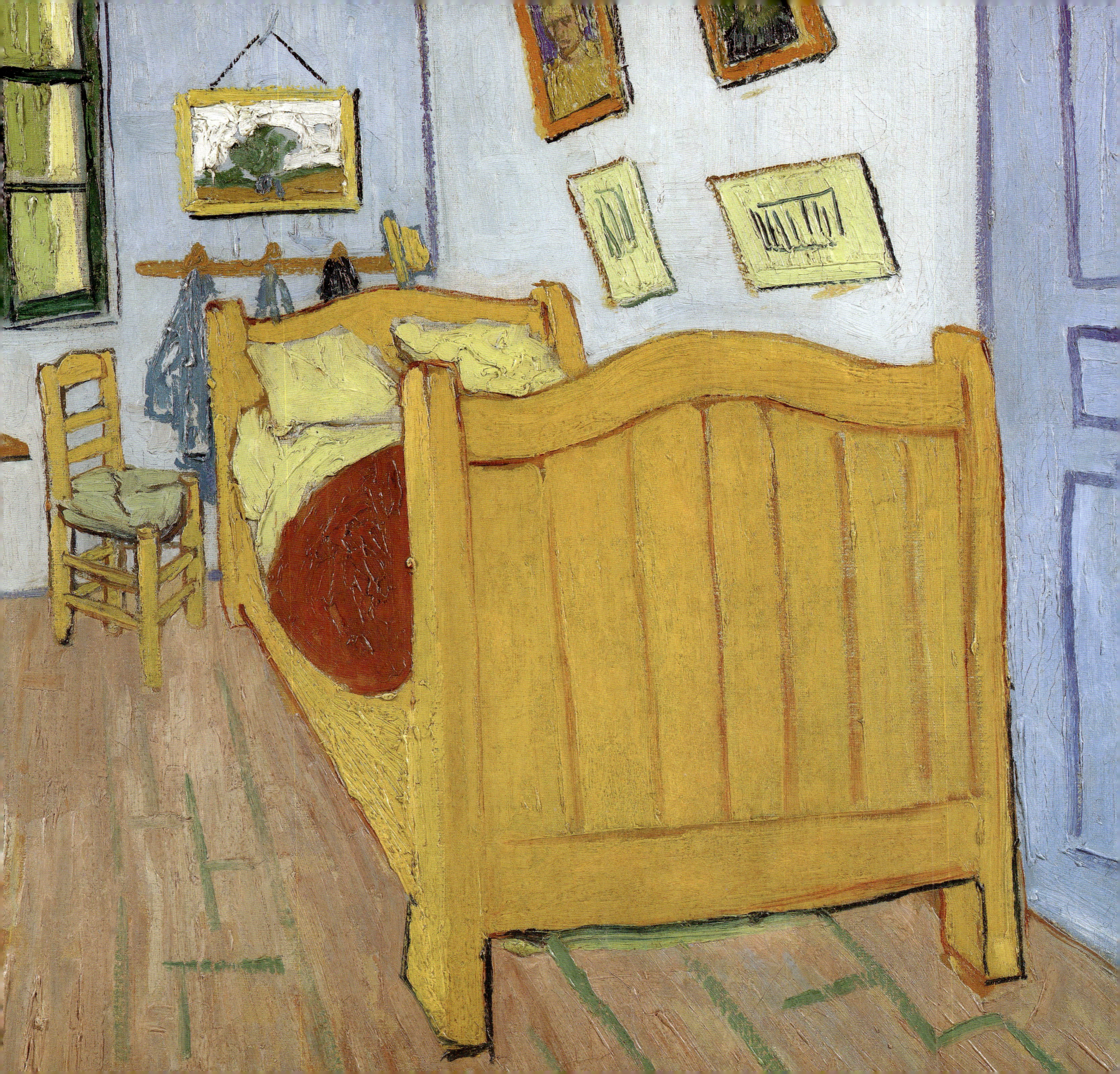

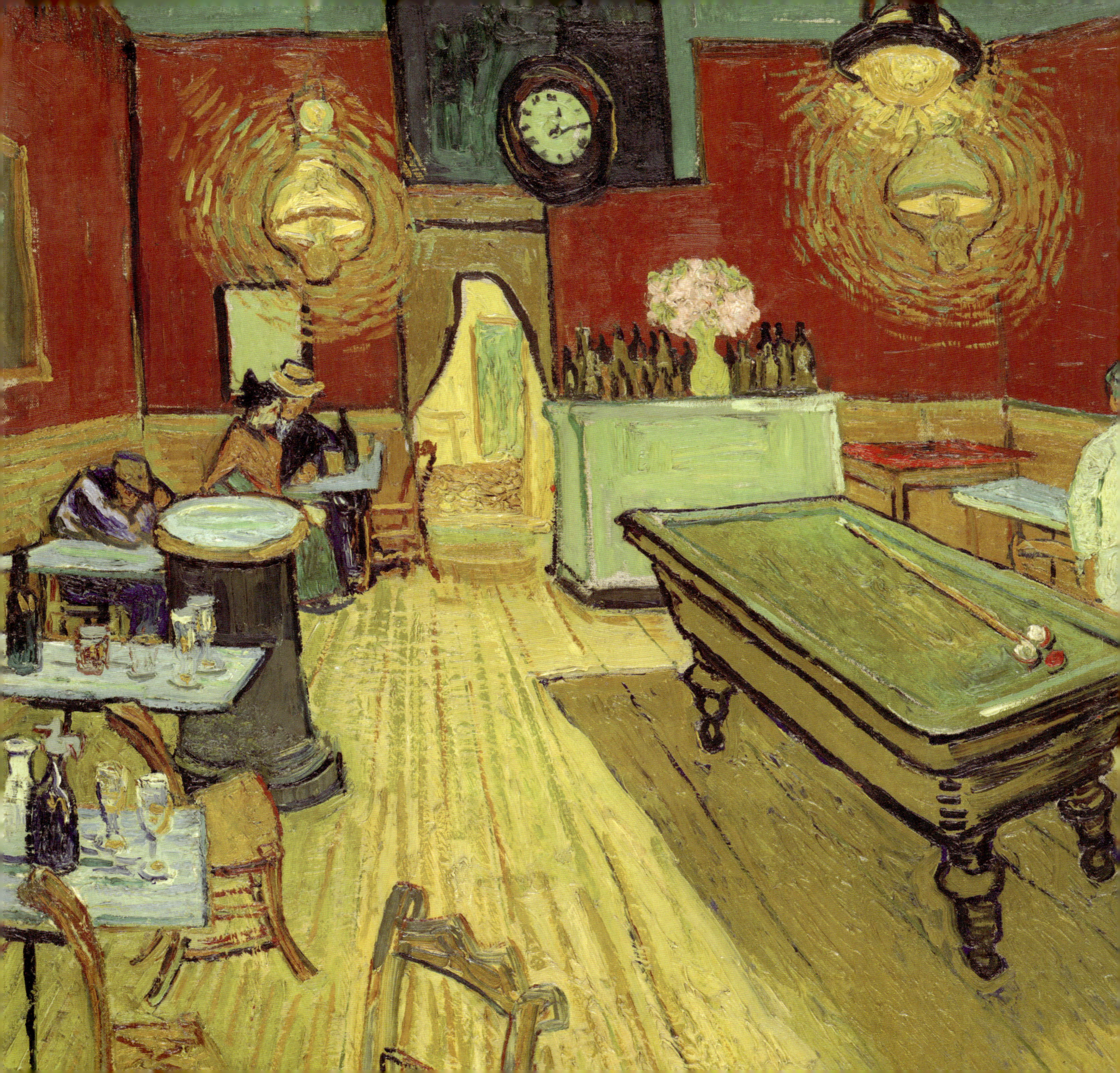

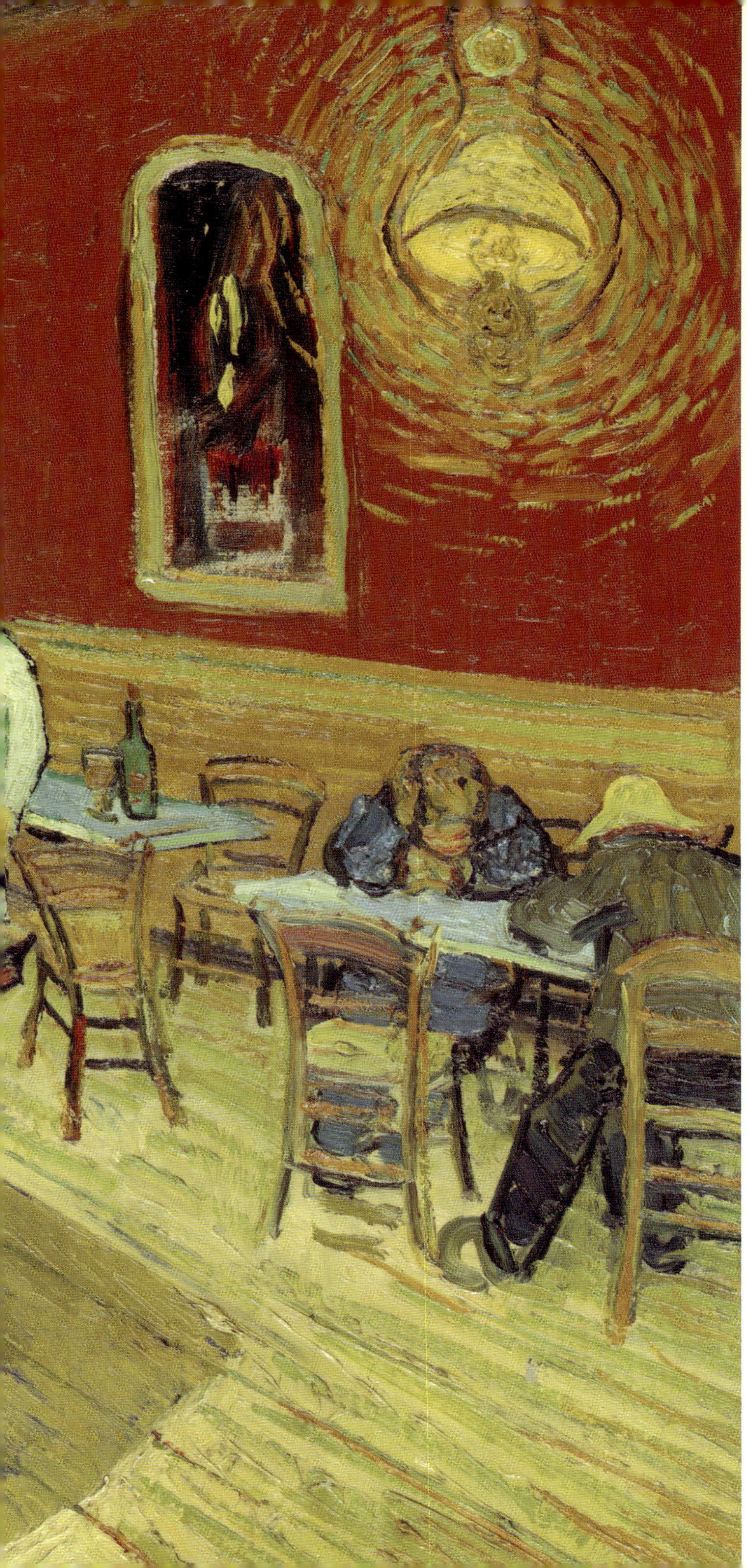

to colour, related to, and yet distinct from, the experiments of Seurat and the Neo-Impressionists, and Gauguin and the Pont-Aven Synthétistes. In the next chapter, we will examine the other pictorial tradition to have had a profound influence on Van Gogh and many of his contemporaries: Japanese prints.

'I have tried to express the terrible passions of humanity by means of red and green.'

Van Gogh

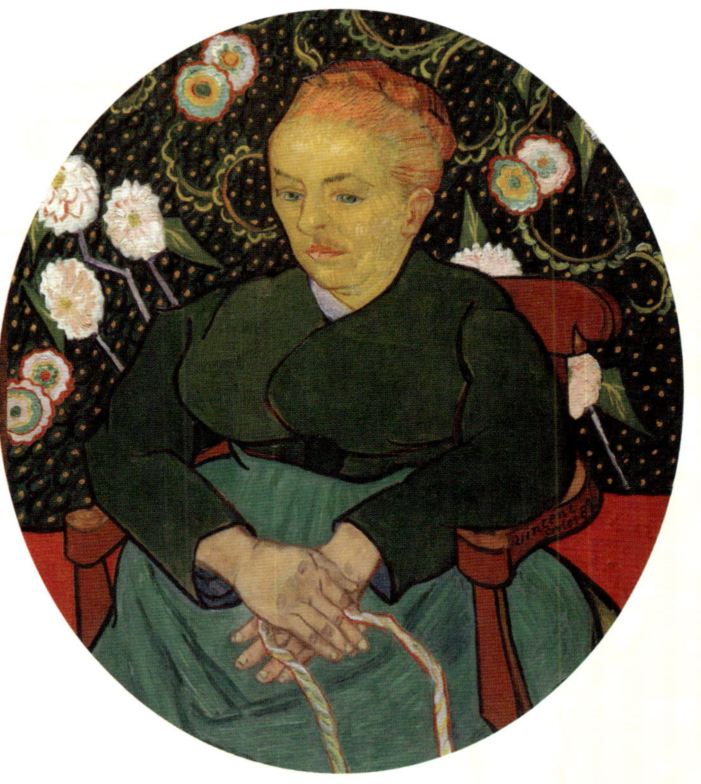

Left : *The Night Café*, 1888, Vincent van Gogh (1853–90)
Detail above : *La Berceuse*, 1889, Vincent van Gogh (1853–90), *see page 22*

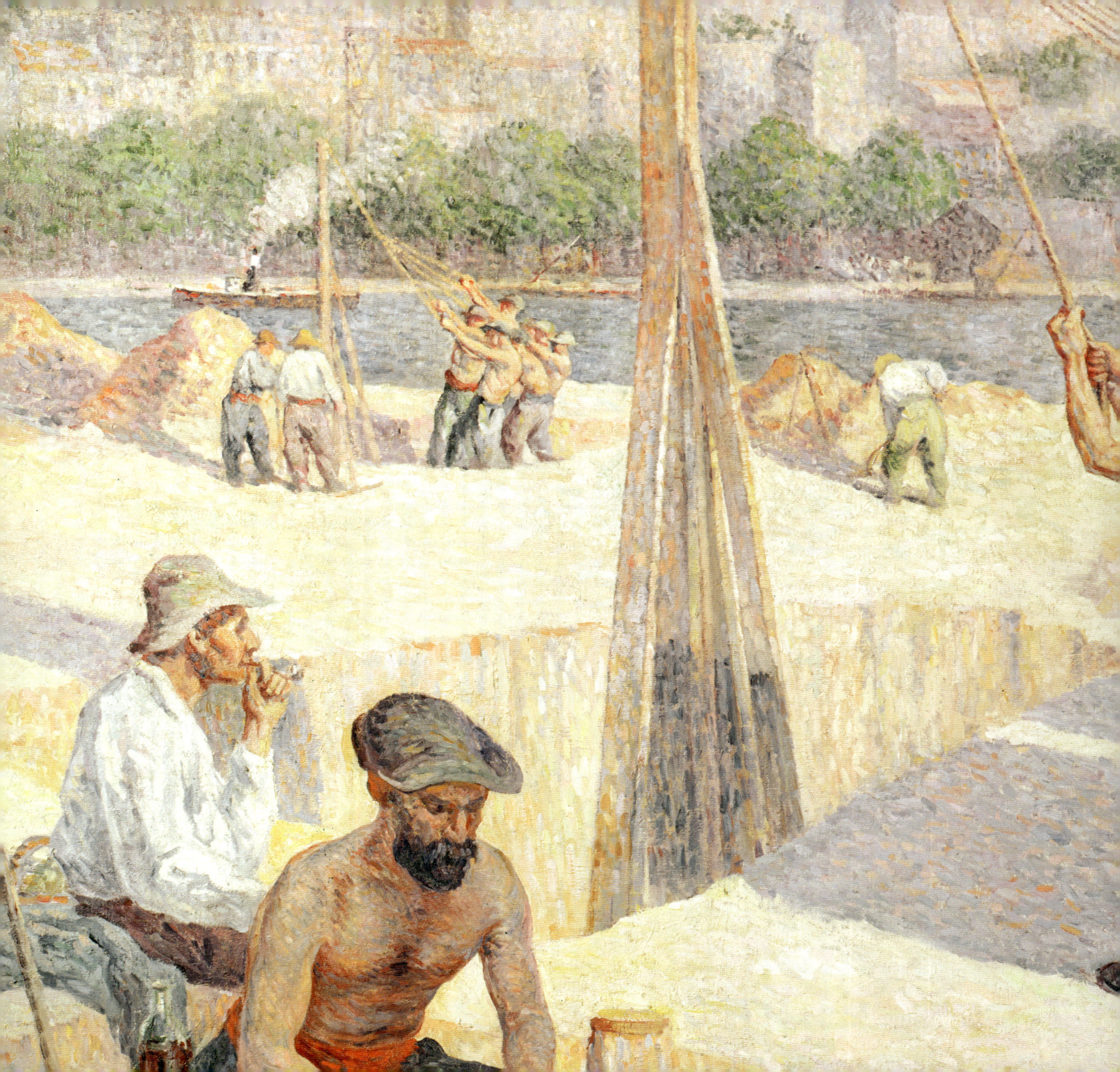

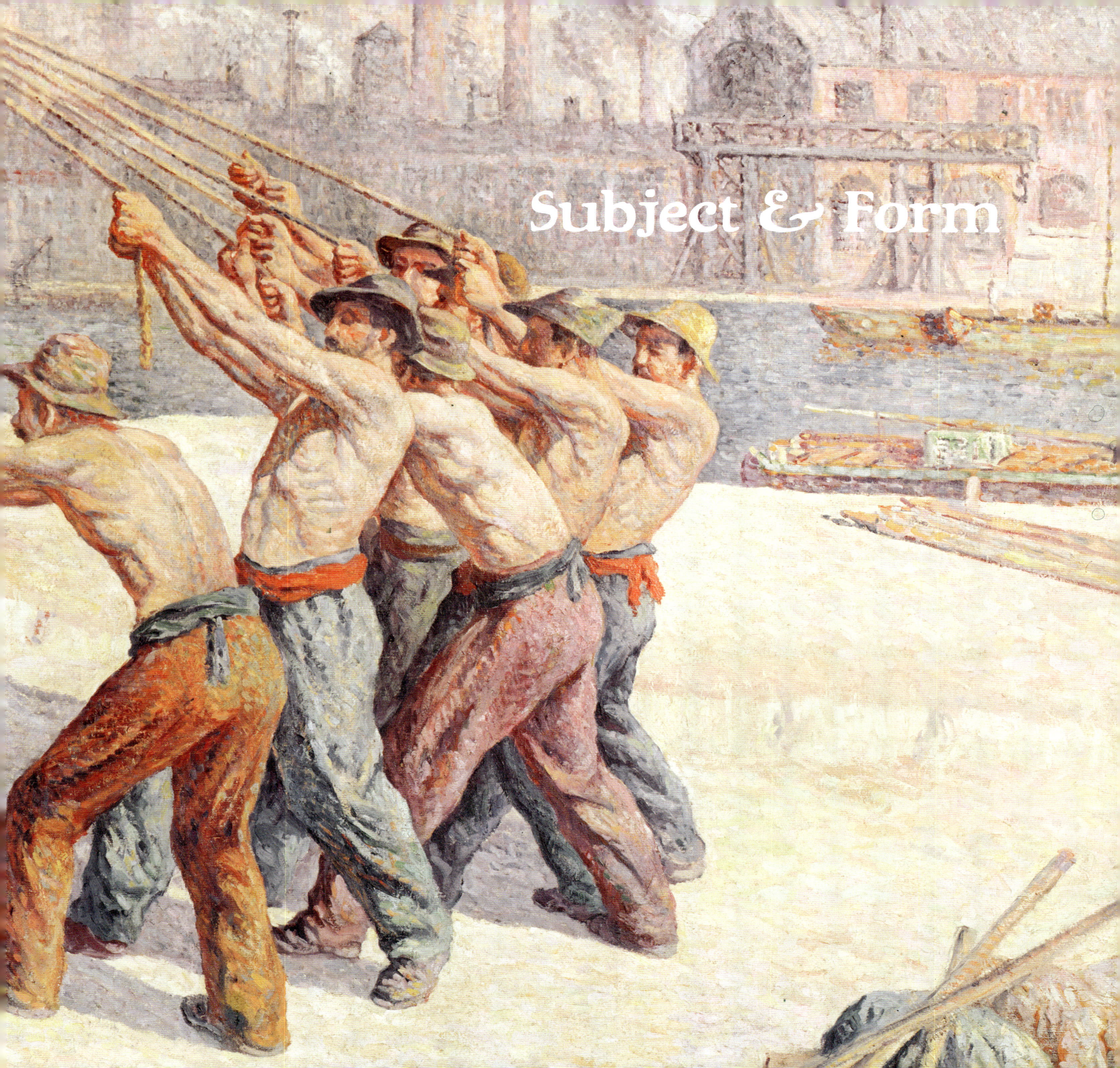
Subject & Form

From Japonisme to Agitation

THERE WERE various factors that influenced the subject matter favoured by the Post-Impressionists, from Japanese prints to anarchist politics.

Van Gogh's Idea of Japan

Van Gogh never tired of extolling to his brother Theo the virtues of Japanese art and culture. 'Come now,' he wrote,

isn't it almost a true religion which these simple Japanese teach us, who live in nature as though they themselves were flowers? And you cannot study Japanese art, it seems to me, without becoming much gayer and happier, and we must return to nature in spite of our education and our work in a world of convention.

For Van Gogh, Japan attained a mythic status in his imagination, on to which he projected the hopes and dreams he cherished for himself and his life in France. After moving to Arles in 1888, he desperately sought to create for himself the utopia of

an artistic community. He wrote to numerous artists, beseeching them to come and paint with him in Arles (in the end, it was only Gauguin who made the trip). In a letter of this sort to Émile Bernard, Van Gogh wrote:

For a long time now I have thought it touching that the Japanese artists used to exchange works among themselves very often. It certainly proves they liked and upheld each other and that there reigned a certain harmony among them; and that they were living in some sort of fraternal community, quite naturally and not in intrigues. The more we are like them in this respect, the better it will be for us. It also appears that the Japanese earned very little money, and lived like simple workmen.

Van Gogh grounded his subjective fantasies, his dream of an artistic utopia in Arles, in the imagined knowledge of a primitive Orient in which all the myriad failings and corruptions of European modernity were resolved. Where European art was weighed down by the prejudice of convention, Japanese art was modest and truthful; whilst European artists toiled away alone, Japanese artists fostered fraternal bonds; where European society was becoming rootless and neurotic, Japanese society was grounded in nature. '[Arles] would be better than the painter's paradise; it would be an absolute Japan.'

Van Gogh's portrait of *Père Tanguy* (1887, *see* right) is especially revealing about the value Japanese art held for him. The subject, Julien-François Tanguy (1825–94), sold art (including Japanese prints) and artistic supplies from a small shop on the rue Clauzel. Van Gogh and he became very close friends. Van Gogh depicts Tanguy in the stiff, frontal pose – with hands firmly interconnected

Right and detail above : *Père Tanguy*, 1887, Vincent van Gogh (1853–90)

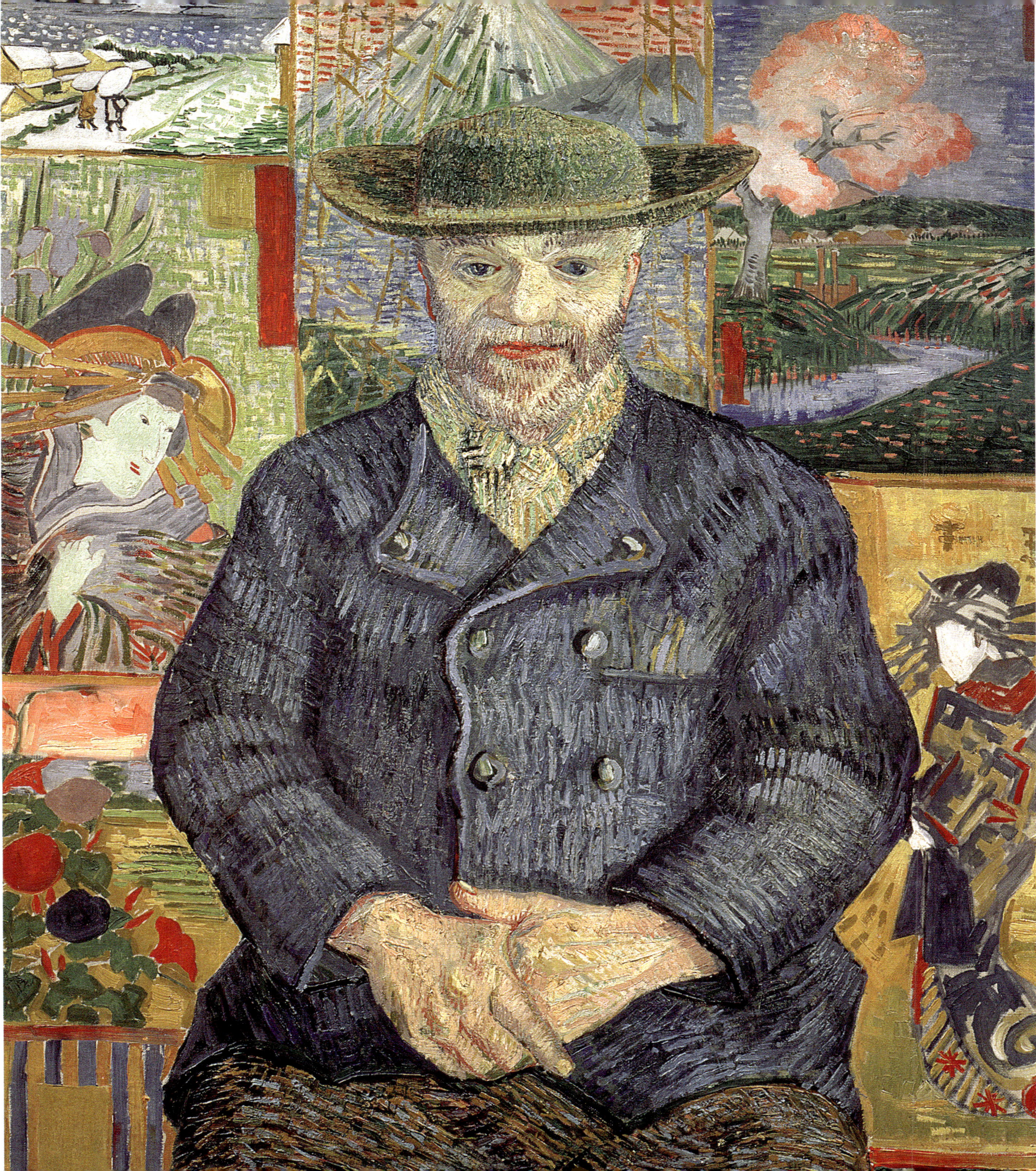

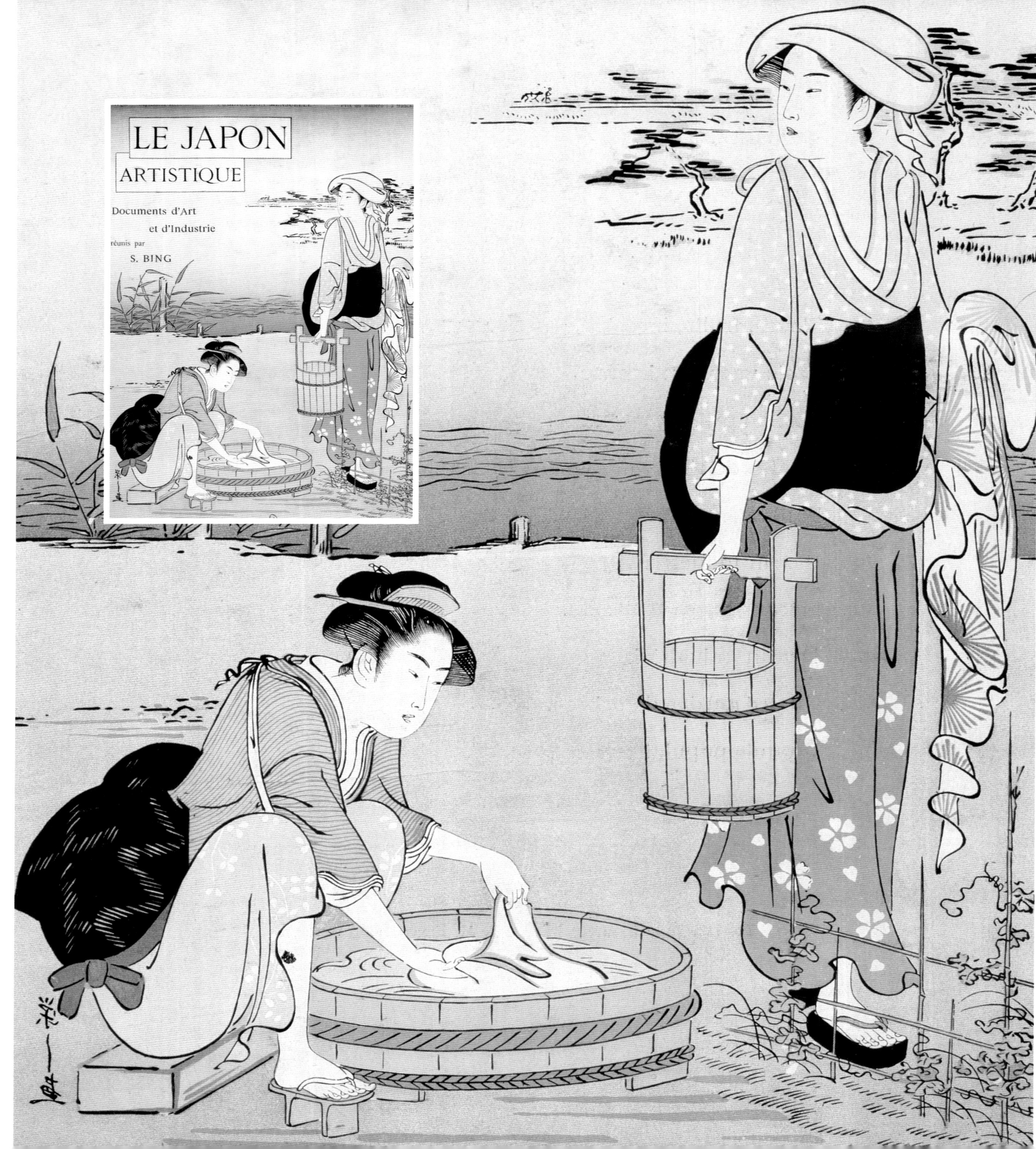

LE JAPON
ARTISTIQUE
Documents d'Art
et d'Industrie
réunis par
S. BING

on his lap, and eyes downcast – typical of representations of Japanese Buddhist monks, heralding his friend as a wise sage of serene temperament. Their kinship was cemented by their shared utopian political beliefs, something that, as we have seen, Van Gogh associated strongly with Japan.

Affixed on the wall behind him are at least five brightly coloured and freely painted Japanese prints depicting landscapes and geishas. Van Gogh was an avid collector of Japanese colour woodblock prints, known as *ukiyo-e* (which translates to 'pictures of the floating world', and connotes the hedonistic lifestyle of the Japanese merchant class who could, starting from the early 1600s, newly afford them). Indeed, Van Gogh even mounted an exhibition of his collection in the café Le Tambourin. Expressing his desire to draw in the manner of the Japanese, Van Gogh here synthesized the Japanese iconography with the impasto, expressive brushwork and the prismatic, harmonic colours he had drawn variously from the Impressionists and Neo-Impressionists.

Van Gogh was not alone in projecting on to Japanese art and decoration his personal hopes for cultural renewal. Van Gogh's two years in Paris between 1886 and 1888 coincided with the peak of a cultural mania for all things Japanese. For the previous two-and-a-half centuries, Japan had been ruled by the feudal Tokugawa Shogunate. Its rulers enforced a policy of *sakoku*, or 'period of national isolation', whereby Japanese exports had been strictly controlled and cultural contact with the outside world was minimized. However, following excursions by American colonialists after 1853, Japan was forcibly opened to Western trade. The superiority of American military technology and the humiliation of the resulting treaties (one in 1854, another in 1858) mortally damaged the prestige of the Shogunate. Uncontrolled foreign trade deeply destabilized Japanese society and its economy. The Shogun's opponents (*ishin shishi*) sensed their opportunity to depose him and restore the strength of Japan. After a short civil war, they succeeded in deposing the Shogun in favour of the Emperor (the Meiji Restoration), who subsequently ended the policy of *sakoku* in 1868.

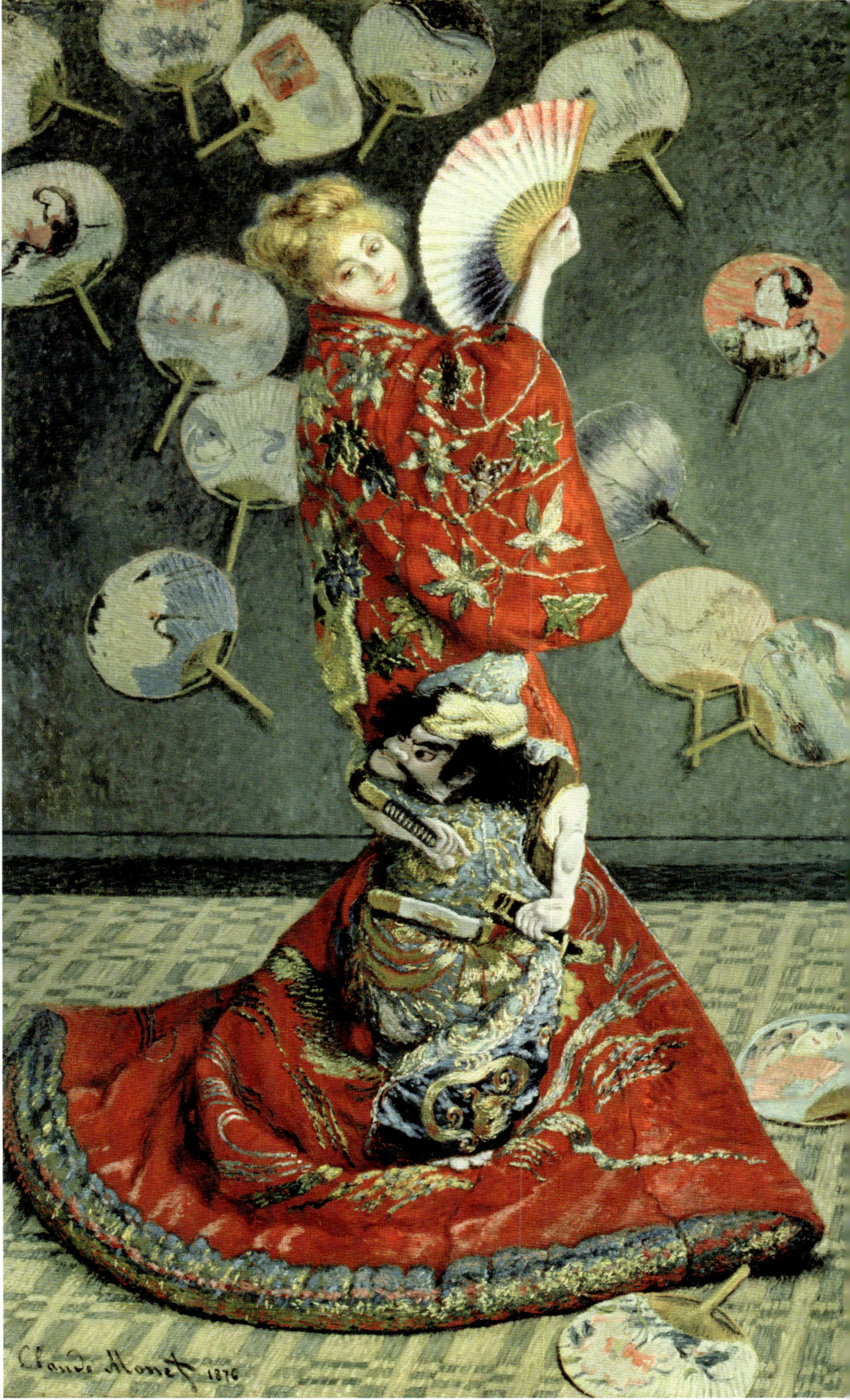

Left : Cover of the magazine *Le Japon artistique*

Above : *Camille Monet in Japanese Costume*, 1876, Claude Monet (1840–1926)

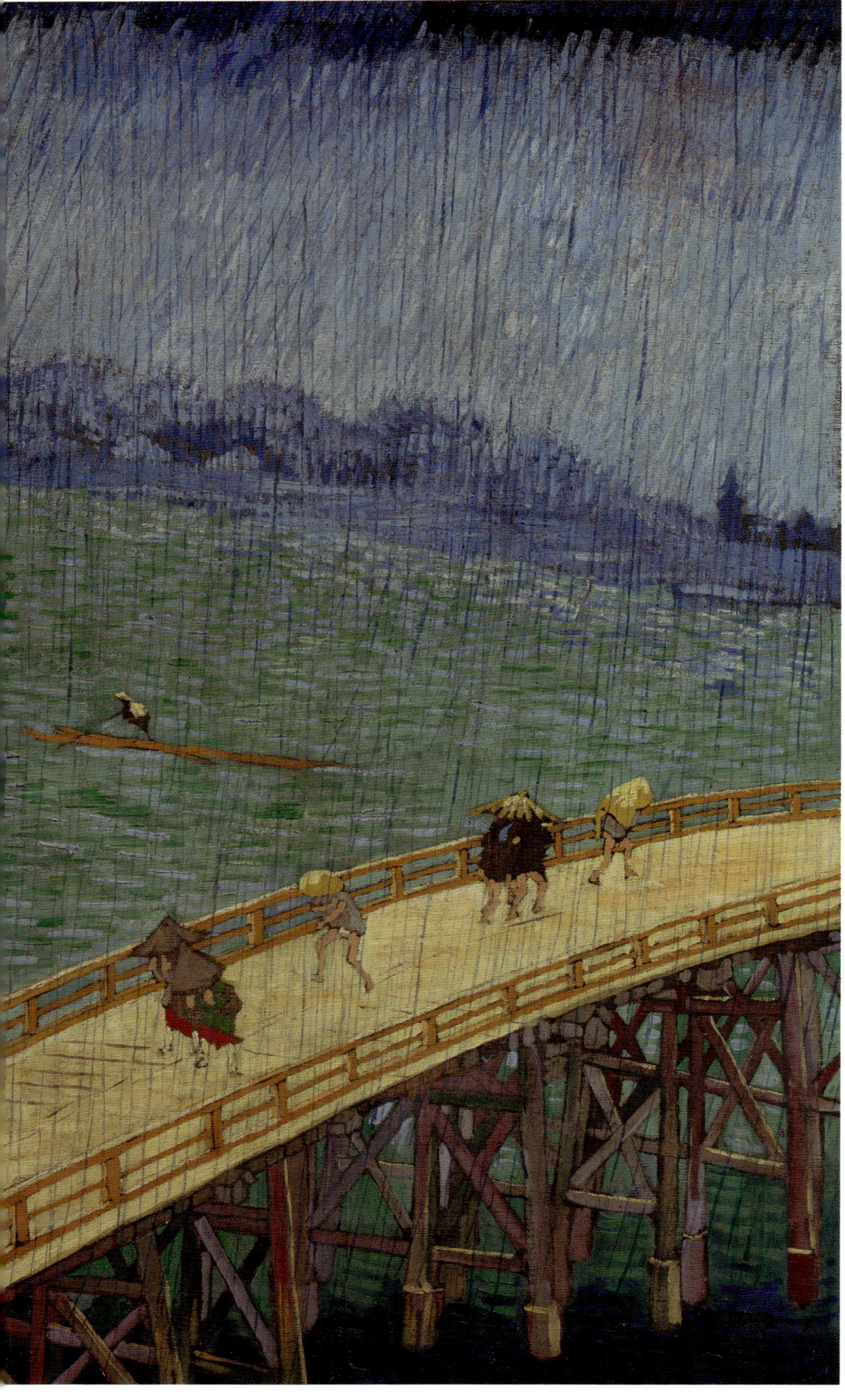

Consequently, in the 1860s, for the first time, French culture was exposed to Japanese exports on a large scale, which included *ukiyo-e* prints, decorative fans, kimonos, furniture, lacquered boxes and assorted bric-a-brac. The Japanese stand at the 1867 Exposition Universelle was the catalyst by which this steady stream became a veritable flood: it was virtually impossible to visit an artist's studio in the 1870s and 1880s without seeing Japanese prints, kimonos or fans. Shops specializing in Japanese products, most notably Siegfried Bing's (1838–1905) gallery, proliferated, as did magazines, books and even clubs devoted to Oriental art. Van Gogh was an avid reader of Bing's magazine *Le Japon artistique* (*see* page 68), published between May 1888 and April 1891. The Société du Jing-lar was one such Japoniste club, founded in 1867 by the art critic Philippe Burty (1830–90), in which members prepared for their 'aesthetic deliberations' by dressing in kimonos and eating Japanese cuisine from tableware decorated in a Japanese style by the painter Félix Bracquemond (1833–1914), who regularly exhibited with the Impressionists.

Japonaiserie

Camille Monet in Japanese Costume (1876, *see* page 69) by Monet and *The Japanese Bath* (1864) by James Tissot (1836–1902) are indicative of this craze of *Japonaiserie*. Monet depicts his wife Camille dressed in a bright red and intricately patterned kimono, twisting her body around its central axis in order to best display its decorative motif. In her right hand, she coquettishly displays a decorative fan, tilting her head and directing her gaze at the viewer. On the back wall and on the floor are arranged numerous Japanese fans of the kind fashionable in the 1870s. The flirtatious appeal of Monet's enrobed wife thus rests in the juxtaposition of tantalizing and novel exoticism and the here-and-now of modern life, a meeting of East and West. Camille wears a blonde wig to highlight her non-Japanese ethnicity and to play on precisely this dynamic.

If Monet hints at the potential for erotic appeal, Tissot positively revels in it: a Western nude wears a patterned kimono, opened invitingly to the viewer,

Above : *Bridge in the Rain (after Hiroshige)*, 1887, Vincent van Gogh (1853–90)

Right : *Sudden Shower on the Great Bridge near Atake*, from the series 'One Hundred Views of Famous Places in Edo', 1857, Utagawa Hiroshige (1797–1858)

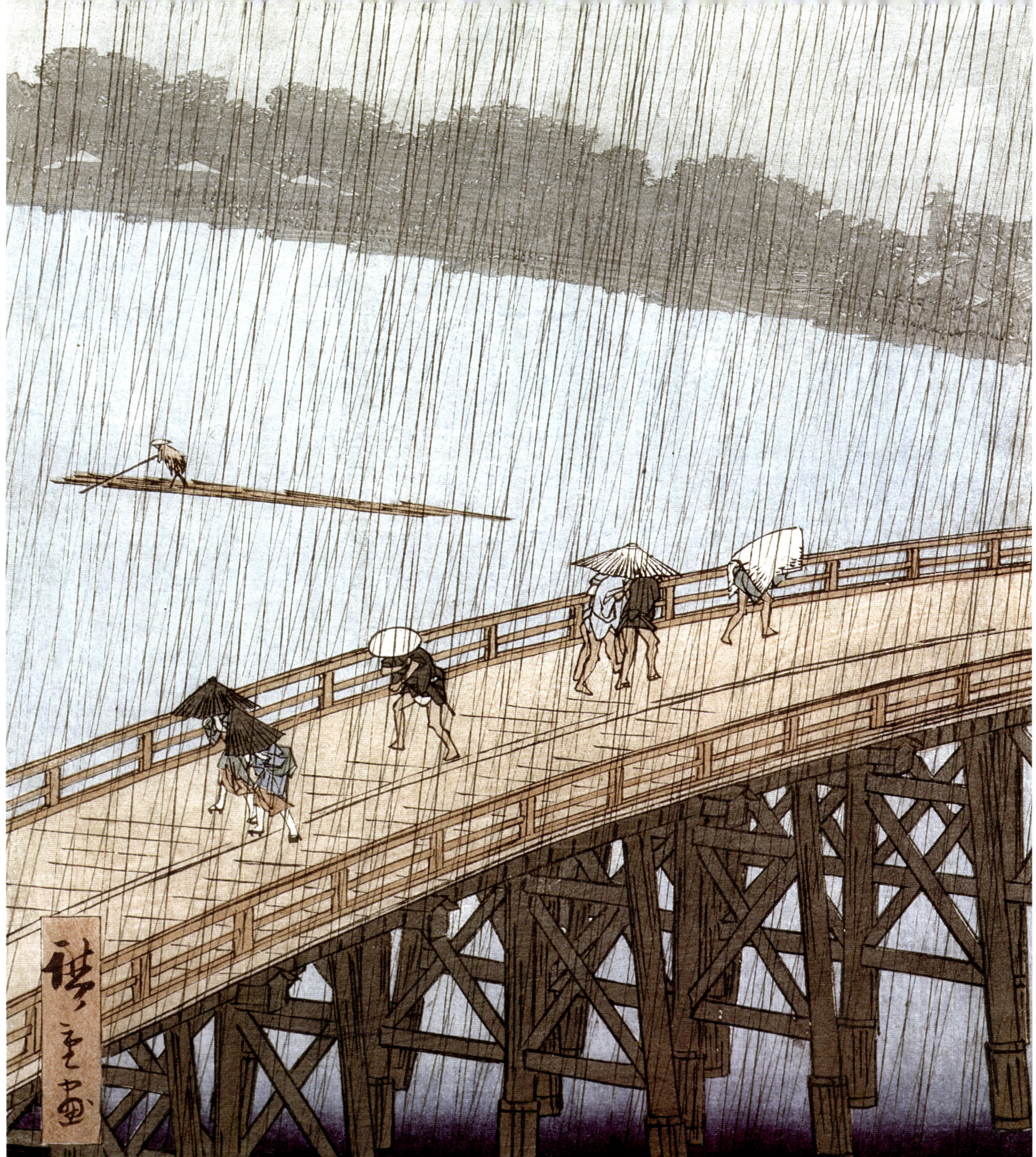

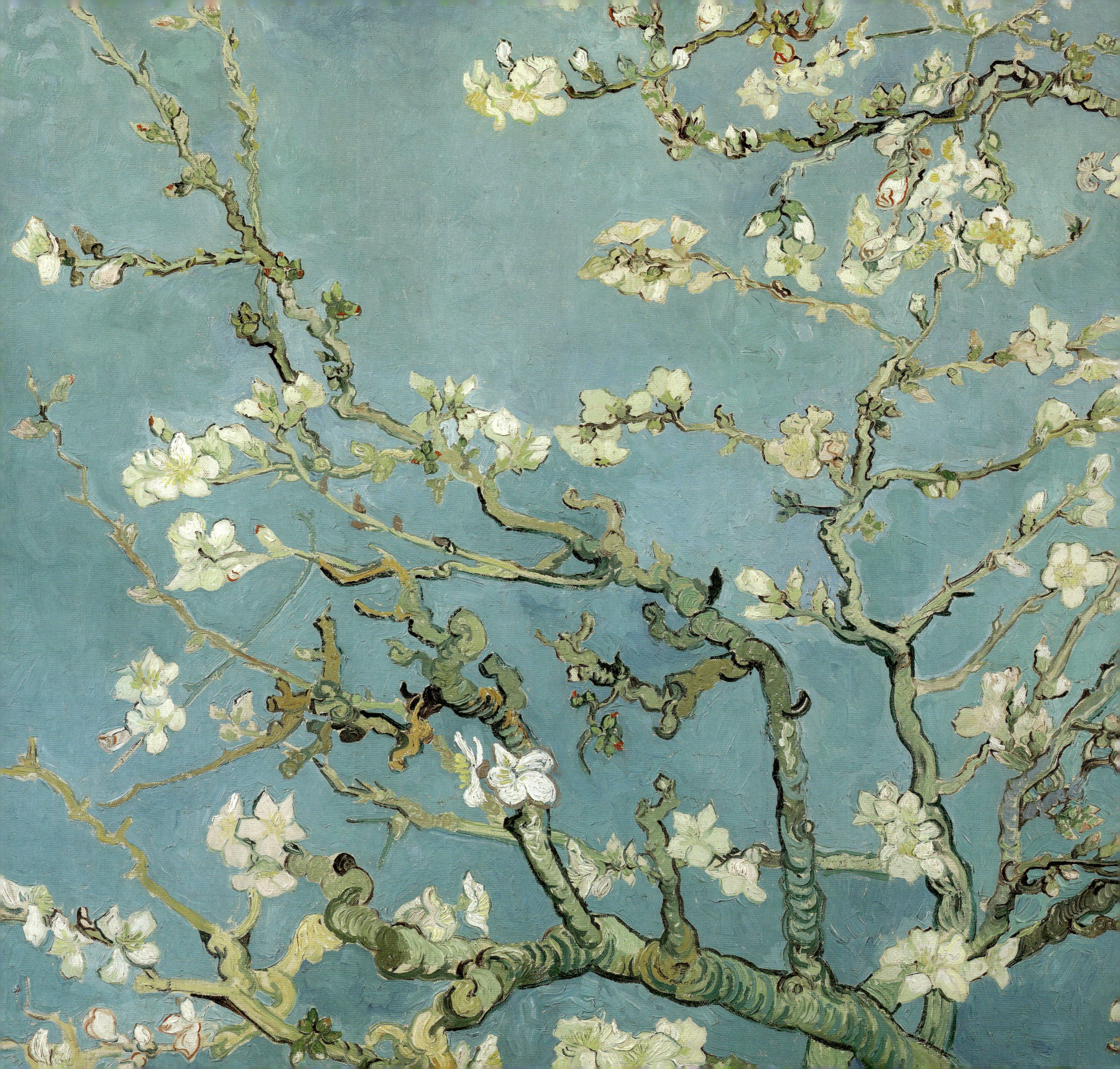

whose gaze she meets with an expression that hovers ambiguously between enticing and challenging. Behind her we see Japanese buildings and a Japanese landscape, complete with cherry blossoms. We are not invited to dwell on how such a scene might, in reality, happen, but rather to suspend our disbelief and enjoy the sensuality of silk on skin, the fantasy of pleasurable escape to a faraway place in which the erotic and the exotic intermingle.

'Come now, isn't it almost a true religion which these simple Japanese teach us, who live in nature as though they themselves were flowers.'

Van Gogh

In these canvases, both Tissot and Monet, literally as well as figuratively, have merely dressed Western forms in Japanese garb, superficially quoting the artefacts circulating amongst their milieu as a point of interest in an otherwise thoroughly European artistic trope, the Impressionist interior or the classically inspired female nude. Although Van Gogh too, in his portrait of Père Tanguy, quoted from Japanese art by including in the background recognizable prints

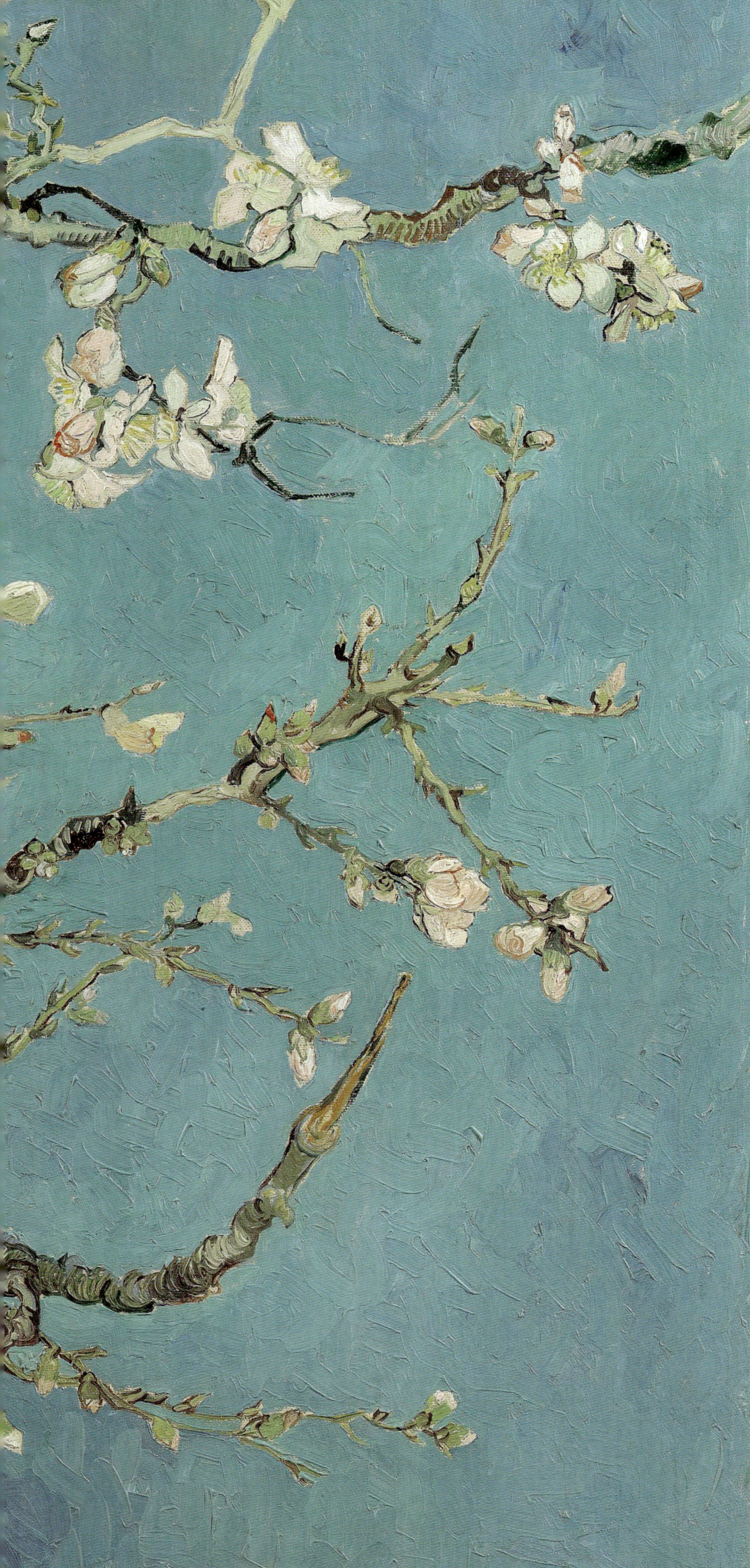

Left : *Almond Blossom*, 1890, Vincent van Gogh (1853–90)

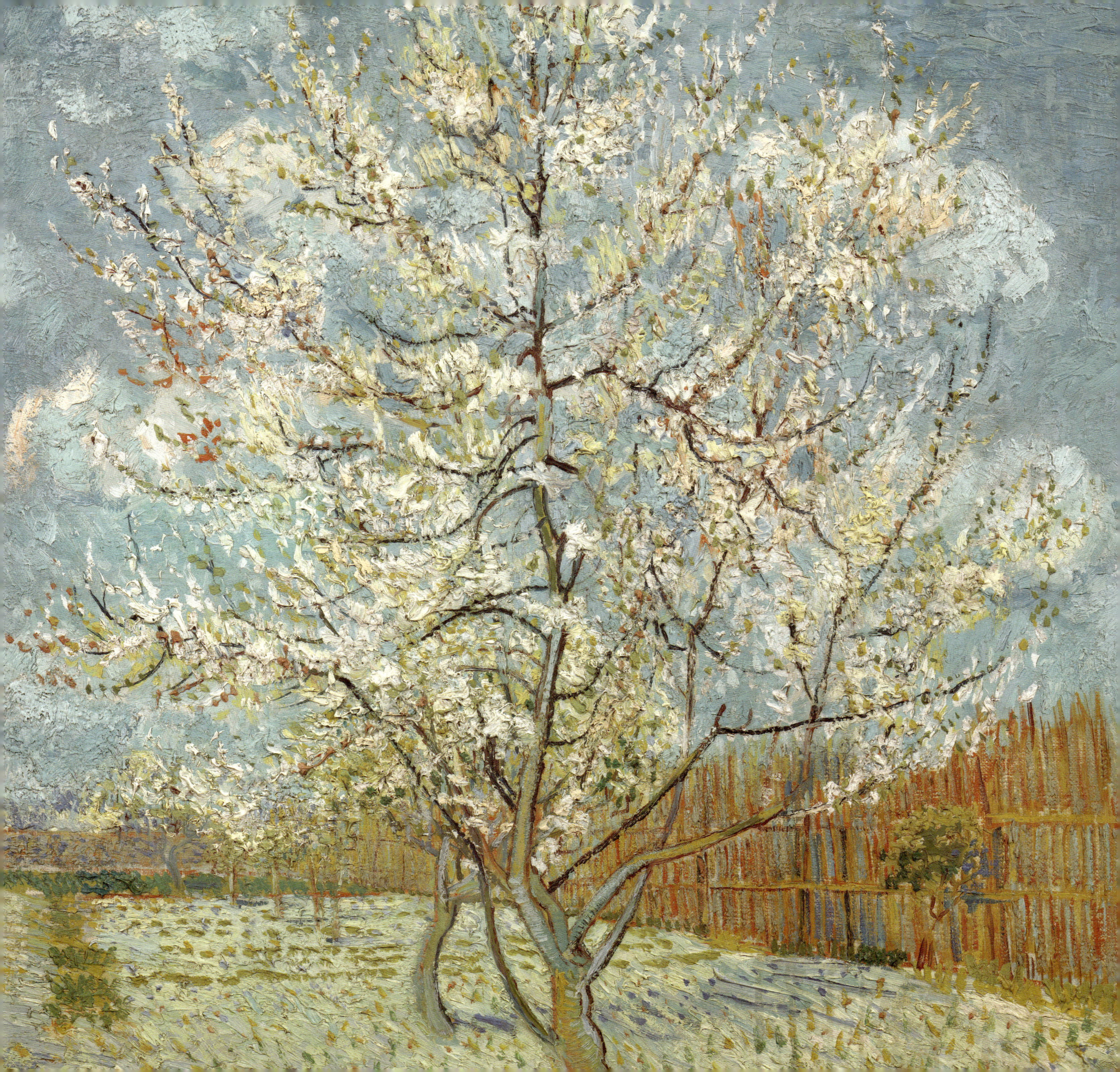

– such as *Ishiyakushi: The Yoshitsune cherry tree near the Noriyori shrine* (1855) by Utagawa Hiroshige (1797–1858), one of the most prominent *ukiyo-e* printmakers – he did so with an altogether different goal of developing a completely new way of seeing.

Not only did Van Gogh collect Japanese woodblocks, he also made a number of meticulous copies after them. His 1887 *Bridge in the Rain (after Hiroshige,* see page 70) is a copy of Hiroshige's *Sudden Shower on the Great Bridge near Atake* (1857, *see* page 71), which is part of a series of 'One Hundred Famous Views of Edo' (there are actually 119 views of Edo, the old name for Tokyo, in the series). Hiroshige depicts five small figures scurrying across the wooden bridge, spanning the Sumida River, in order to escape a sudden rain shower, while a solitary boatman punts his log raft along the middle of the water without hope of ready shelter. The print offers an everyday scene of contemporary city life and a motif popular with *haiku* poets and *ukiyo-e* artists. The top and bottom edges of the print are darkened (achieved by a technique known as *bokashi,* where the printmaker would attain the gradation of colour by manually applying ink to the moistened block) to represent thunderous clouds and deep water respectively. The composition is radically unbalanced and asymmetrical: the off-centre elevated viewpoint and diagonal horizon line give the scene a deliberately skewed perspective such that the bridge, rather than penetrating into space, seems instead to spread out across it.

The raised vantage-point likewise allows Hiroshige to leave large sections of the print completely empty, save the subtly gradated, almost decorative, pattern of blue ink and the fine, criss-crossing lines of the rain. The use of flat fields of largely unmodulated colour is replicated in the bridge and in the figures rushing across it, who are elucidated with an almost calligraphic economy of line. The lack of modelling or shadows, in conjunction with the rejection of perspective, and the unbalanced composition (in which swathes of the image are given over to abstract patterning), give the work a fresh, dynamic and decorative effect that was to transfix Van Gogh. Not just a copyist, in paintings such as 1888's *The Pink Peach Tree (see* left), Van Gogh creatively translates Hiroshige's compositional techniques

Left : *The Pink Peach Tree,* 1888, Vincent van Gogh (1853–90)

'[in Japanese art, painters] found confirmation of rather than an inspiration for their personal ways of seeing, feeling, understanding and interpreting nature.'
Ernest Chesneau

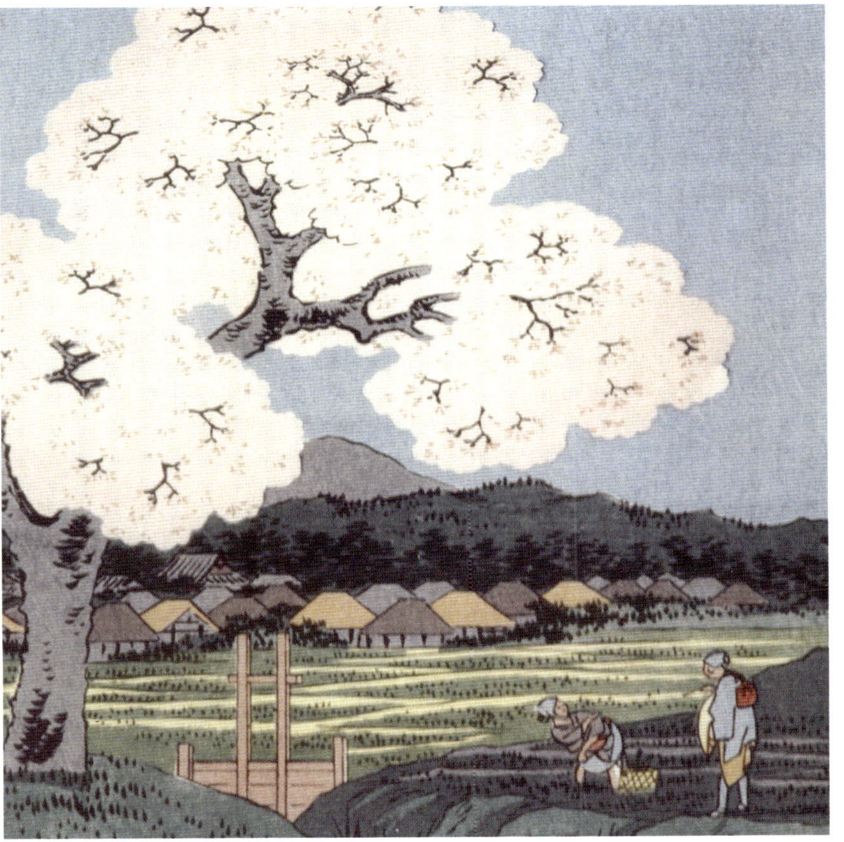

Above : *Ishiyakushi: The Yoshitsune Cherry Tree near the Noriyori Shrine,* 1855, Utagawa Hiroshige (1797–1858)

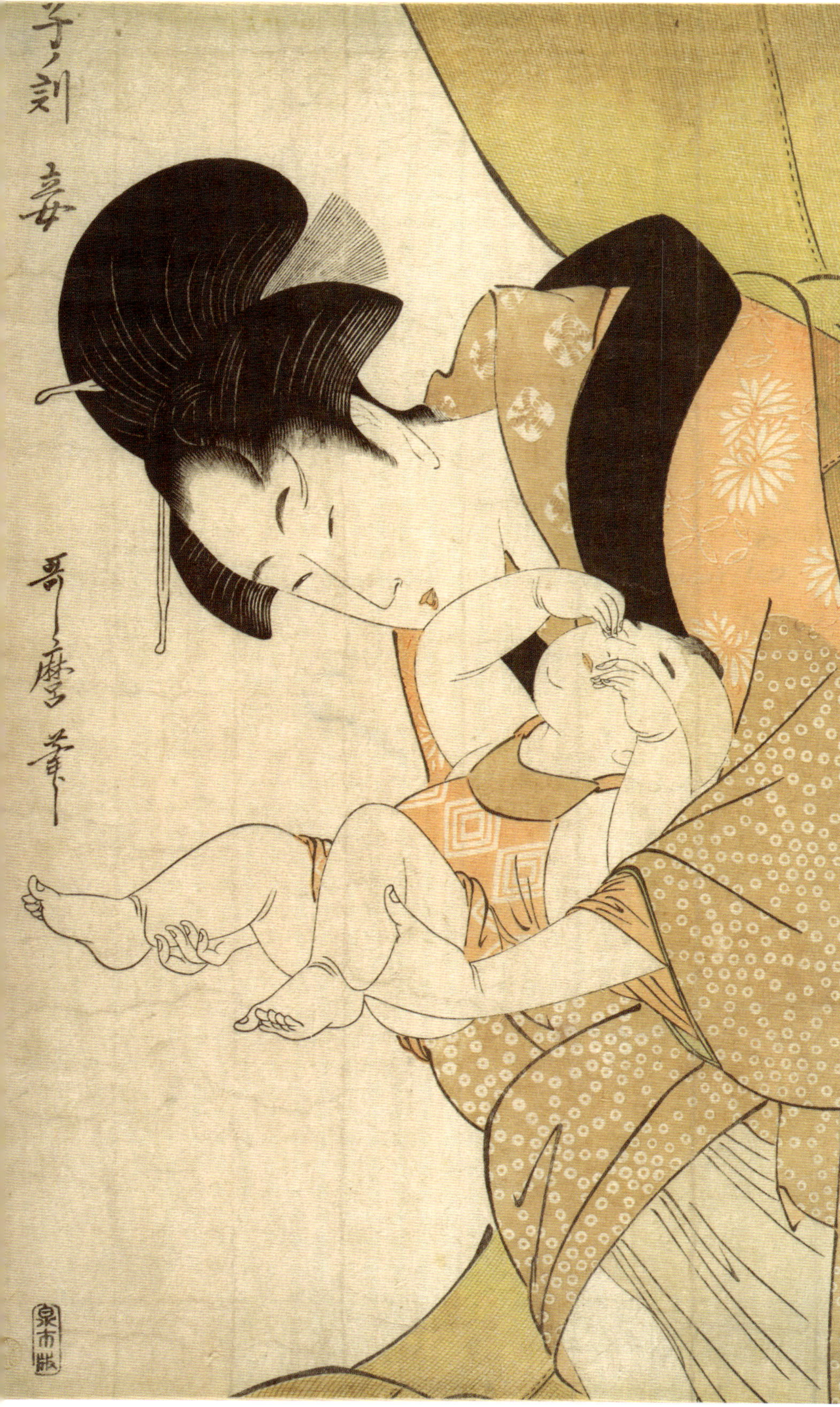

and calligraphic style. The decorative form of Hiroshige's *Yoshitsune Cherry Tree* (*see* page 75) – a flat patch of pink, atop a boldly outlined trunk, set against an unmodulated blue sky – familiar to Van Gogh since at least 1887, may well have been the driving influence behind Van Gogh's 1890 *Almond Blossom* (*see* page 72).

Cassatt

Van Gogh was not alone in his deep analysis and innovative adaptation of Japanese prints. Mary Cassatt, an American Impressionist working in Paris, executed a series of prints in the 1890s that document the daily rituals of her domestic life. The restrictive social mores of bourgeois Parisians severely curtailed the freedoms of women, who, if lacking a male chaperone, were confined to their homes. Unable to wander the streets as might the *flâneur* of Baudelaire's imagination (and indeed, like her male Impressionist colleagues), Cassatt found in *ukiyo-e* prints a refreshing celebration of her quotidian domestic experience. Cassatt adapted the graphic idiom of prints like Kitagawa Utamaro's (*c.* 1753–1806) *Midnight: Mother and Sleepy Child* (1790, *see* left) in works such as *Maternal Caress* (1890–91, *see* right). She combined large, flat areas of pure colour with economic yet sinuous lines to produce a scene suspended in time, stripped of all narrative specificity. The quiet harmony of line, pattern and colour (the gradation of hue from the pure orange of the bed, floor and floral pattern of the wallpaper and chair to the flesh tones of mother and child), all set within a flattened space, offer an elegant and intimate vision of domestic femininity.

Bonnard

Male artists likewise found stimulus in pictures from Japan's 'floating world'. In 1899, Pierre Bonnard, taking inspiration from Hiroshige's 'One Hundred Famous Views of Edo', produced a series of 12 lithographs depicting 'Some Views of Parisian Life'. Like Hiroshige's *Sudden Shower on the Great Bridge near*

Above : *Midnight: Mother and Sleepy Child,* 1790, Kitagawa Utamaro (1753–1806)

Right : *Maternal Caress,* 1890–91, Mary Cassatt (1844–1926)

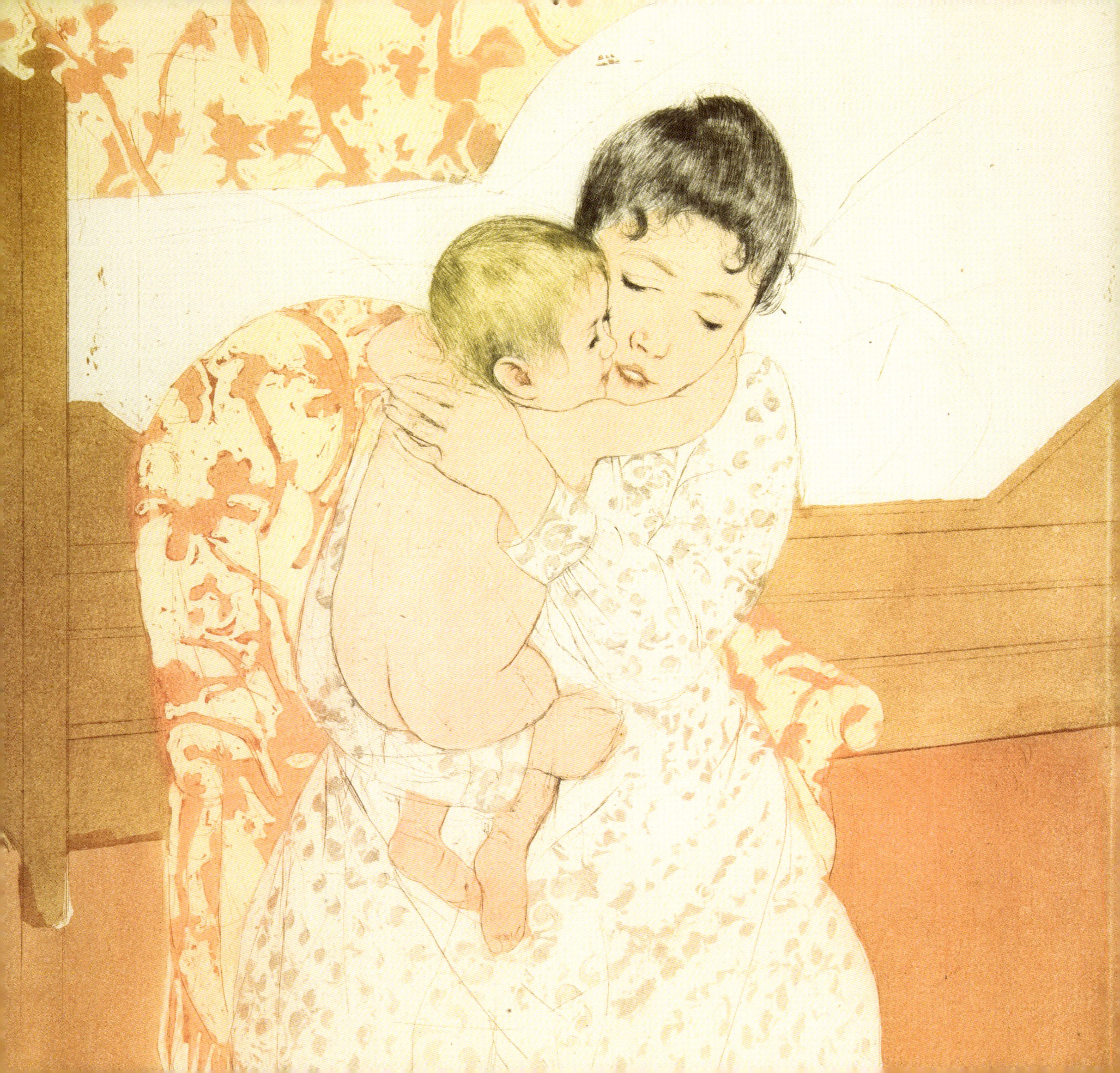

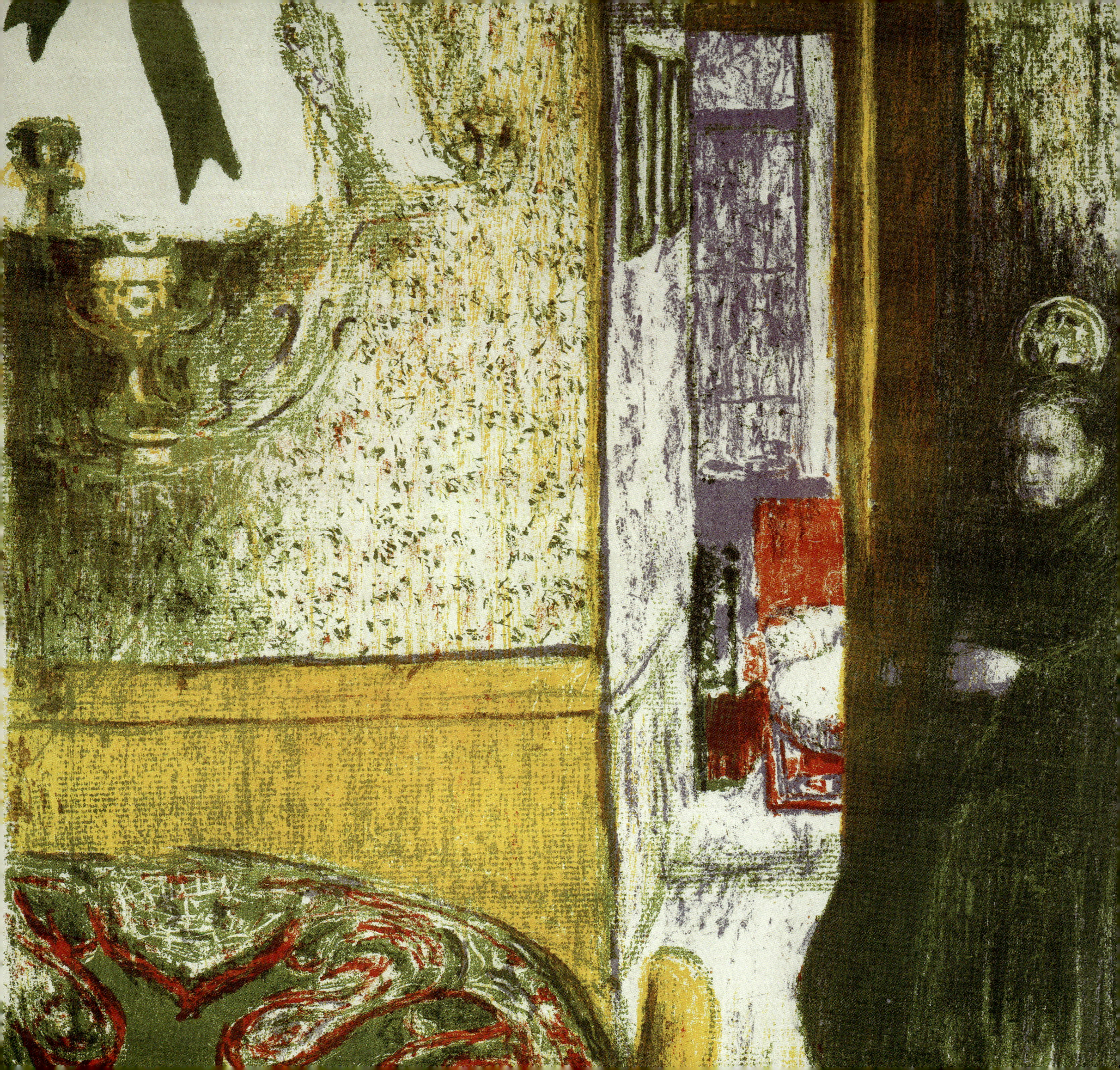

Atake (*see* page 71) or *View of the Saruwakach Street by Night* (1856), Bonnard's *Street Corner* (c. 1897) adopts an unusual viewpoint for an everyday street scene, with figures distributed without regard to balance or focus. Negative space calls attention to the flatness of the sheet rather than the ostensible three-dimensionality of the space. Bonnard was so taken with Japanese prints as to have been called 'le Nabi très Japonard' by his contemporaries.

Vuillard

Édouard Vuillard, Bonnard's fellow Nabi and close friend, likewise experimented with synthesizing an abstruse symbolism that bypassed rationalism with the abstract and decorative qualities of the Japanese masters. In a series combining 'Landscapes and Interiors', Vuillard's *Interior with a Hanging Lamp* (1899, *see* left) lacks the calligraphic clarity of Hiroshige, but adopts his flat, decorated surfaces, colour relations and unusual viewpoint. The massive gas lamp that dominates the composition is a direct reference to the equally large festival lantern in Hiroshige's 1856 woodblock of *Kinryūsan Temple at Asakusa*, in order to render a domestic interior that oscillates between the cosy and the anxious.

Toulouse-Lautrec

Perhaps the most famous printmaker of the late nineteenth century was Henri de Toulouse-Lautrec (1864–1901). A self-styled bohemian, Toulouse-Lautrec's aristocratic heritage, physical deformity and alcohol-fuelled depression only served to cement his legendary status around the dance halls, cabarets, café-concerts and brothels of Montmartre, his home after January 1884. Toulouse-Lautrec suffered from a disability (reportedly a consequence of his parents' consanguineous marriage) that gave him short, fragile legs, great difficulty walking and restricted his height to 152 cm (5 ft). Although he had a traditional artistic training under the Academic Realist Léon Bonnat (1833–1922) and

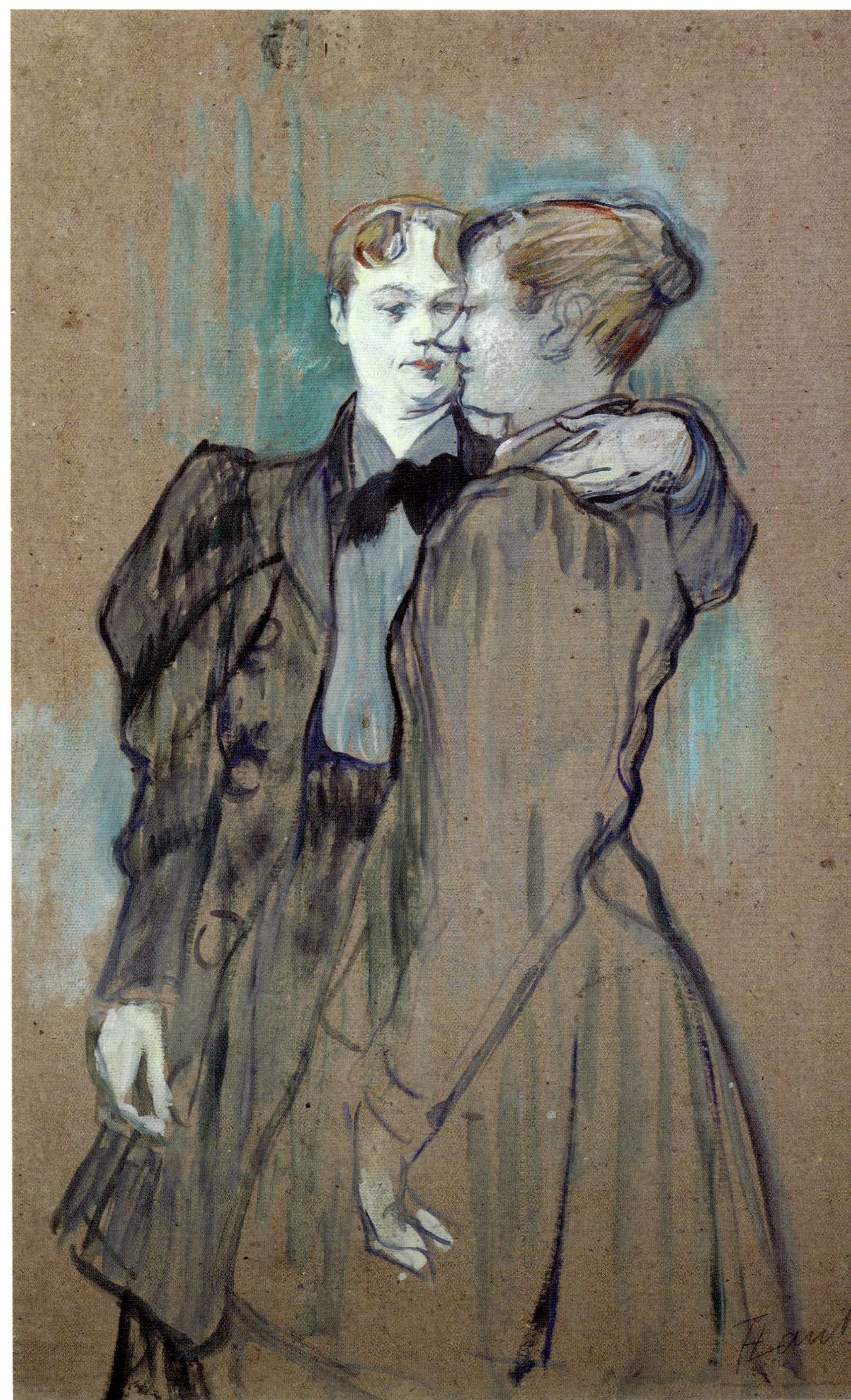

Above : *At the Moulin Rouge: Two Women Waltzing*, 1892, Henri de Toulouse-Lautrec (1864–1901)

Left : *Interior with a Hanging Lamp*, 1899, Édouard Vuillard (1868–1940)

then with Fernand Cormon – in whose studio he met Louis Anquetin (1861–1932), Bernard and Van Gogh – Toulouse-Lautrec was nevertheless determined to blaze his own trail. Combining a profound depth of sympathy for socially marginalized groups with a penetrating intellect, in works such as *At the Moulin Rouge: Two Women Waltzing* (1892, *see* page 79) and *In Bed* (*c.* 1892, *see* right), Toulouse-Lautrec documented the varied lives of the Montmartrois underclass amongst whom he lived and worked.

The Art of the Poster

However, it was in his designs for posters that Toulouse-Lautrec drew most consciously from the wellspring of Japanese prints. His first commission advertised the *Moulin Rouge: La Goulue* (1891, *see* page 82), 'the glutton', a cancan performer whose trademark finale involved lifting her skirt. This poster, nearly 2 metres (6½ feet) tall, made Toulouse-Lautrec a household name overnight. Its boldly outlined forms, patches of flat colour, lack of tonal

'The normal and final
goal of painting, as of
all the arts, cannot
be direct presentation
of objects.'
Albert Aurier

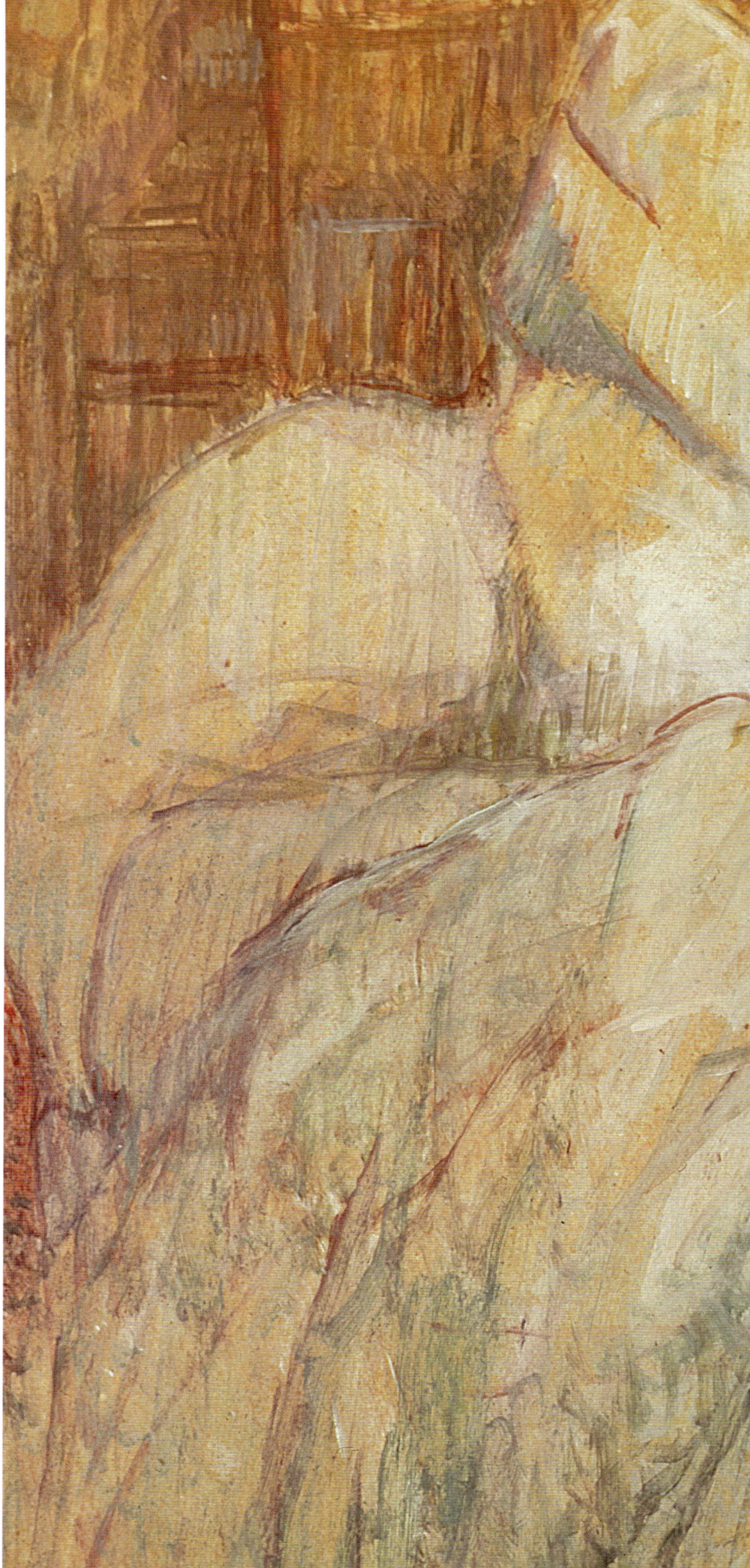

Right : *In Bed*, c. 1892, Henri de Toulouse-Lautrec (1864–1901)

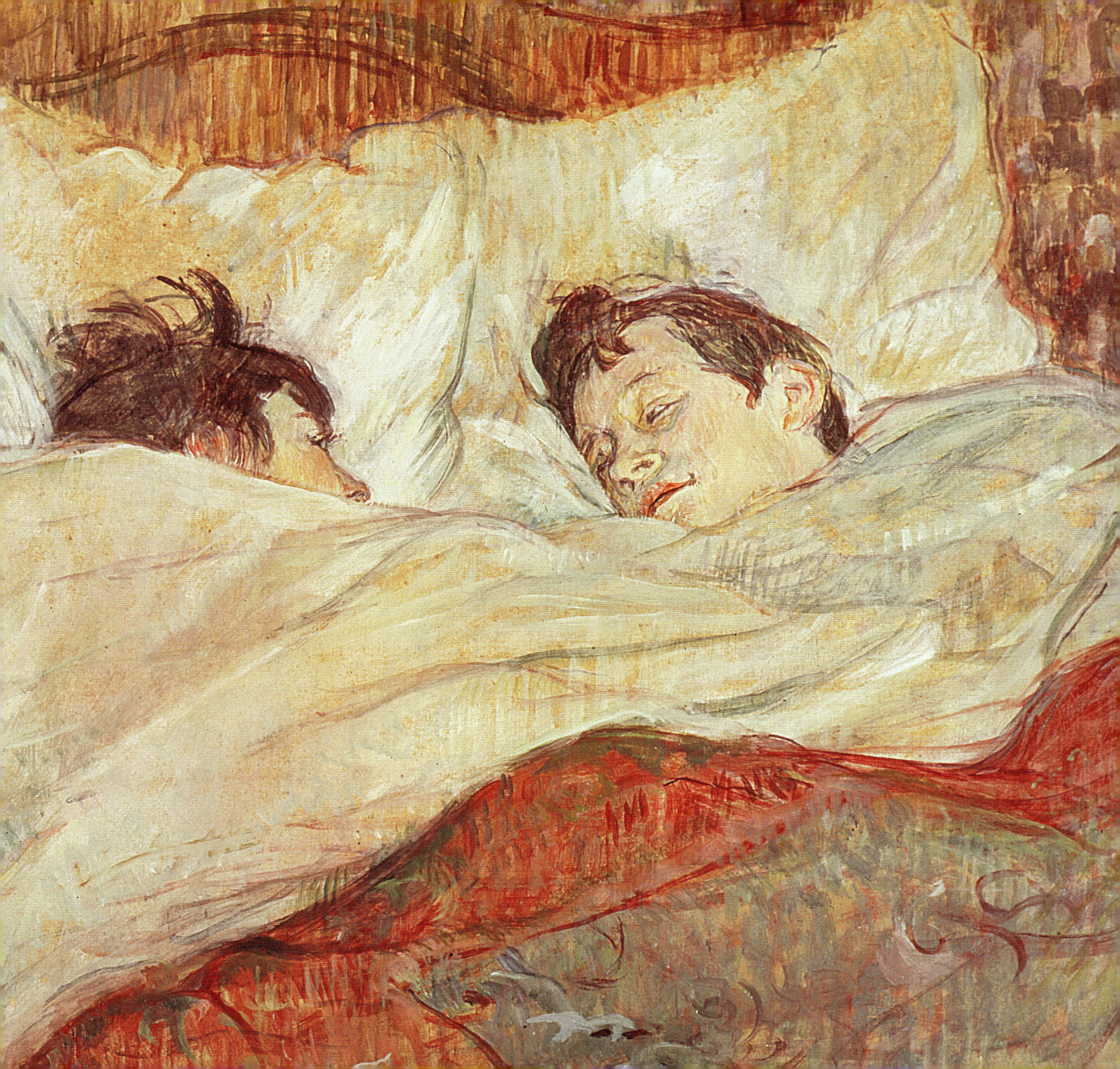

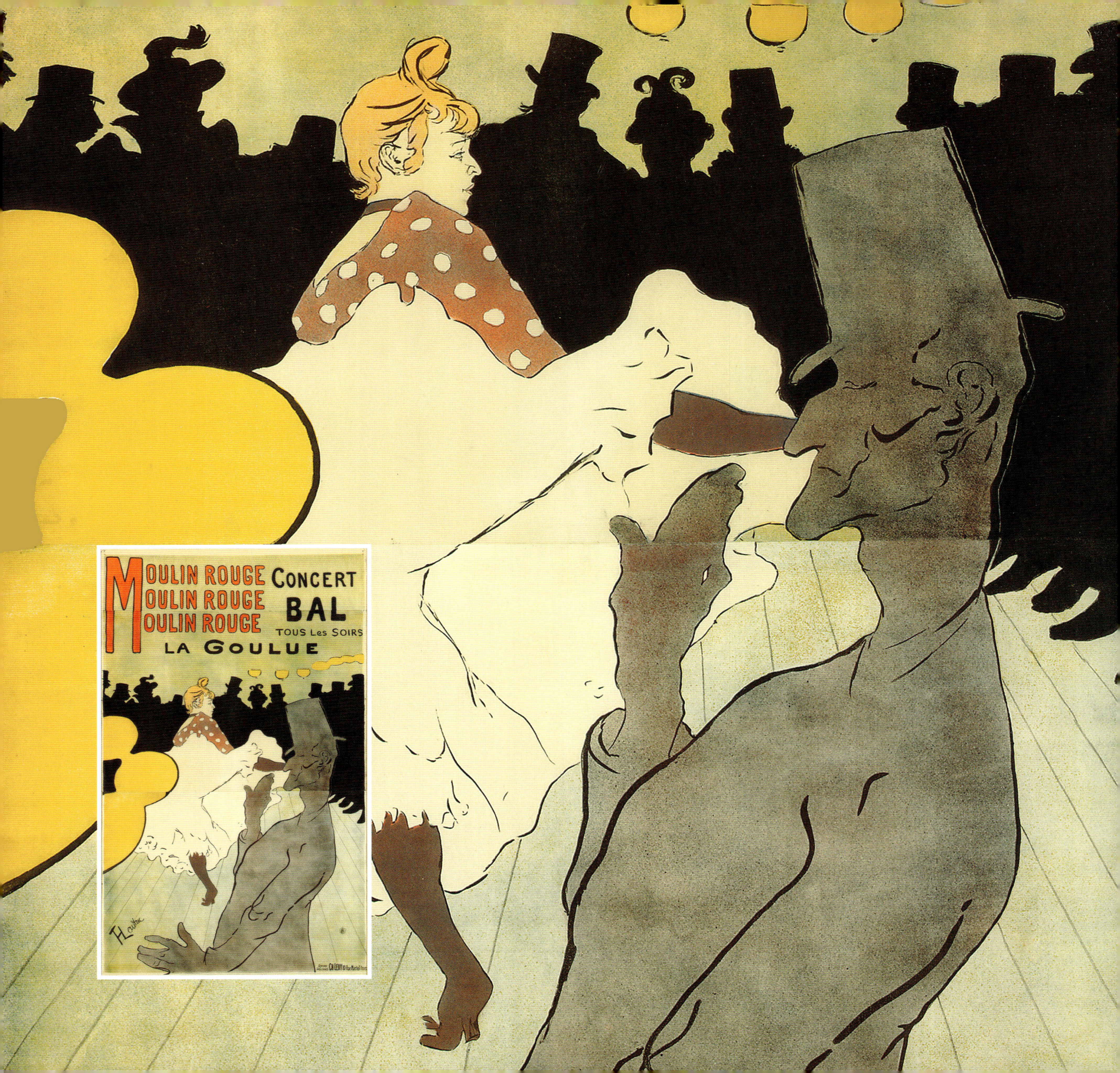

Moulin Rouge
Moulin Rouge
Moulin Rouge
LA GOULUE
CONCERT
BAL
TOUS LES SOIRS

modulation, spatial incongruities, expressive colours and daringly humorous composition all recall Japanese prints. They also reveal the influence of his Post-Impressionist friends: Anquetin, Bernard, Van Gogh and the Nabis Bonnard and Vuillard. Inspired by the performance at the Folies Bergère of Loïe Fuller – a pioneering American dancer best known for her billowing silk costumes, twirling choreography and multicoloured lighting sets – Toulouse-Lautrec produced around 60 impressions of a lithograph, *Miss Loïe Fuller* (1893) in a variety of colours (some dusted with experimental metallic pigments). The motif is pared back to its absolute essence: a twirl of colours, arabesque lines and a glimpse of the performer's head and legs. In a work that evokes rather than describes (mere visual descriptiveness could not do justice to Fuller's performance), Toulouse-Lautrec eliminated all extraneous detail. This included the illusion of perspectival depth, chiaroscuro (modelling of forms using light and shade), naturalistic detail, and with it the central illusion that had sustained Western art from the Renaissance to the Impressionists – against which many artists at this moment were rebelling – that the picture represents a window on to reality.

'To the eyes of the artist objects are meaningless as objects. They can only appear to him as signs…'

Albert Aurier

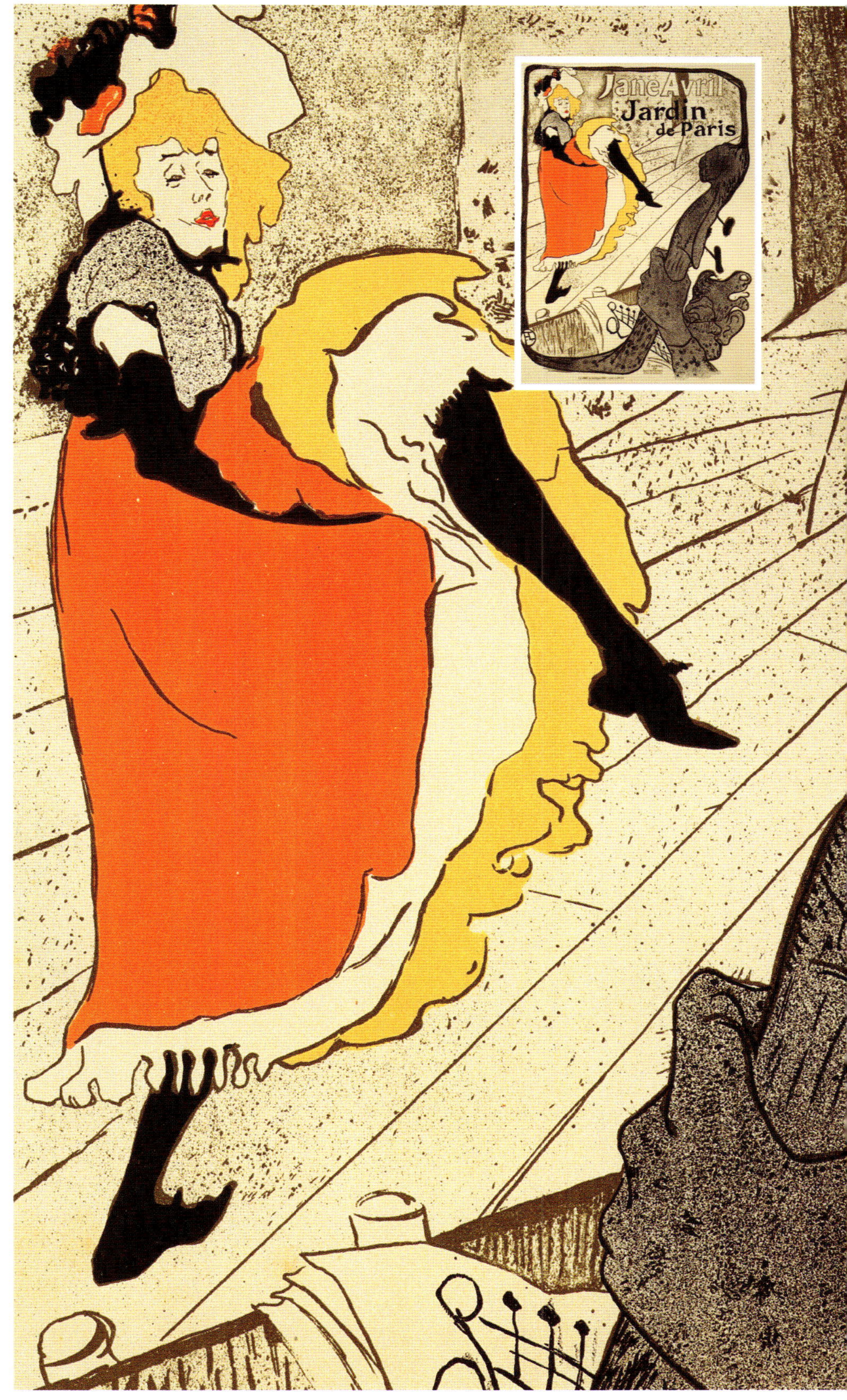

Left : *Moulin Rouge: La Goulue*, 1891, Henri de Toulouse-Lautrec (1864–1901)

Above : *Jane Avril at the Jardin de Paris* (reproduction), 1893, Henri de Toulouse-Lautrec (1864–1901)

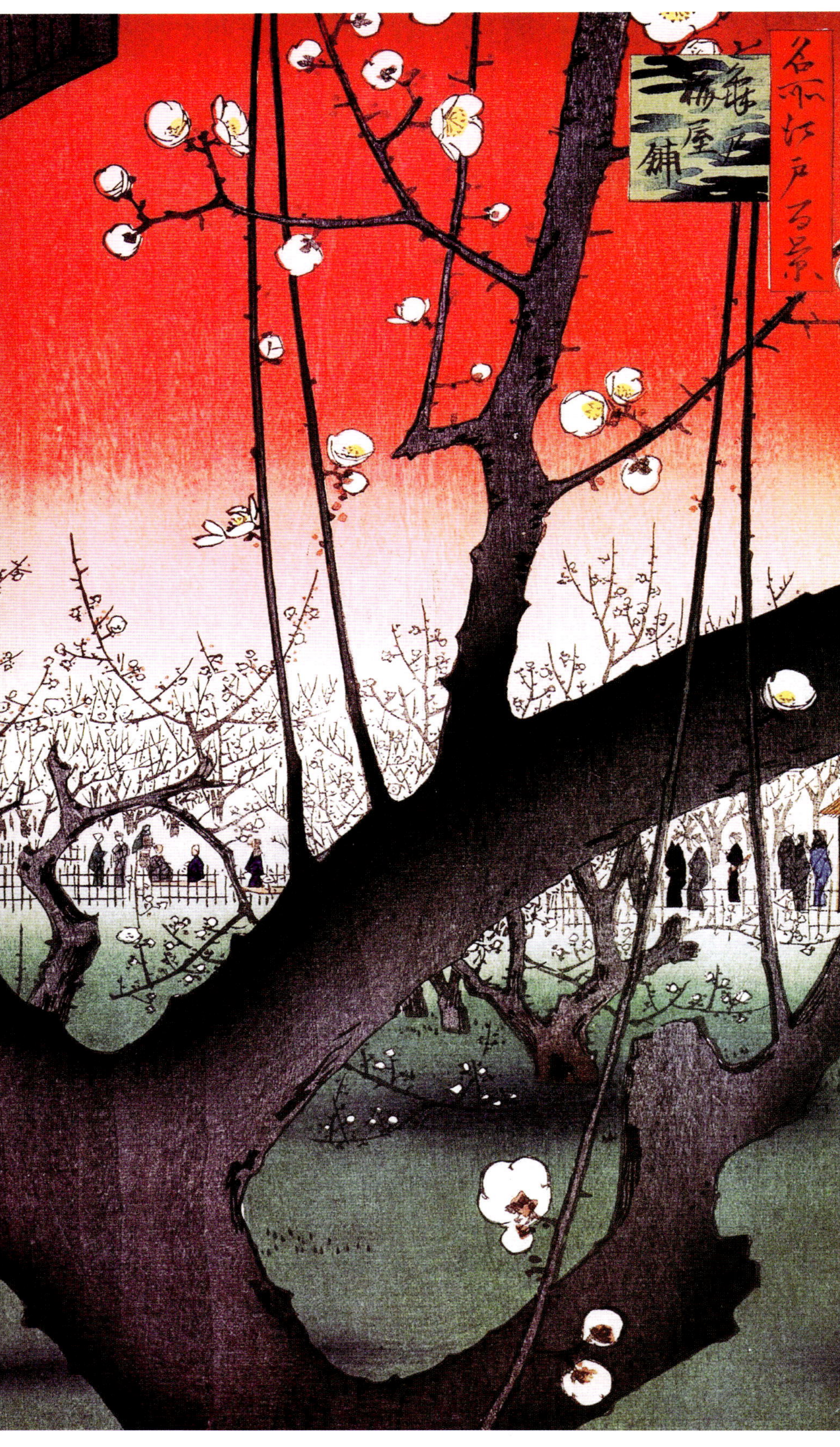

Above : *Plum Park in Kameido*, 1857, Utagawa Hiroshige (1797–1858)

Gauguin's 'Japonisme'

Towards the end of the 1880s, Gauguin was drawing inspiration from the rustic simplicity and devout piety of the 'primitive' people of Brittany. In *Vision of the Sermon: Jacob Wrestling with the Angel* (*see* page 52), Gauguin collapsed his double rebellion – against naturalism and against modernity – on to a people whose distinctively pre-modern way of life, and non-naturalistic art, seemed to offer an inspirational and legitimizing model for him. However, in producing this vision of primitive Breton belief, Gauguin nevertheless cross-pollinated the lessons of Bernard's *Buckwheat Harvest* and *Breton Women in a Meadow* with the aesthetic forms we have been examining as being characteristic of Japanese prints. The flattened colour, unusual viewpoint and diagonally placed tree are all directly related to devices used by Hiroshige (*Plum Park in Kameido*, 1857, *see left*) and copied by Van Gogh (*Flowering Plum Orchard (after Hiroshige)*, 1887, *see right*). Bernard himself identified a study of wrestlers by Katsushika Hokusai (1760–1849), contained within the Hokusai manga, as the source for Gauguin's own wrestling figure group. In searching for, as he put it in a letter to Van Gogh, 'figures [… with] a great rustic and superstitious simplicity'. Gauguin was thus content with a kind of mix-and-match approach to cultural otherness.

In *Yellow Christ* (1889, *see* page 86), Gauguin depicts three Breton women gathered at the foot of the crucified Christ (or a sculpture of the Crucifixion). The same vibrant yellow, bounded within bold blue outlines, is used to articulate Christ's body and the wheatfields. Stone walls undulate and flat, red trees float into the landscape like wisps of smoke. Gauguin was deeply moved by the polychrome (painted) wooden Christ in the rustic chapel of Trémalo near Pont-Aven; his painting seeks to borrow the unpretentiousness and direct appeal of such artefacts, dispensing with the sophisticated illusions of high art in favour of a decorative schema that synthesized his feelings, outward appearances and abstract form. The events that Gauguin depicts in

Right : *Flowering Plum Orchard (after Hiroshige)*, 1887, Vincent van Gogh (1853–90)

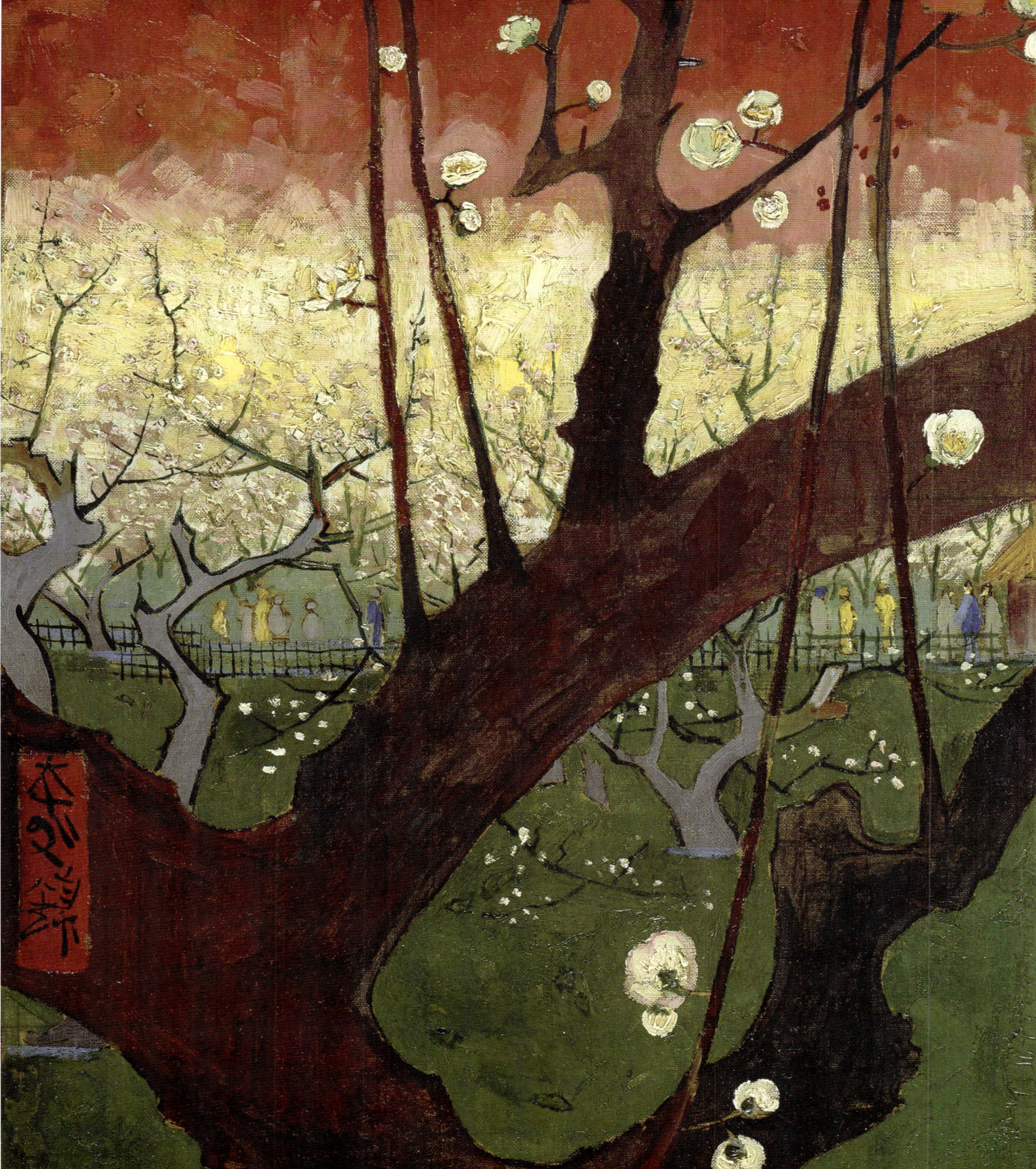

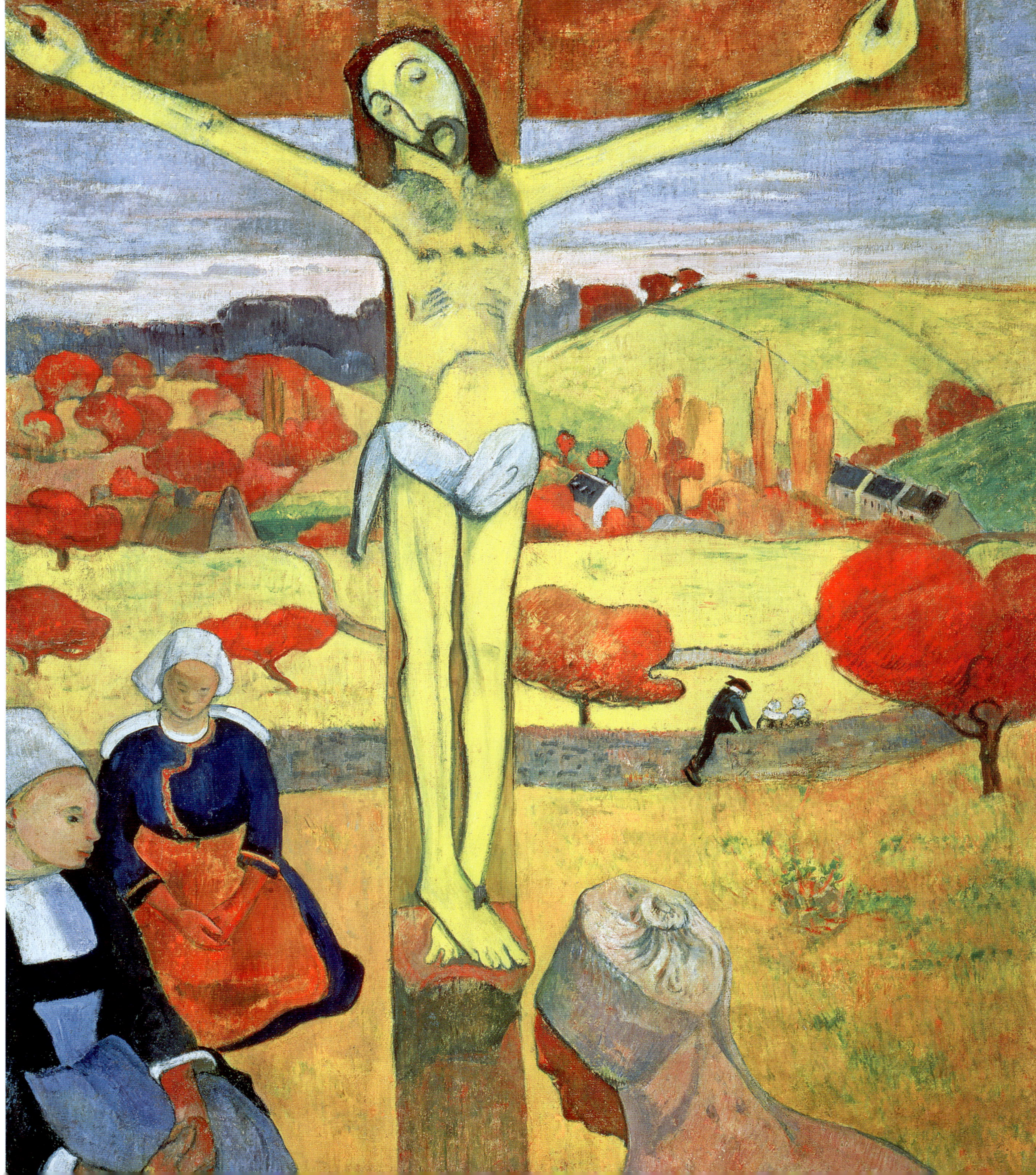

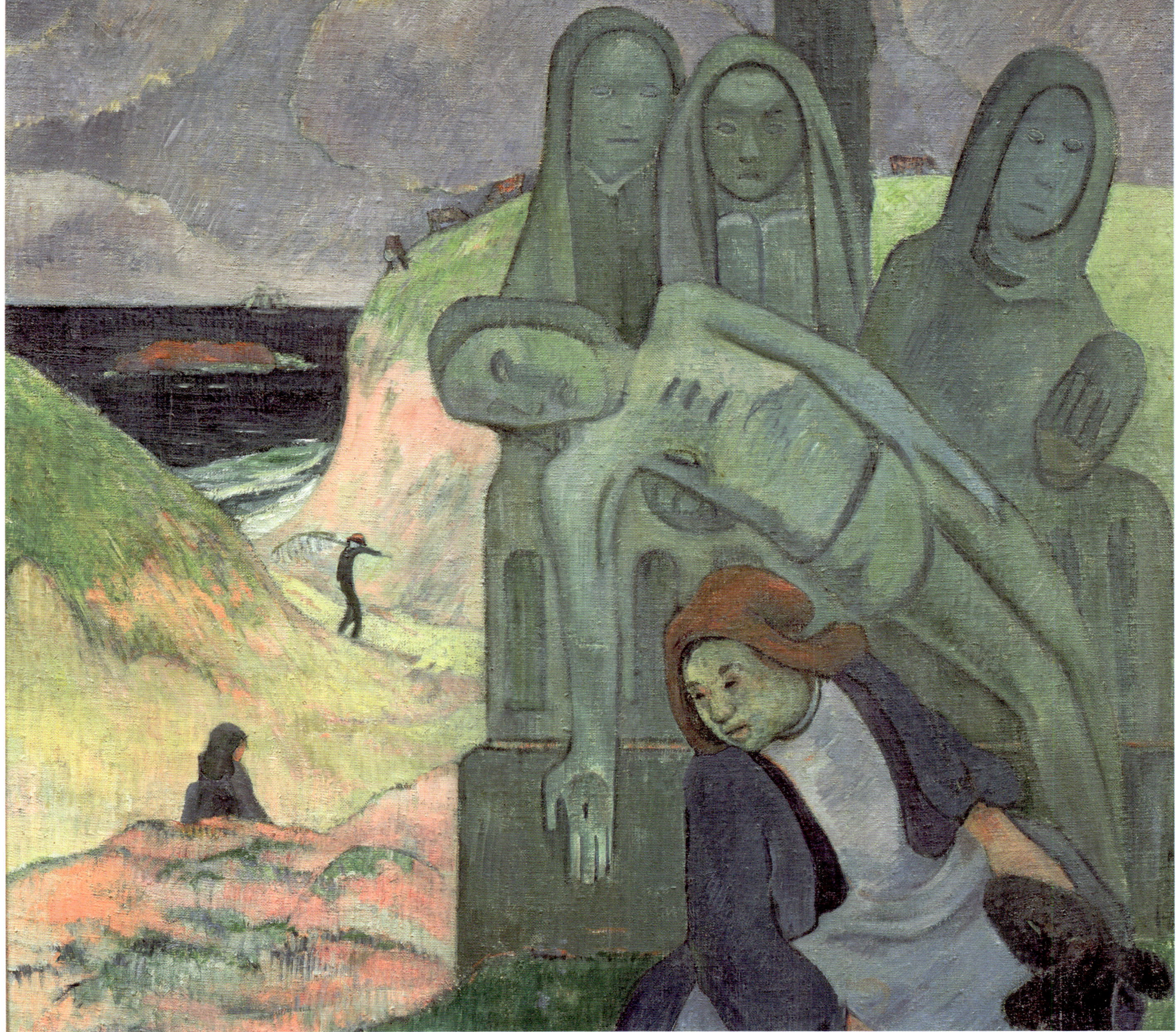

the *Yellow Christ*, and in the closely related *Green Christ* (1889, *see* above), which depicts a Breton woman at the foot of a *calvaire* (a public sculpture of the Crucifixion common across Brittany), are ambiguous, neither clearly historical nor contemporary, neither purely real nor completely imaginary, caught between the decorative and the detailed. This ambiguity was precisely the point, since it was the means by which Gauguin hoped to evoke the mysterious realm of the mind beyond thought that was impossible to directly describe. The art critic Octave Mirbeau (1848–1917) was a firm

Left : *Yellow Christ*, 1889, Paul Gauguin (1848–1903)

Above : *Green Christ*, 1889, Paul Gauguin (1848–1903)

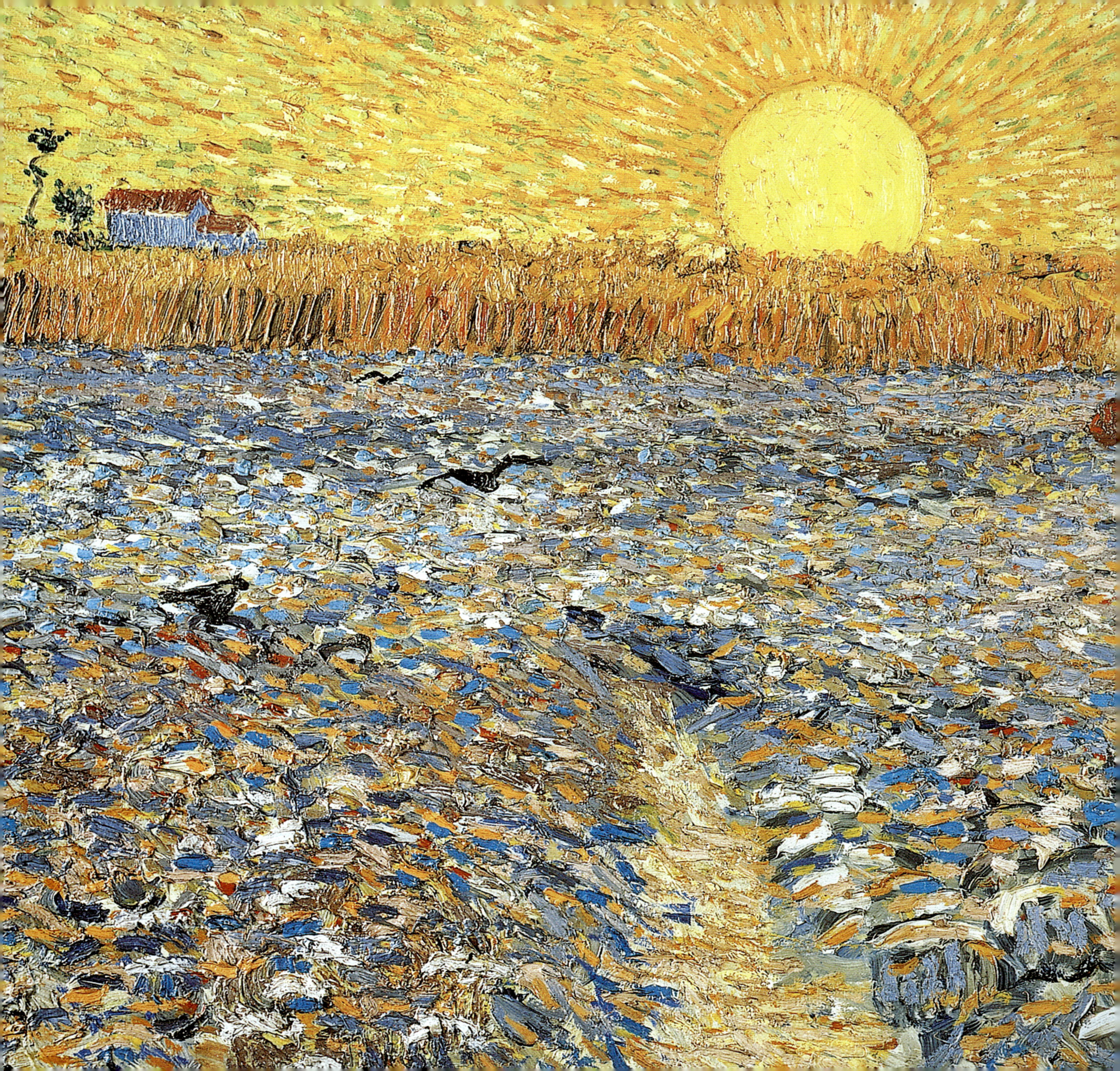

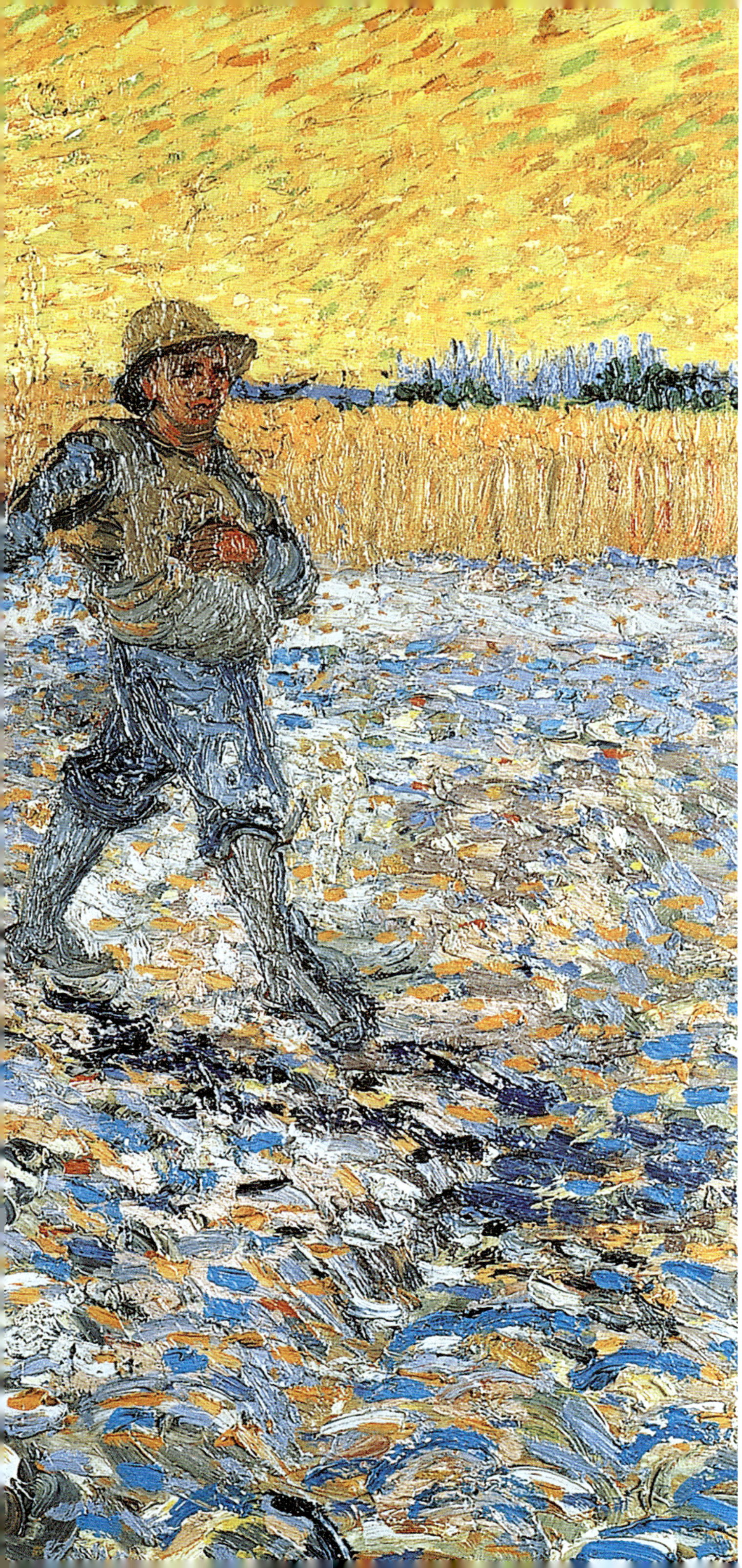

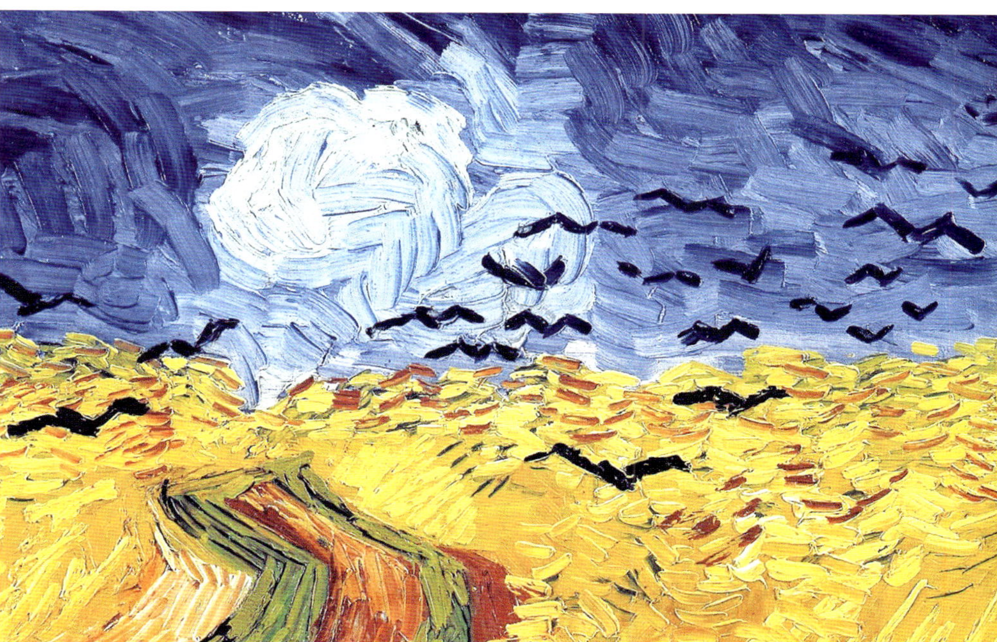

believer in the evocative power of Gauguin's abstruse symbolism and multi-origin primitivism, describing the *Yellow Christ* as 'a rich, disturbing blend of barbaric splendour, Catholic liturgy, Hindu reverie, Gothic imagery, and obscure yet subtle symbolism'.

The Superficiality of Japonisme

It has been argued that the impact of Japanese art was not felt by its introducing completely new aesthetic forms, styles, techniques or categories, but rather in how it seemed to offer external validation for the innovations French painters were already making. In 1878, Ernest Chesneau (1833–90) expressed this very point when he wrote that '[p]ainters found confirmation rather than an inspiration for their personal ways of seeing, feeling, understanding and interpreting nature. The result was a redoubling of individual originality.' Whilst sold as 'Japanese' (literally as well as figuratively: *Japonisme* was big business), what the new cultural commodities and aesthetic forms that fuelled the French vogue for all things Japan really represented was an almost purely imagined place. It was 'Japan'

Left : *The Sower*, 1888, Vincent van Gogh (1853–90)
Detail above : *Wheatfield with Crows*, 1890, Vincent van Gogh (1853–90), *see page 23*

'I must draw diggers, sowers, men and women at the plough, without cease.... I no longer stand as helpless before nature as I used to do.'

Van Gogh

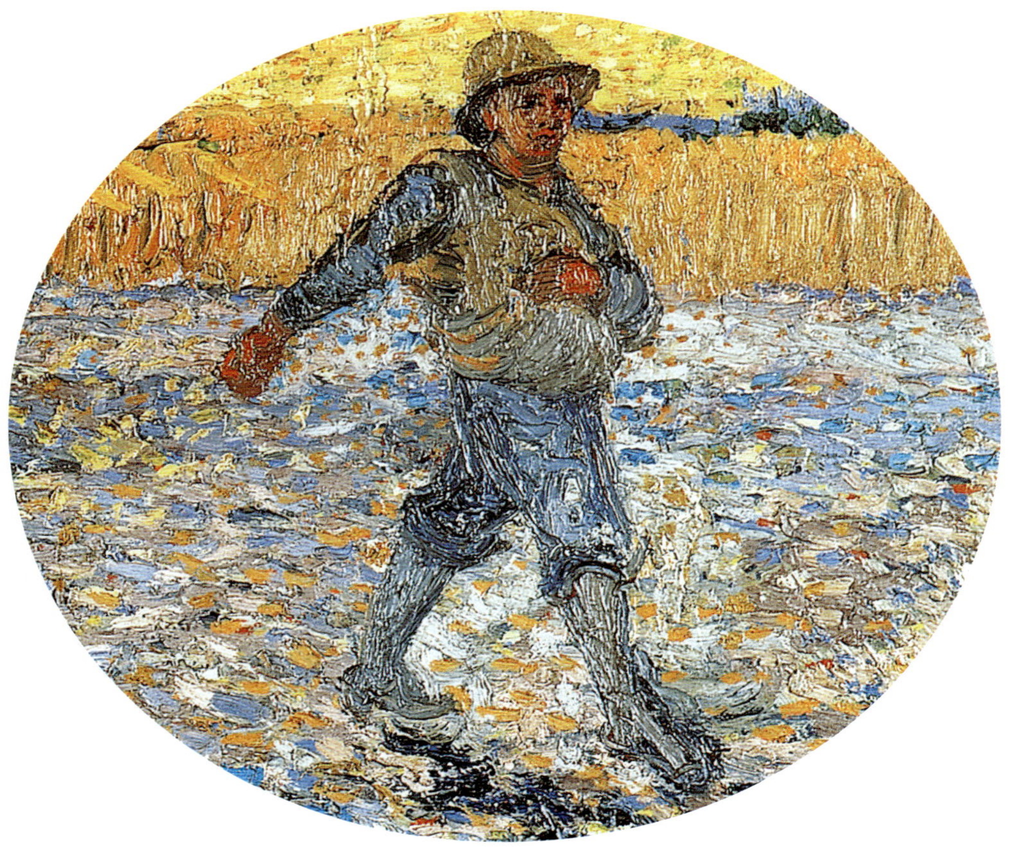

as it existed for the Western imagination, internal to Western systems of thought and frameworks of cultural reference. For the European mind of the late nineteenth century, it was the generic quality of 'otherness', of being alien, that mattered more than the specific characteristic by which it was 'other'. That Gauguin's idea of superstitious simplicity was a liberal mélange from various sources, combined without consideration for their conceptual compatibility, illustrates precisely this way of thinking.

Art and Politics

It was not only contact with other cultures that spurred Post-Impressionists to revolutionize their subject and form in these years; political conviction was an equally robust catalyst. Before encountering Japanese prints, Van Gogh's motivation was a burning passion of democratic, egalitarian politics borne of religious commitment. His early Realist works, which combine a deliberately vernacular style with the (sometimes shockingly) frank depiction of workers' everyday hardships, are especially revealing about his political commitments. The sower was a significant figure in both Christian mythology and French democratic politics. For example, Jean-François Millet's (1814–75) *The Sower* (1850, *see right*), which depicts in an intentionally crude manner a peasant distributing grain – striding forward illuminated by the dawn rays of the rising sun – was an icon of both Realism and democratic politics. Critics in the 1850s saw in Millet's strong and strident peasant a seditious harbinger of social revolution.

Van Gogh revered Millet, and sought to emulate his many treatments of the sower theme, writing that 'I must draw diggers, sowers, men & women at the plough, without cease…. I no longer stand as helpless before nature as I used to do.' His own *Sower* (1888, *see left* and page 88) draws from Millet's sunrise setting, the peasant's pose and the textural materiality of his paint handling, but seeks to explicitly overlay Christian notions regarding the natural cycles of death and rebirth. Van Gogh's peasant does not threaten to march towards the

Detail above : *The Sower*, 1888, Vincent van Gogh (1853–90), *see page 88*

Right : *The Sower*, 1850, Jean-François Millet (1814–75)

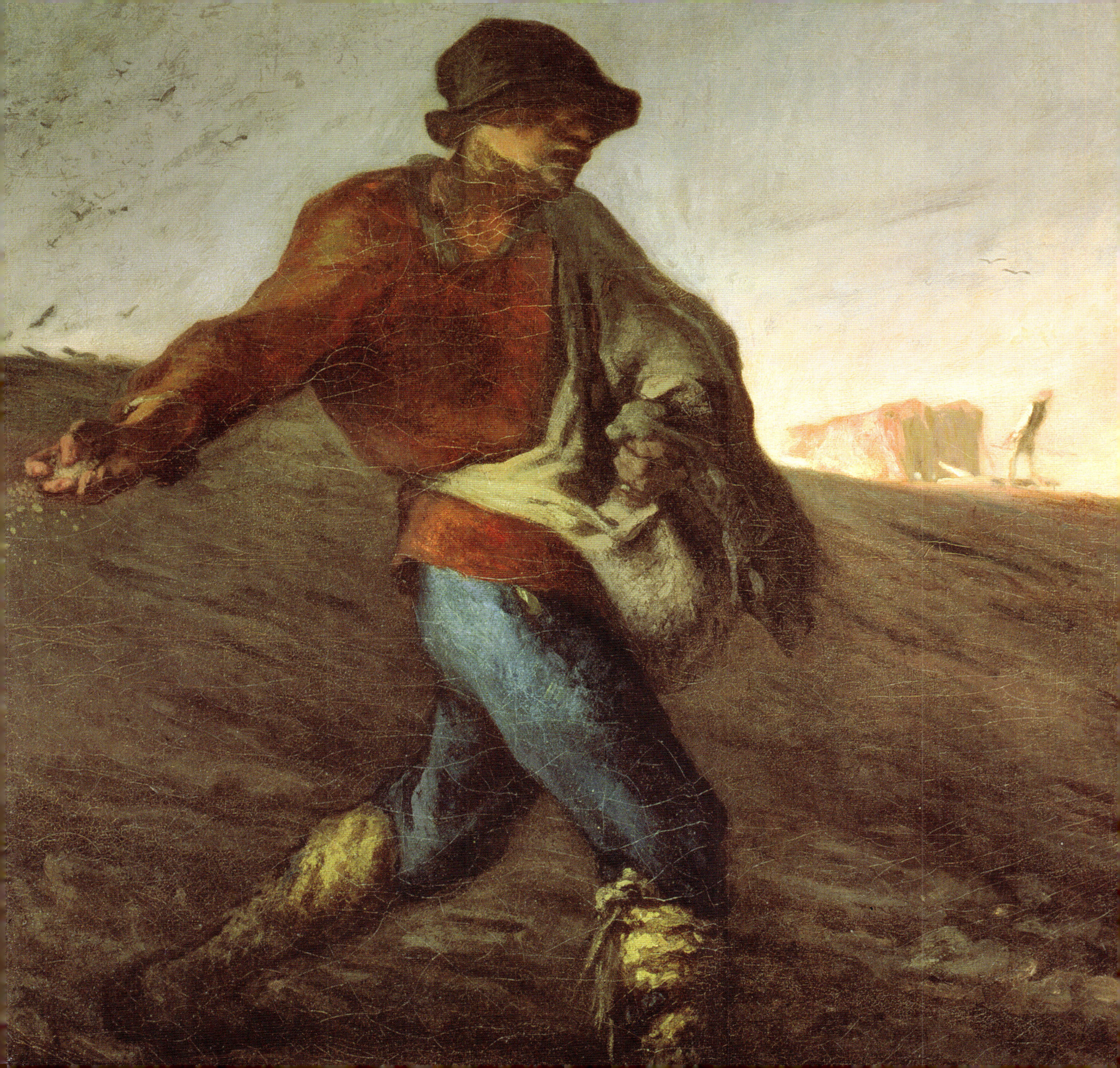

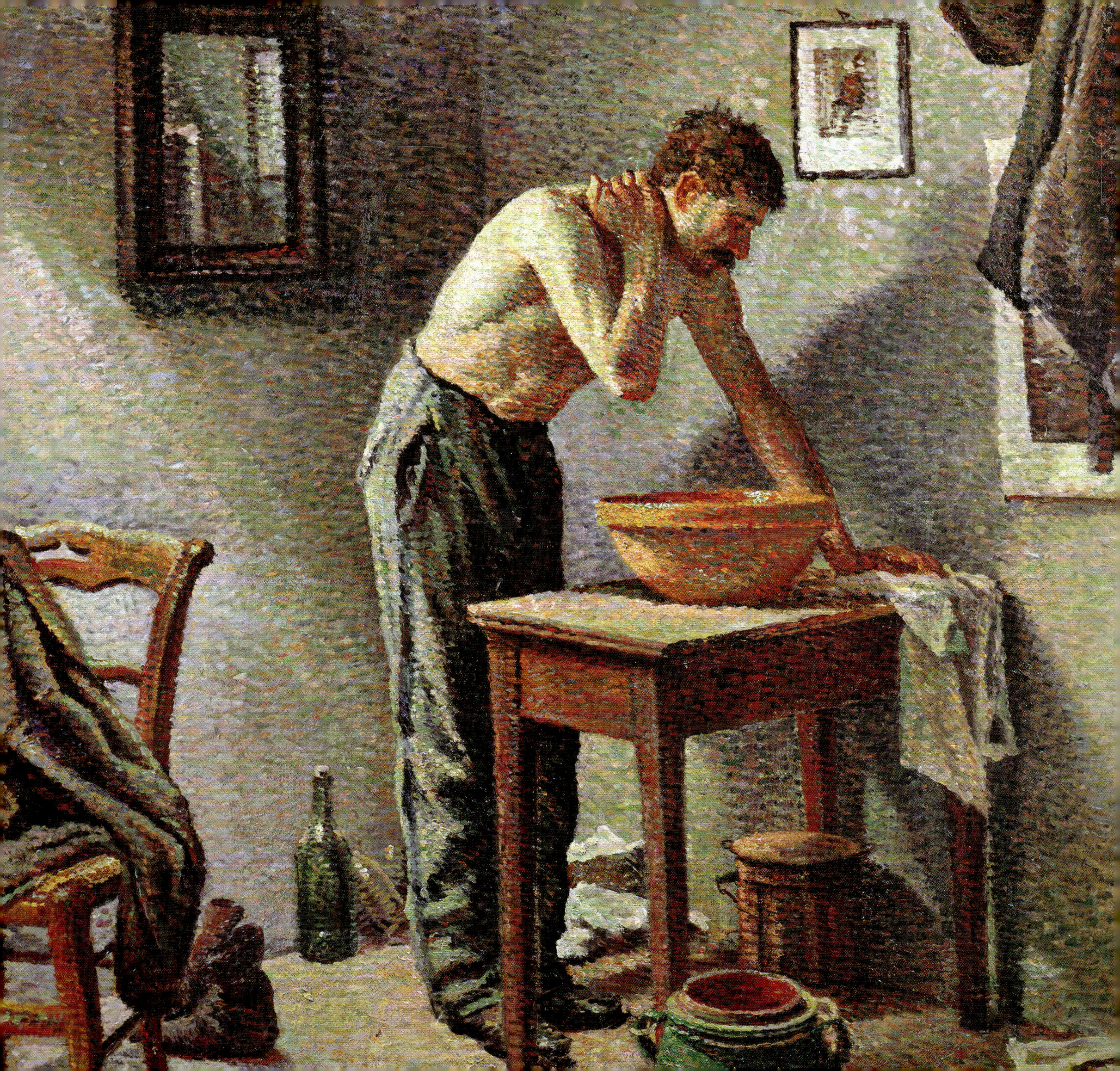

viewer, but is rather situated firmly within the endless agricultural cycle. As we have seen, his overriding longing was for utopia, neither exclusively socialist, Christian nor Japanese, but an idiosyncratic admixture. However, less than three years after Van Gogh completed *The Sower*, more ideologically strident groups were to rock the French establishment to its core.

'The Propaganda of the Deed'

In the 1890s, France was gripped by a wave of anarchist, Marxist and socialist agitation calling for France's labouring population to violently overthrow their bourgeois oppressors and eradicate the capitalist system through strike action. Anarchist groups undertook a covert series of direct retaliations against the state, in revenge for the arrest of some of their number at a protest in Clichy on 1 May 1891. François Claudius Koenigstein (1859–92), known as Ravachol, set off bombs in the flats of the judges who had sentenced the Clichy anarchists. The following year, Auguste Vaillant (1861–94) threw a bomb into the French parliament and, although nobody was killed, the middle-class élite was terrified. In 1894, a week after Vaillant's execution, Émile Henry (1872–94) set off a bomb in the Gare Saint-Lazare (the station depicted by Monet in 1877), killing one and wounding 20. These atrocities culminated in the assassination of the president, Marie François Sadi Carnot (1837–94), who was stabbed to death on 24 June 1894 in Lyon by an Italian anarchist, Sante Geronimo Caserio (1873–94). The

government reacted with a draconian crackdown in the form of the so-called *lois scélérates* ('villainous laws'), which restricted press freedom and essentially criminalized anarchist politics *in toto*. Under these laws, 30 leading anarchists were arrested and tried for their anarchist associations in 1894. Amongst the defendants, in what was known as the 'Trial of the Thirty', was art critic and advocate of Neo-Impressionism Félix Fénéon.

The authorities could not establish any criminal links between 'the thirty', and 27 were acquitted, Fénéon among them. However, Fénéon certainly was an anarchist. Moreover, he thoroughly approved of, and sometimes abetted, the practice of 'propaganda by the deed' (it has been suggested, without firm evidence, that he was responsible for the bombing of the fashionable Foyot restaurant in 1894). After the 'Trial of the Thirty', a consensus emerged in anarchist circles that violent terrorism was no longer an effective strategy, and instead 'propaganda of the word' came to be the prevailing *modus operandi*, a non-violent strategy with a more definable role for artists.

Félix Fénéon and Maximilien Luce

There were intimate connections between anarchist philosophers and Neo-Impressionist painters. Maximilien Luce (1858–1941), born into the working class, was radicalized early, having witnessed a massacre of Communards by government troops at the age of 13. Luce, 'a tough, loyal fellow with a

Left : *Man Washing*, 1887, Maximilien Luce (1858–1941)

Detail above : *Morning, Interior*, 1890, Maximilen Luce (1858–1941), *see page 96*

primitive, muscular talent' as Fénéon described him, routinely published illustrations with the anarchist press, including Émile Pouget's (1860–1931) anarchist weekly *Le Père Peinard* (for which he designed the frontispieces and to which Fénéon was a contributor) and Jean Grave's (1854–1939) *La Révolté*, later renamed *Les Temps nouveaux*. Luce's lithographs were not executed in Pointillist technique (which would have been ill-suited to the medium), but with a clear and graphic simplicity ideal for their propagandist purpose. In an illustration for *Les Temps nouveaux* (1895), Luce depicts a large female figure, an allegory of anarchism, striding forward, with arms outstretched. The sun rises on a new dawn, illuminating a group of bare-chested labourers as they bury the weapons and crowns made obsolete by the coming utopia; still in shadow, a woman beckons to Anarchy, mirroring her gesture of outstretched arms, calling her forth to banish the decay and suffering of toil under the shadow of capitalism.

In his paintings, no longer restricted by the need to inexpensively reproduce his design by lithographic printing, Luce returned to full-colour Pointillism. His subject matter, however, mirrored that of his illustrations and accorded closely with the anarchist ideas espoused by writers like Fénéon. The valorization and idealization of the honest labourer, for example, was a persistent subject for Luce. In *Man Washing* (1887, *see* page 92), exhibited at the Salon des Indépendants alongside Signac's *The Dining Room, Breakfast*, Luce depicts the morning ablutions of a solitary man, standing at his toilet in a sparsely decorated interior. Clear, white light illuminates both the room and the man's semi-nude torso from a window to the left of the scene, out of frame. The man's simple clothes and boots are dotted around the room; on the walls are a small mirror and a pair of unidentifiable prints. Catching him at a rare moment of introspective calm, Luce emphasizes the worker's hard, muscular body and his psychological autonomy. Luce's later *Piledrivers* (1902–03, *see* right), again exhibited at the Salon des Indépendants, could almost be this work's pendant: a group of muscular workers, stripped to the waist strain against the resistance and inertia of the ground, into which

Right : *Piledrivers*, 1902–03, Maximilien Luce (1858–1941)

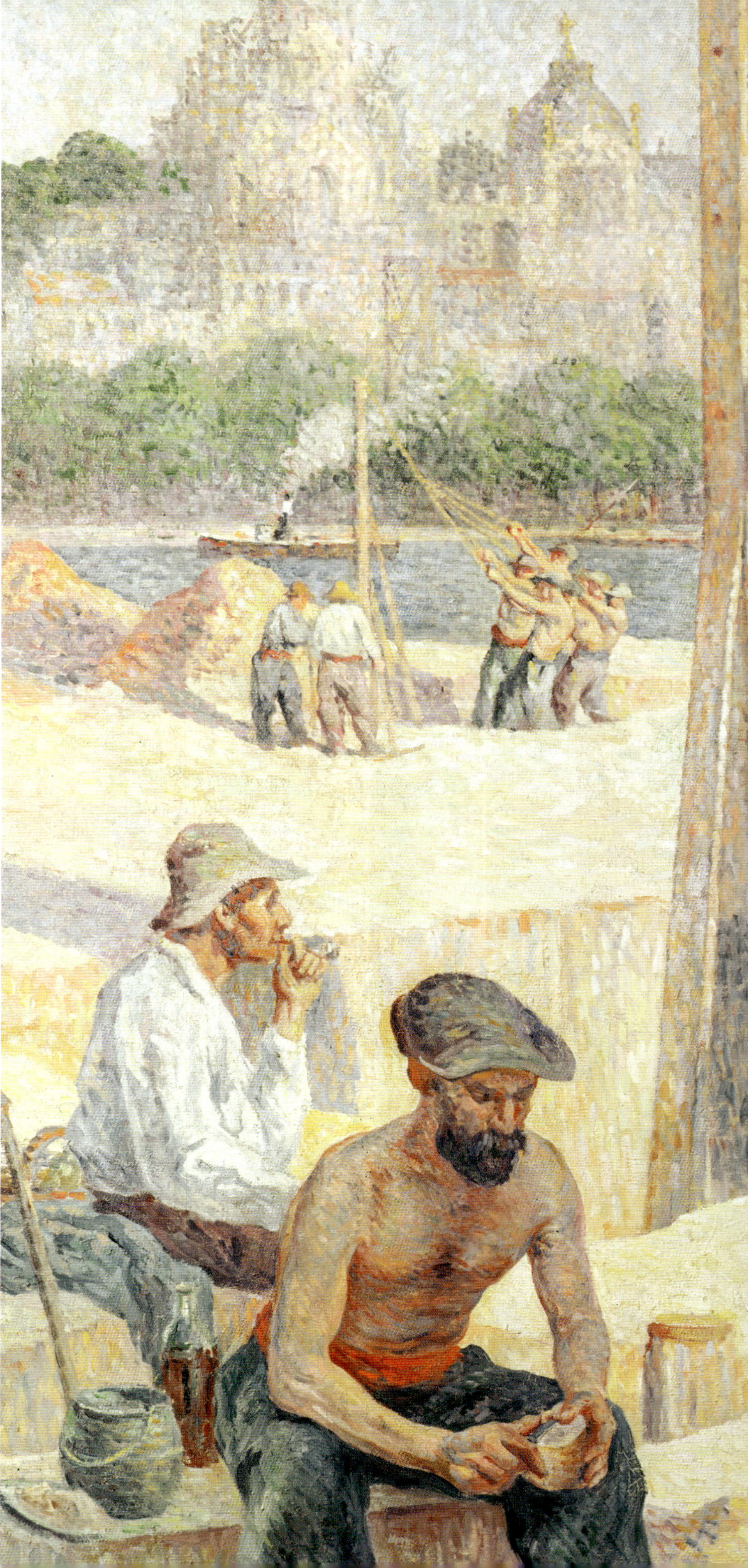

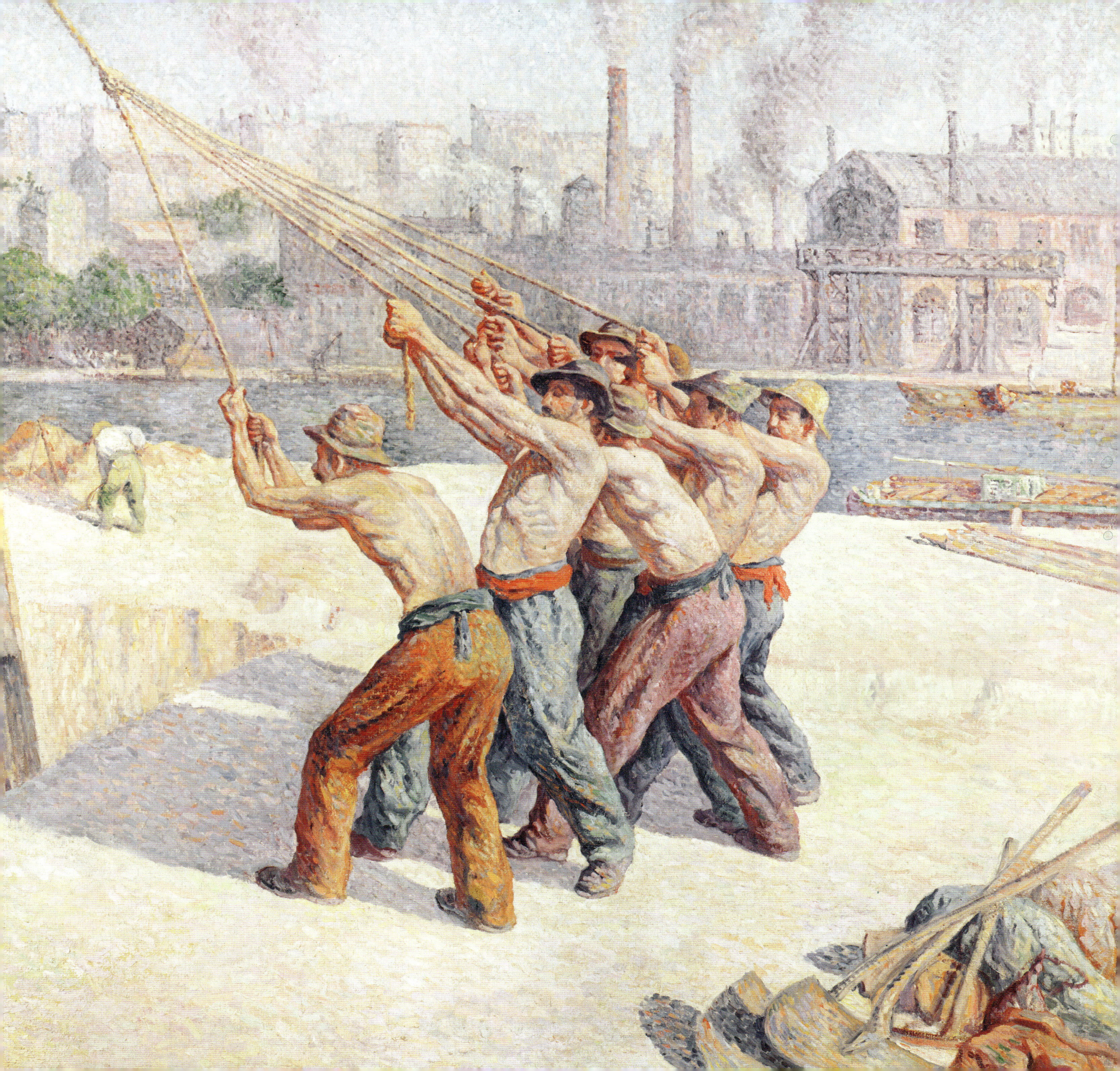

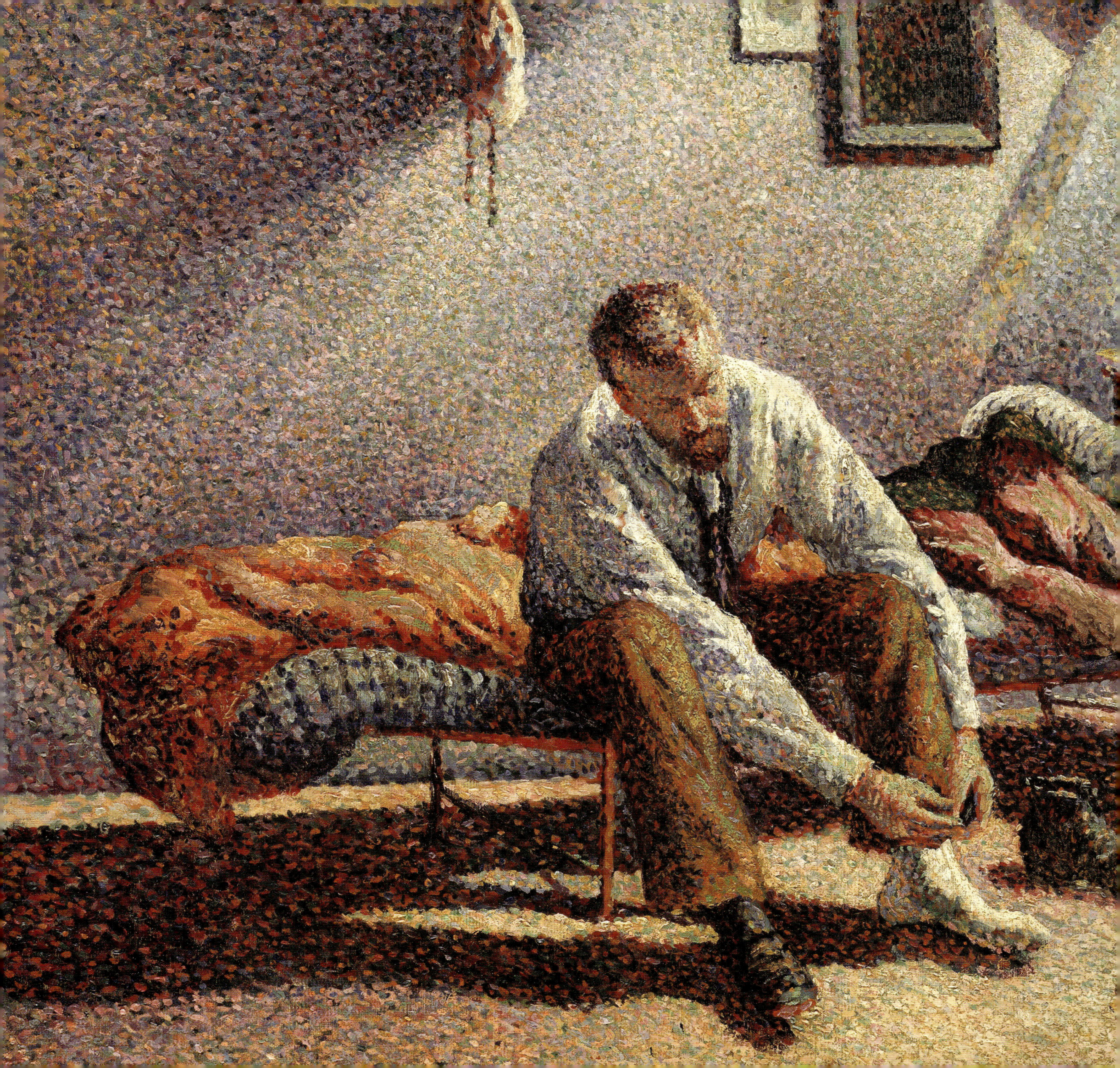

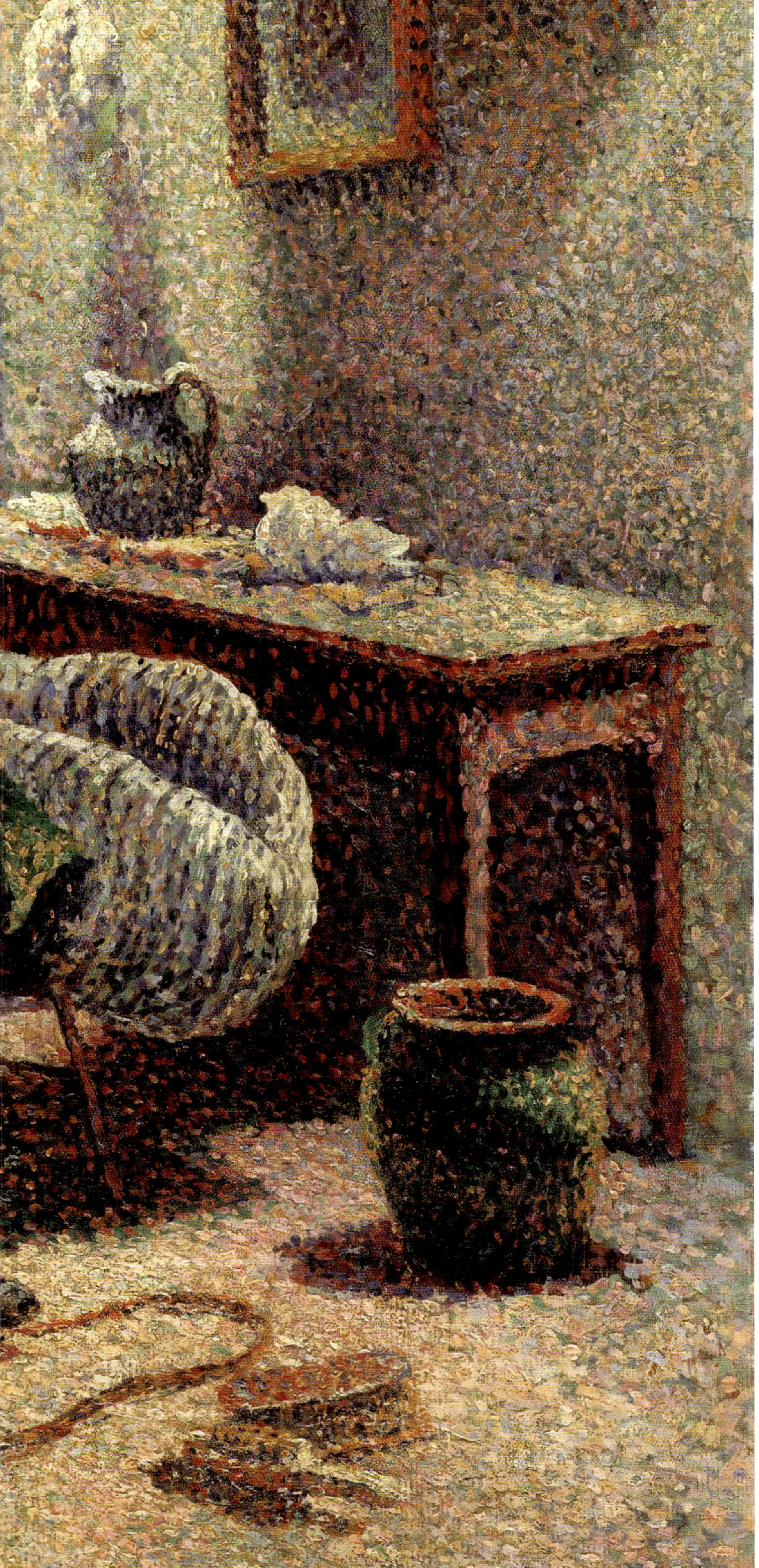

they are driving a pile. Stressing both the brute physicality and communal endeavour of their task, Luce makes use of Neo-Impressionism's supposed scientific objectivity to document the everyday life of Paris's working class. Factories billow on the opposite bank of the Seine, a worker in the foreground rests, while another group in the background pulls with equal vigour.

Morning, Interior (1890, *see* left), painted three years after *Man Washing*, again captures an undramatic scene of temporary stillness in the life of a working man. Once more in spartan surroundings, the subject this time is Luce's friend and fellow Neo-Impressionist painter Gustave Perrot (about whom little is known), who sits on his flimsy bed and puts on his shoes. Luce's perceptive depiction of the effect of light, as it illuminates the room and transforms its colour, locates the painting at dawn, playing on a tension between, on the one hand, new possibilities (of the kind signified in his illustration for *Les Temps nouveaux*) and, on the other, rest disturbed prematurely by the duties of labour. Perrot appears as a humble craftsman; through his rigorous applications of dots and careful attention to colour, so does Luce.

Signac's Utopia

In addition to offering clear-sighted documents of the reality of labour in the present moment, Neo-Impressionists also looked forward, imagining the future utopia of anarchist liberation. Signac's *In the Time of Harmony. The Golden Age is not in the Past, it is in the Future* (1893–95, *see* page 99) is precisely one such utopia. Signac, like Luce, was primarily influenced by the political philosophy of Pyotr Kropotkin (1842–1921) and Elisée Reclus (1830–1905), anarcho-communists who advocated collective ownership of the means of production, social equality and the abolition of private property. The society they envisioned was made up of small units (often the size of a neighbourhood) in which the individual never lost their autonomy or freedom. Signac depicts this ideal society, living in harmony with each other and with nature; no longer

Left : *Morning, Interior*, 1890, Maximilien Luce (1858–1941)

compelled to labour for the profit of capitalists, work and leisure are intertwined as the basis for personal fulfilment and collective prosperity. While people sow seeds or gather fruit, others read, dance, play and paint. Although containing anarchist symbols – such as the sower and the cockerel – the painting is not overly dogmatic or propagandist. Rather, it sought to provoke in its viewers precisely the yearning for social harmony that motivated Signac and his fellow anarchists. A diffuse and unifying golden light spreads over the landscape and the figures, making them cohere into a legible whole.

Anarchist in Subject and Form

It was not simply in terms of their subject matter that the Neo-Impressionist anarchists sought to contribute to the cause of socio-economic renewal. As we have noted, the strand of anarchist philosophy to which the Neo-Impressionists were most attracted, the anarcho-communism of Kropotkin and Reclus, held that individual autonomy was the basis for collective harmony. The building block of their society was the individual liberated from all coercive mechanisms. Overall harmony was the product of harmonious relations between free individuals: 'Social interest and individual interest can never be antagonistic in a well-equilibrated society,' as Jean Grave put it in his journal *Le Révolté*. This view of harmony as a function of autonomy finds its direct parallel in the form and technique of Neo-Impressionism. Take Signac's 1890 *Opus 217. Against the Enamel of a Background Rhythmic with Beats and Angles, Tones, and Tints, Portrait of M. Félix Fénéon in 1890* (*see* page 100), a portrait of a key advocate of anarchism

and Neo-Impressionism against an abstract, kaleidoscopic swirl of colours and patterns. Fénéon, holding a flower in one hand, a top hat and walking stick in the other, is shown in profile sporting his characteristic goatee. The background reveals Signac's interest in the science of colour theory, specifically the writing of Charles Henry (1859–1926), whose colour wheel Signac here adapts.

Across the flat, decorative surface are tiny dots of approximately equal size, applied in a uniform, egalitarian manner. Without losing their specific integrity, they nevertheless interact with their neighbours and, at the appropriate viewing distance, come together to form a unified whole. Moreover, harmonious and equilibrious relations are assured through the application of Chevreul's theory of simultaneous contrast: 'For a colour to be beautiful,' as Signac paraphrased it, 'it should influence its neighbour by harmonizing with it and subduing it, for their common benefit. From this charming duo is born perfect harmony.' In the language of Neo-Impressionism, it is thus colours and dots that take the place of individuals in anarchist writing, a confluence that Signac deliberately encouraged: 'Justice in sociology, harmony in art; the same thing.' The Neo-Impressionist surface was thus the metaphorical re-enactment of the social configuration conceived by anarchist thinkers.

Seurat's Social Critique

Although not as fervently anarchist as Signac, Luce or Fénéon, Seurat nevertheless shared their interest in tackling the social issues of French

Detail above : *Apple Picking*, 1886, Camille Pissarro (1830–1903), see page 40

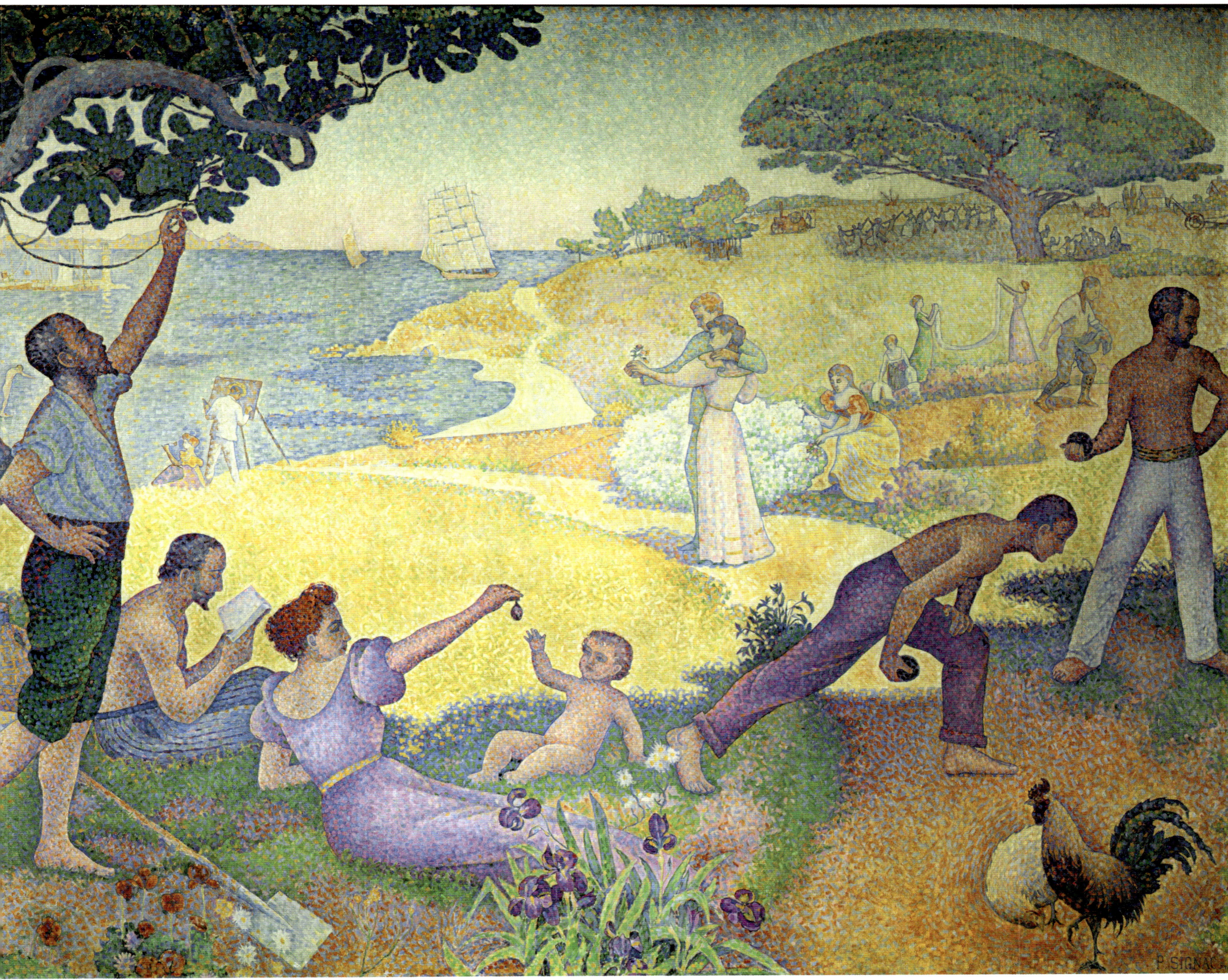

Above : *In the Time of Harmony. The Golden Age is not in the Past, it is in the Future, 1892–95, Paul Signac (1863–1935)*

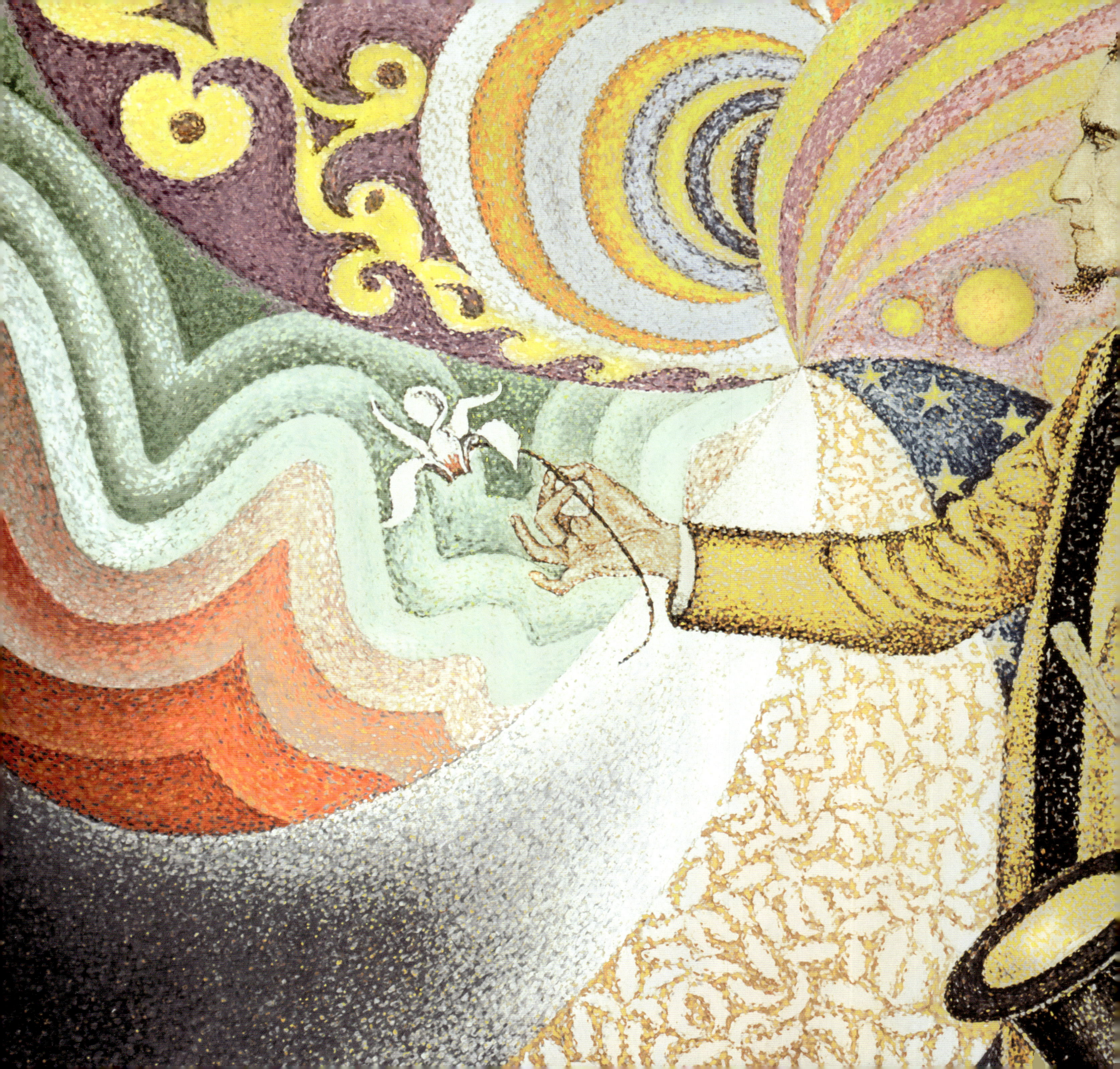

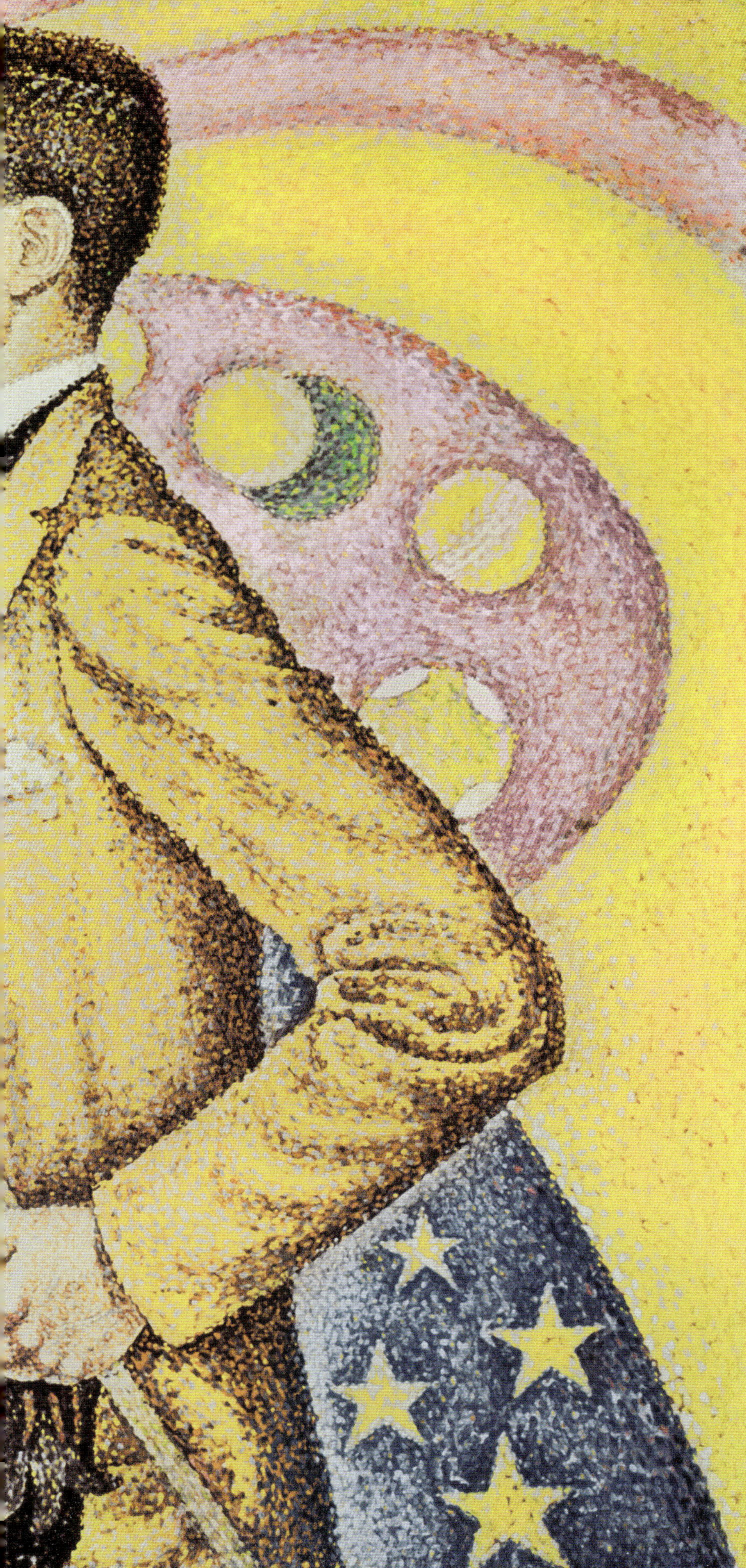

society in the late nineteenth century. Indeed, his *Grande Jatte* and *Bathers* represent two poles of France's increasingly bifurcated class structure: the working class in Asnières (the porous and contaminated margin between city and suburb) separated from the bourgeoisie on the Grande Jatte. The two canvases should be considered as forming a pendant: not only did Seurat commence the *Grande Jatte* very shortly after completing the *Bathers*, the two scenes mirror each other across the same stretch of water. The stretch of earth and trees on the upper right of *Bathers* is actually the island of the *Grande Jatte*; the boy who cups his hands to his mouth is shouting across the river to the crowd we see assembled in the later painting. Given their pairing, how can we explain the obvious formal discrepancies? How can we square the flatness of *Grande Jatte* – whose curiously static cast of characters are captured without the modelling of light and shade that would render them legible as three-dimensional objects in space – with the more statuesque (even monumental) *Bathers*? How do we explain the shift in palette from the soothing blues of Asnières to the astringent green of the Grande Jatte? Seurat even modified his brushwork between the two, adopting a strict Pointillist method in the later work, where before he had opted for traditional blending of brushstrokes (overlain with patches of Pointillist detailing, added later).

Vitruvian Harmony

The stiff and upright posture of the bourgeois pleasure-seekers, captured flat against the canvas surface, are spread horizontally as if in an ancient frieze. Their bodily proportions are determined by a strict adherence to the same Classical formula studied by Leonardo in his *Vitruvian Man* (c. 1490). For Seurat's contemporaries, these devices would have recalled the Arcadian murals of Pierre Puvis de Chavannes (1824–98), perhaps the pre-eminent artist of his day, acclaimed by critics and painters of every aesthetic and political affiliation. In works such as *Inter artes et naturam (Between Art and Nature)* (*see pages 102–103*) of 1888–90, Puvis offers a soothing vision of a timeless and placeless utopia (the

Left : *Opus 217. Against the Enamel of a Background Rhythmic with Beats and Angles, Tones, and Tints, Portrait of M. Félix Fénéon in 1890*, 1890, Paul Signac (1863–1935)

landscape, whilst ostensibly of Rouen, is heavily idealized). Figure-groups are carefully arranged across a flattened, frieze-like space; in varying states of dress (some are classically attired, some half-nude, and some in more modern garb) but always graceful, the figures engage in allegorical gestures denoting the study of nature and architecture. It was precisely the tradition of Puvis's murals from which Signac was drawing in *In the Time of Harmony*. Yet where Puvis located the golden age in a vague (temporal and geographical) past, Signac, in the very title of the work, struck the political claim that The Golden Age is not in the Past, it is in the Future.

'Puvis de Chavannes gone modern'

While referencing a Classical tradition (Seurat himself compared *Grande Jatte* to the Parthenon frieze in Athens) whose most prominent contemporaneous manifestation was Puvis's Arcadianism, Seurat nevertheless modified and disturbed it, not least by bringing it into the modern age. Unlike the multiple interacting figure-groups that populate the garden of Puvis's *Inter artes et naturam*, none of the characters in Seurat's work communicate with one another. Their stiffness contrasts sharply with the graceful and dynamic elegance of Puvis's figures. The order and timelessness that infuses Puvis's mural, in being updated to represent modern forms, in being made to coexist with the ostensibly modern science of colour relations, collapses in on itself. Harmony degenerates into stasis. The *Bathers* would thus seem closer to this Classical ideal: more 'fleshed out', dynamic and soothing. Seen in this way, the two canvases thus represent two very different modernizations of Puvis's utopia, one positive, one negative. Indeed, Fénéon himself saw in the *Grande Jatte* 'a Puvis de Chavannes gone modern'.

For the critic and writer Joris-Karl Huysmans (1848–1907), the stiffness of the *Grande Jatte* was a significant defect: 'I am decidedly afraid that there is … not enough of the flame that ignites, not enough life!' He noted:

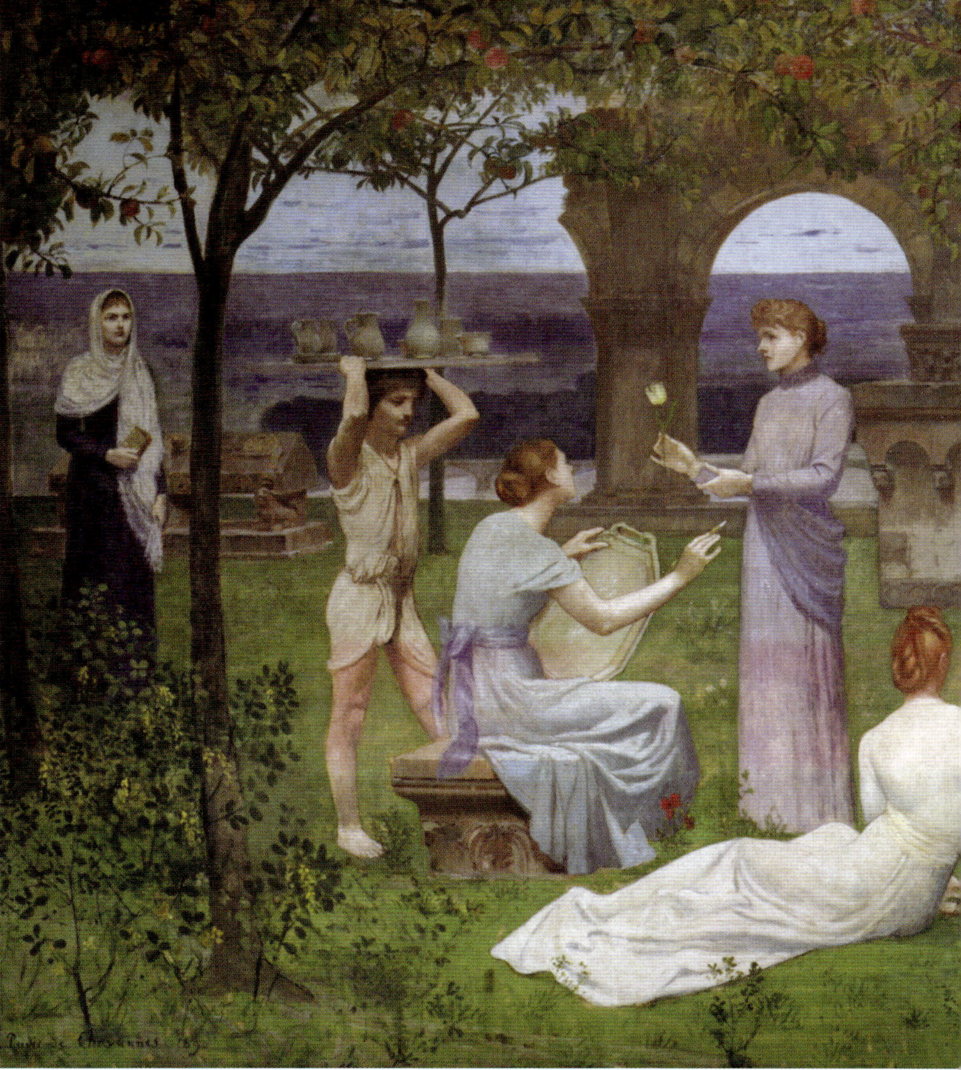

Strip his figures of the coloured fleas with which they are covered, and underneath there is nothing, no soul, no thought, nothing. Nothingness in a body of which only the contour exists. Thus in his pictures of the Grande Jatte the human armature becomes rigid and hard; everything is immobilized and congealed.

However, for the anarchist critic Paul Adam (1862–1920), this was precisely the point: 'Even the stiffness of the people, the ready-made forms, help give the sound of modernity, the recall of our tight clothing, glued to the body, the reserved gestures, the British manner everywhere imitated.' Seurat's subject, for

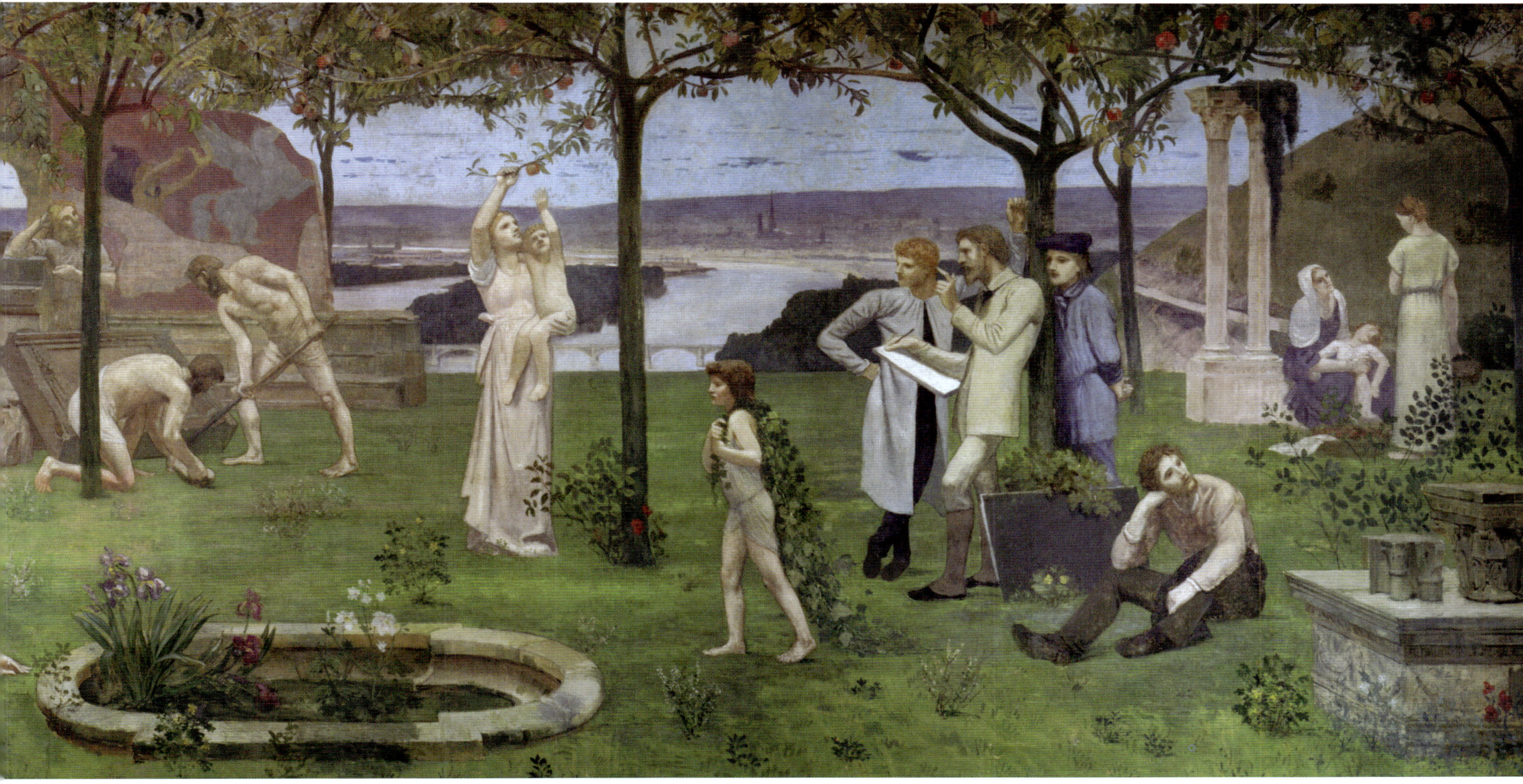

Henry Fèvre, was 'the rigidity of Parisian leisure, tired and stiff, where even recreation is a matter of striking poses'. We might be more precise and say bourgeois leisure – the workers on the opposite bank are nowhere near as stilted or affected.

Justice in Sociology, Harmony in Art

The absurd formality of the figures in the *Grande Jatte* is thus one of superficial appearances, of social expectations, of the 'British manner'. The formal flatness of the figures is an allegory for their flatness as people; even in their leisure time, their class-bound reserve prevents them from fully enjoying themselves. For the anarchists of Seurat's circle, life in modern Paris, under the rule of the bourgeois Republican government committed to liberal (free market) capitalism, was not only intolerably unjust but also profoundly alienating. If anarchists offered political renewal hand-in-hand with Neo-Impressionism's provision of aesthetic harmony ('Justice in sociology, harmony in art; the same thing'), then Seurat seems to have been pinning his hopes squarely on the denizens of Asnières, whose clarion call, like Signac's rising sun, is both a provocation and a celebration.

Above : *Inter artes et naturam (Between Art and Nature)*, 1888–90, Pierre Puvis de Chavannes (1824–98)

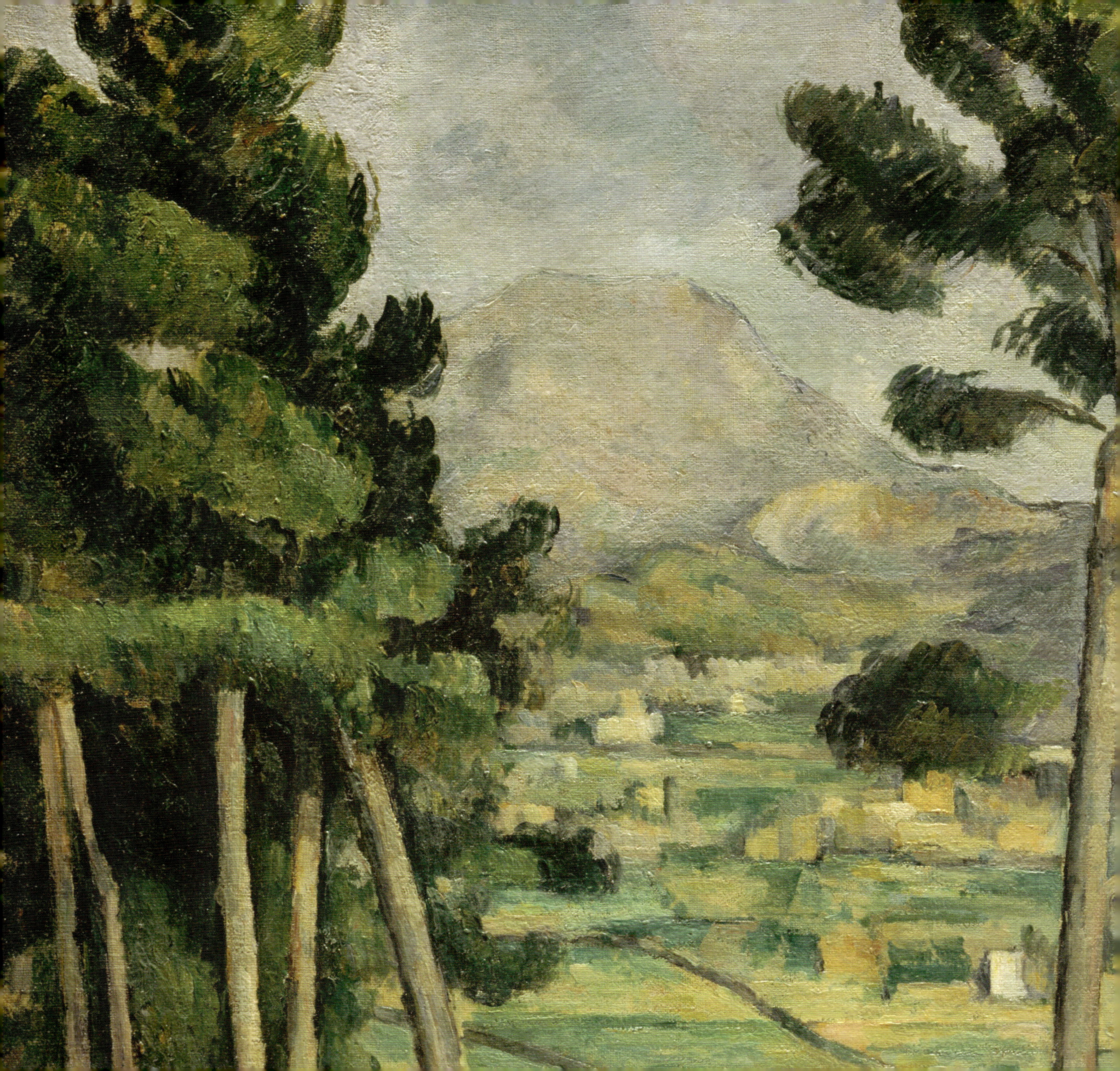

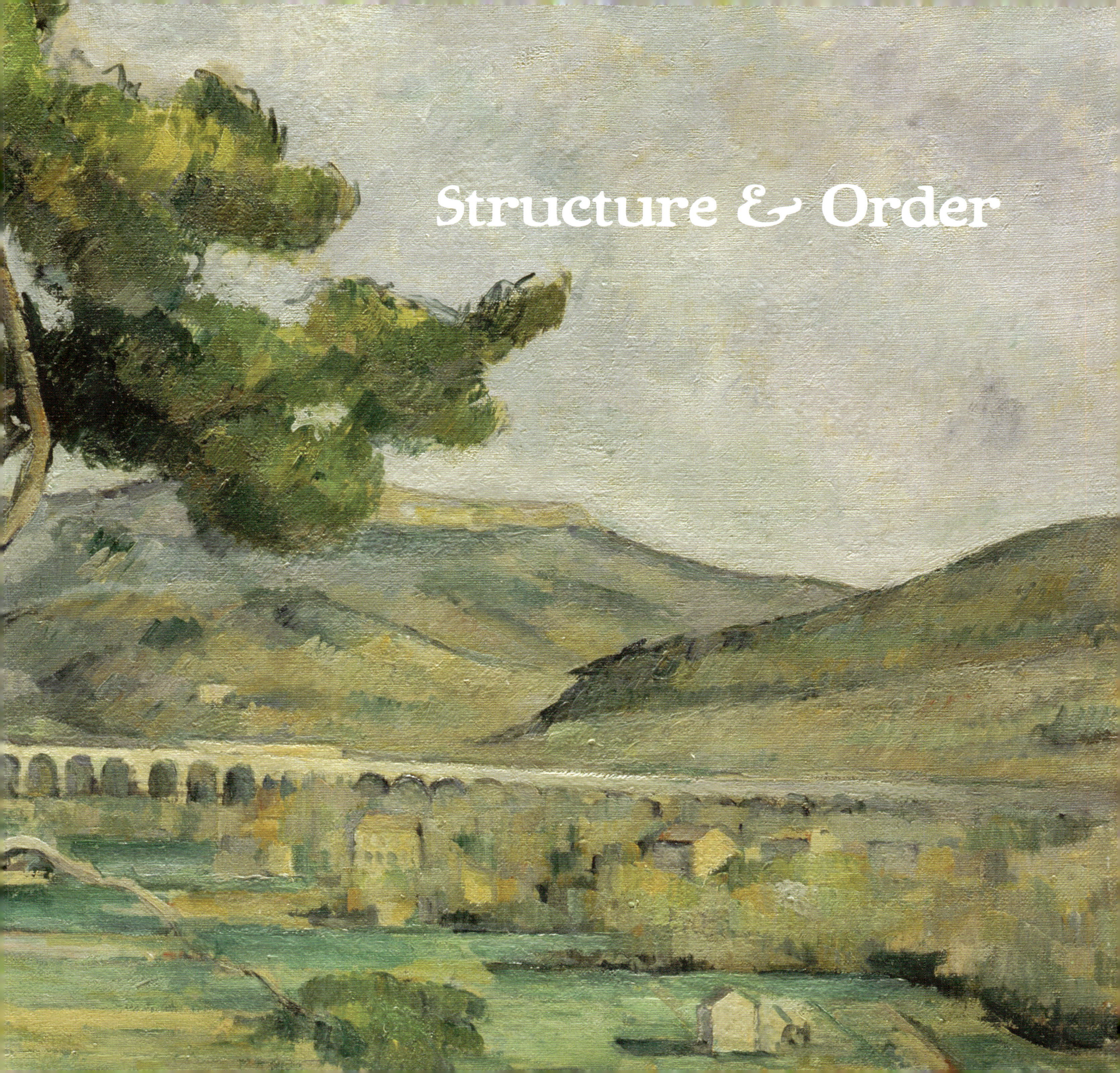
Structure & Order

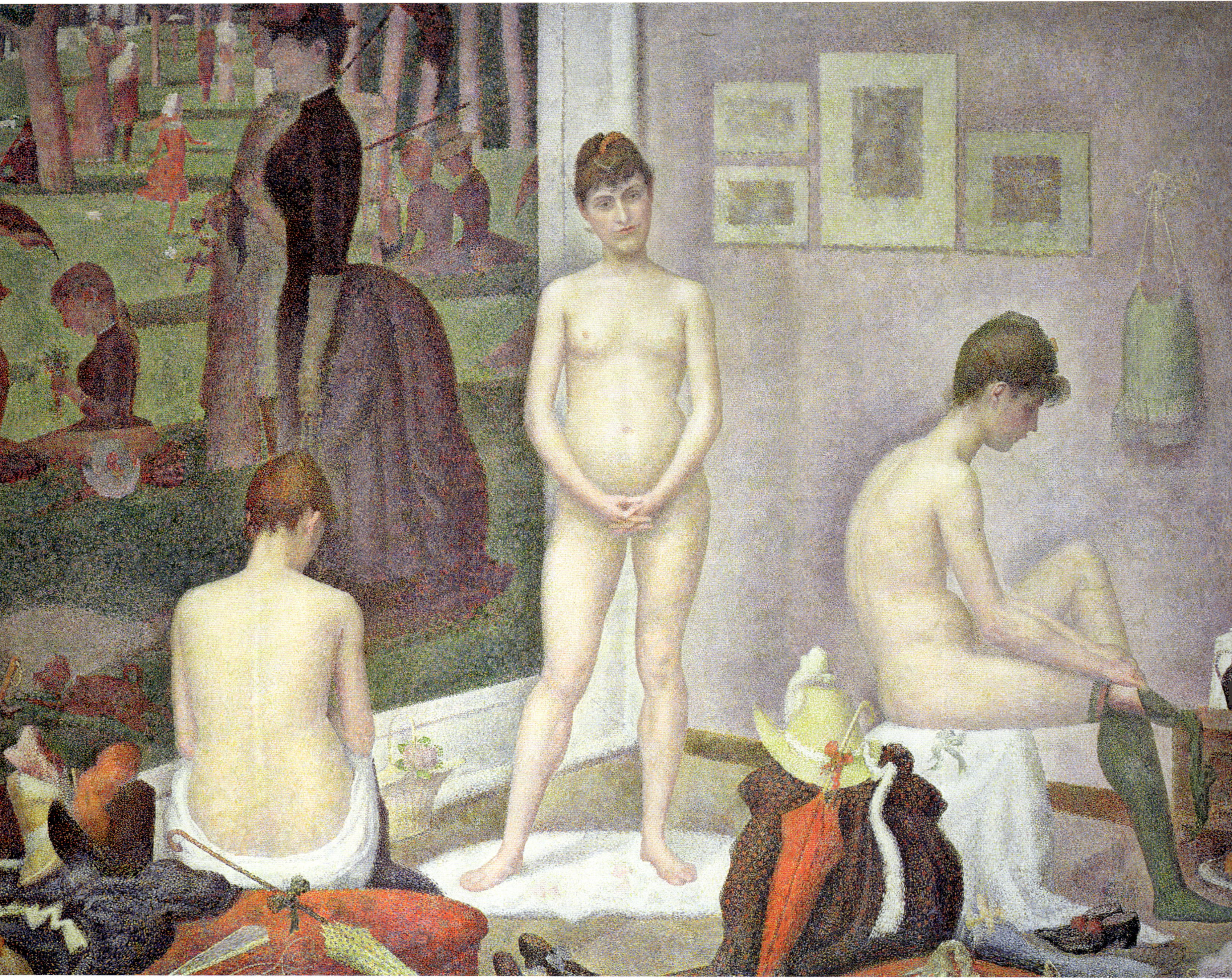

Above : *The Models*, 1888, Georges Seurat (1859–91)

Interrelation of Forms

FOR SEURAT AND CÉZANNE, the canvas surface was a space in which the artist imposed order; however, each developed a very different method for doing so.

The Models

Seurat was deeply wounded by accusations that his *Grande Jatte* was evidence of his inability to paint the human form, and so resolved to prove them wrong. In 1888, he unveiled *The Models* (1888, *see* left), an enormous canvas (207.6 x 308 cm/81¾ x 121¼ inches) at the Salon des Indépendants. Three nude figures, posing in various states (back to us, facing us and in profile), present themselves to the viewer. We are situated in an interior, specifically in Seurat's studio: along the back left wall we see his *Grande Jatte*, and scattered across the floor are the clothes and accoutrements (or props) of the models, organized as if representing shades from a colour wheel.

The critic Arsène Alexandre (1859–1937) recorded how he met Seurat 'working away with unbelievable

concentration, cloistered in a little studio on the boulevard de Clichy, denying himself everything, spending all his slender means on expensive work. This time he meant to prove that his theory, so well suited to *plein-air* subjects, was applicable to large-scale figures and interiors, and he did his canvas *Poseuses*.' To stage a work in one's own studio, featuring one's own paintings was, like the female nude, something of a traditional subject. Similarly, scholars have identified numerous sources for the poses and composition of Seurat's three nudes, from antiquity (Seurat studied the Louvre's second-century B.C. Roman copy after the Greek *Three Graces* as a student), Raphael's *Three Graces* (1504–05) and Perugino's *Apollo and Marsyas* (1495, although in 1888 it was attributed to Raphael), to more contemporary examples in Manet, Puvis, Cézanne and Renoir.

The original French title for the work – *Poseuses* – is curious. While *poser* meant 'to pose' ('to assume an attitude for the purpose of being drawn or painted'), the subject doing the posing would be referred to as *modèle* – model. *Poseur*

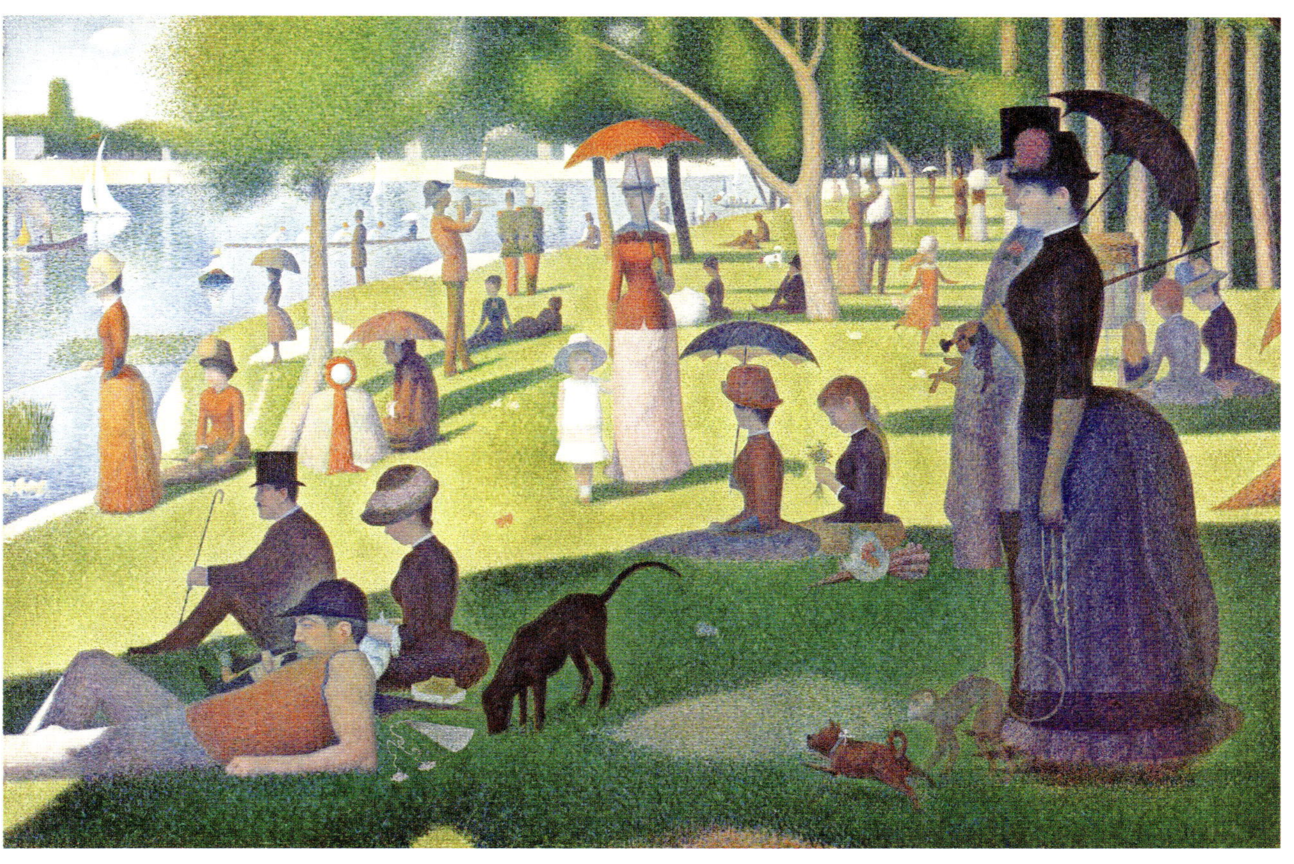

Above : *A Sunday Afternoon on the Island of the Grande Jatte*, 1884–86, Georges Seurat (1859–91)

referred instead to either, firstly, the kind of working man who installs parquet flooring, hardware or tracks or, secondly, 'one whose attitudes, gestures, looks are studied for effect' or 'one who, out of vanity, seeks to attract notice by an artificial or affected manner'. Consequently, following this second definition, the title of the painting could just as easily be referring to the female figures in the *Grande Jatte* on the back wall as to the models in Seurat's studio. This collapsing of the identity of his models on to the well-heeled and fashionably attired bourgeois women he had captured in 1886 was a witty, subtle and subversive statement, and one that unlocks the deeper political meaning of the work.

In the *Grande Jatte*, Seurat had critiqued the alienated superficiality of the bourgeoisie who hide their shallowness behind appearances; while the stripped-off *Bathers* offered an altogether more genuine counterpoint. However, the smartly dressed female in the foreground of *Grande Jatte*, and singled out in *The Models*, hides more than her superficiality: at her feet plays a monkey, or *singesse* in French, a word which, in addition to denoting the animal, was also a slang term for a prostitute. Hanging on the arm of her client, made up to play the part of his wife, at this site of polite bourgeois sociability, then, is a prostitute. Covertly, in the presence of respectable women and children, bodies are being sold; the bourgeois pretence to their moral superiority is thus exposed to be only skin (or, more accurately, dress) deep.

What Seurat had left implicit in 1886 he now made explicit in 1888: the clothes that the models have shed – hats, gloves, fans, parasols, shoes, garters and stockings – correlate directly with the kinds of clothes being worn in the painting within the painting. It is as if they have walked directly out of the *Grande Jatte* and disrobed before us. While also making a witty and humorous allusion to the artifice inherent in art, Seurat thus unmasks the more sordid truth behind bourgeois pretentions: prostitutes and models were, in nineteenth-century Paris, largely drawn from the same milieu. The bodies of the models, pliant yet poised, 'precociously pubescent' (in the

Right : *Circus Sideshow (Parade de cirque)*, 1887–88, Georges Seurat (1859–91)

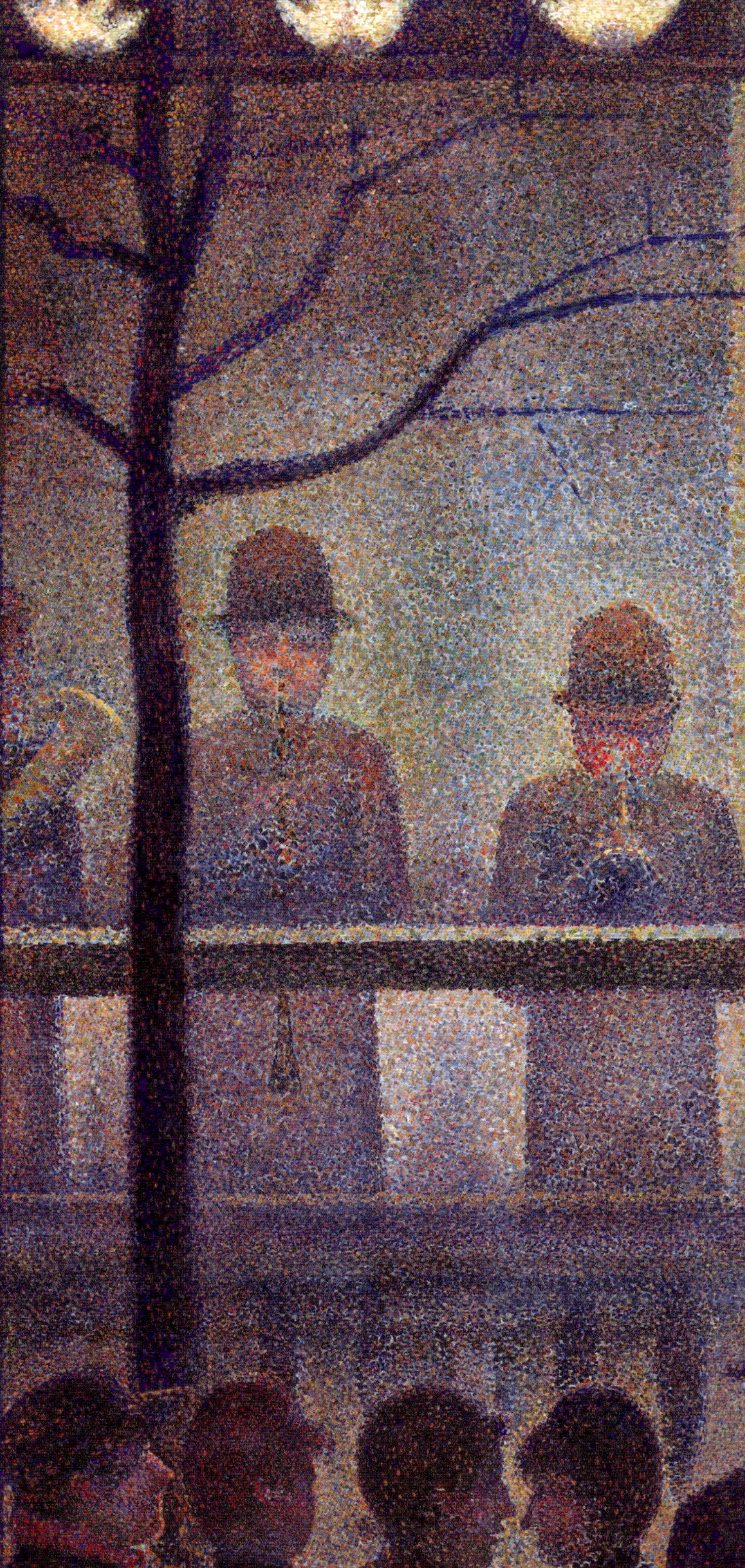

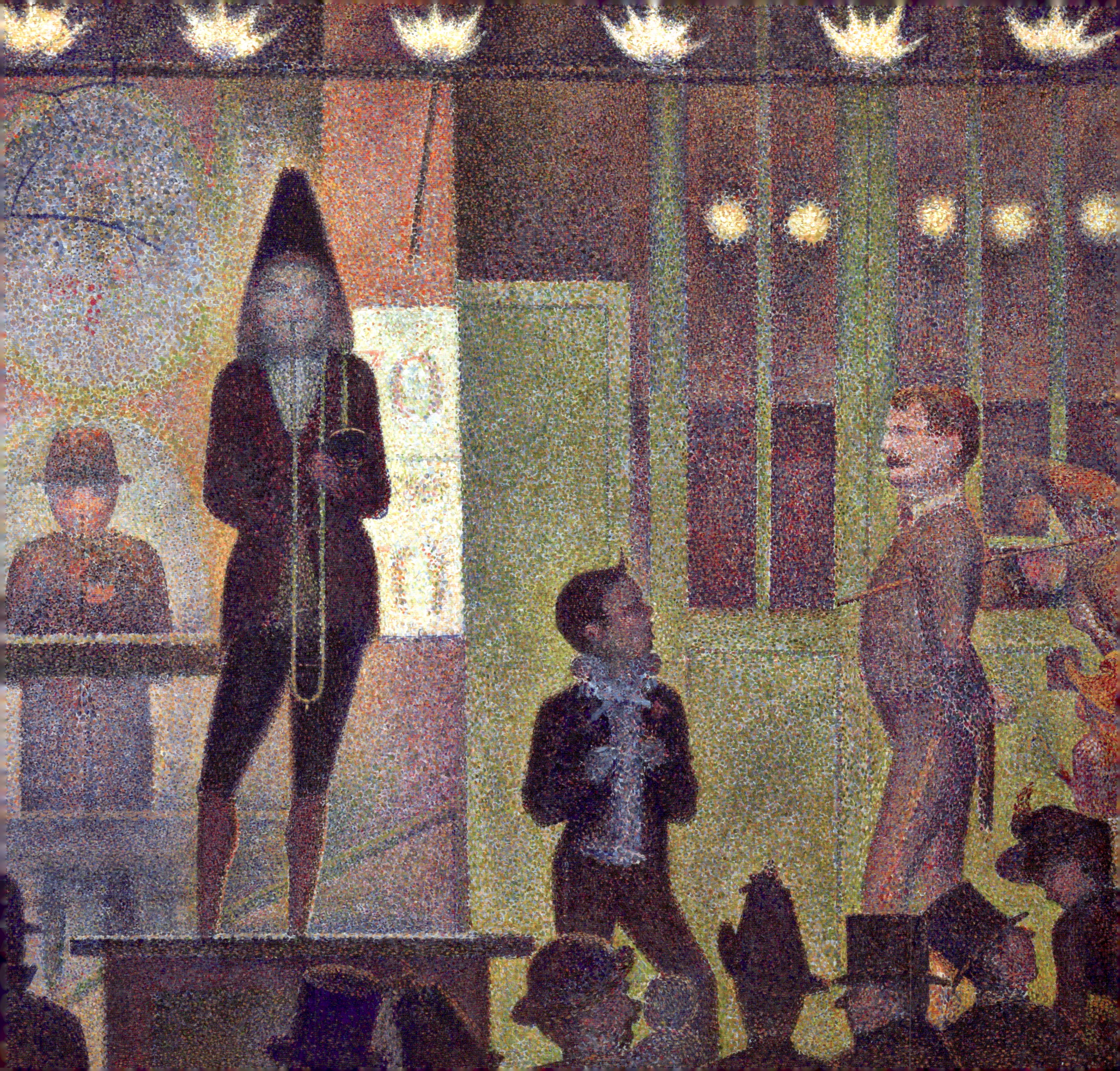

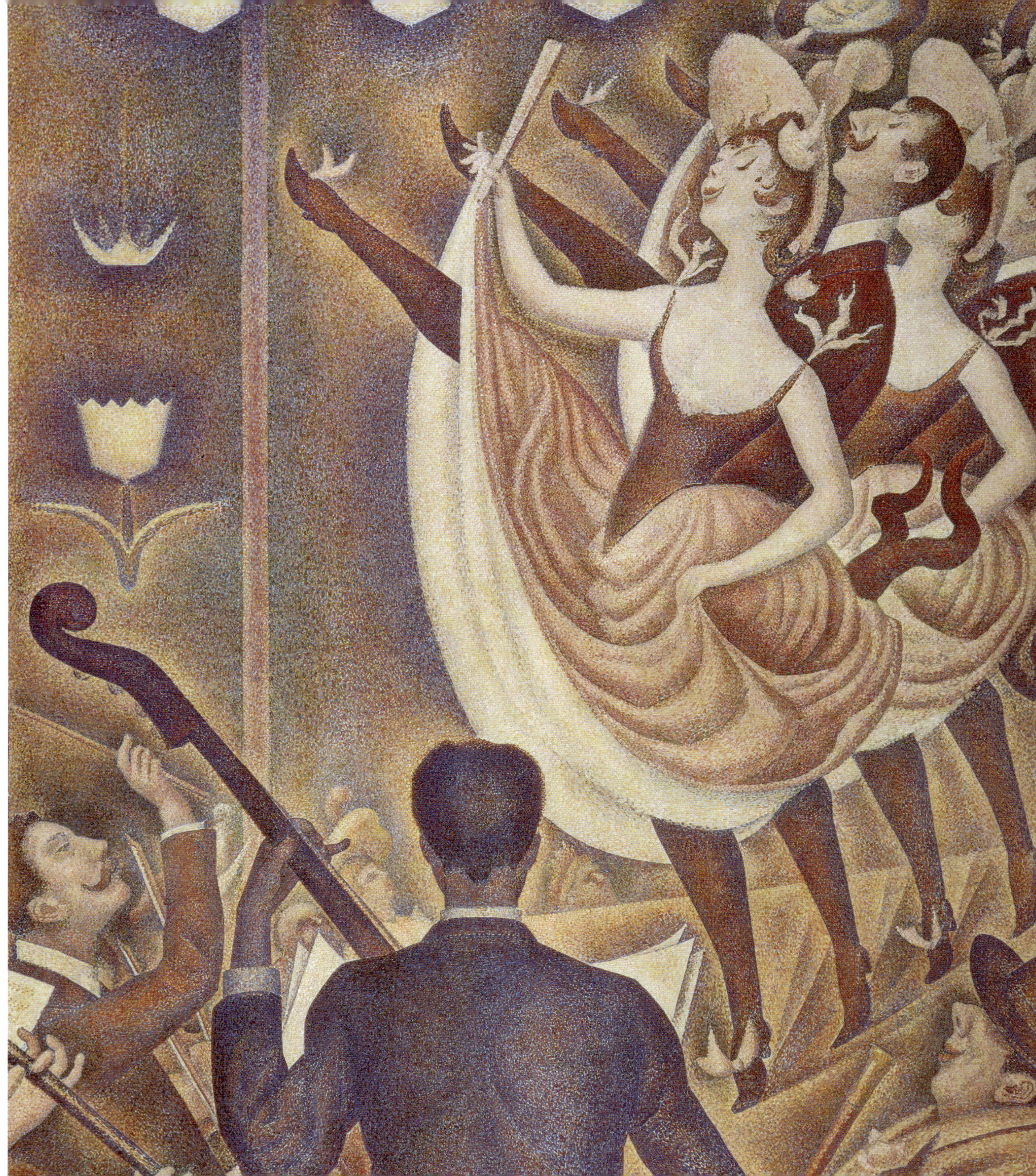

words of Gustave Geffroy, 1855–1926), straightforwardly posing, are thus a frank admission of the truth, an intervention into Western art history and a continuation of an ongoing social critique.

Mass Entertainment

Exhibited alongside *The Models*, and almost completely overshadowed by it in the press (not least because it was only half its size), was *Circus Sideshow (Parade de cirque)* (1887–88, *see* page 109). If *The Models* was, in part, an exercise in demonstrating the versatility of Neo-Impressionism (applying the technique in an indoor, naturally lit scene), then *Circus Sideshow*, a nocturnal scene under artificial lighting, offered yet another bravura display. The painting depicts the Circus Corvi at the annual Gingerbread Fair, held in a working-class area of eastern Paris, around the Place de la Nation. Sideshows such as this were staged for free, in order to entice passers-by to purchase tickets for the main event.

Such forms of spectacular mass entertainment were enjoying a peak of popularity in the late nineteenth century. As France's delayed industrial revolution was transforming patterns of labour, so too did leisure practices transform in concert. With employers now demanding set work hours and enforcing stricter discipline, the appetite of the labouring population to be entertained in their precious and delimited time off grew considerably.

Thus we see assembled in the foreground the potential patrons of the Circus Corvi, gathered to watch the performance of the band. To the right, a queue of people ascend the steps, waiting for their turn at the green-coloured box office. Under the gas lighting, the colours possess a dream-like ethereality. The space of the scene has been almost completely flattened; it is difficult to discern the planes of three-dimensional space and the relative positions of the figures within them. The highlights which illuminate the back of the trombone player's legs indicate him to be before the light source (relative to the viewer) and thus in front of the rest of the band, whose bright orange faces reveal them to be standing directly under the gas lights. The dim blue of the attendant crowd intimate that they are in the very foreground. This use of lighting and colour to signify spatial relations was a breakthrough innovation of Seurat's Neo-Impressionist technique; it offered a startling alternative paradigm for depicting space to the use of traditional perspective.

The calming effect of the palette is strengthened by the rhythmical and logical way in which the composition has been constructed, governed by basic mathematical ratios. Seurat may also have been inspired by the powerfully evocative poems of Arthur Rimbaud (1854–91) and Jules Laforgue (1860–87). In 'La parade', published in *La vogue* on 13 May 1886, Rimbaud described:

Sturdy enough jesters. Several have exploited your worlds. Devoid of need, in no hurry to make play of their brilliant faculties or their knowledge of your conscience. How ripe they are! Eyes dazed like the summer night, red and black, tricolours, steel pricked with golden stars; features deformed, leaden,

pallid, on fire; hoarse-throated frolickers!… They're sent out soliciting in city

streets, decked out in disgusting luxury….

In improvised costumes of nightmarish taste they play romances, tragedies

of bandits and demigods, spiritual as the tales and religions never

were…. Master jugglers, they transform people and

places and reveal magnetic stagecraft. Eyes

inflamed, blood sings, bones thicken, tears

and trickles of rouge stream down.

Their raillery and their terror lasts

a moment, or months entire.

I alone hold the key to this

savage parade.

Around 1880, Laforgue wrote in
'Soir de carnaval':

Paris kicks up his heels in the gaslight.
The clock like a knell sounds one A.M.
Sing! dance! Life is short, all is in vain. […]
Oh, life is too sad, incurably sad. At festivals here and
there I have always sobbed: 'Vanity, vanity, all is only vanity!' –Then
I think: where are the ashes of the psalmist?

For both Laforgue and Rimbaud, the banal and gaudy tricks of the circus
sideshow prompt melancholy reflection on the pointlessness of life and the
inevitable demise of all civilization. Seurat was almost certainly familiar with
both these poems; indeed, part of the ambiguity in his own work rests in his
paradoxical combination of ordered structure and evocative contents, of
pleasurable entertainment and disquieting temptation.

Structured Order

Seurat's final two masterpieces, *The Can-Can* (1889–90, *see* page 110) and
The Circus (1890–91, *see* right), were similarly on the theme of cheap,
modern mass entertainment. However, where the structure of *Circus
Sideshow* was only approximately mathematical, these later two
works were much more ambitiously rigorous. We have
encountered Charles Henry as a source for
the abstract kaleidoscope against which
Signac positioned Félix Fénéon in his
1890 portrait *Opus 217. Against the
Enamel of a Background Rhythmic
with Beats and Angles, Tones,
and Tints, Portrait of M. Félix
Fénéon in 1890.* However,
Henry's influence on the
Neo-Impressionists was much
more profound than merely this
provision of a motif. A friend of
Fénéon's, Henry was a mathematician,
aesthetician and librarian at the Sorbonne;
he was especially interested in finding a way
to mathematically and scientifically quantify the
relationship between aesthetic forms, physiological sensations and
psychological phenomena.

Charles Henry

Henry followed the nineteenth-century scientific mainstream in understanding
emotion to be caused by physiological activity (nerves and muscles) prompted
by outside stimulus. When hearing good news, one leaps upwards and

Detail above : *The Can-Can, 1889–90, Georges Seurat (1859–91), see page 110*

Right : *The Circus, 1890–91, Georges Seurat (1859–91)*

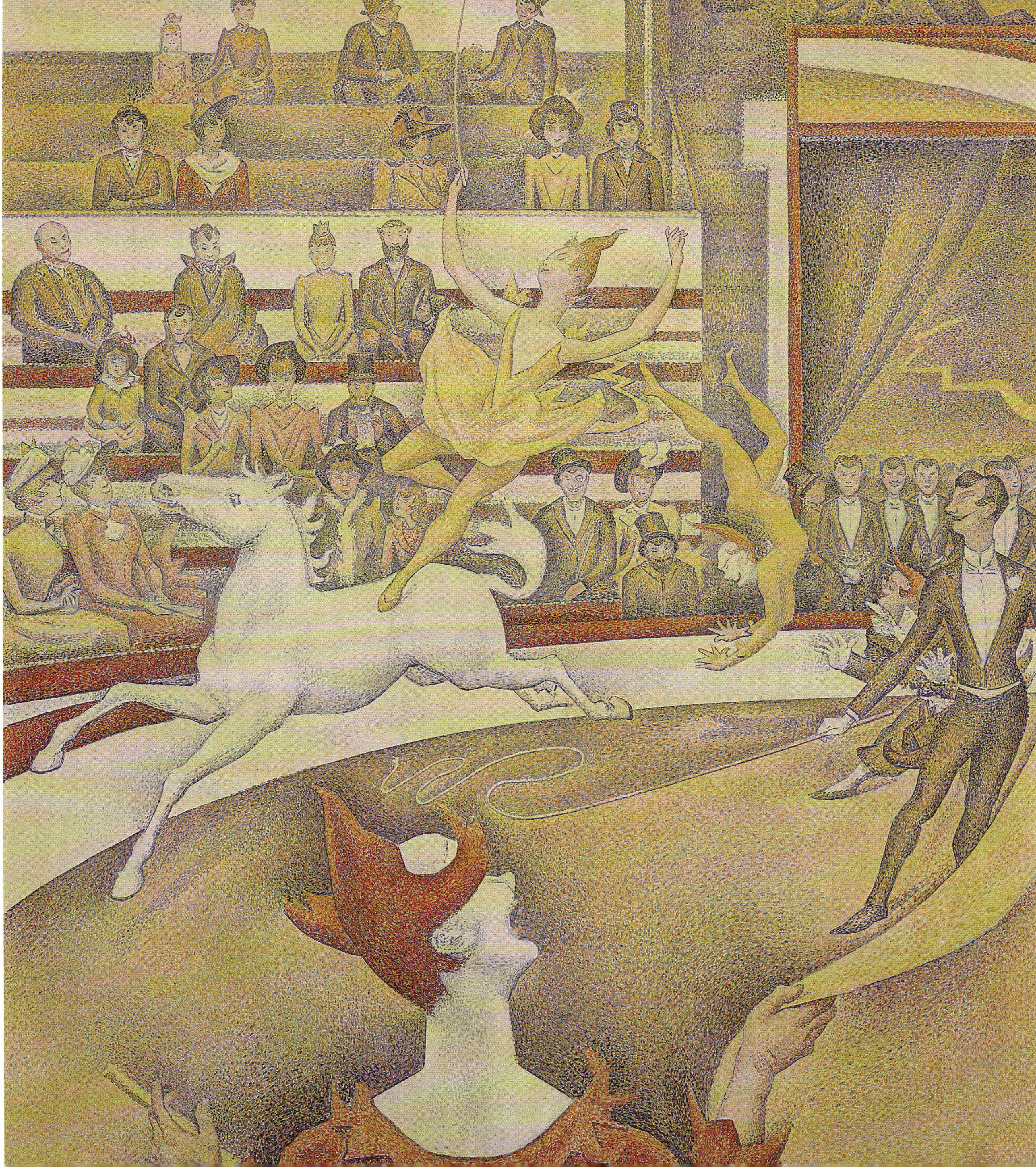

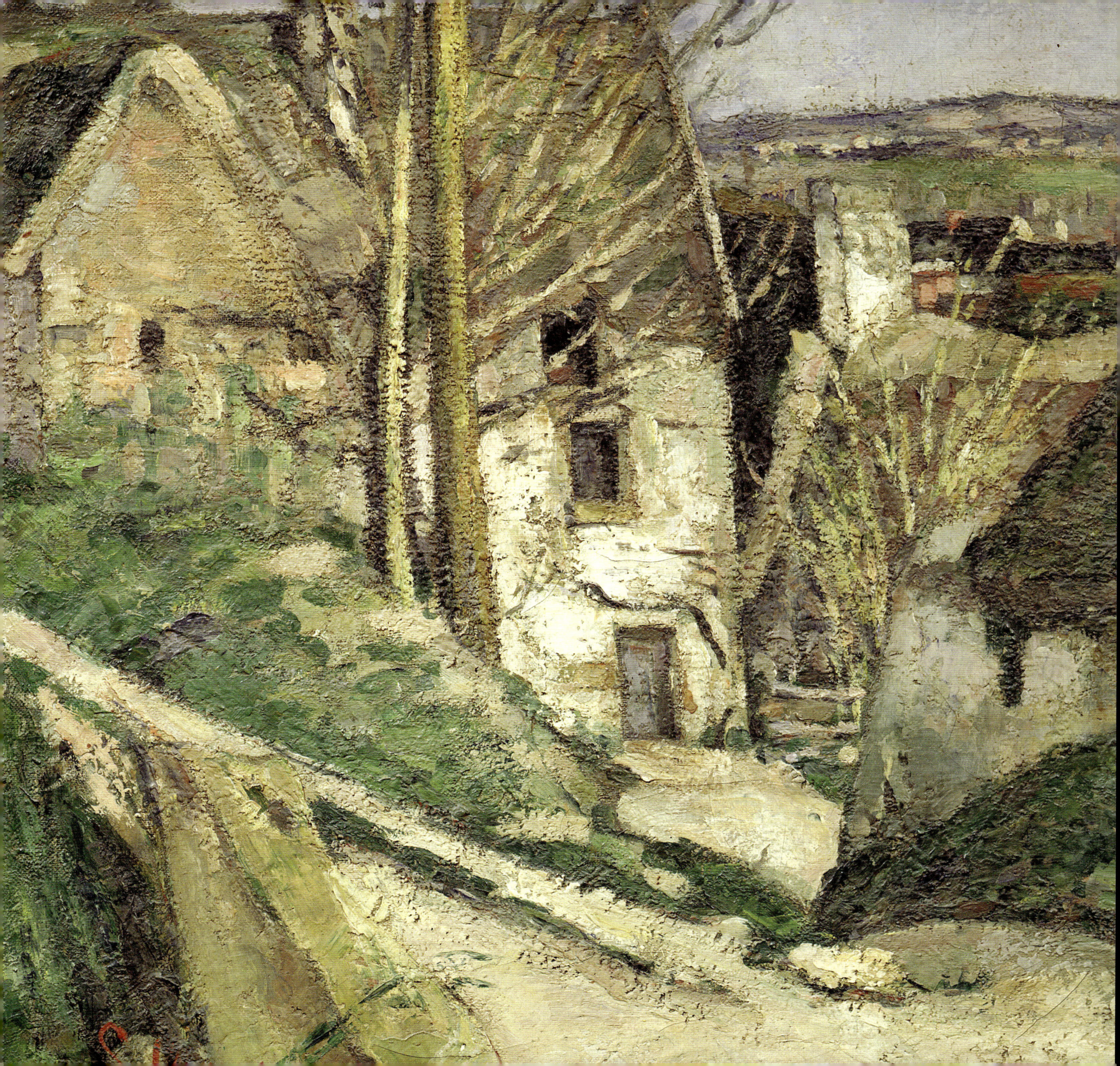

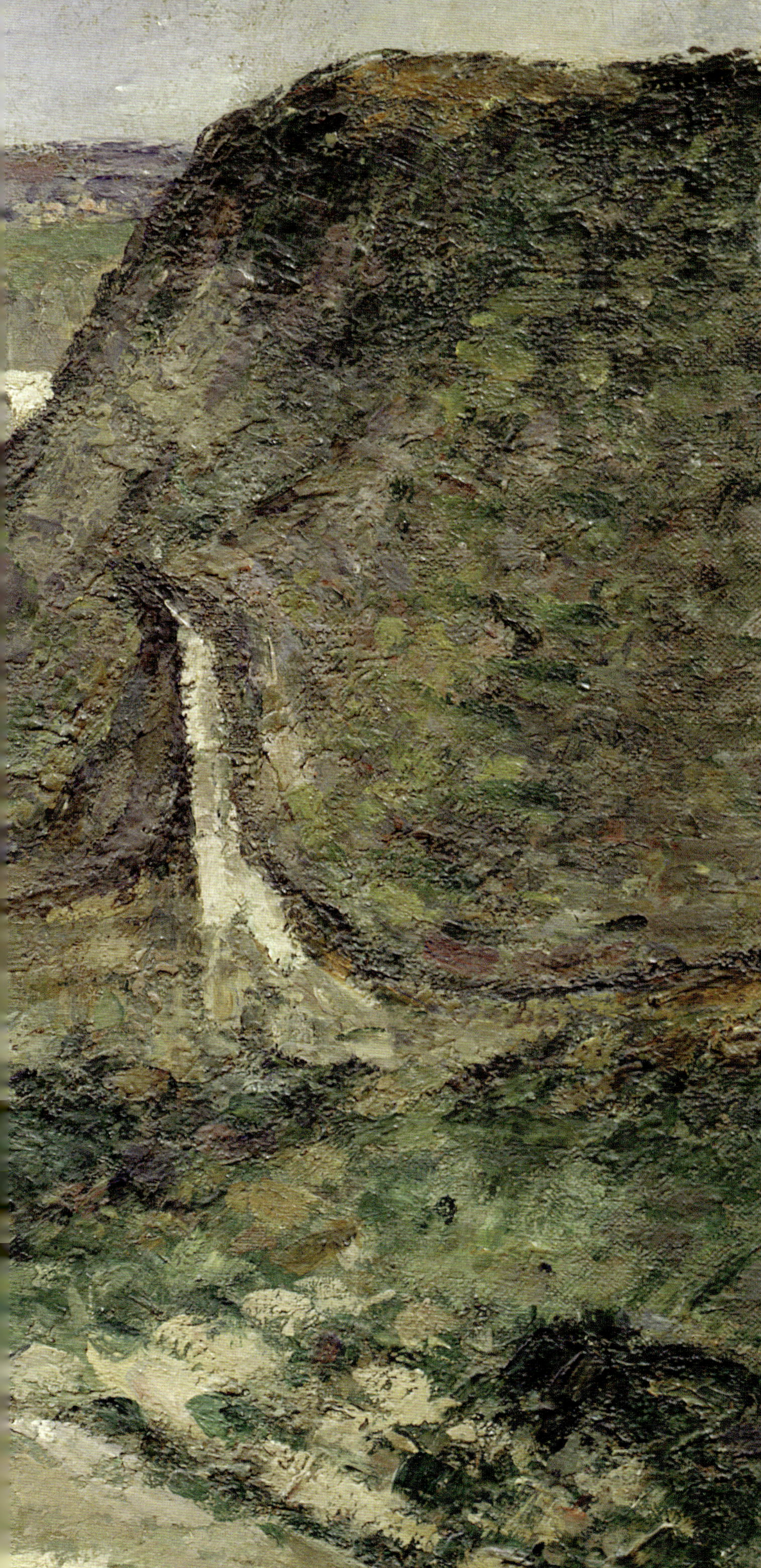

experiences joy; when witnessing some tragic scene, one slumps downwards and experiences sorrow. Turning a crank in the usual clockwise direction is pleasurable (Henry theorized), anticlockwise unpleasurable. When art constituted this stimulus, Henry proposed that line and colour possess both an abstract persistence and a psychic resonance: for example, a chevron (^) can be used by an artist to describe the top of a window or the roof of a house; whatever it describes, it nevertheless remains legible as a chevron, as an upward-oriented line, in the abstract sense.

When we perceive this abstract residue in viewing, say, the window in the picture, we instinctively associate it with the 'agreeable' emotional response connected to the line's upward gesture. Conversely, when we perceive a V shape, we unconsciously experience the sorrow associated with descending gestures. Colour, for Henry, was intimately tied to line in that each colour stimulated a specific physiological (and therefore emotional) reaction: red, orange and yellow were 'dynamogenic', allied to upward lines; blue, green and violet were 'inhibitory' and linked to downward lines. The composition, the arrangement of these abstract elements, could possess a rhythm that was either pleasing or not, depending on how it matched the biorhythms of human physiology.

Art is Harmony

The formal structure of the picture could thus be theoretically engineered to elicit a very specific emotional response on the part of the viewer. For Seurat, the painting's structure ought to be harmonious in the sense that it unified opposites in such a way as to stimulate an emotion. In response to the inquiry of a journalist, Maurice Beaubourg (1866–1943), in 1890 Seurat set out to quantify his theory of aesthetics, which he struggled over four separate drafts to achieve. In the end, he was able to summarize it thus:

Left : *The House of the Hanged Man, in Auvers-sur-Oise*, 1873, Paul Cézanne (1839–1906)

Art is Harmony.

Harmony is the analogy of opposites, the analogy of similarities of tone, of tint, of line taking account of a dominant and under the influence of the lighting, in combinations that are gay, calm or sad

Opposites are:

for tone, a more luminous/lighter one for a darker one.

for tint, the complementaries, that is, a certain red opposed to its complementary, etc.

> *Red—Green*
>
> *Orange—Blue*
>
> *Yellow—Violet*

for line, those making a right angle.

Gaiety of tone is the luminous dominant, of tint, the warm dominant, of line, lines above the horizontal.

Calmness of tone is the equality of dark and light; of tint, of warm and cool, and the horizontal for line.

Sadness of tone is the dark dominant; of tint, the cool dominant, and of line, downward directions.

We can observe how Seurat has put these principles into practice in *The Can-Can*. The painting depicts two men and two women on stage performing a vulgar dance known as the '*Chahut*' on a stage in a Montmartre dance hall (almost certainly the café-concert *Le Divan Japonaise*). We witness the dénouement of their performance, when the dancers salute the assembled audience with a series of high kicks. In the orchestra pit (and the extreme foreground of the picture), the bassist stands with his back to us; to his left, we see only the fingering hands of the flautist and two fiddlers' bows; the moustachioed conductor, gazing up at the performers (up the foreground performer's skirt?) is the only musician whose face we see. The audience, intermingled with the musicians, includes the 'pig-snouted' (in the words of critic Gustave Kahn, 1859–1936) gentleman on the right of the canvas, and the well-dressed group sporting flamboyant millinery in the background.

'The muffled harmony in M. Paul Gauguin's paintings flows from the close-set tones he uses'.

Felix Fénéon

The composition is dominated by the upward and linear thrust of the dancers' legs, poised improbably in the air. The bass, too, is tilted along that same upward axis, as is the flute and the fiddler's bows. Even the men's moustaches are curled upwards. The shadows of the performers, cast on the stage under the glare of the gaslights, are schematized into sharply pointed and highly dynamic chevrons. Such areas of gay linearity correspond to the areas in which warm tints dominate.

However, has the unification of 'agreeable' lines ('above the horizontal') in warm ('dynamogenic') tones – offset only slightly by the 'inhibitory' blue shadows that form a nimbus around the downward oriented light fixtures – produced, as the theory would suggest, an image of pure happiness? Critics at the time compared Seurat's painting to caricatures and posters, highlighting its decorative flatness, schematized forms, and repetitive and forceful rhythms. Seurat's portrayal of the *Circus Sideshow*, as we have seen, drew from poems that played on the contradictory nature of modern forms of mass entertainment: the promise of unadulterated pleasure on the one hand, and the crude and hollow reality of alienated degradation on the other. Here too, the rictus grin of the performers and the lustful sneer of the pig-snouted patron, combined with the stifling atmosphere 'under the influence of the lighting', seem to counteract the agreeable mood Seurat has ostensibly encoded into the painting's form. This tension between pleasure and alienation is not resolved, but rather permeates the canvas, which thus becomes a complex, multilayered satire on modern life and modern pleasure.

Right : *Woman in Front of a Still Life by Cézanne*, 1890, Paul Gauguin (1848–1903)

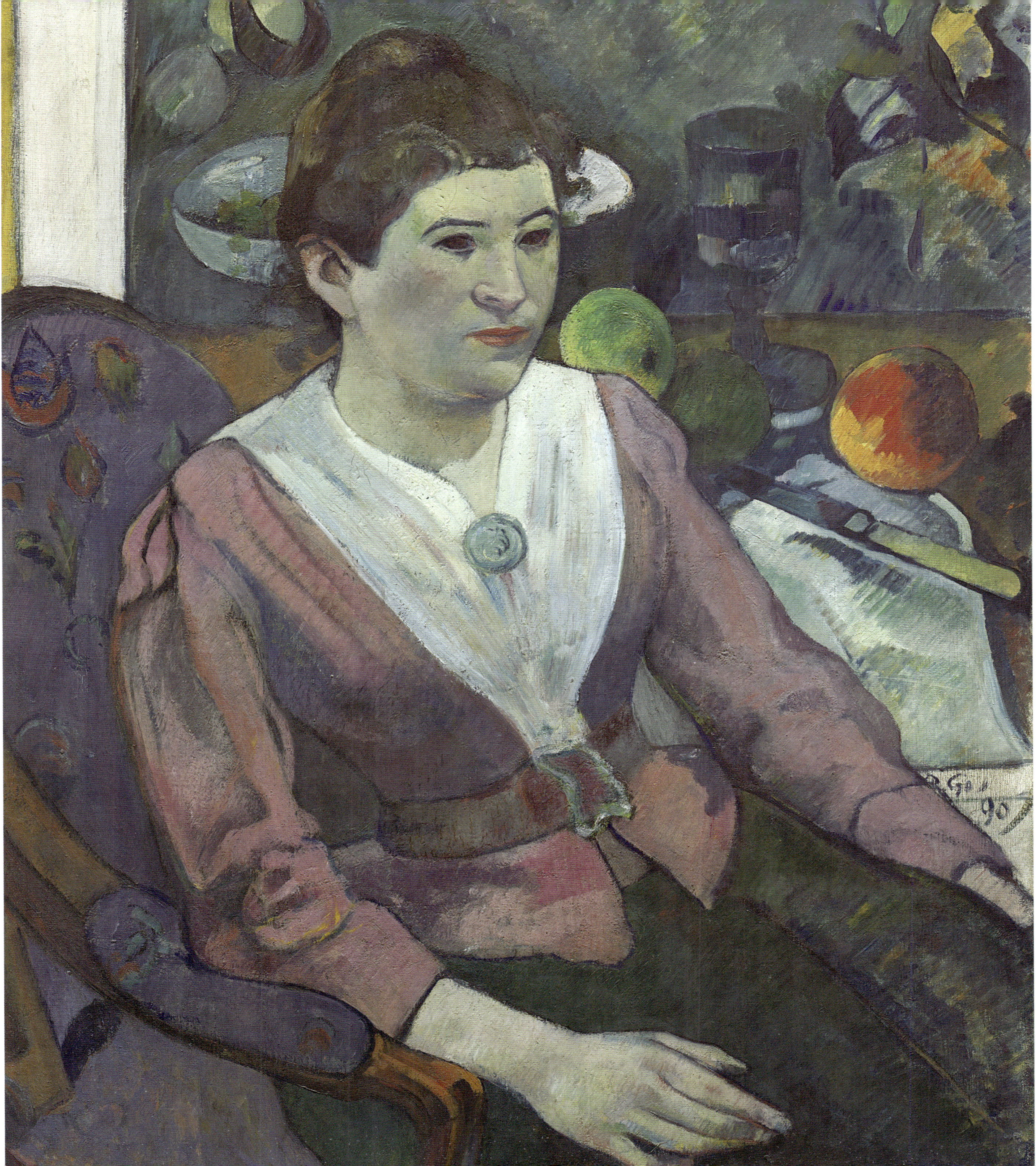

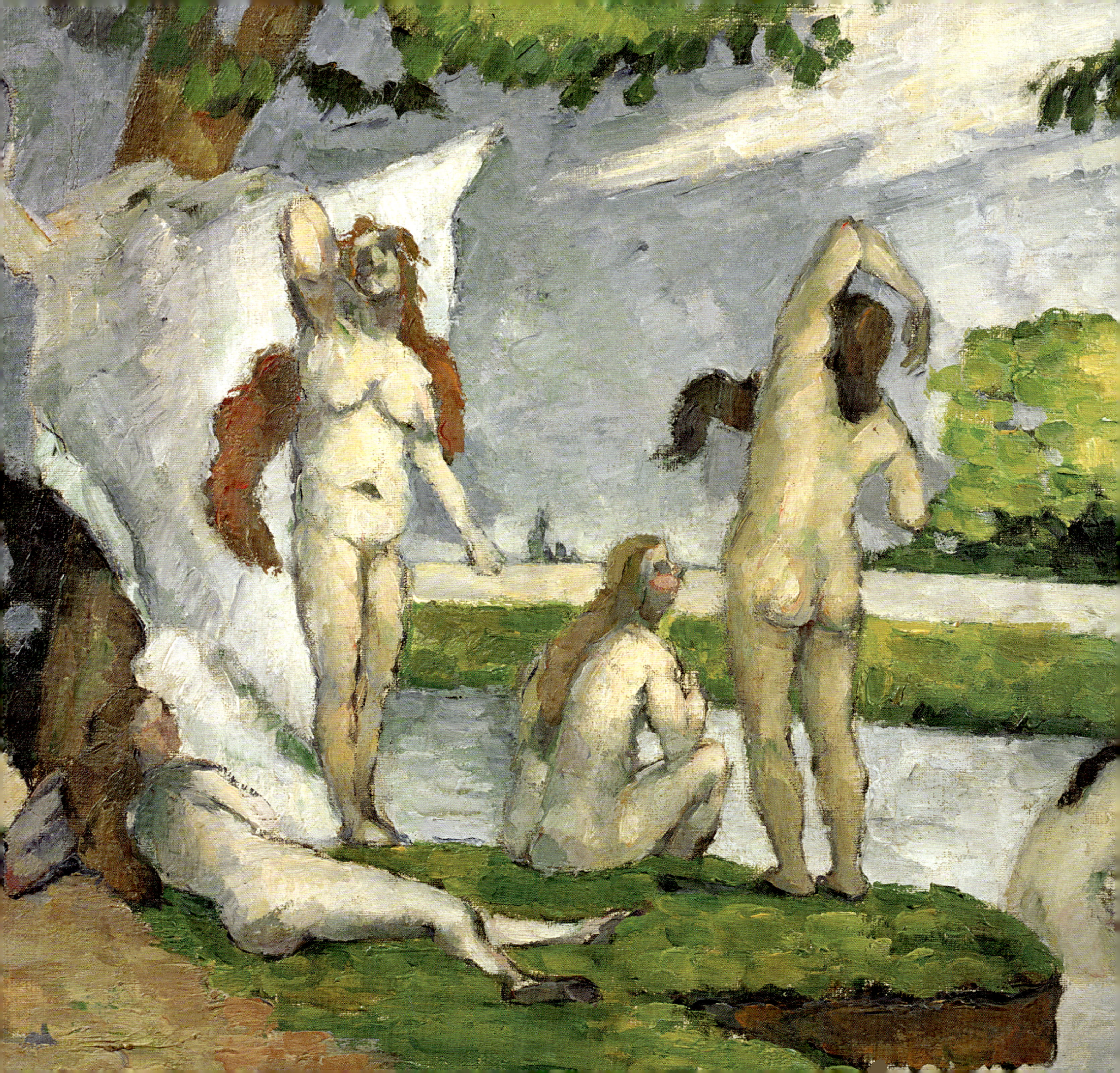

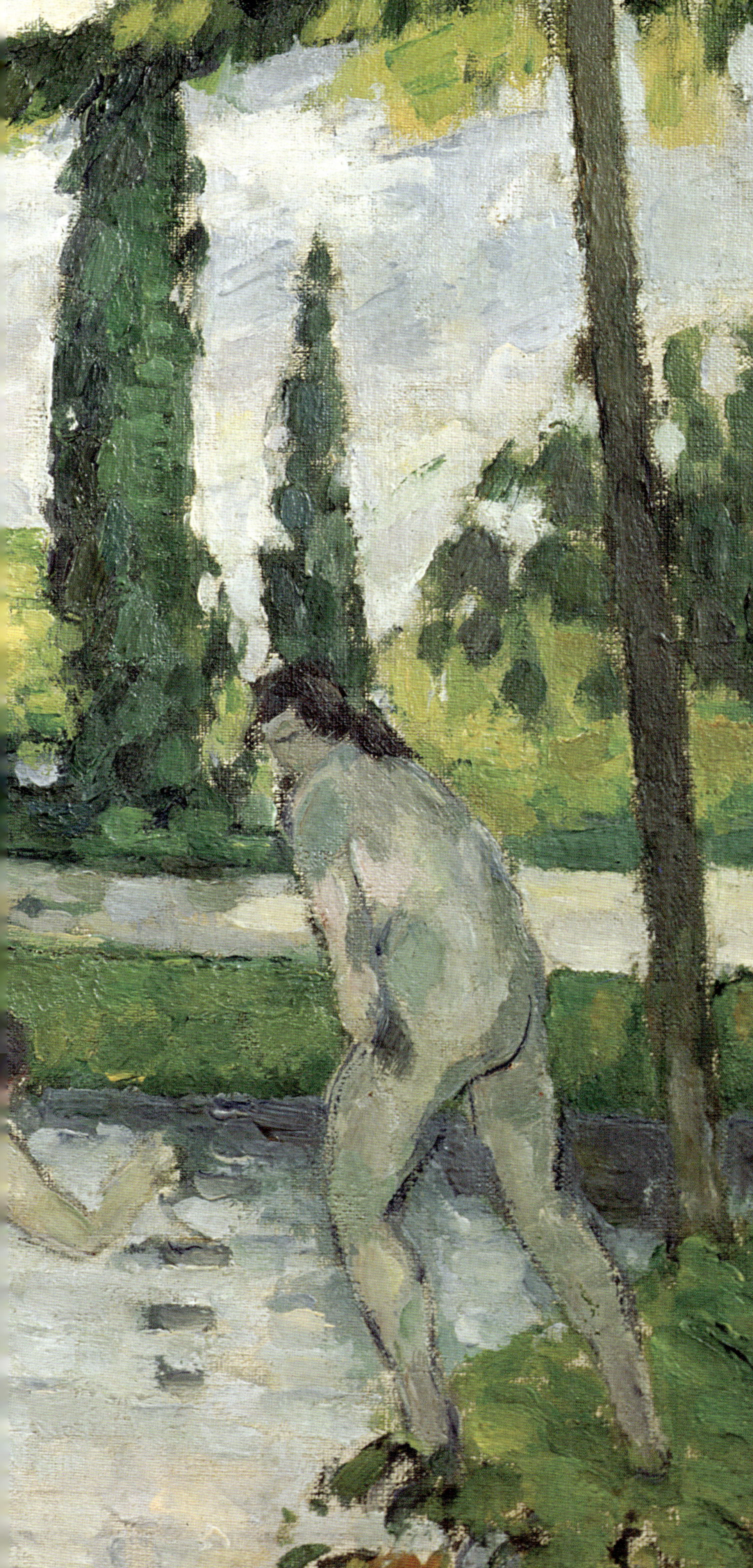

Like the sideshow and the café-concert, the circus was becoming increasingly popular in the last decades of the nineteenth century. As in his depiction of *Le Divan Japonaise*, in picturing the Circus Fernando, Seurat again focused on foregrounding expressive vertical gestures and creating a linear and chromatic compositional rhythm. The clockwise motion of the horse, the ascending gesture of the rider, the dynamic tension of the clown caught mid-flip and the fluttering of the foreground clown's ribbon draw the eye up and around in theoretically pleasing ways.

However, some critics saw in the composition a 'demonic rhythm'; in the spectators, the grimness of 'complete passivity' and 'lazy elbow-leaning'; and in the simplified, artificial palette, scant recompense for 'errors of draftsmanship'. Seurat, the ultimate theoretical artist, had gone too far. For Alphonse Germain (1861–1938),

> *In The Circus everything has been put together according to harmony by analogy, the reconciliation of opposites, with gaiety in mind: ascending lines in complementary directions (attitudes of the figures, details of the costume, placement of objects); as much photographic warmth as its author's delicate, grey vision can provide; finally, thanks to the successive contrast of tones, a very strong orange dominant, accentuated by a frame opposed in its tones and tines to the whole. The theorem is rigorously demonstrated, if anything too much so … the figures in The Circus, presented geometrically (especially the yellow clown), have the stiffness of automatons.*

Yet, for the generation that was to follow, it was precisely this geometric stiffness that endeared Seurat. For the painter Lucie Cousturier (1876–1925), *The Circus* was an affirmation of Seurat's 'unwavering conviction that natural phenomena are to be considered according to their expressive value, not according to their real existence, and must even be denied if necessary'. Seurat's breakthrough was in finding a way to combine the seemingly competing demands of scientific objectivity and expressive abstraction.

Left : *Bathers*, 1874–75, Paul Cézanne (1839–1906)

Guillaume Apollinaire (1880–1918) and André Salmon (1881–1969), both poets and early supporters of Cubism, identified *The Circus* as an 'icon' revered by two artists themselves grappling with the formal paradoxes inherent in representation: Picasso and Georges Braque (1882–1963). Seurat seemed to offer them proof that the liberation of painting's abstract elements need not entail a retreat from the tangible and the physical. Another key influence on this generation was Cézanne's rigorous analysis of the geometric substructures underpinning natural phenomena.

Cézanne

Cézanne was born in the Provençale town of Aix-en-Provence, about 20 km north-northeast of Marseilles. Cézanne's childhood, indeed the entirety of his life, was marked by, firstly, a profoundly difficult relationship with his father, a successful banker who disapproved of his son's ambition to be a painter, and, secondly, a deep attachment to Provence. One of Cézanne's closest childhood friends was the naturalist writer and theoretician Émile Zola, who moved to Paris in 1858 in order to advance his career. Cézanne's desire to follow him was frustrated by his father until 1861, who, in eventually consenting to his son's abandonment of legal studies, nonetheless provided him with only meagre financial support.

In Paris, Cézanne worked at the Académie Suisse, where he became acquainted with Pissarro and, through Zola, the circle coalescing around the pioneering Manet. Pissarro's *Portrait of Paul Cézanne* (1874) provides an insight as to how

Cézanne presented himself to the Parisian art world in these years: rough, unsophisticated, provincial and anti-authoritarian. Looking down from a caricature on the wall behind is the figure of Gustave Courbet (1819–77), the mid-century Realist painter known for his radical democratic art and his participation in the Paris Commune. The obvious allusion is that Cézanne is a modern Courbet. Indeed, like Courbet (a native of the rural and intransigent Franche-Comté region), Cézanne deliberately played up his regional accent and provincial (lack of) manners, proud of his outsider status with respect to the metropolitan, bourgeois élite that would later become indelibly associated with Impressionism.

Cézanne's early works were darkly Romantic figure paintings, often around the theme of sexual violence. *The Abduction* (1867), which he gifted to Zola, is typical: set in a shadowy and mysterious landscape, two large and expressively coloured figures contort around each other to create a wild fantasy of sexualized and dynamic violence. Cézanne's *Portrait of the Artist's Father Reading L'Evénement* (1866, *see* page 123) echoes this heavy style, where the figure is built up from thick smears of oil paint applied not with the brush, but with the palette knife.

Cézanne's encounter with Impressionism, specifically Pissarro's Impressionism, was to be a decisive turning point in his artistic development. In 1872, Cézanne took his mistress Hortense Fiquet and their son Paul to Pontoise, so that he could paint with Pissarro. The elder Impressionist's rustic landscapes and commitment to *plein-air* painting made a deep impression on Cézanne,

Detail above : *The Gulf of Marseille Seen from L'Estaque*, c. 1886, Paul Cézanne (1839–1906), *see page 126*

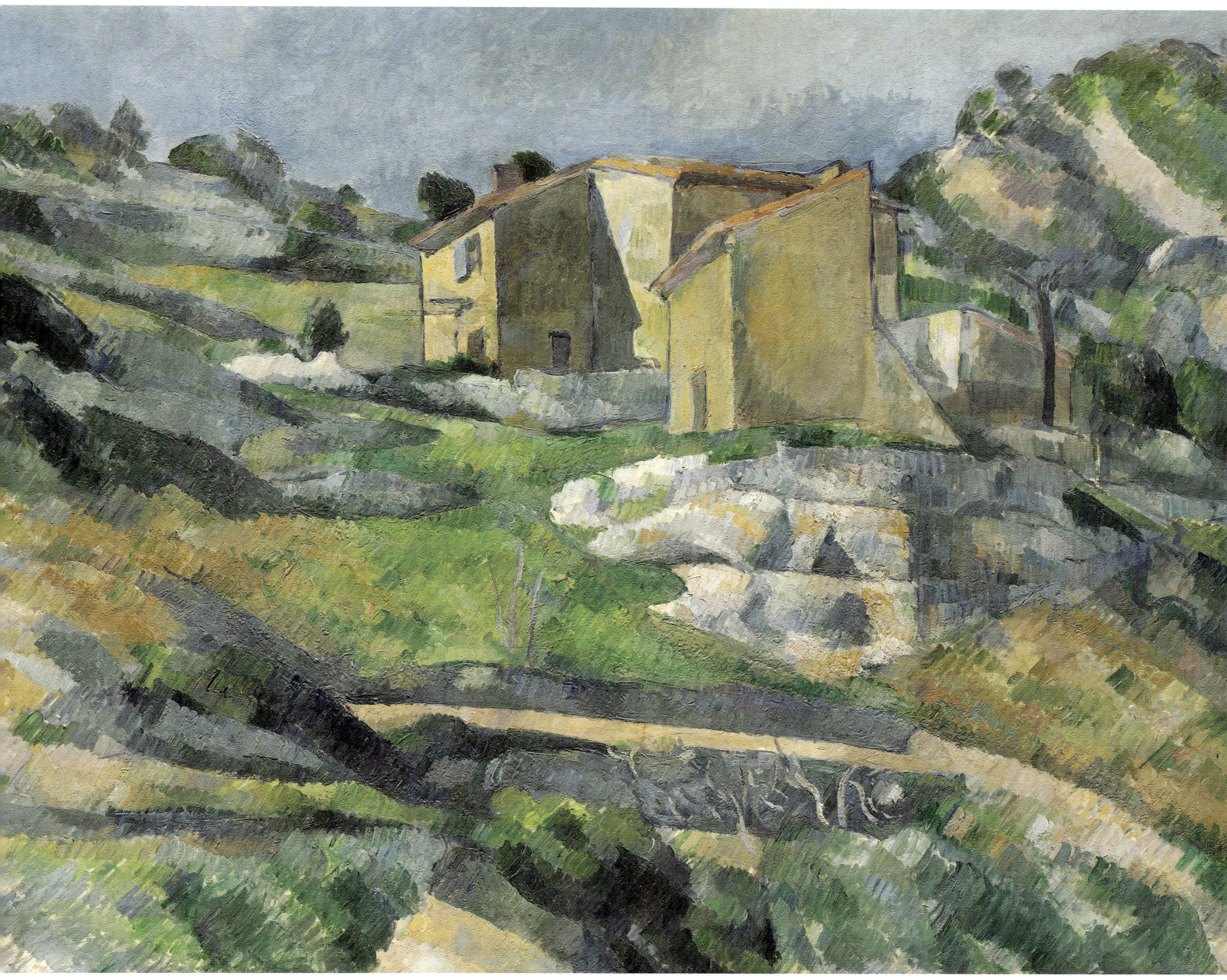

Above : *Houses in Provence: The Riaux Valley near L'Estaque*, 1883, Paul Cézanne (1839–1906)

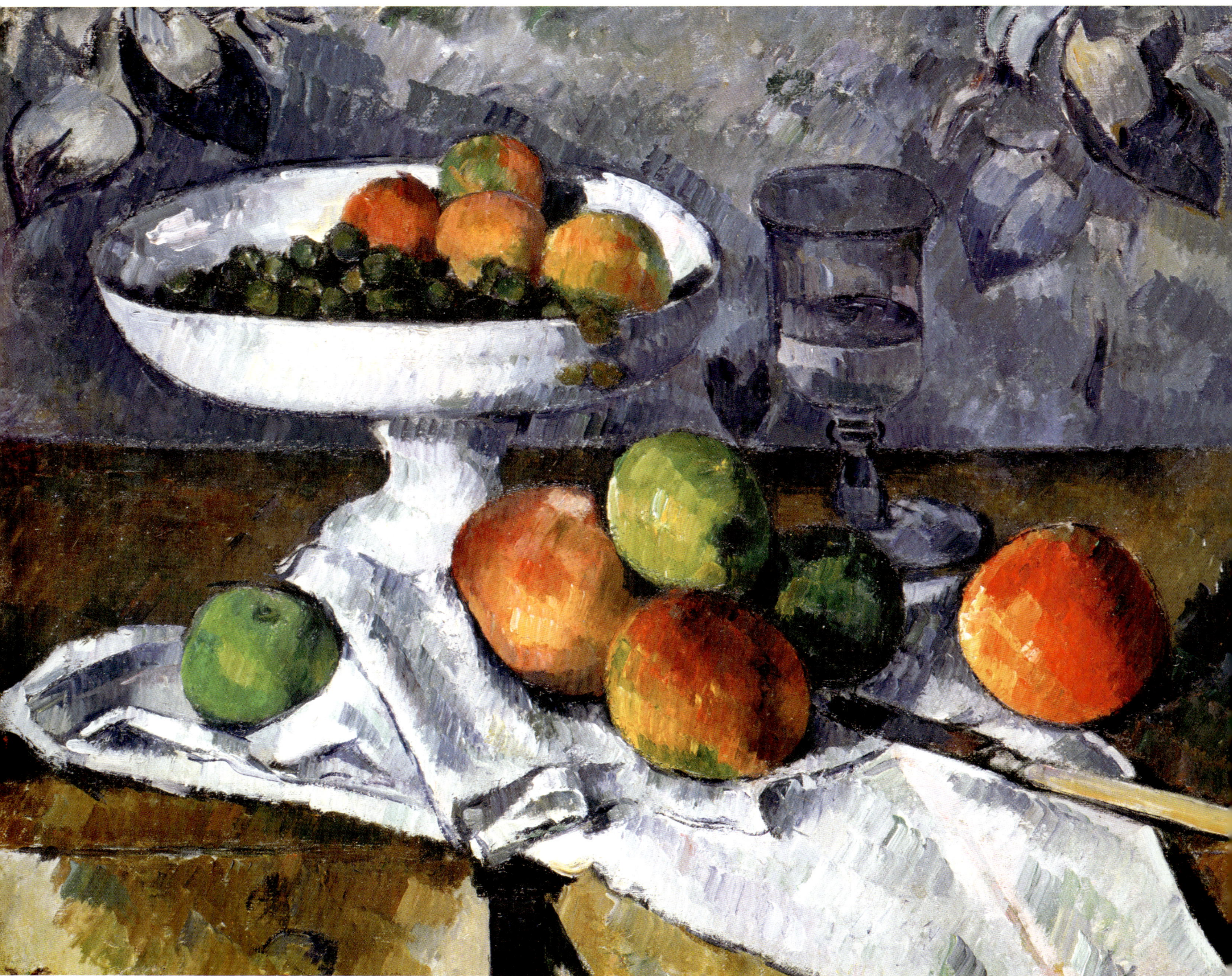

Above : *Still Life with Compotier, c. 1879–80*, Paul Cézanne (1839–1906)

who was himself seeking a style truthful to both nature and his own subjective experience, sensibility and 'sensations'. Zola, who had remained close to Cézanne after his move to Paris, was advocating in the Parisian press for art that married sensibility and nature: for him, art was 'a corner of creation seen through a temperament'. Under Pissarro's amenable tutelage ('Pissarro has a high opinion of me,' he wrote to his mother in 1874, 'and I have a high opinion of myself'), in works such as *The House of the Hanged Man, in Auvers-sur-Oise* (1873, *see* page 114), Cézanne learned how to synthesize his personal passions with the visual impact of nature. This suggestively titled painting (the house was named after the suicide of its owner) was exhibited at the First Impressionist Exhibition in 1874, and reveals at once Cézanne's growing proximity to Impressionism and his resistance against a total assimilation of its tenets. Where Cézanne adopted the Impressionist broken brushstrokes and penchant for roadside landscapes, painted on the spot, the spatial vertigo induced by the plunging road and conoidal view through the buildings, in conjunction with his heavy-handed application of paint, marked his individuality.

In the mid-1870s, Cézanne produced his first works on a theme that was to become something of an obsession: bathers. He produced a number of bathing scenes, both male (*Bathers Resting*, 1876–77, *see* page 125) and female (*Bathers*, 1874–75, *see* page 118), of both individuals and groups, that combined verdant *plein-air* landscapes with human figures drawn largely from the artist's imagination. While these early bathers recall happy childhood memories of bathing with Zola and other friends, Cézanne's prolonged and indecisive preparations (for *Bathers Resting*, he made numerous studies experimenting with the sex, arrangement and pose of the bathers), and his embarrassment before the nude model encode something of the frustrated sexuality that motivated his work in the 1860s. Cézanne habitually reused figures in multiple paintings, to save him having to make more life studies. The longer he painted bathers the more pronounced this pathological sexual investment in the imagined human form became.

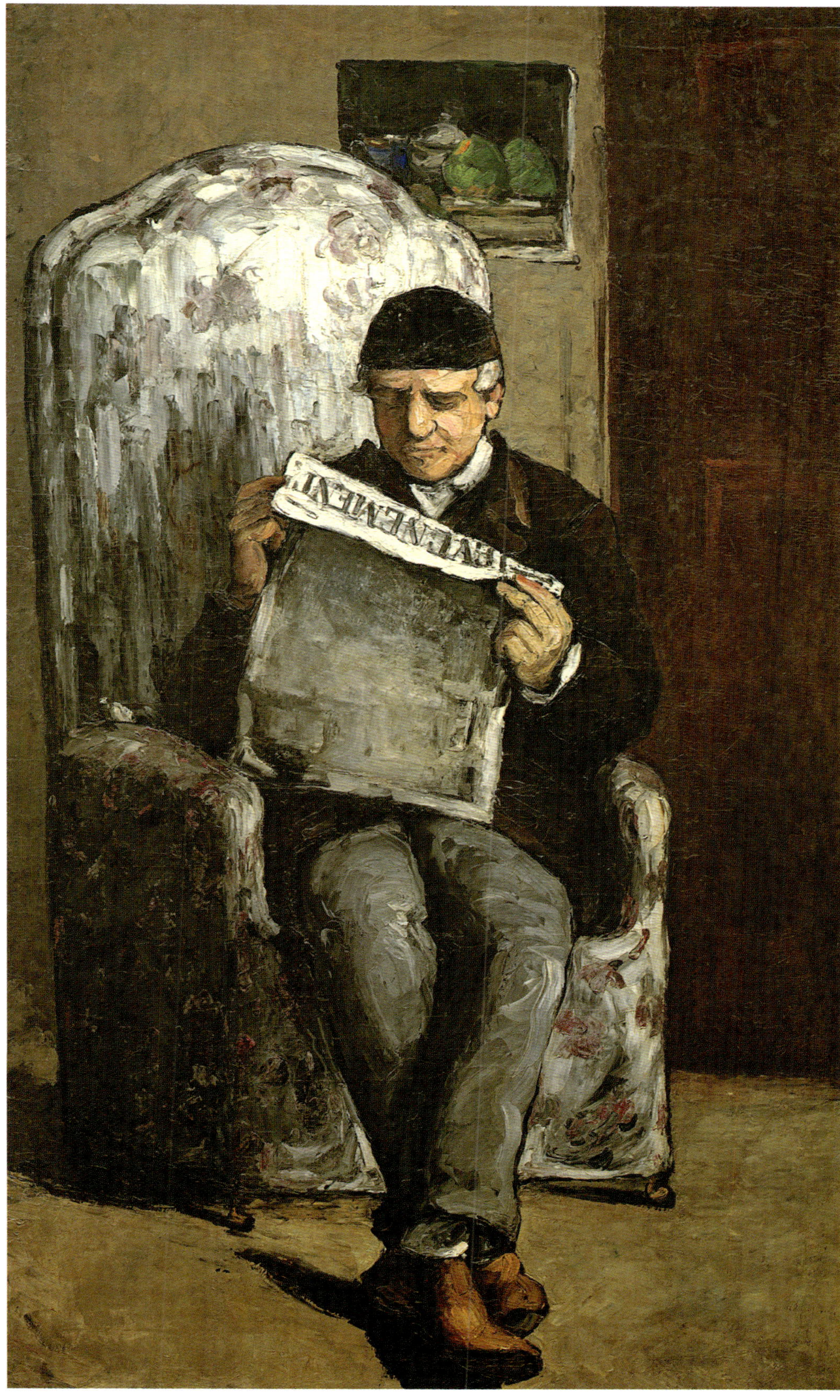

Above : *Portrait of the Artist's Father Reading L'Evénement*, 1866, Paul Cézanne (1839–1906)

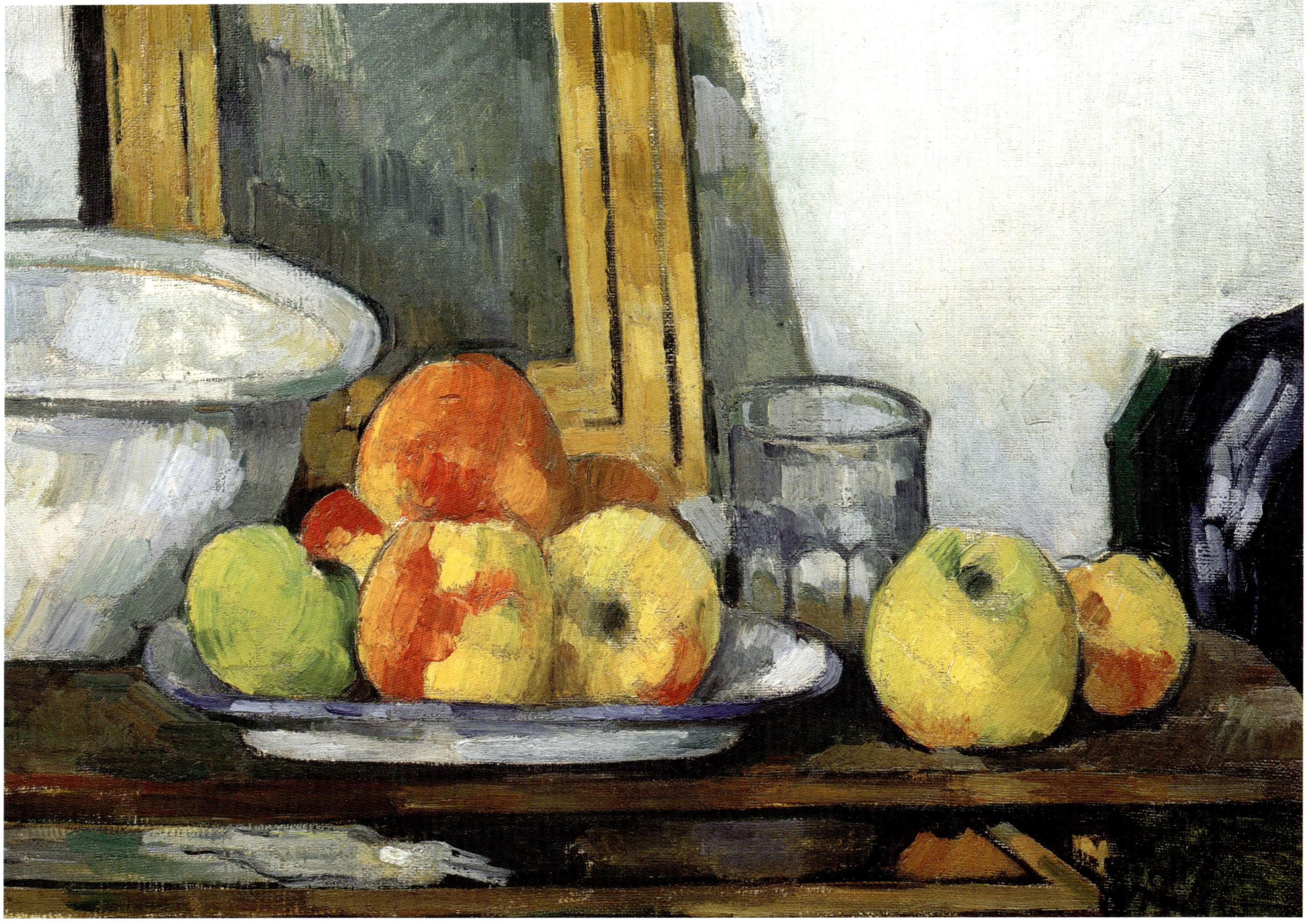

The Constructive Stroke

In his landscapes from this period, Cézanne experimented with what has become known as his 'constructive stroke': the systematic application of short brushstrokes of changing hue, arranged in parallel to each other. In *Houses in Provence: The Riaux Valley near L'Estaque* (*c*. 1883, *see* page 121), Cézanne combined the prolonged, analytical scrutiny implied by the constructive stroke with an audacious rejection of traditional standards of finish. His cerebral abstraction of natural forms draws attention to his painterly process, to the fact of his having worked, physically and mentally, to transliterate his 'sensations' before nature into an image that simultaneously signified both. His concern for solidity and structure marked a rejection of Impressionism's insubstantiality. This breakthrough was a particular

Above : *Still Life with an Open Drawer, 1867–69, Paul Cézanne (1839–1906)*

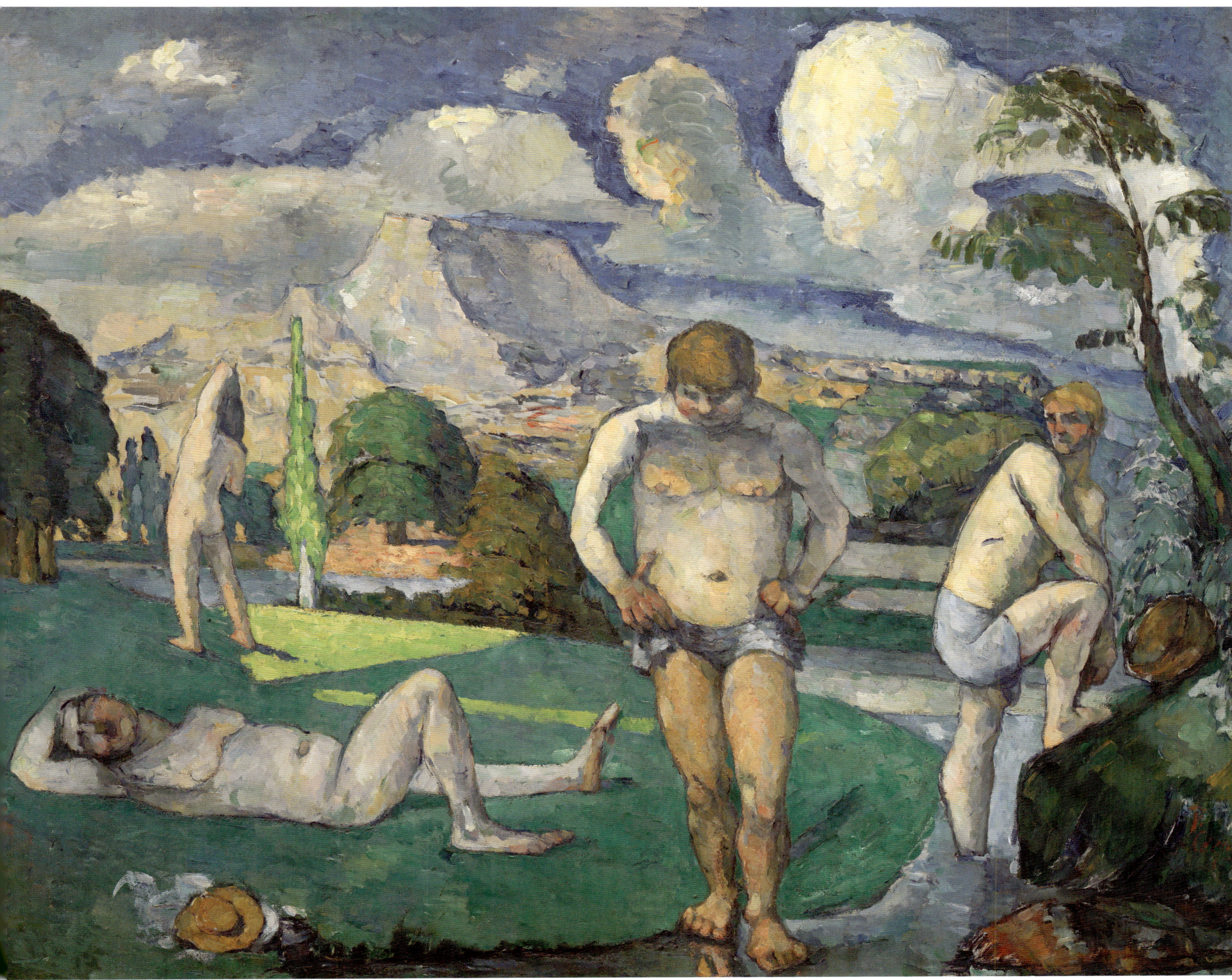

Above : *Bathers Resting,* 1876–77, Paul Cézanne (1839–1906)

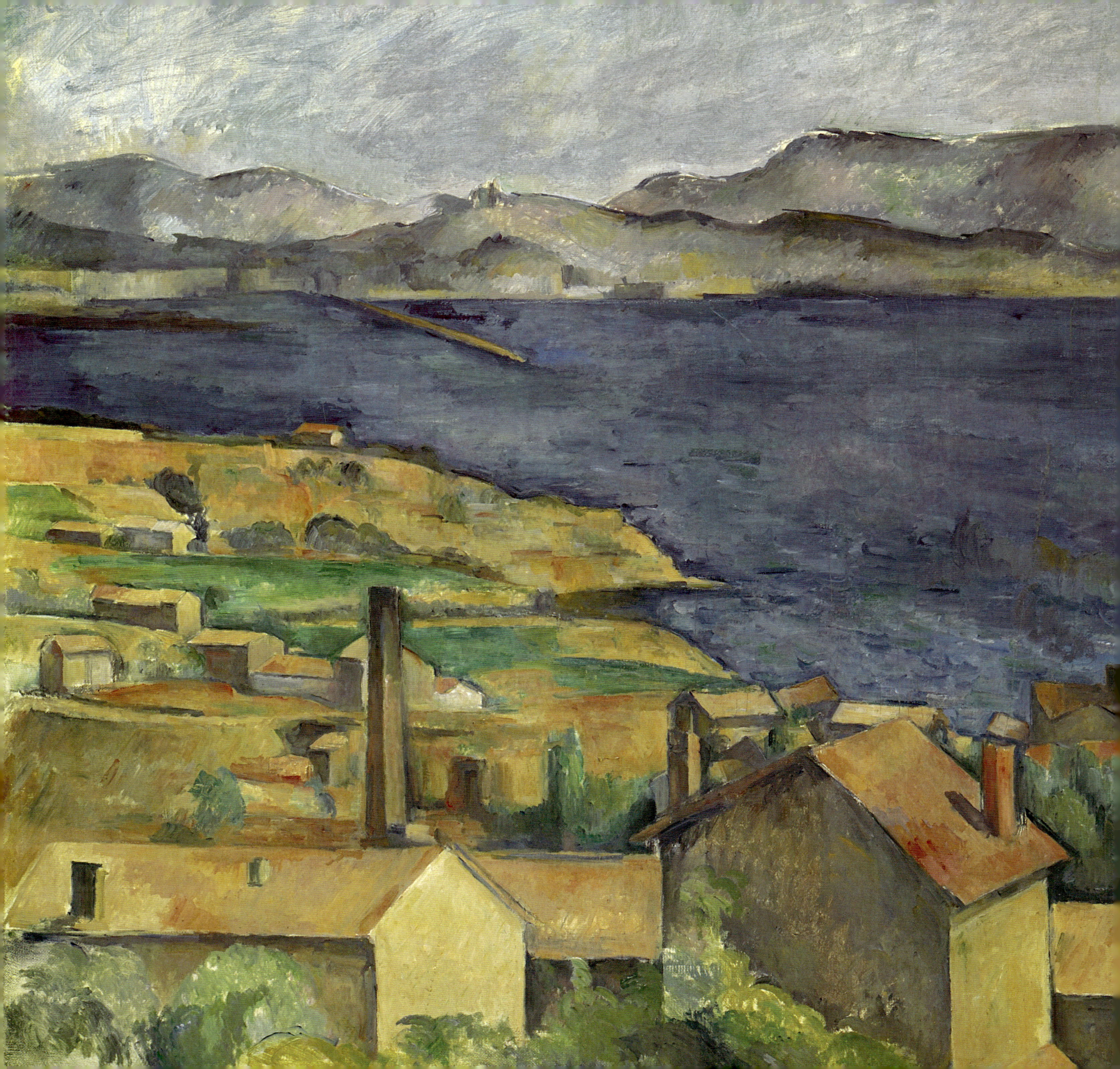

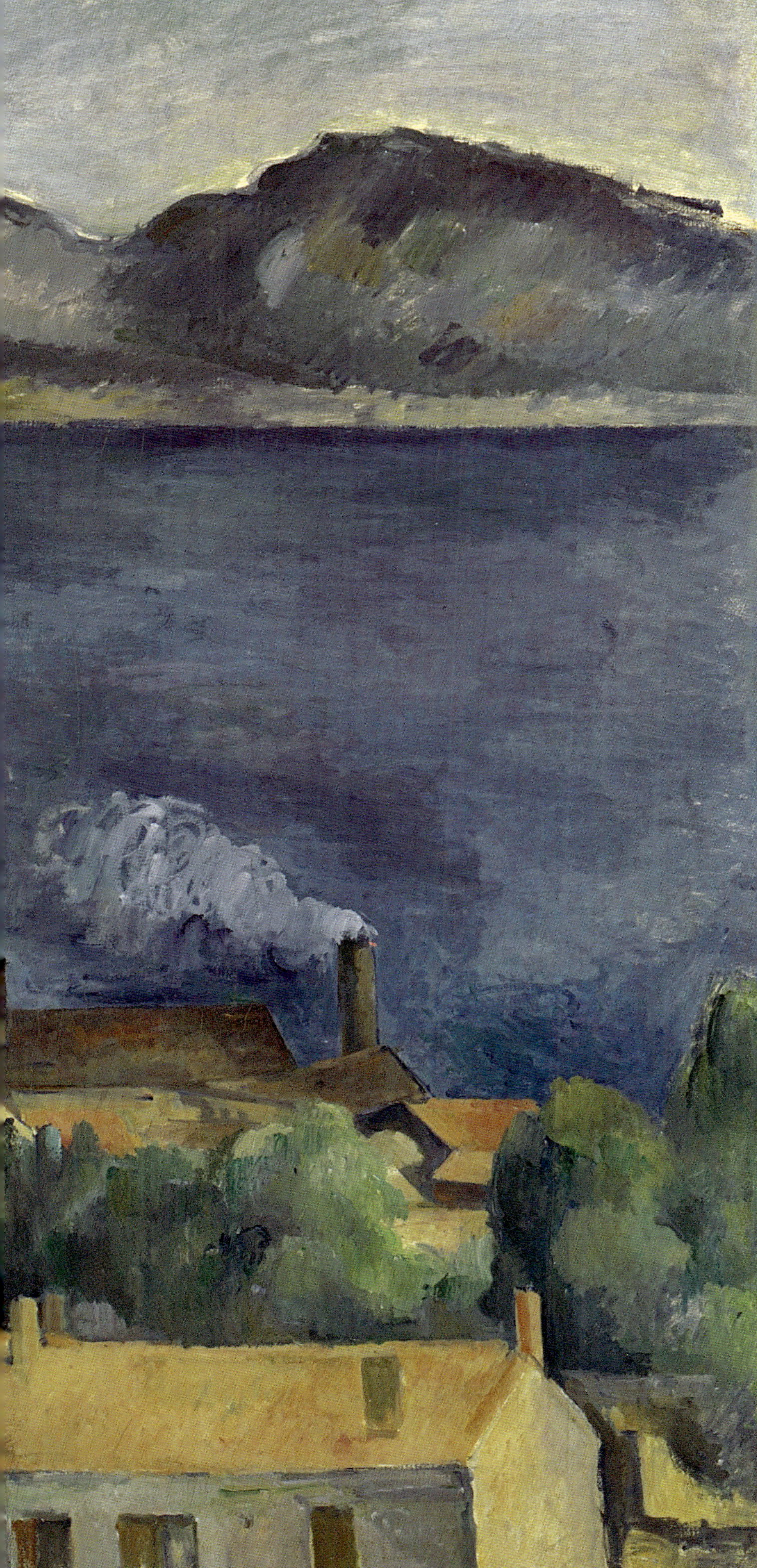

revelation for Gauguin who, as we have seen, worked alongside Pissarro and Cézanne in Pontoise in 1879.

Cézanne oscillated between Paris and Provence during this period. However, he increasingly came to identify with his Provençale roots, finding in its towns and villages a retreat from hectic modern life and the superficial culture epitomized by Impressionism. The basis of Cézanne's critique of Monet for being 'nothing but an eye' was his belief in the importance of thoughtful analysis. Cézanne spent the bulk of his time between 1883 and 1885 in Aix and in L'Estaque (a nearby village), and produced a number of landscapes in which his identity as a painter was progressively intertwined with his specifically Provençale subject matter. In *The Gulf of Marseille Seen from L'Estaque* (*c.* 1886, *see* left), Cézanne's radical and geometrical abstraction of the natural landscape is taken even further, as he searches for the underlying structure that will give the scene a kind of timeless solidity. Devoid of figures, the delicately composed and highly architectural scene – in which blue balances orange, buildings balance mountains – represents the height of Cézanne's desired synthesis of brain and eye.

In the traditional artistic opinion, the multiple genres of painting were stratified into a hierarchy according to their capacity to communicate noble truths and stimulate pensive erudition. At the top was history painting – large-scale historical, allegorical or mythological scenes with multiple, idealized figures with a didactic and noble message – at the bottom (sandwiching portraiture, landscapes and genre painting) was still life. Cézanne, however, saw in the still-life genre an opportunity to experiment and hone his pictorial innovations. His earliest attempts, such as *Still Life with an Open Drawer* (1867–69, *see* page 124), share the heavy, viscous materiality of his Romantic figure scenes. In *The Black Clock* (*c.* 1870, *see* page 128), Cézanne nods to the Dutch still-life tradition. For Dutch and Flemish painters of the seventeenth century, the still life (known as '*stilleven*', and later '*natures mortes*') was a way to tackle themes of decay, the inevitability of death and the futility of worldly or materialistic concerns.

Left : *The Gulf of Marseille Seen from L'Estaque*, c. 1886, Paul Cézanne (1839–1906)

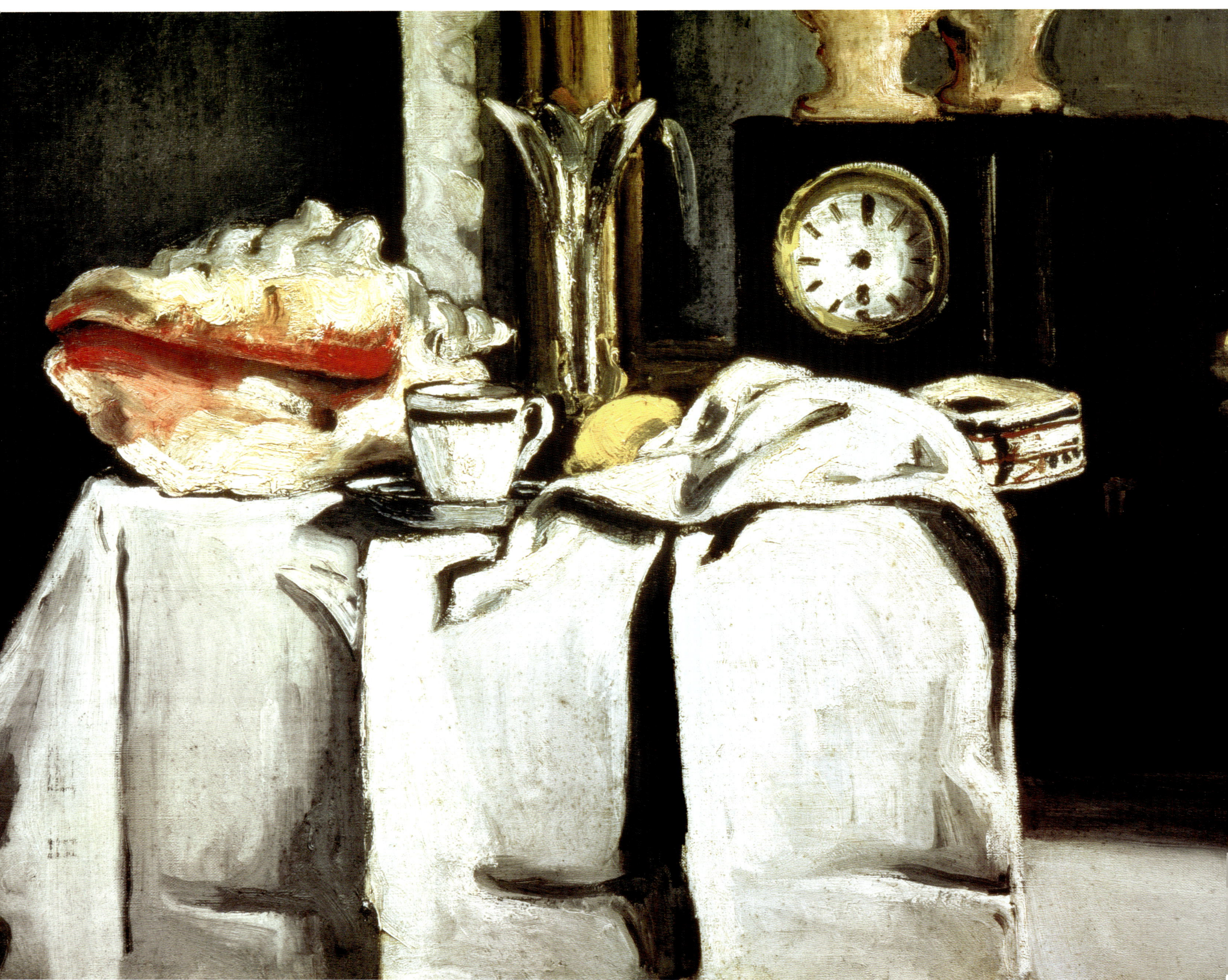

Above : *The Black Clock, c.* 1870, Paul Cézanne (1839–1906)

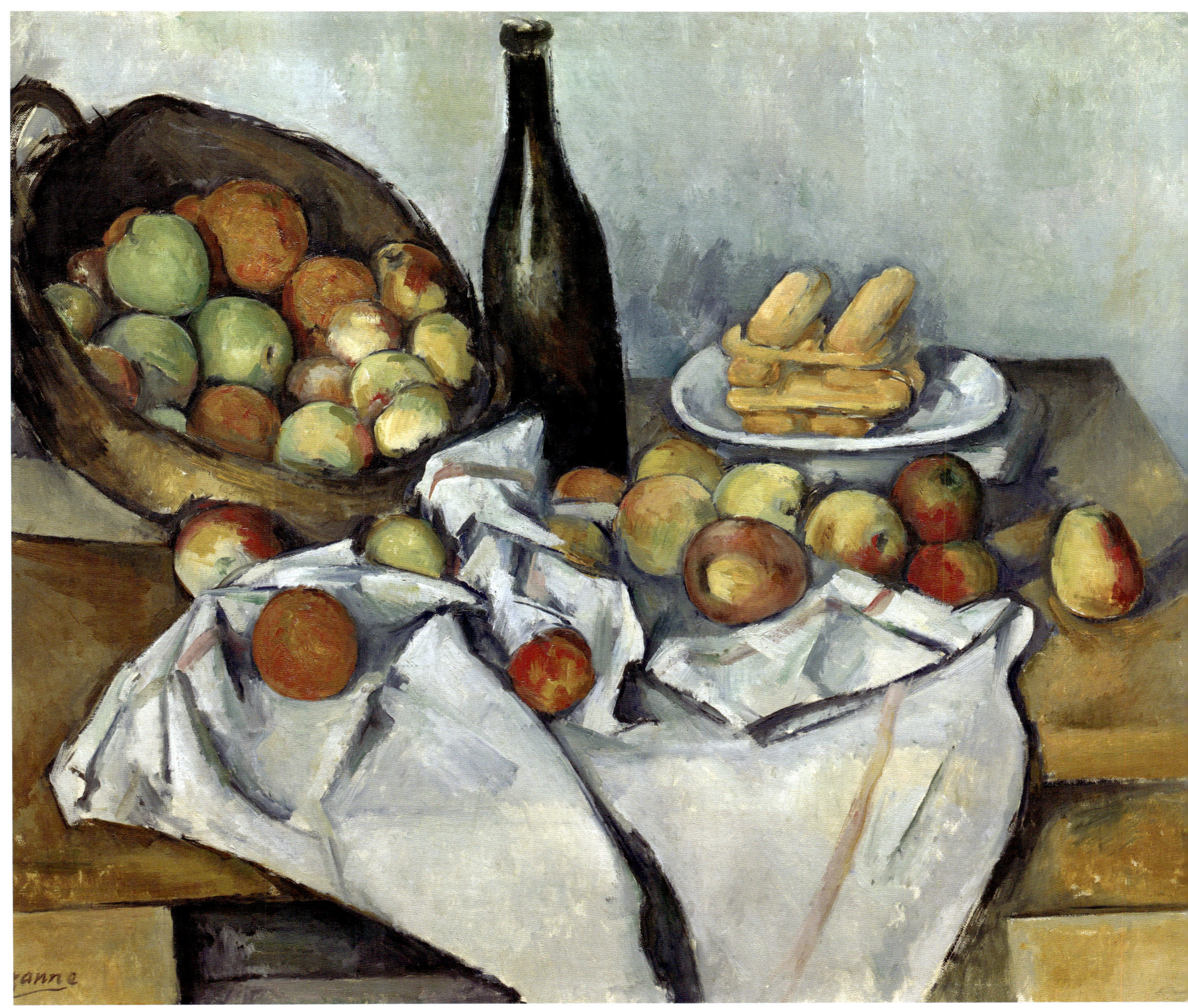

Above : *The Basket of Apples*, 1890–94, Paul Cézanne (1839–1906)

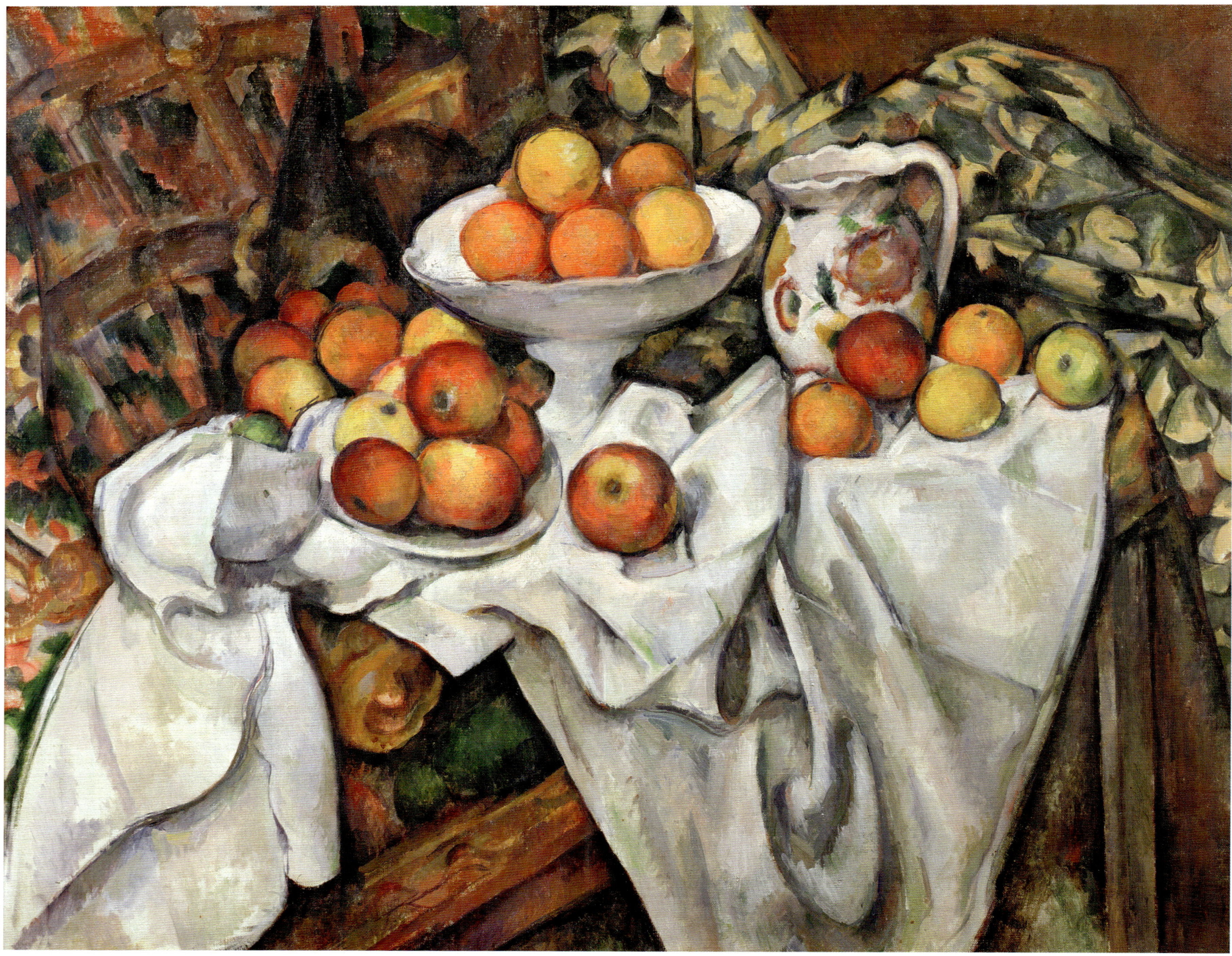

Cézanne borrowed their characteristic symbolism and presented a seemingly arbitrary assortment of man-made and natural objects; the arrestingly vulvic seashell jars with the sterility of the empty vase; the handless clock connotes a precarious and rootless atemporality.

Building on his achievements in landscapes however, over the 1870s, Cézanne would move away from this deeply symbolic modality towards producing still lifes concerned with the problems of perception and representation. In *Still Life with Compotier* (*c.* 1879–80, *see* page 122), Cézanne applied his

Above : *Apples and Oranges, c. 1895–1900, Paul Cézanne (1839–1906)*

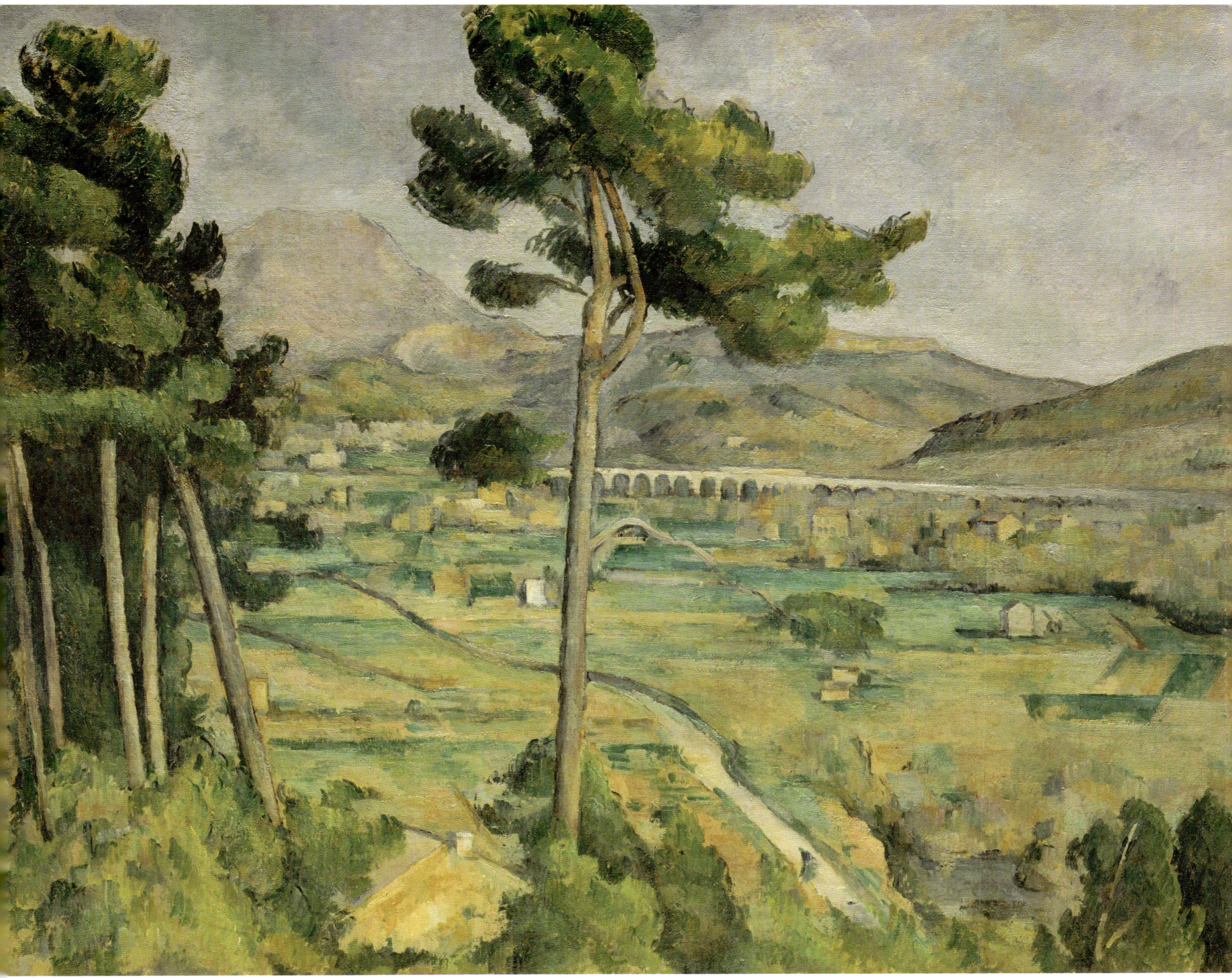

Above : *Mont Sainte-Victoire and the Viaduct of the Arc River Valley, 1882–85, Paul Cézanne (1839–1906)*

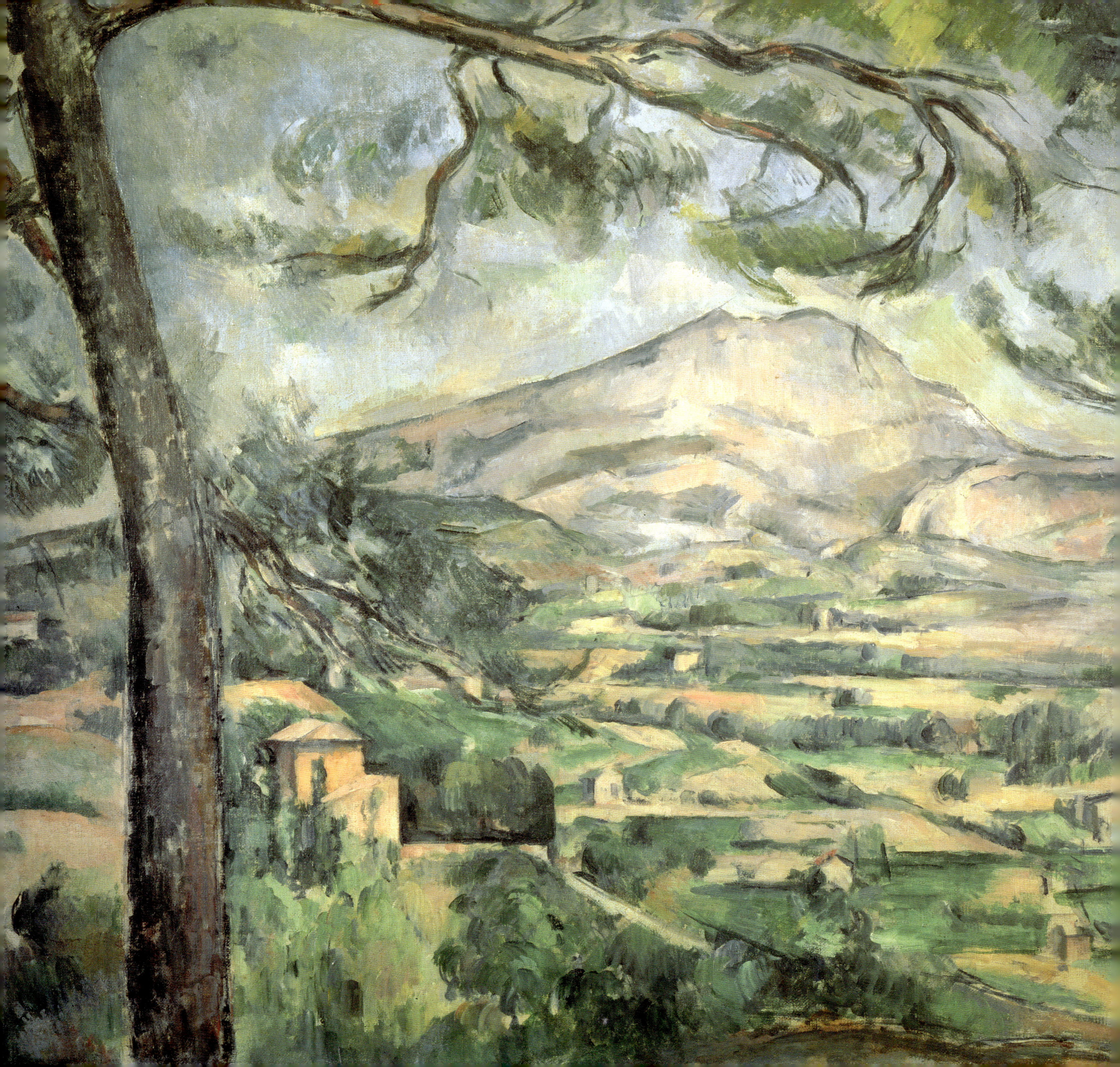

characteristic constructive stroke evenly across the canvas in such a way as to equalize various objects and to flatten space. The apples are modelled through modulation in hue between such brushstrokes, yet their overriding planarity and materiality impresses upon us that what we see are not apples but rather the representation of apples, echoing Maurice Denis' (1870–1943) statement that 'a picture before being a battle horse, a nude woman, or some anecdote, is essentially a flat surface covered with colours assembled in a certain order'.

The wallpaper functions as both a flat, decorative background and a void of indeterminate space, before which objects seem to float. The bunched-up tablecloth, rather than offering a neutral support, is an integral component in the composition, its folds giving it a spatial and material presence. In this radically pioneering painting, then, objects become surfaces and surfaces become objects. Gauguin, the painting's jealous owner ('[t]his Cézanne that you ask me for is a pearl of exceptional quality and I already have refused three hundred francs for it; it is

'I discovered that sunlight... could not be reproduced; it had to be represented by something else – by colour.'
Paul Cézanne

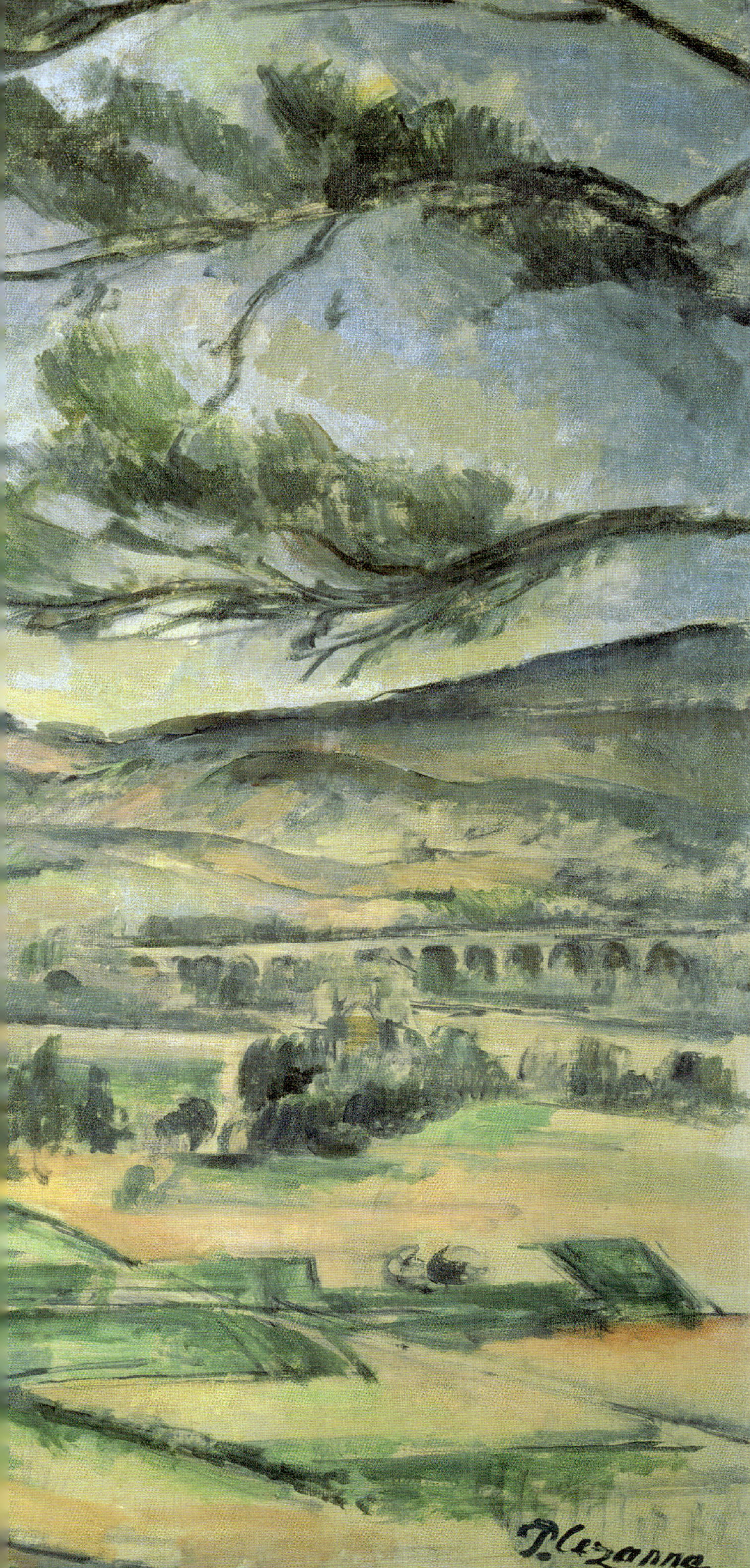

Left : *Mont Sainte-Victoire with Large Pine*, c. 1887, Paul Cézanne (1839–1906)

one of my most treasured possessions, and except in absolute necessity, I would give up my last shirt before the picture'), would include it in the background of his portrait of an unidentified *Woman in Front of a Still Life by Cézanne* (1890, *see* page 117), imposing his own name over its white frame, as if to appropriate Cézanne's achievements.

Apples would continue to be the focus of Cézanne's pioneering late still lifes. In *The Basket of Apples* (1890–94, *see* page 129) and *Apples and Oranges* (*c*. 1895–1900, *see* page 130), the tablecloth is possessed of an ever more exaggerated structural integrity, its sculptural folds seeming to defy gravity. Cézanne's belief that art ought to be 'a harmony running parallel to nature', that is, not an imitation of it ('[p]ainting from nature is not copying the object, it is realizing one's sensations') underpins the structure and form of these works, in which Cézanne abandoned illusionism and drew his viewer's attention to the materiality of the painted object. The fruit he paints are not apples but a certain configuration of brushstrokes engineered to signify apples.

The tables in each work tilt forward and threaten to spill their contents over the threshold of the frame. In *The Basket of Apples*, the tablecloth seems to conceal some structural rupture in the table itself, whose left side looms forward, whilst its right side recedes; the back edge is far lower on the left than on the right. In this visual essay on perception and analysis, Cézanne encodes his prolonged contemplation by including multiple viewpoints; the left side of the table seems to tilt forward because we see it from a more elevated vantage point than the right half, as if we are physically moving through and around the presented scene.

The year 1886 would prove to be a watershed for Cézanne. In March, Émile Zola published a novel entitled *L'Œuvre*, whose protagonist was a failed artist named Claude Lantier. Cézanne took this character, who constantly failed to finish his works or live up to his revolutionary potential, to be a slight aimed

Right : *Mont Sainte-Victoire and Château Noir*, 1904–05, Paul Cézanne (1839–1906)

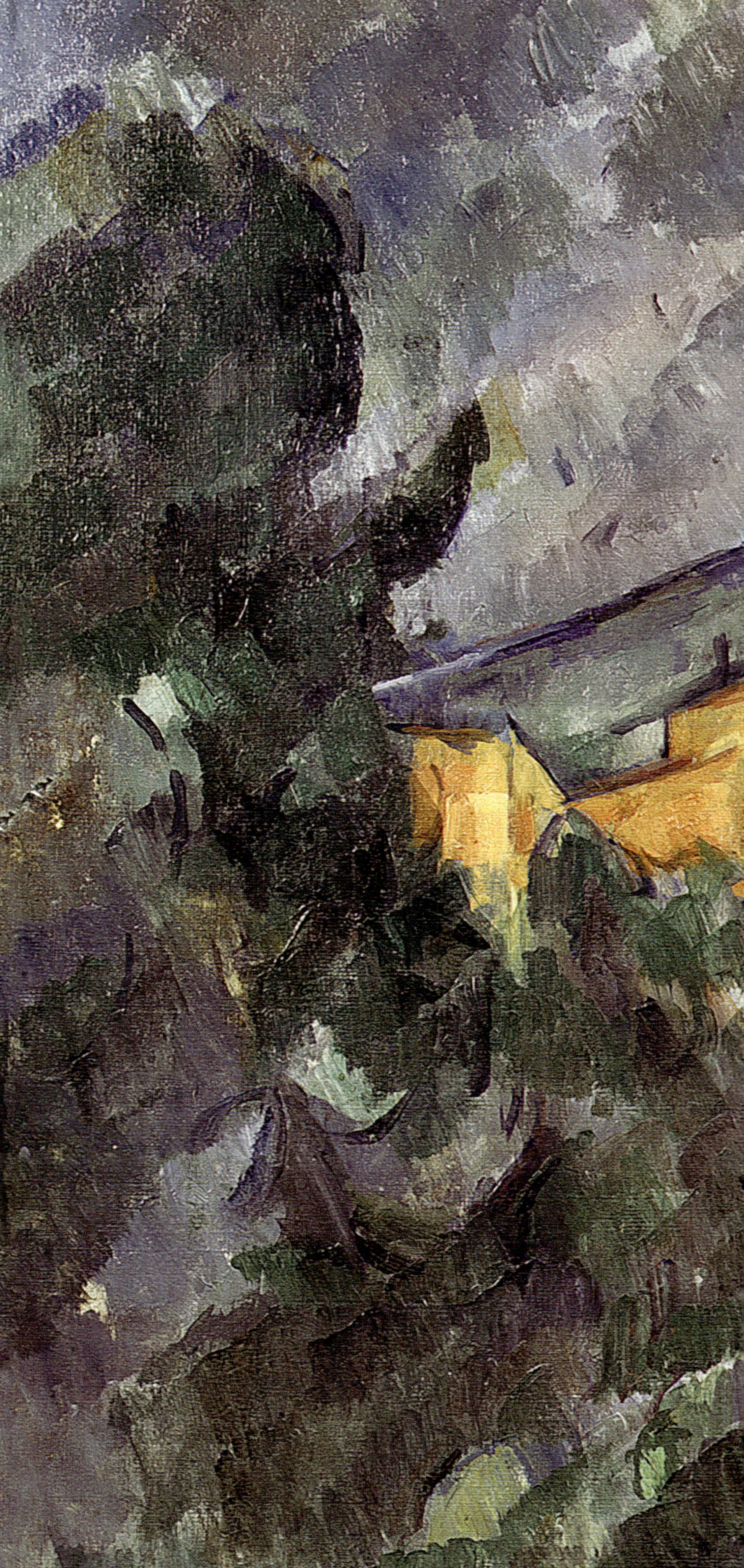

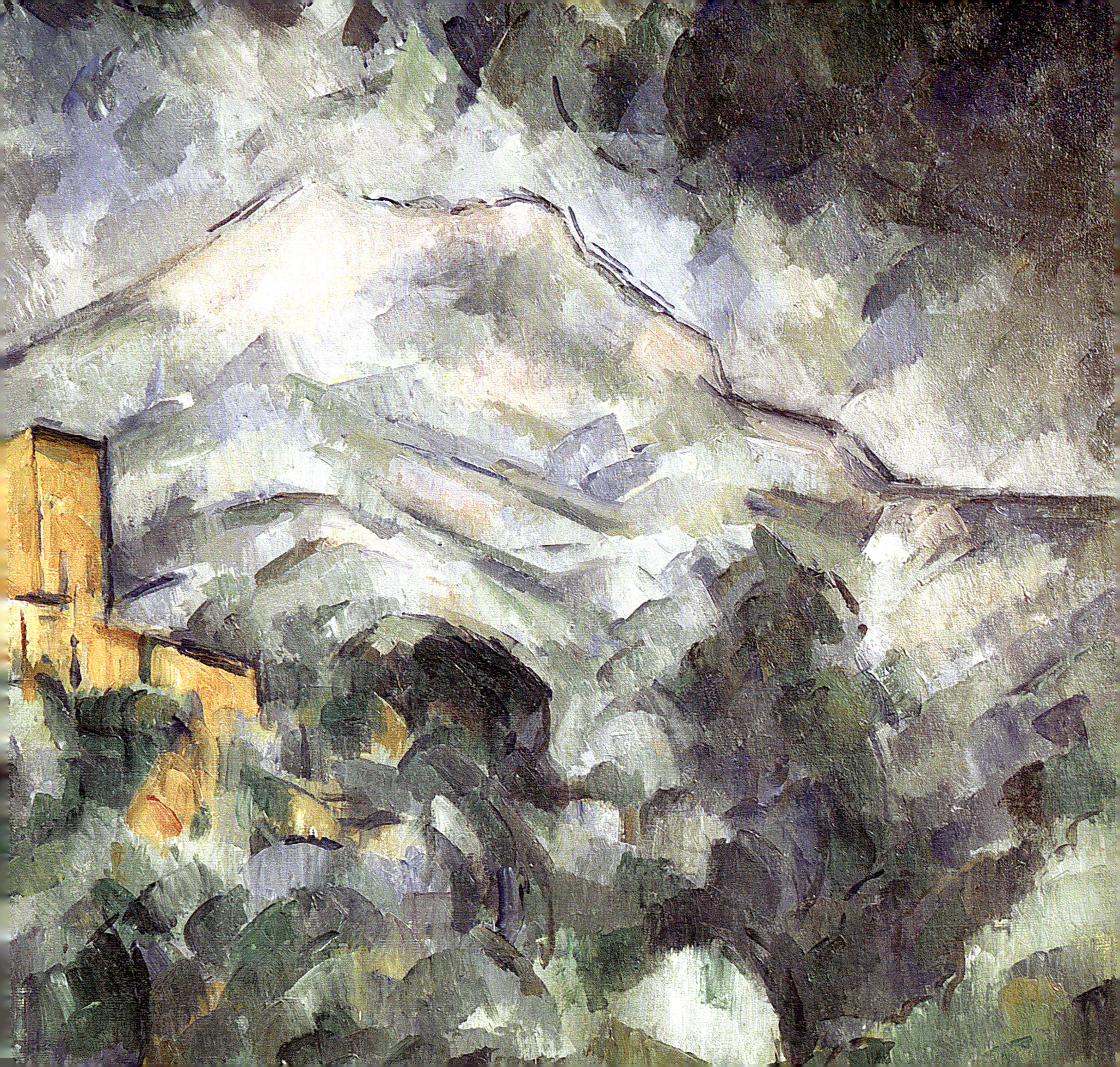

> *'Even the stiffness of the people, the ready-made forms, help give the sound of modernity...'*
> Paul Adam (on Seurat's Grande Jatte)

directly at him. Although the character was in reality a composite of Cézanne and other artists (such as Monet and Manet), Zola's 1896 judgement in *Le Figaro* that Cézanne was 'an aborted great talent' perhaps justifies Cézanne's vexation. Lantier's suicide could well have been a metaphor for Cézanne and Zola's friendship: they never spoke again. In April, his overbearing father having fallen ill and (perhaps prescient of his impending death) finally consented, Cézanne married Hortense and legitimated their son. In October, his father died, leaving Cézanne a sizeable inheritance.

In response to such personal turbulence, Cézanne retreated even further into his Provençale haven, above which towered the iconic Mont Sainte-Victoire. This limestone mountain, jutting 1,011 m (3,317 ft) above the pine forests, overlooks Aix, and is visible from the Aix-Marseilles train line, which opened on 15 October 1877. As he had in his paintings from

L'Estaque – in which he sought to create an idealized vision of Provence that, by the very ostentatiousness of the mechanism of its idealization, would simultaneously facilitate a fantasy of retreat and signify his painterly labour – in the 1880s, 1890s and 1900s, Cézanne redoubled his attention on the rich Provençale landscape.

Cézanne painted *Mont Sainte-Victoire and the Viaduct of the Arc River Valley* (1882–85, *see* page 131) atop a hill just behind his sister's house. The Arc valley is contained and compressed between (in the background and on the right) Mont Sainte-Victoire and its foothills, and a pine forest on the left. The patchwork of fields is elucidated through horizontal brushstrokes of varying tones, in which are positioned highly schematized buildings, which give only the merest hint of three-dimensionality to an otherwise insistently one-dimensional, flat space. Cézanne has deliberately heightened a sense of spatial ambiguity by overlapping brushstrokes that ought to describe separate objects in separate spatial planes. Note how the sky is blended into the foliage and how the rightmost branch of the pine tree blends into the fields. The result of this overlapping of brushstrokes is the eradication of depth.

Like the Art of Museums

Cézanne sought to transform Impressionism into 'something solid and durable, like the art of museums'. The viaduct helped him in achieving this in two ways. Firstly, the geometrical strength of the cross formed by the pine intersecting the viaduct forms the painting's structure, to which everything else submits. Secondly, this solid and stable framework recalls the balanced harmony of Renaissance landscapes, where the drive for compositional unity overrode any concern for naturalism. The viaduct, which evokes the form of a Roman aqueduct, also specifically references the master of the Classical landscape, Nicolas Poussin (1594–1665).

Right : *The Card Players*, 1892–95, Paul Cézanne (1839–1906)

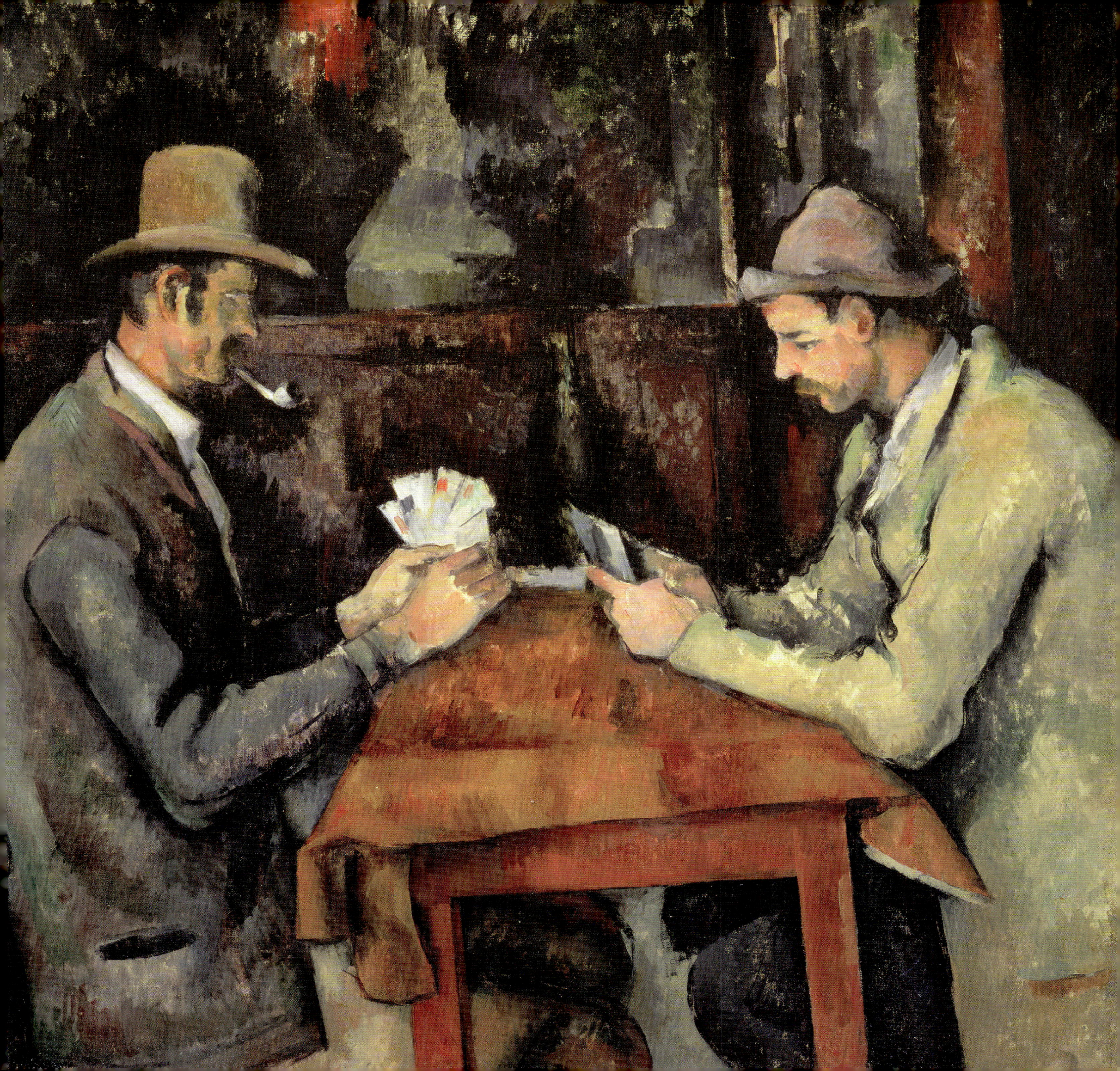

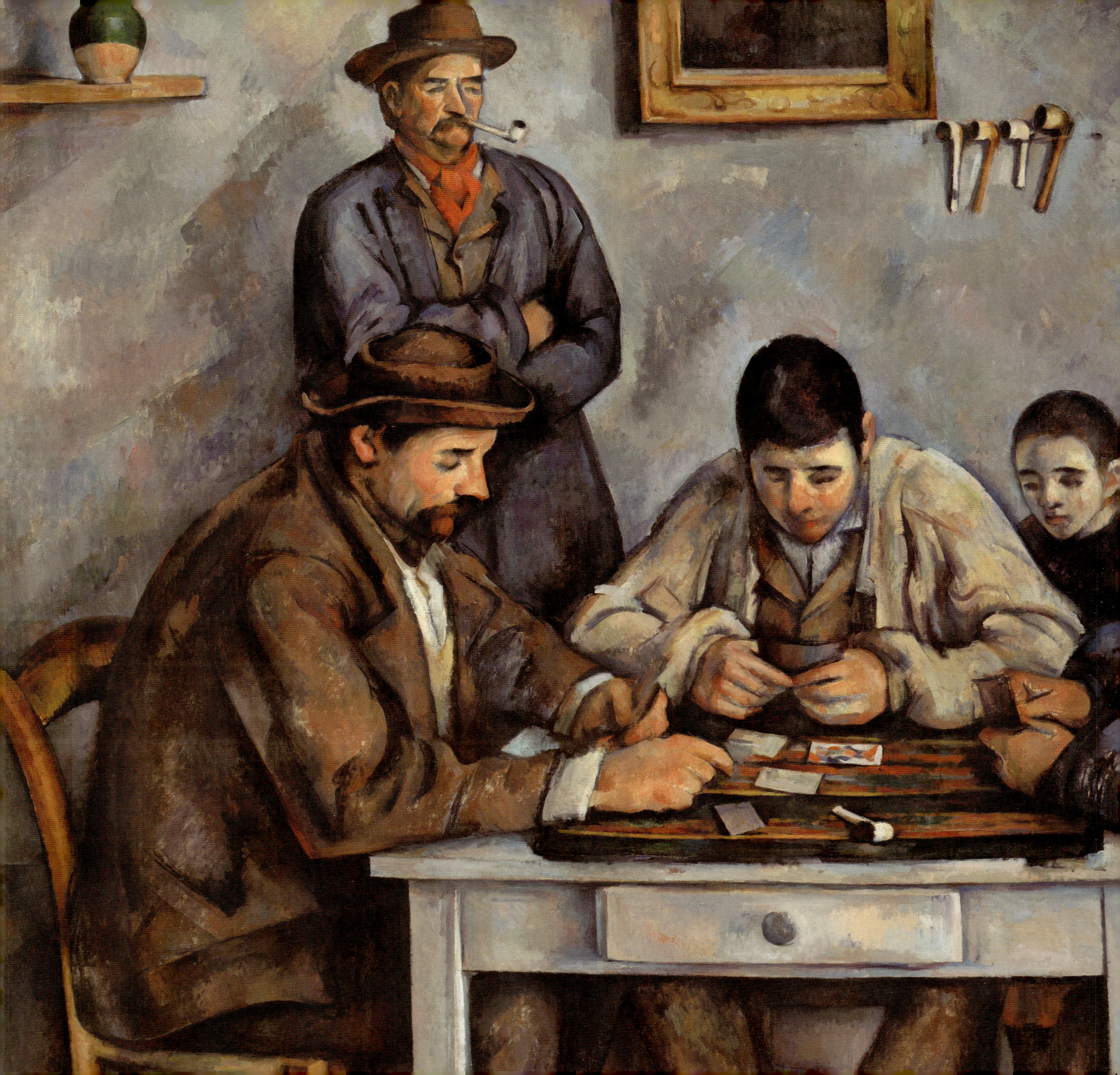

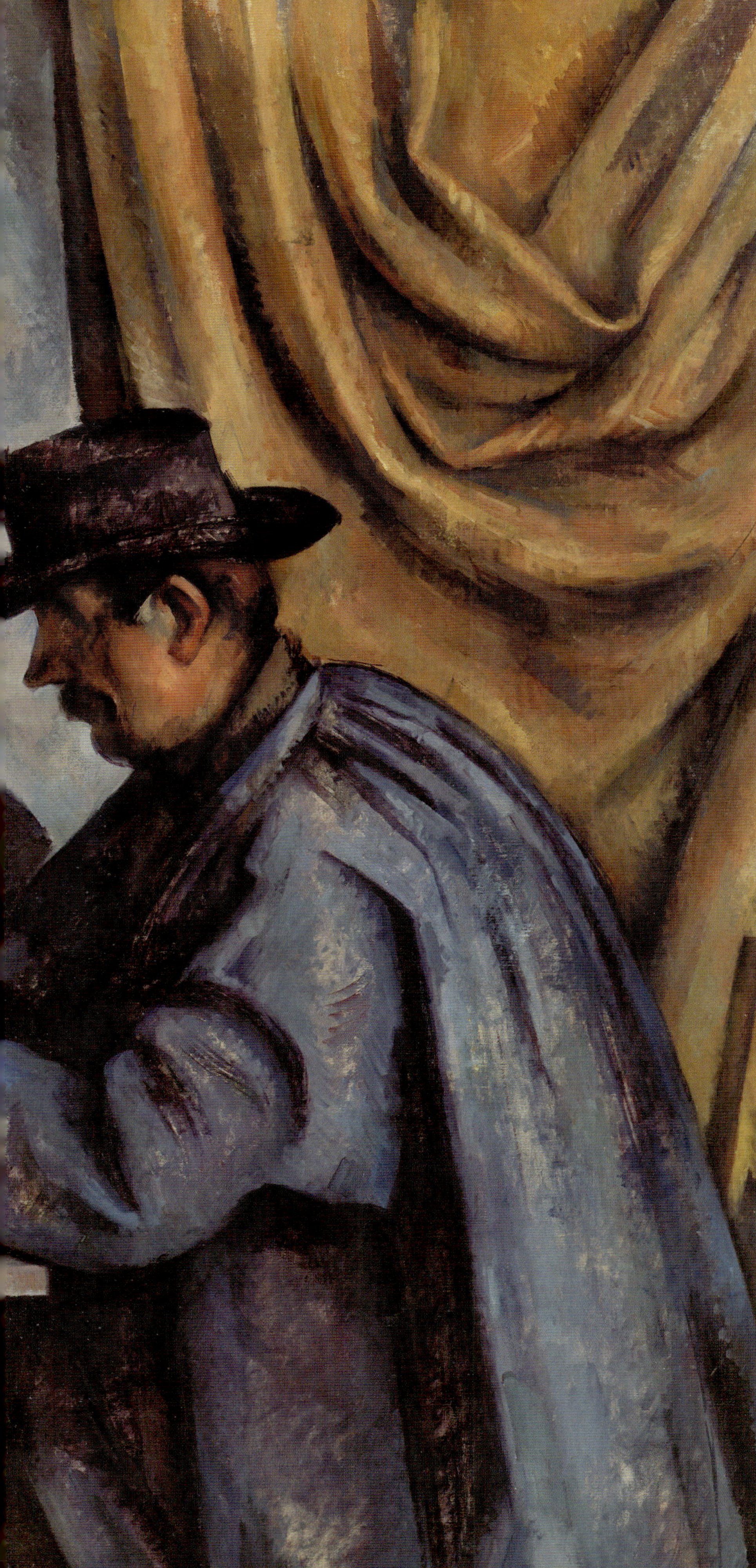

This desire to 'paint Poussin over again after nature', central to Cézanne's conception of the significance of his art, is likewise appreciable in his later paintings of the mountain. In *Mont Sainte-Victoire with Large Pine* (c. 1887, *see* page 132), the branches of the tree harmonically echo the ridges and outline of the mountain, creating a sense of serene balance. In *Mont Sainte-Victoire and Château Noir* (1904–05, *see* page 135), Cézanne has taken his geometricizing, abstracting idiom to its logical conclusion. Stripping away all extraneous detail, Cézanne conveys only the most essential underlying form of the landscape, its flora and buildings.

In addition to his serial interest in Mont Sainte-Victoire, which he painted over 40 times in the 1890s and 1900s, Cézanne developed two other major series: of card players and of bathers. Cézanne first became interested in the motif of men playing cards in the autumn of 1890, and over the next decade he completed five canvases of varying size, composition, framing, colouration and number of figures. Debate still rages as to the precise chronology of the canvases, but it is believed that the brighter, multi-figure compositions – such as the Barnes Foundation's *The Card Players* (1890–92, *see* left) – predate the darker, two figure scenes, which include the Courtauld Gallery's *The Card Players* (1892–95, *see* page 137).

Cézanne used local peasants as models for the card players, some of whom worked on his late father's estate in Jas de Bouffan (including the pipe-smoking player on the left of the Courtauld version: 'Père Alexandre', the gardener). The Provençale men who tilled the same earth over which Cézanne laboured are painted with the solidity and heft that Cézanne had previously reserved for Mont Sainte-Victoire. Like the mountain, these men are sturdy and timeless representatives of Provence's eternal essence. Their intense concentration on the liminal moment before the wager produces a narrative tension which resonates between the timelessness encoded in their form and the worldly, mundane nature of their activity.

Left : *The Card Players*, 1890–92, Paul Cézanne (1839–1906)

Cézanne, Chardin, Caravaggio

The simple composition and gravity of these works mark a knowing departure from traditional representations of the motif with which Cézanne was certainly familiar, a tradition of dynamism, restlessness and animation stretching from Caravaggio (1571–1610) to The Brothers Le Nain (Antoine *c.* 1599–1648; Louis *c.* 1593-1648; Mathieu 1607–77) and Jean-Baptiste-Siméon Chardin (1699–1779). Chardin's variations on the theme of a boy building a house of cards imparts a symbolism of precariousness and alludes to the frivolity of earthly distractions. This kind of heavy philosophical message, as we know from his early still lifes, was not completely alien to Cézanne.

Cézanne's final major series focused on *Large Bathers* (*see* right and page 142), of which he produced three versions roughly in concert. As we have seen, the theme of nudes in a landscape had both personal and art historical significance for Cézanne, possessing both a grand nobility and the potential for nostalgia and sexual investment. Looking back to a tradition that included Poussin and Titian, Cézanne worked almost obsessively on these canvases, seemingly unable to bring himself to finish.

In contrast to his early bathers, in these late works, the exclusively female bodies are more integrated with the landscape, in terms of tone, texture and structure. While solid, they nevertheless possess a certain ambiguity, especially at those points where they are almost absorbed by the surrounding foliage. The figures lack any individuality, revealing that they originated not in a moment of observation but one of imagination. These ostentatiously unreal bodies are thus brazen in their assertion that they are not bodies but rather patches of paint; that they have been created, rather than described, by the artist. Paradoxically, they simultaneously also signify sexual desire, lurid fantasies of unrestrained sexual contact, of the sexual touch pleasurably blurring the boundaries between them.

Right : *Large Bathers*, 1894–1905, Paul Cézanne (1839–1906)

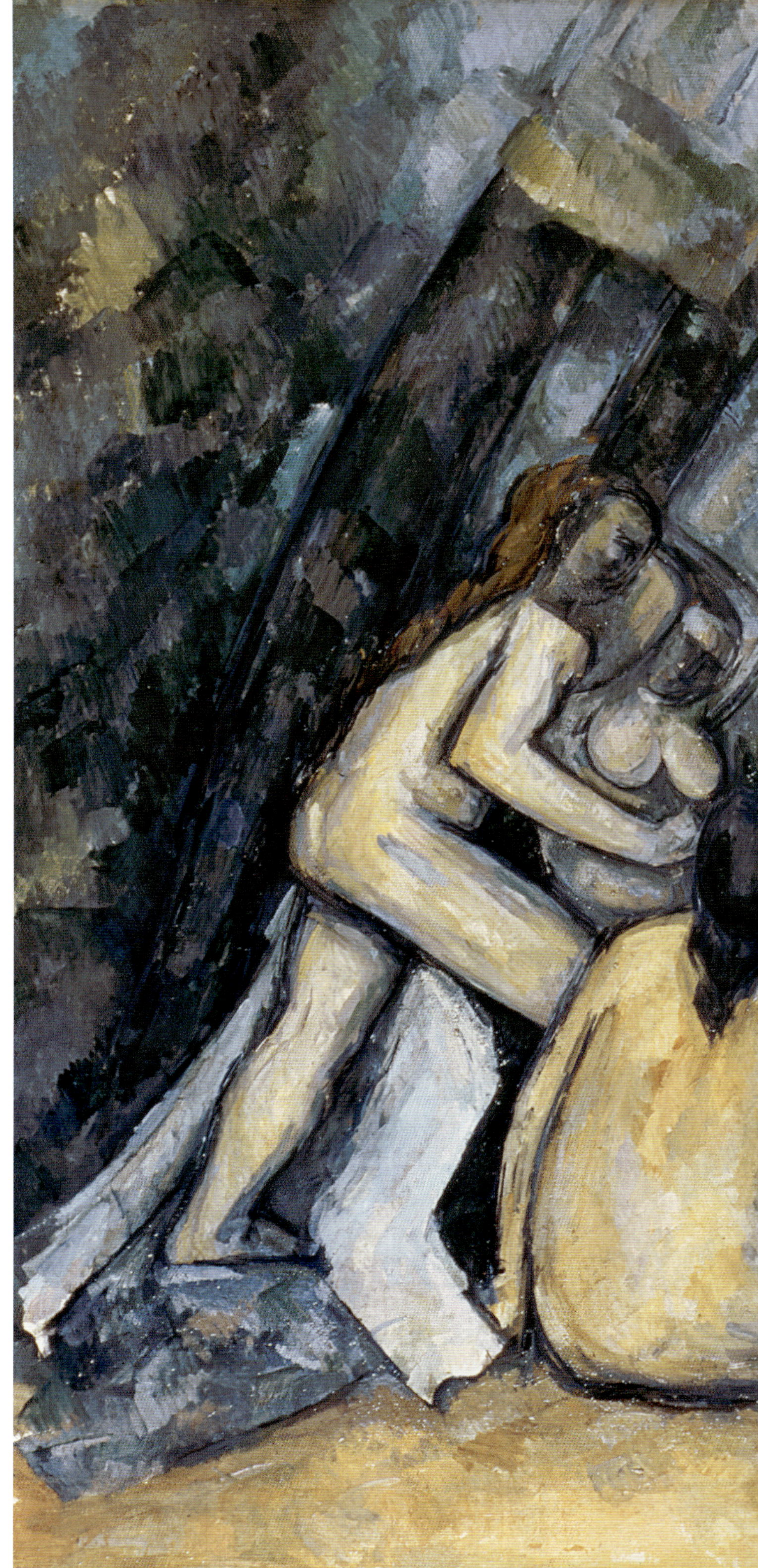

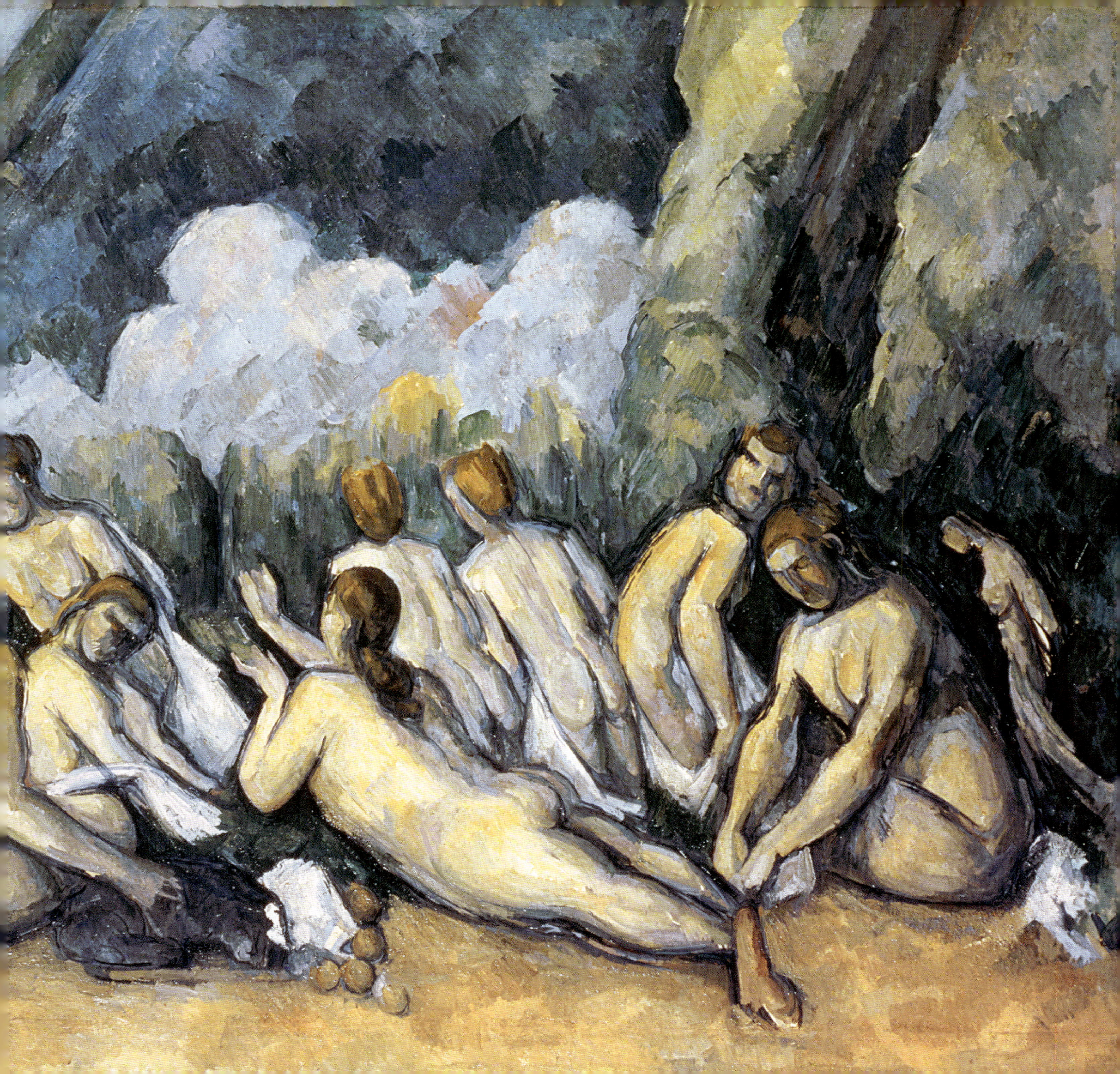

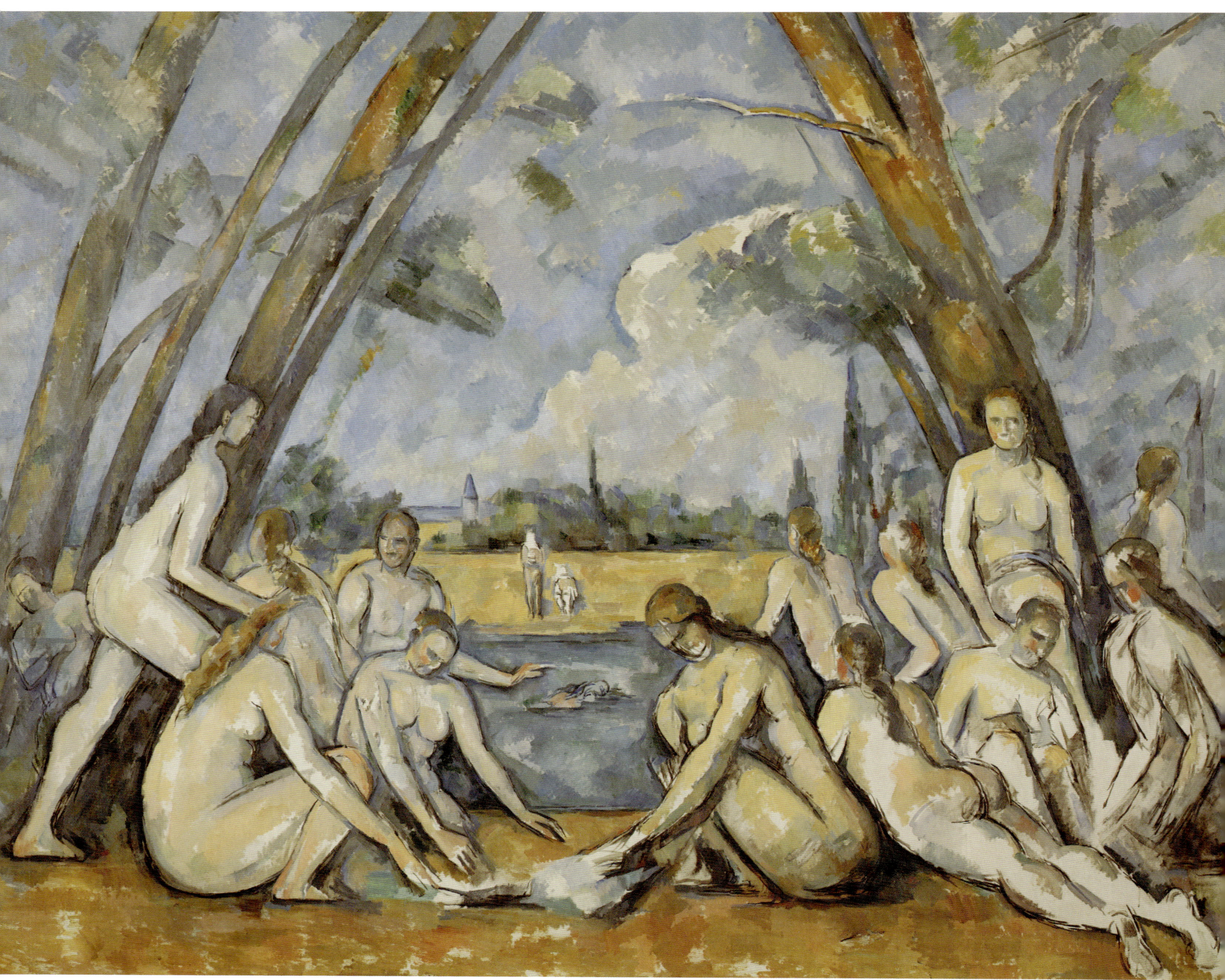

Above : *The Large Bathers*, 1900–06, Paul Cézanne (1839–1906)

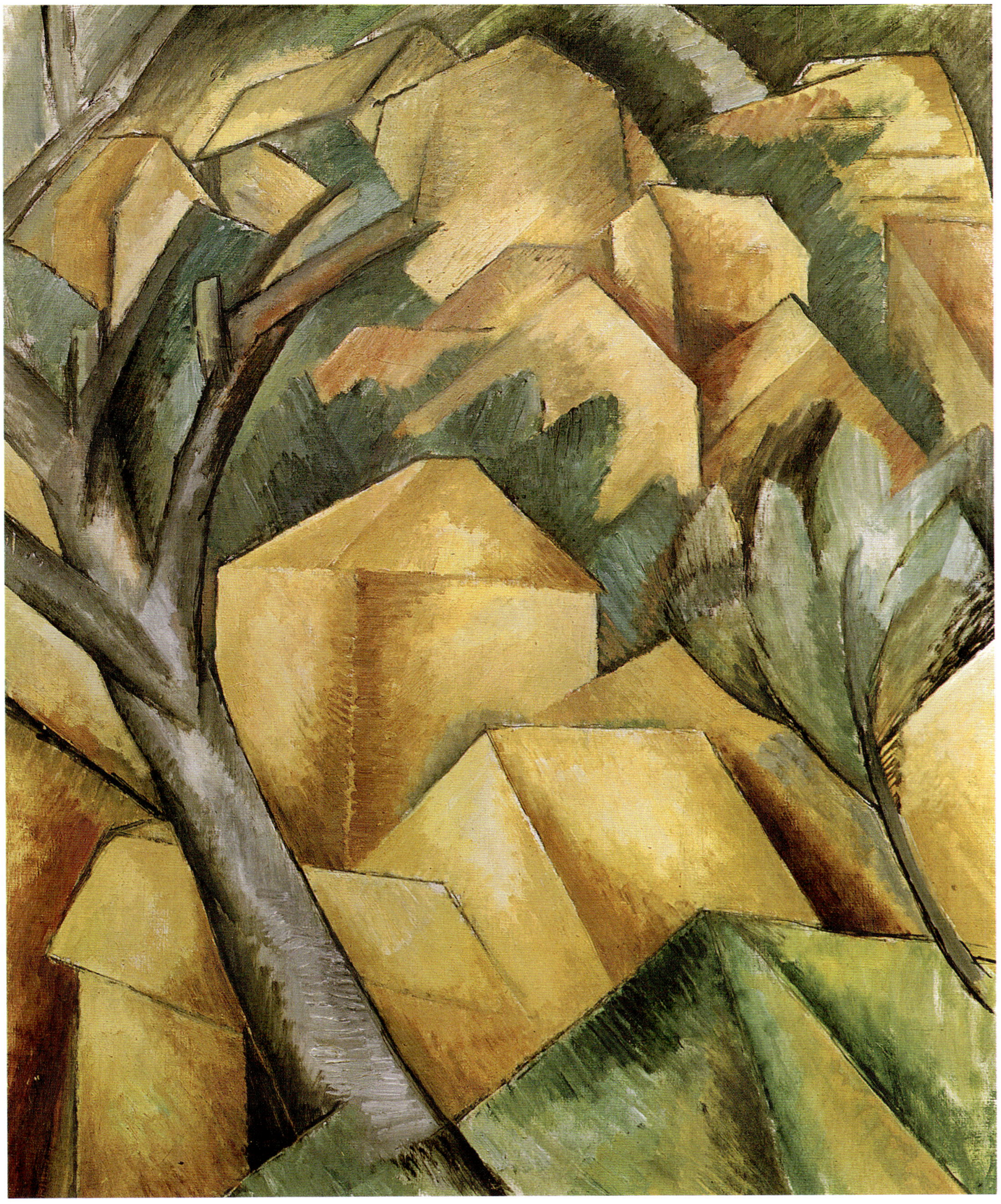

Above : *Houses at L'Estaque*, 1908, Georges Braque (1882–1963)

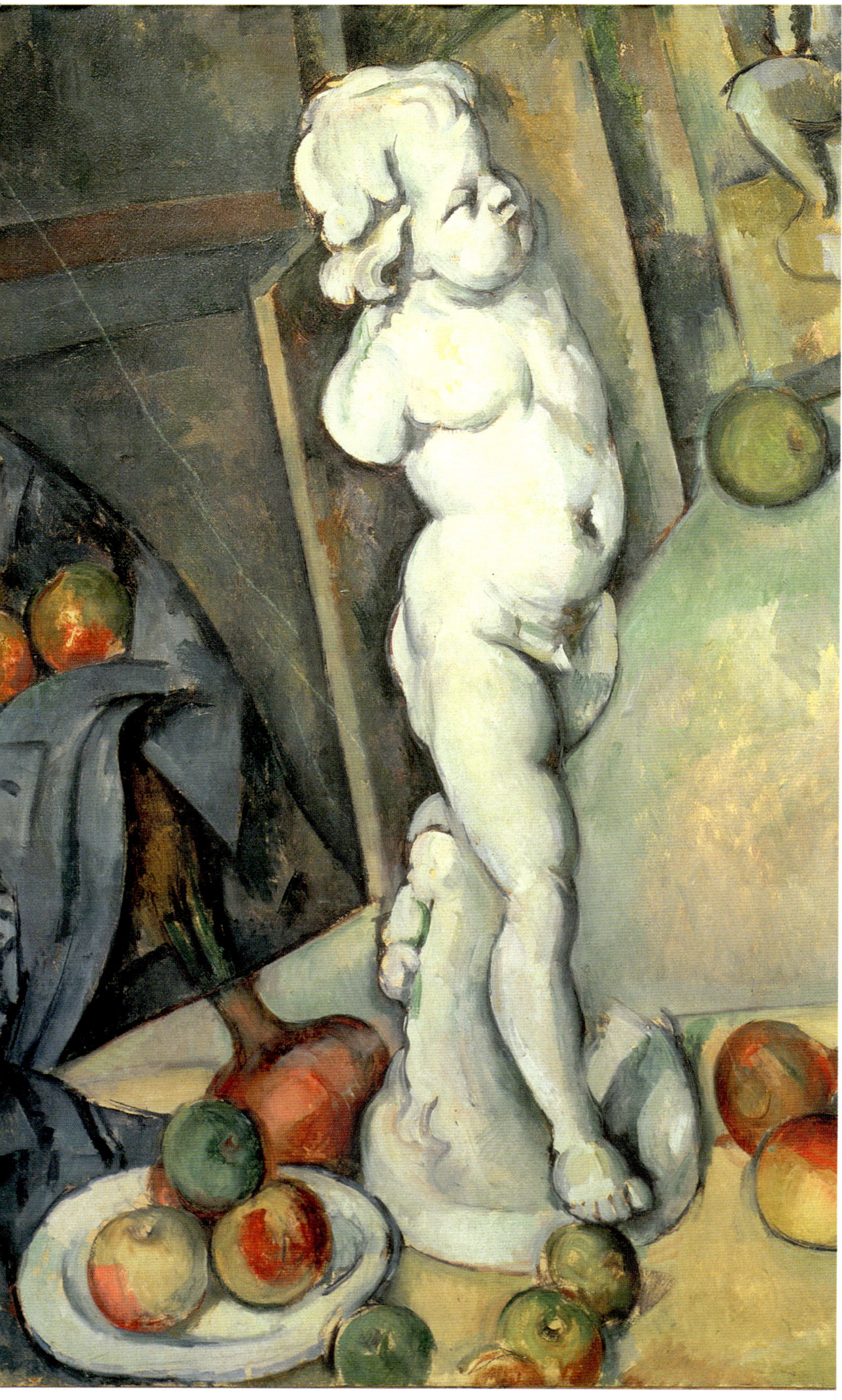

Above : *Still Life with Cherub*, 1895, Paul Cézanne (1839–1906)

Cézanne's Influence on Cubism

Cézanne's influence on subsequent generations of artists cannot be overstated. Starting in 1895, Cézanne terminated his self-imposed exile in Provence (he had exhibited only infrequently after his contributions to the 1874 and 1877 Impressionist exhibitions were roundly mocked) and consented to exhibitions of his works being staged by his dealer, Ambrose Vollard (1866–1939). Among those excited by Cézanne's achievements were Picasso and Braque. In 1908, Braque painted a scene of *Houses at L'Estaque* (1908, *see* page 143) that was a direct response to Cézanne. Braque applied the older artist's method of geometricized abstraction to an even greater degree, as if taking Cézanne's 1904 advice to Émile Bernard to 'deal with nature by means of the cylinder, the sphere and the cone' entirely at face value.

Cézanne's still lifes, such as *Still Life with Cherub* (1895, *see* left), would also prove to be a revelation. If we compare it with Picasso's *Still Life with a Bottle of Rum* (1911) or even the slightly later *Still Life* of 1912 (*see* right), we see the same Cézannesque geometrical schematization of forms that underpinned Braque's proto-Cubist landscape. Cézanne's practice of including multiple viewpoints has again been applied and exaggerated. Cézanne's still lifes relate to the extended moment of subjective perception, the real way in which we see, rather than the 'knowledge' of how an object 'ought to look'. It is precisely this sense of 'lived perspective' that Picasso's Analytical Cubism seeks to convey, with its fragmented appearance of many viewpoints and flattened, overlapping planes. Picasso well understood that Cézanne had revealed the arbitrary relationship between the painted mark and the object it represented. Thus, in reconstructing the objects before him, Picasso used the painted mark to form a language that would communicate without imitating. Picasso is said to have called Cézanne the 'father of us all': whether or not he actually vocalized it, it was certainly true.

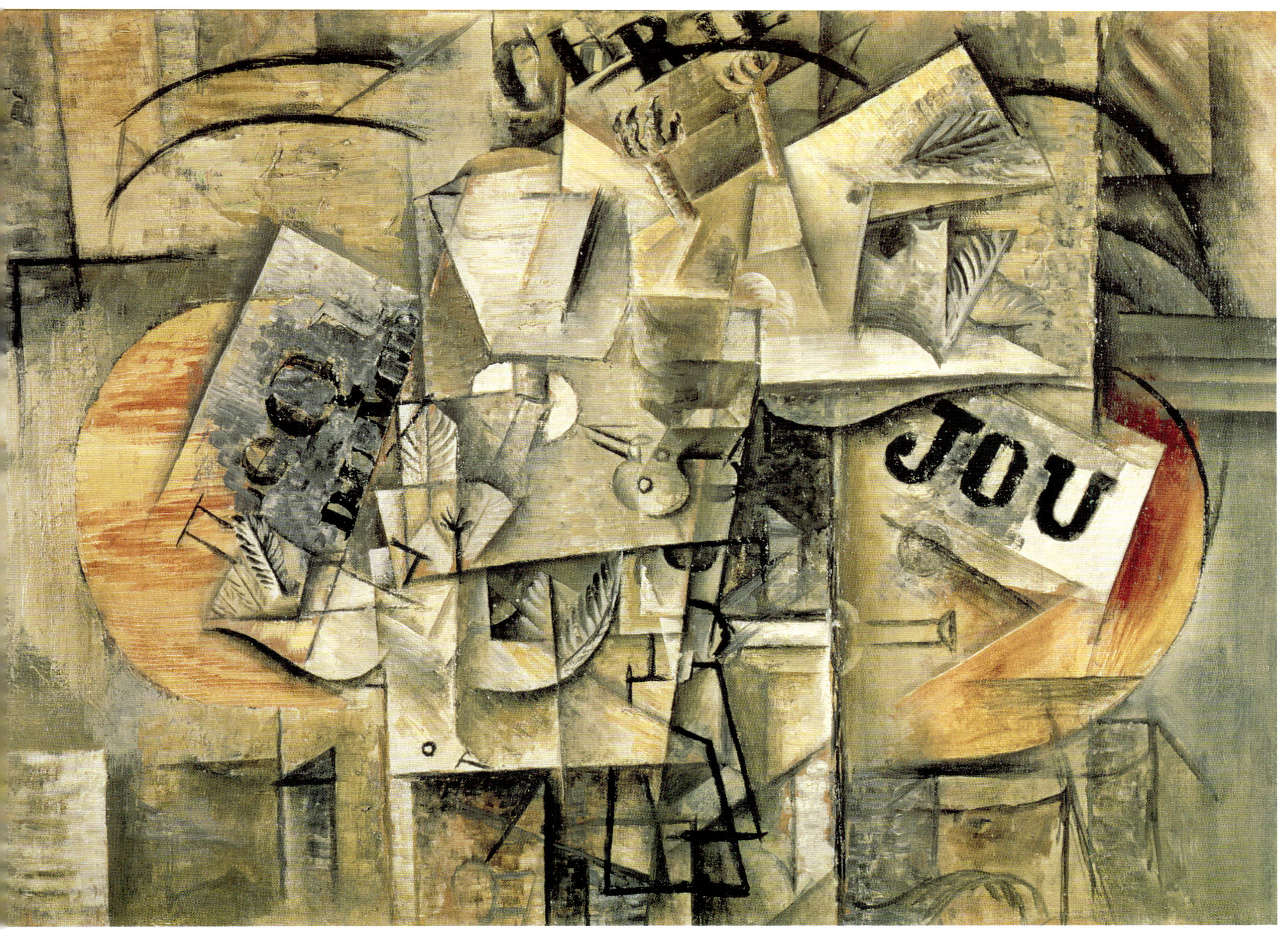

Above : *Still Life*, 1912, Pablo Picasso (1881–1973)

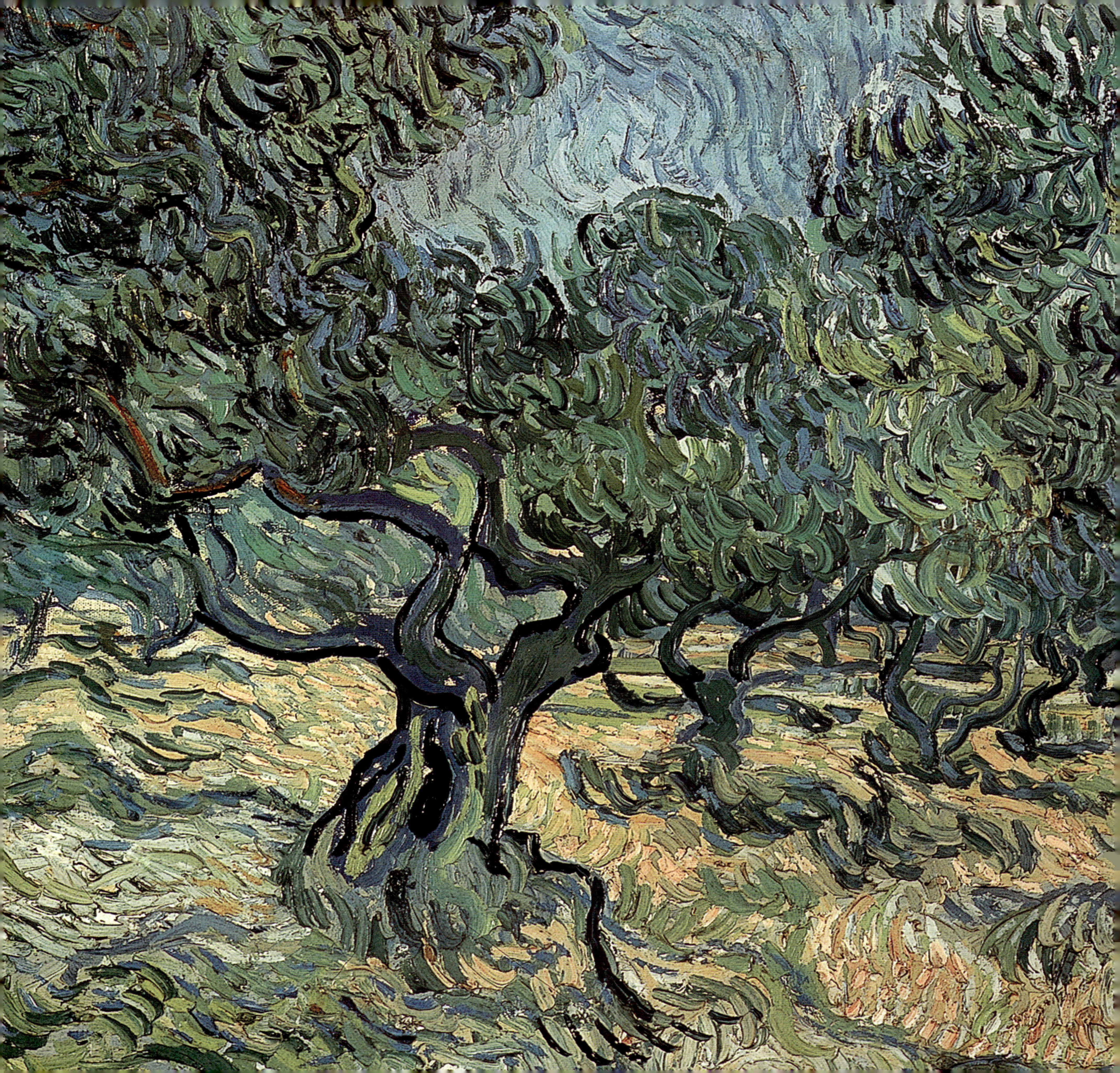

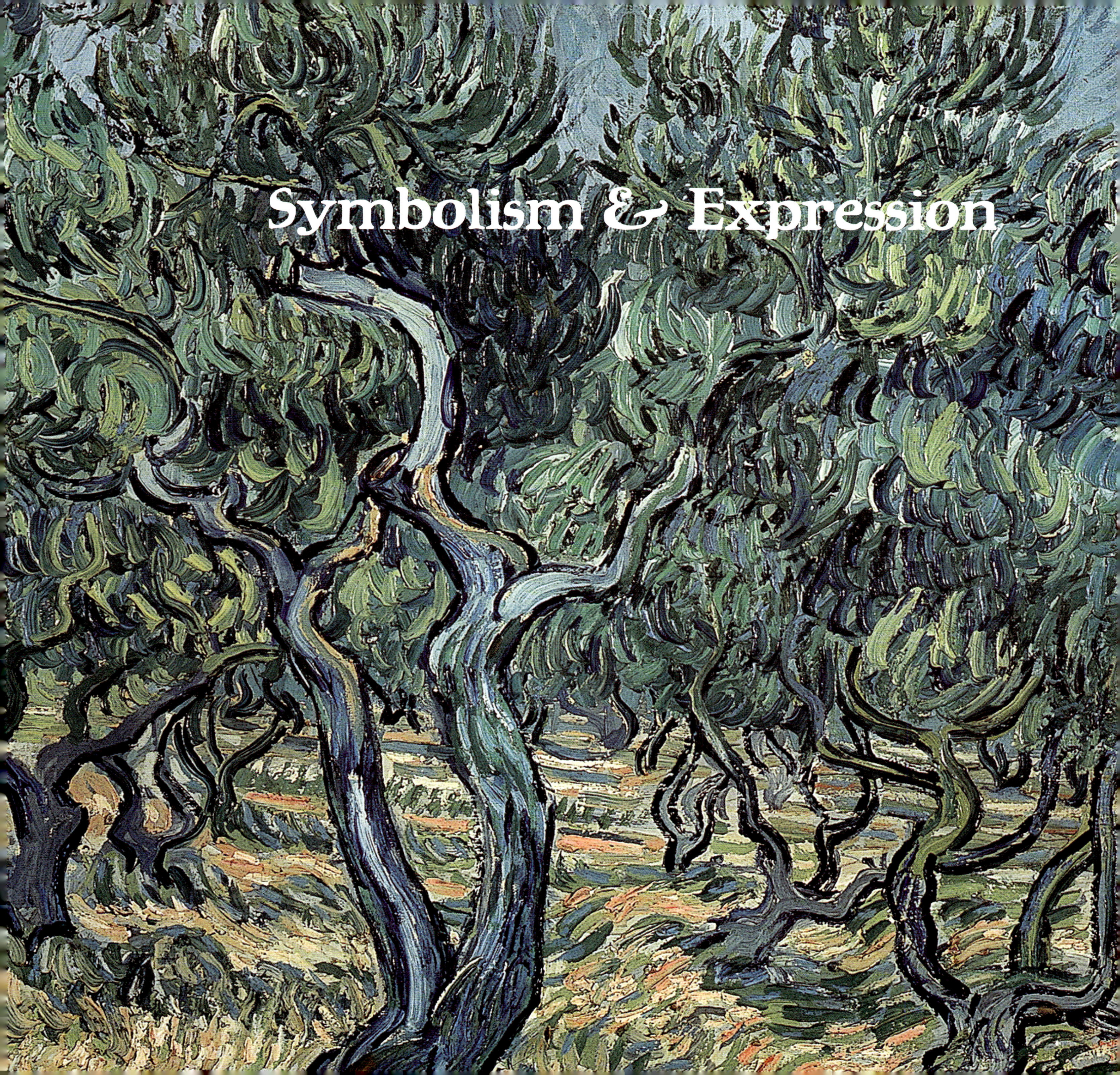
Symbolism & Expression

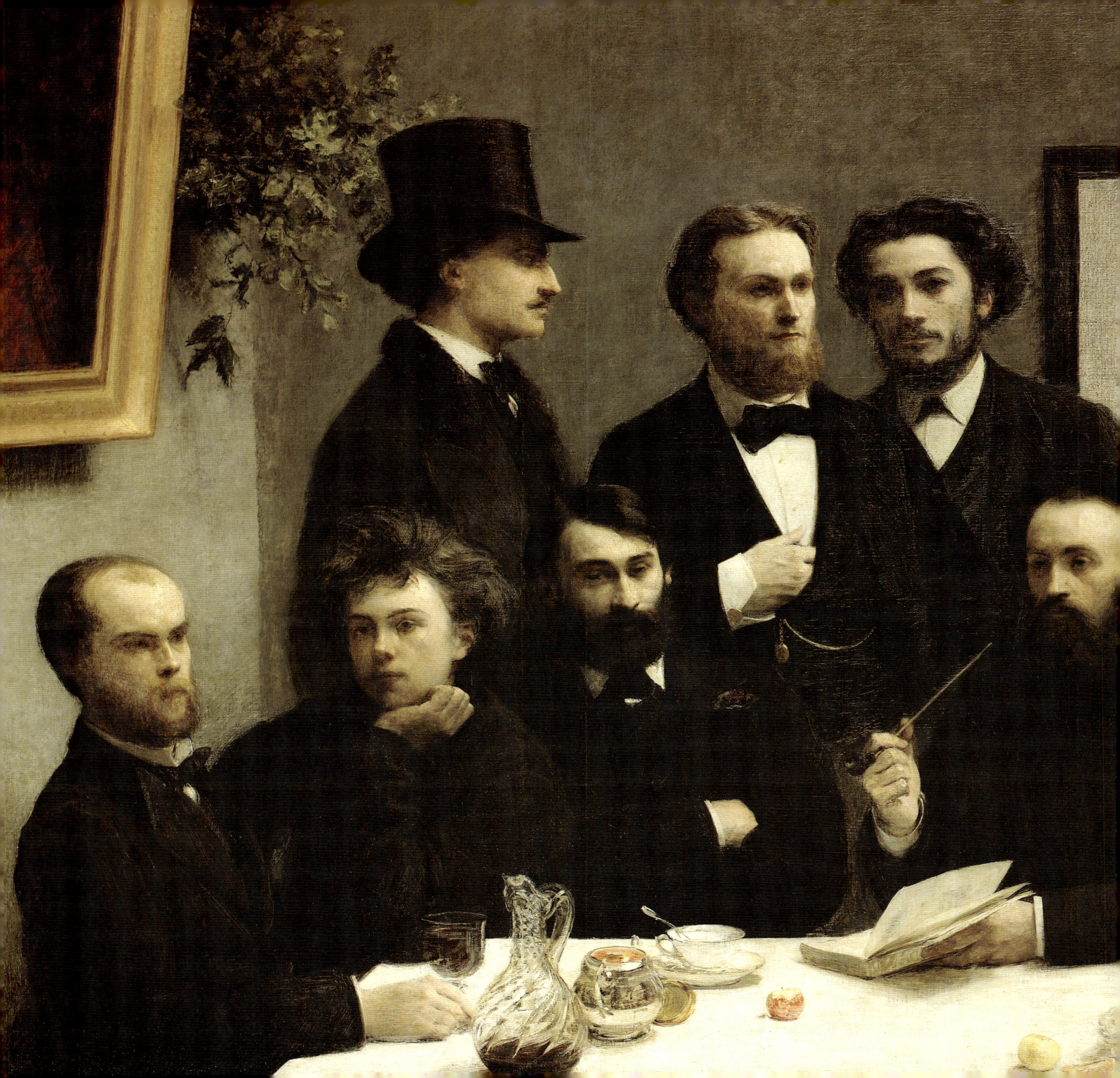

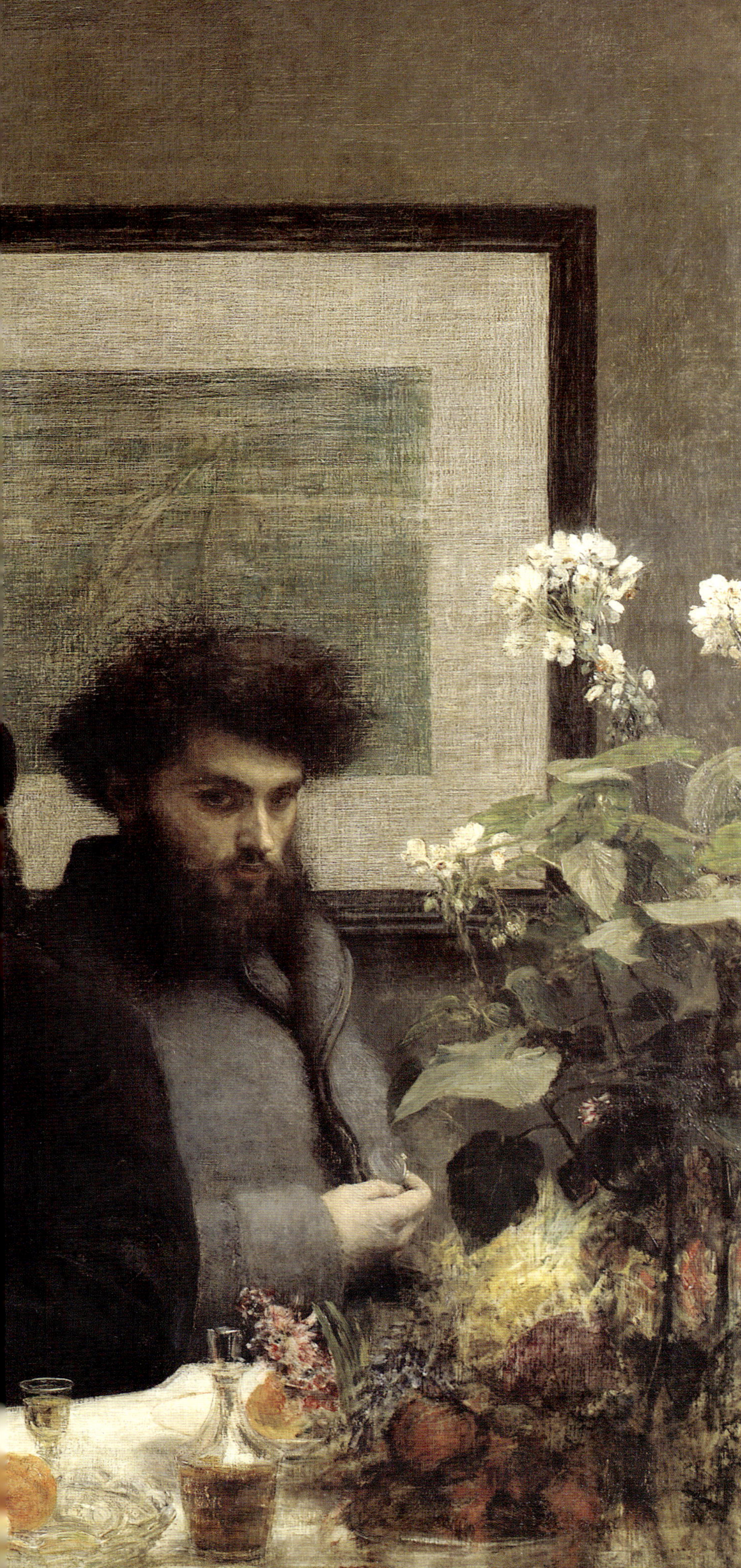

Internal Worlds

FOR SOME ARTISTS at this time, the attraction of painting was not that it offered a way to bring order to nature, but rather that it was a vehicle for representing a world beyond words. Rather than reinterpret their physical environs, some Post-Impressionist painters gave vent to their tumultuous inner minds or sought to realize a vision of the mystical, metaphysical plane of reality that existed beyond the concrete world of material things.

La Renaissance littéraire et artistique

Henri Fantin-Latour's *By the Table* (1872, *see* left) depicts, clustered into a corner of an unassuming interior, a group of men finishing a meal together. One of them smokes a long-stemmed pipe and stares into the middle distance, as if lost in a reverie contemplating the meaning of the book before him. This gesture is significant, not least because the psychological interiority it connotes seems to be shared by other members of the group, only three of whom acknowledge our presence as viewers. Having, in his 1870 *A Studio in the Batignolles Quarter* (*see* page 12), depicted his contemporary painters (including Manet, Renoir, Monet and Bazille), in this painting, Fantin-Latour has turned his attention to poets. On the far left, Paul Verlaine (1844–96) sits beside Arthur Rimbaud, the most important members in the group that also includes Émile Blémont (1839–1927), Pierre Elzéar (1849–1916), Jean Aicard (1848–1921), Léon Valade (1841–83), Ernest d'Hervilly (1838–1911) and Camille Pelletan (1846–1915).

What united these men was their shared interest in *La Renaissance littéraire et artistique*, a poetry review that ran from April 1872 until May 1874, and

Left : *By the Table*, 1872, Henri Fantin-Latour (1836–1904)

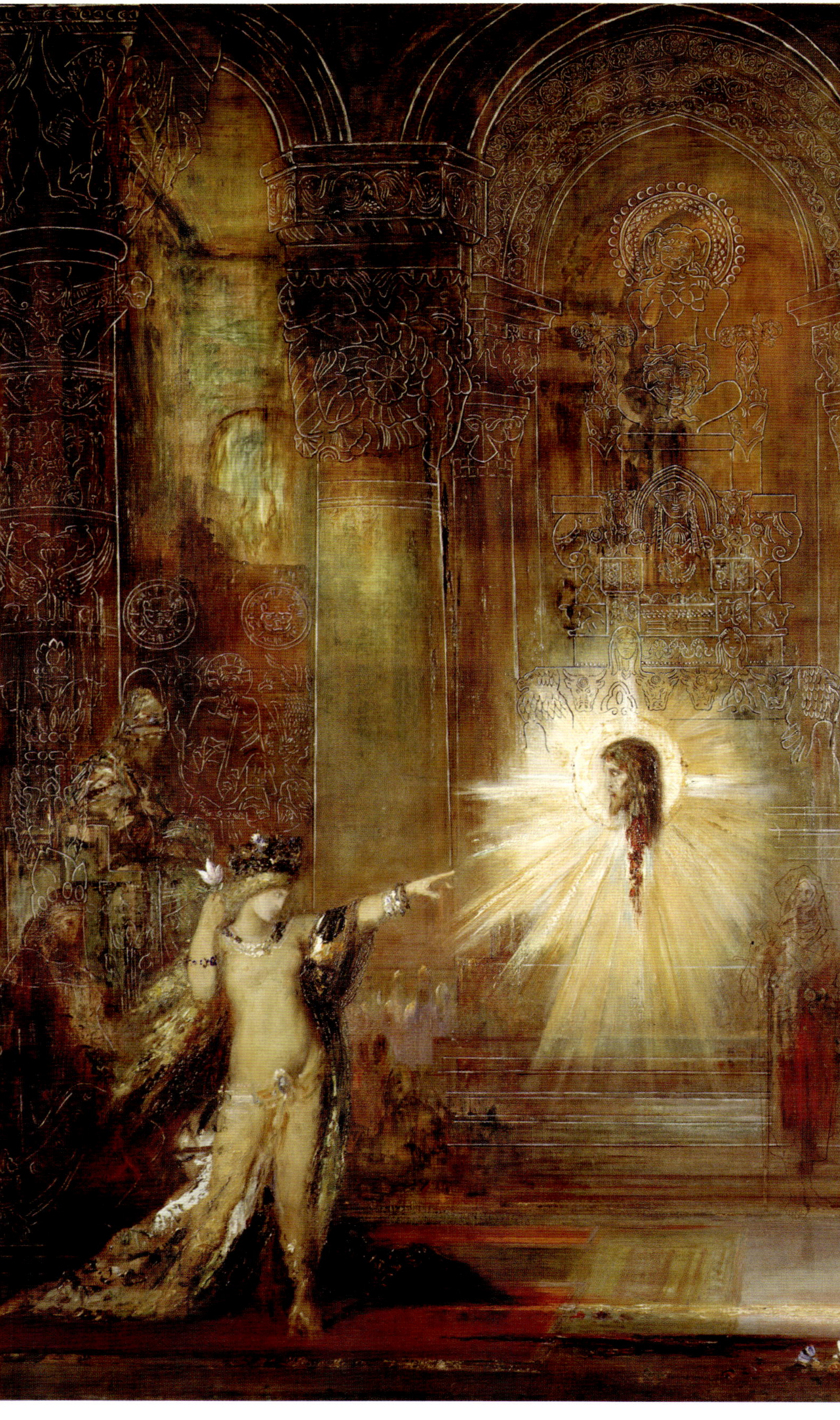

published works by, among others, Verlaine, Stéphane Mallarmé (1842–98) and Walt Whitman (1819–92); Blémont was its chief editor. *La Renaissance littéraire et artistique* was one of a number of publications that advocated a style of poetry known as Parnassianism. Influenced by a dogma of *l'art pour l'art* (art for art's sake), Parnassian poets valued a lyrical and impersonal form and the use of classical subjects, instead of the subjective, emotional vigour and political radicalism of the Romantic poets that had come before.

Two years after Fantin-Latour painted his portrait, Verlaine published a manifesto-cum-poem entitled *L'art poétique*, in which he argued for a poetry of musicality and ambiguity. Mallarmé, not pictured but associated with the group, similarly favoured ambiguity, proposing that poetry should not describe but rather slowly evoke an ideal world, that is, the 'pure concept, unlinked to any related or material form'. Rimbaud's *Une Saison en Enfer* (1873), a diary-like prose poem of nine parts, was a deliberately frustrating investigation of the limits of self and spirituality in which the author abstracted language to the point of its fragmentation. Baudelaire's infamous collection of poems, *Les Fleurs du Mal* (1857), was a touchstone for this generation of poets. In a poem entitled 'Correspondances', Baudelaire described how '[i]n Nature's temple, living pillars rise, Speaking sometimes in words of abstruse sense; Man walks through forests of symbols, dark and dense, Which gaze at him with fond familiar eyes'. Verlaine, Mallarmé, Rimbaud and others would spend the last decades of the nineteenth century wandering though Baudelaire's forest of symbols, sharing with their readers words of abstruse sense that would evoke the reality beyond appearances. In 1886, Jean Moréas (1856–1910) published the *Symbolist Manifesto*, which tied together these developments under a single banner: Symbolism.

Moreau

Gustave Moreau's (1826–98) *The Apparition* (1874–76, *see* left) offers an early example of how artists put into practice these literary ideas. The painting

Above : *The Apparition*, 1876, Gustave Moreau (1826–98)

Right : *Young Girls on the Edge of the Sea*, 1879, Pierre Puvis de Chavannes (1824–98)

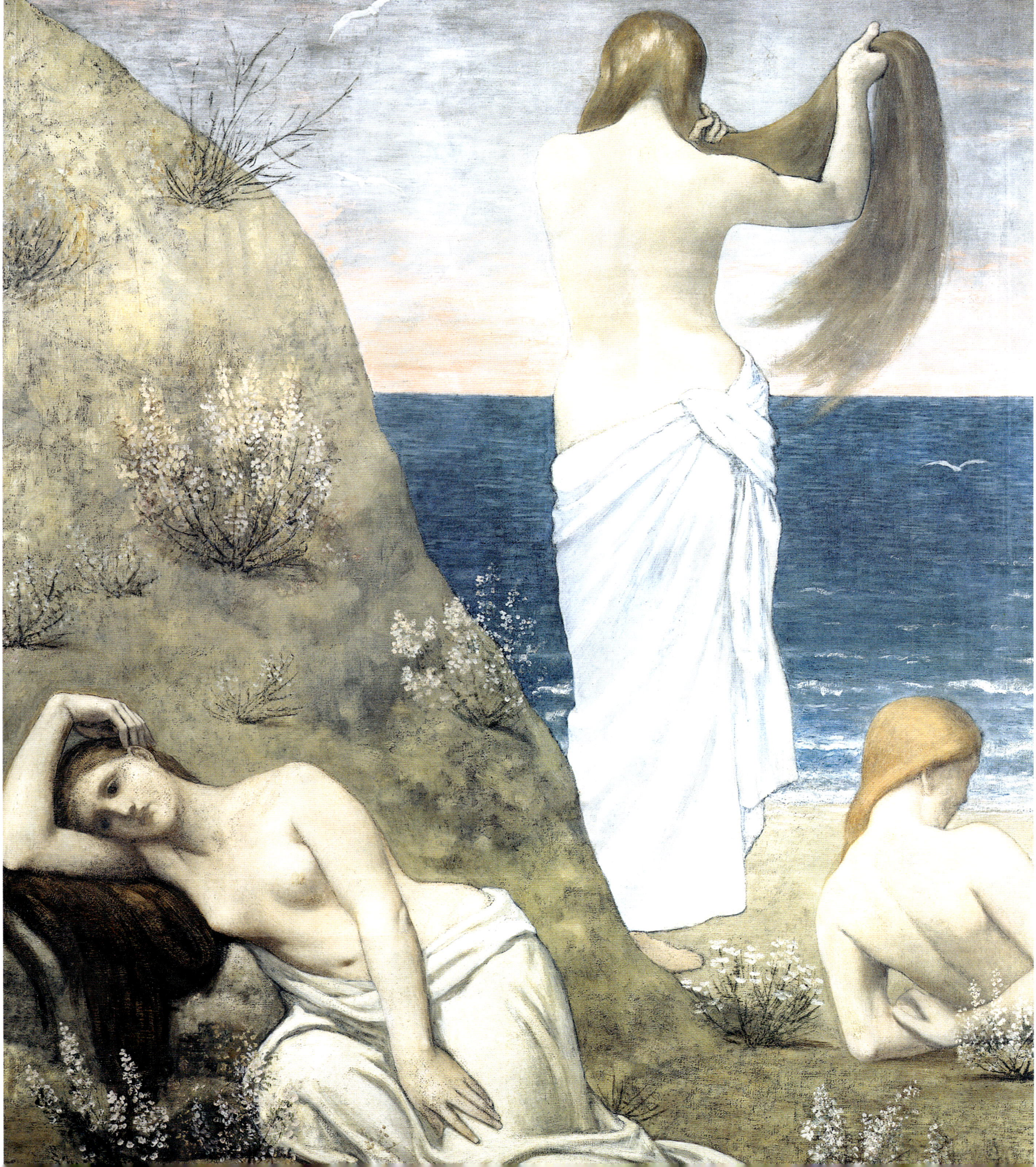

illustrates the dance of Salomé before King Herod Antipas who, thus enthralled, consents to her desire to be presented St John the Baptist's severed head on a charger. However, Moreau has deliberately left it ambiguous as to precisely which moment in the biblical narrative we see.

Do we witness Salomé's enchanting dance and the materialization of her desire; or are we at the moment of remorse, after the murder has been committed, with the physical head revealing its spiritual essence? In depicting a scene of Christian mythology, Moreau nevertheless created a mystical and evocative Oriental setting by combining elements from Japanese prints and Benvenuto Cellini's (1500–71) bronze *Medusa* (1545) – for the haloed head of St John – and – for the palace's decoration – from the Alhambra in Granada. Not only were the themes of exoticism, sexual desire, death and regret deeply stirring, but Moreau's ambiguous collision of the tangible and the intangible was profoundly influential.

Symbolist ideas were especially attractive and influential for painters dissatisfied with Impressionism's obsessive focus on appearances. For Gauguin, Sérusier and the rest of the Nabis – Maurice Denis, Pierre Bonnard, Paul Ranson, Ker-Xavier Roussel, Henri-Gabriel Ibels and Édouard Vuillard – Symbolist poetry inspired an esoteric brand of Post-Impressionism saturated with complex signs, hidden meanings and mystical resonance.

Puvis de Chavannes

Another artist to whom later painters would look admiringly was Pierre Puvis de Chavannes. Puvis produced two distinct kinds of work: grand public murals of the kind that inspired Seurat, which celebrated the values of bourgeois France – for example *Inter artes et naturam* (*Between Art and Nature*) (1888–90) – and smaller-scale easel paintings, which depicted psychologically challenging, ambiguous and disturbing scenes. Like Moreau, in each mode, Puvis found the

Right : *Christ in the Garden of Olives*, 1889, Paul Gauguin (1848–1903)

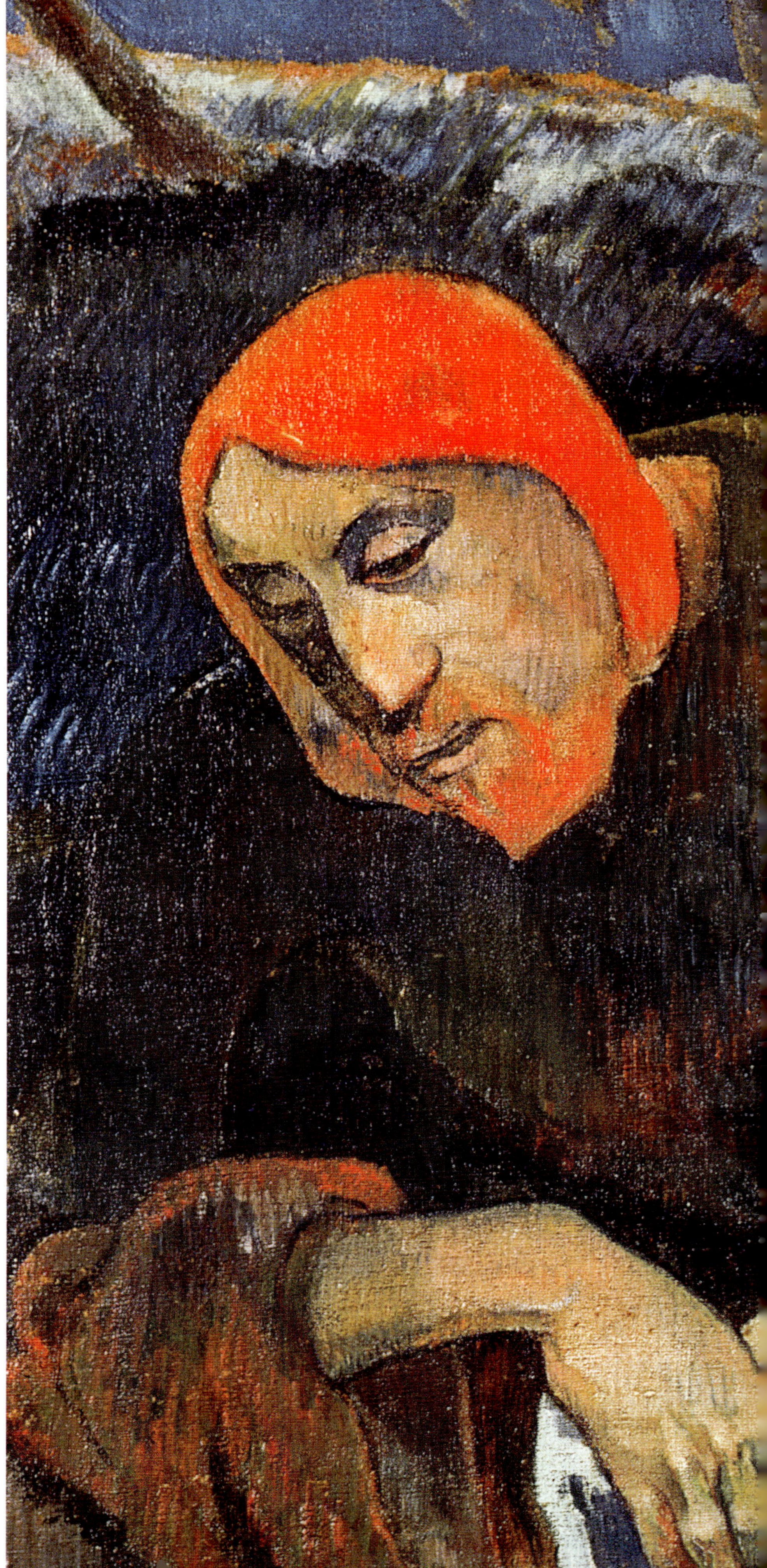

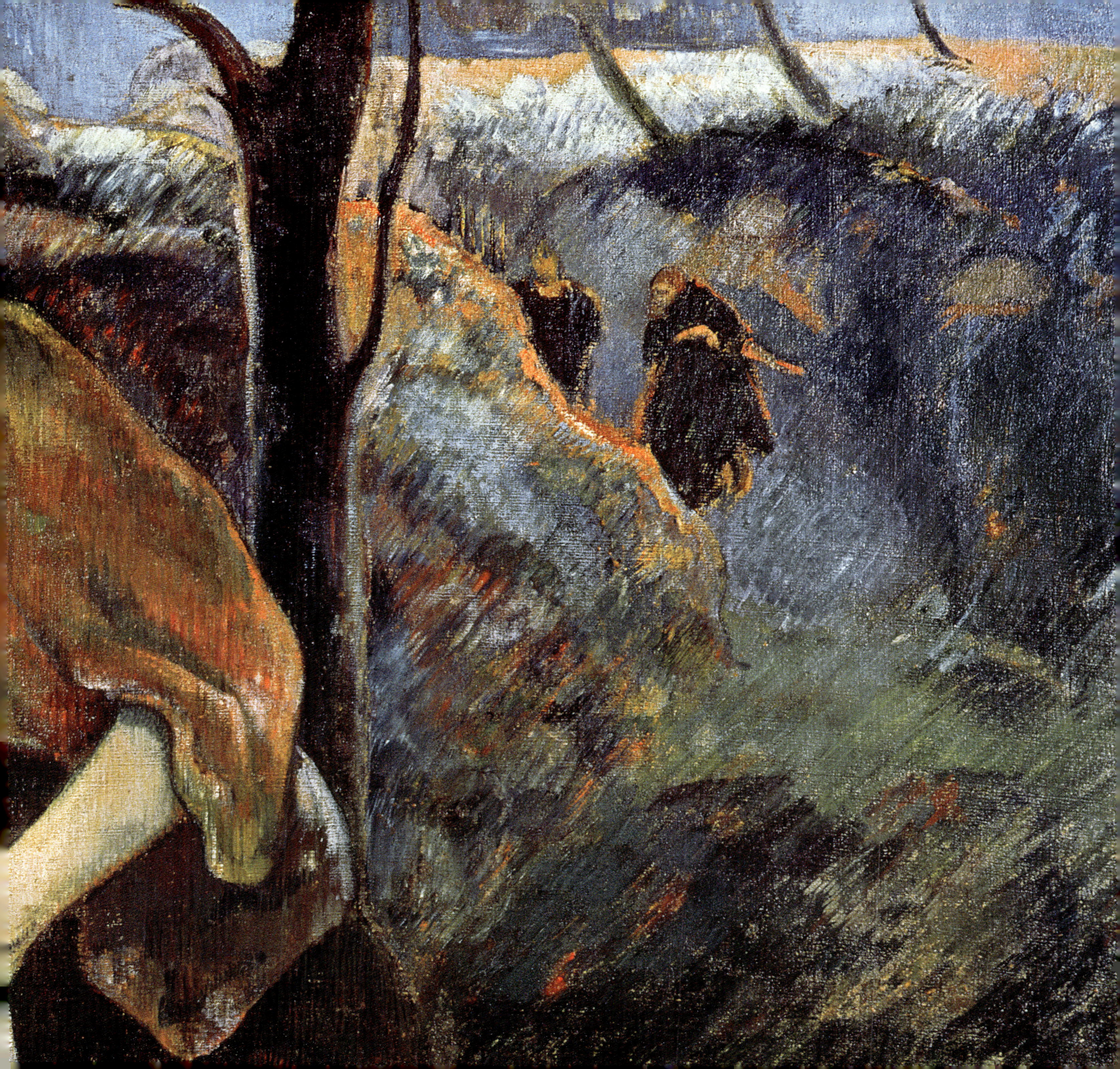

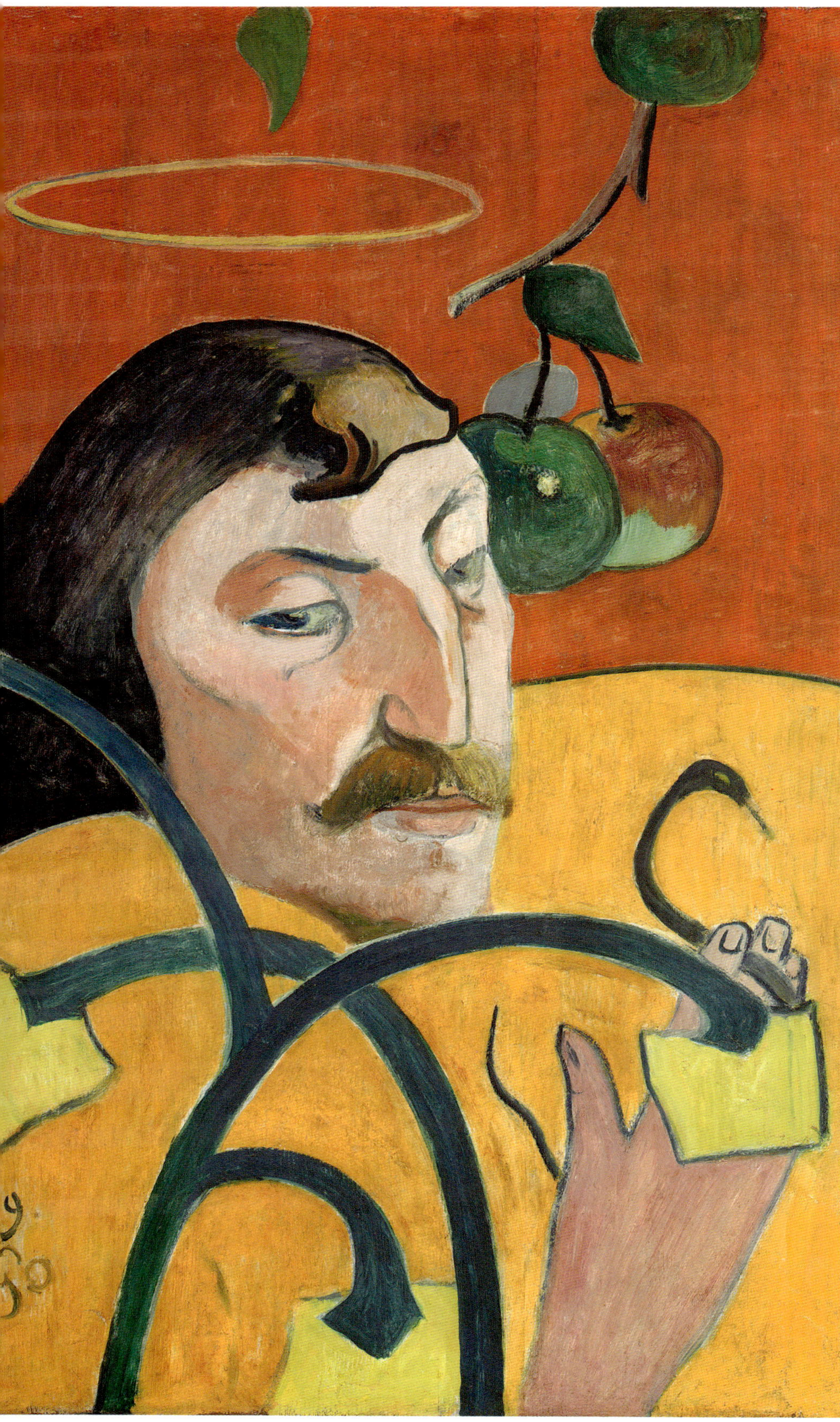

Above : *Self-Portrait*, 1889, Paul Gauguin (1848–1903)

female body a convenient carrier for meaning, be it harmony with nature or, as in *Young Girls on the Edge of the Sea* (1879, *see page 151*), wistful longing. Puvis's paintings and murals shared a neutral palette, matte texture, flattened and schematized forms, rhythmic compositions and economy of line. It was in turning his mainstream decorative idiom (suitable for didactic murals) towards the realm of the psychological that Puvis was most inspirational.

Symbolism in Painting

In March 1891, the art critic and Symbolist poet Albert Aurier (1865–92) published an essay entitled 'Symbolism in Painting: Paul Gauguin'. In this landmark essay, Aurier effectively summarized the hopes and ambitions of the Symbolist generation of painters. After castigating Impressionism for capturing appearances and nothing more, Aurier went on,

The normal and final goal of painting, as of all the arts, cannot be a direct presentation of objects. Its ultimate aim is to express Ideas by translating them into a special language. To the eyes of the artist objects are meaningless as objects. They can only appear to him as signs…. The artist will … have the right … to exaggerate, to accentuate, to deform those directly significant elements of form, line, colour, not only according to his individual vision, but also to make any deformations needed to express the Idea.

Thus to sum up, the work of art, as I have chosen to evoke it logically will be:

1. *Ideological, because its sole ideal is the expression of the Idea.*

2. *Symbolist, because it expresses the Idea through forms.*

3. *Synthetic, because it presents these forms, these signs in such a way that they can be generally understood.*

4. *Subjective, because the object presented is considered not merely as an object, but as the sign of an idea suggested by the subject.*

5. *(And therefore) Decorative, since truly decorative painting as conceived*

Right : *The Buddha*, 1906–07, Odilon Redon (1840–1916)

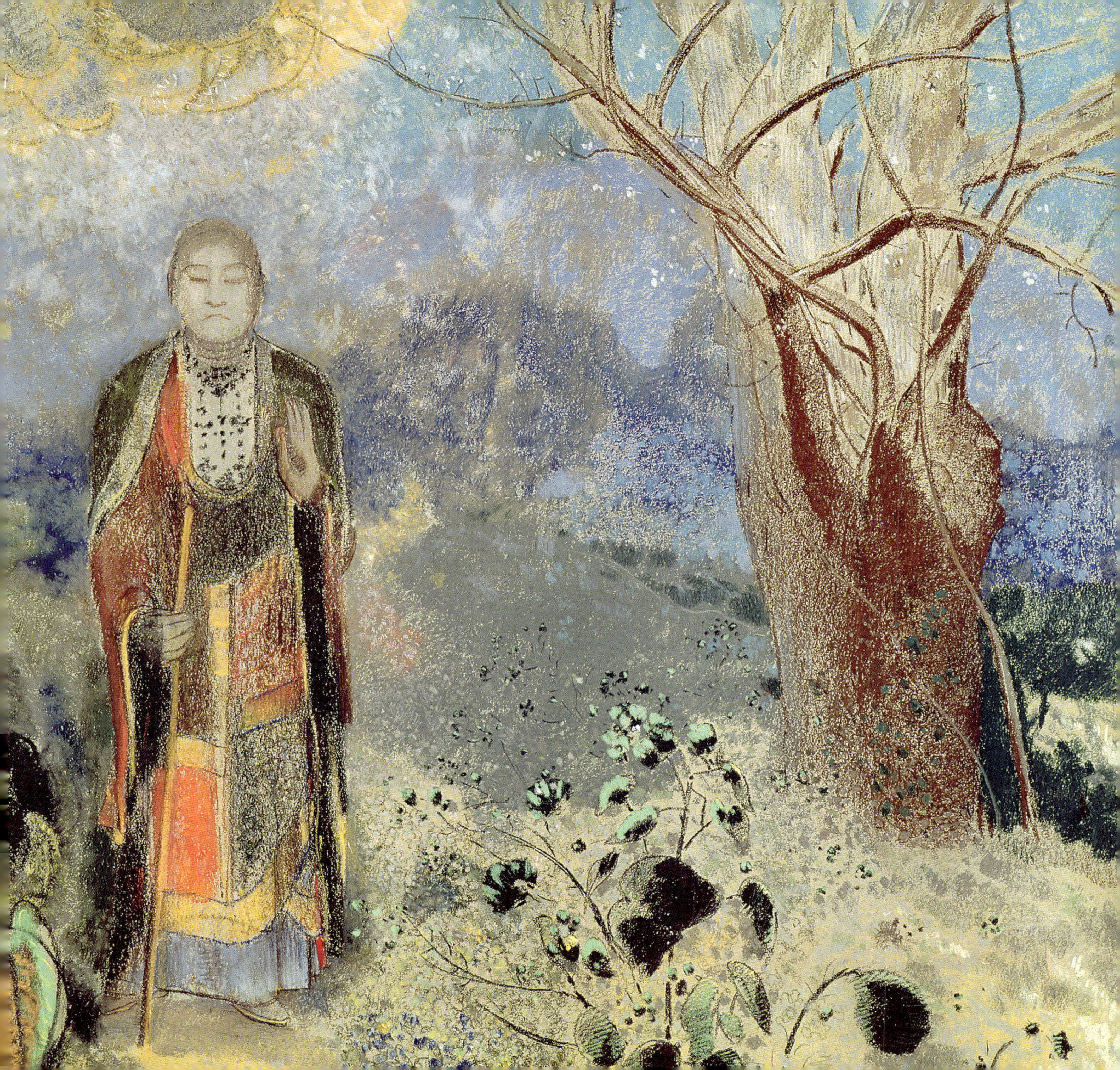

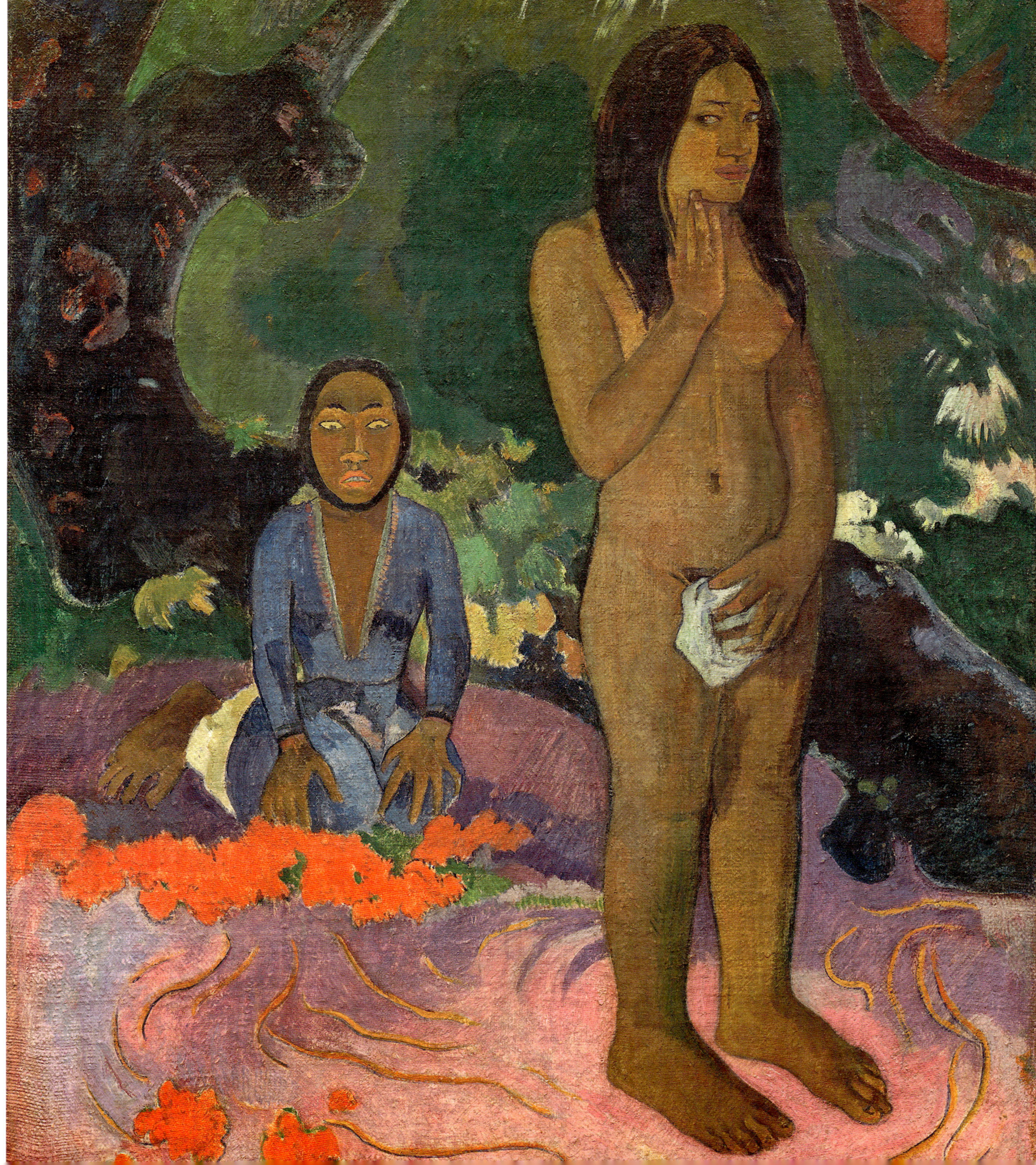

*by the Egyptians and probably by the Greeks and the primitives, is
nothing but a manifestation of art which is at the same time subjective
and synthetic.*

As we have seen, it was the encounter with Émile Bernard in 1888 that turned Gauguin's art decidedly towards Symbolism. Starting with *Vision of the Sermon* (1888) and developing in works such as *Yellow Christ* (1889) and *Green Christ* (1889), Gauguin came to intertwine his anti-naturalistic, decorative abstraction with a symbolism drawn from Christian mythology. It was not just his style that Gauguin sought to assimilate, but also his identity: in *Christ in the Garden of Olives* (1889, *see* page 153), Gauguin transposes his own features on to those of Christ. Of this work, Gauguin explained: 'I have painted my own portrait … but it also represents the crushing of an ideal, and a pain that is both divine and human. Jesus is totally abandoned; his disciples are leaving him, in a setting as sad as his soul.' As his identification with the betrayed Christ suggests, Gauguin was at this time becoming increasingly dissatisfied with life in France.

Gauguin's first move was from Pont-Aven to the village of Le Pouldu, where he remained over the winter of 1889 and 1890. One of the works he produced during this time, *Self-Portrait* (1889, *see* page 154), continued to collapse Gauguin's idea of himself on to Christian symbols of mankind persecuted: Gauguin's disembodied right hand fondles the serpent of temptation; the forbidden fruit float in a field of unmodulated red pigment. Of

his nimbused head, Gauguin wrote that it was a 'symbol of the contemporary Impressionist painter', possessing 'the face of an outlaw … with an inner nobility and gentleness', and presenting 'a portrait of all wretched victims of society'. Gauguin's morose restlessness had thus not been ameliorated by the move to Le Pouldu; by December 1889, he was fantasizing about distant shores, writing to Bernard that '[t]he West is now in a state of decay'.

Encouraged by fellow Symbolist painter, Odilon Redon (1840–1916) and his Réunionese wife Ari, Gauguin soon settled on a move to Madagascar, located, like Réunion, in the Indian Ocean and, at that moment, in the process of succumbing to French colonial rule. Like Gauguin, Redon's work drew from a vague Oriental mysticism, as in *The Buddha* (1906–07, *see* page 155), and sought to evoke metaphysical ideas though abstruse and arresting symbols, as in *The Eye Like a Strange Balloon Mounts Toward Infinity* (1882, *see* left). When Gustave Kahn wrote that 'the essential aim of our art is to objectify the subjective (the externalization of the Idea) instead of subjectifying the objective (nature seen through the eyes of a temperament)', his formula applied to Redon as much as to Gauguin, each of whom explicitly rejected Zola's Naturalist credo that art is 'a corner of creation seen through a temperament'.

Seeking a tropical paradise far away from the restrictive mores of Western civilization, where the women were, 'so to speak, obligatory' (as Gauguin put it, relishing a steady supply of models and sexual partners), Gauguin

Left : *Parau na te Varua ino (Words of the Devil)*, 1892, Paul Gauguin (1848–1903)

Above : *The Eye Like a Strange Balloon Mounts Toward Infinity*, 1882, Odilon Redon (1840–1916)

nevertheless came to believe that 'Madagascar is still too close to the civilized world: I am going to Tahiti and I hope to finish my life there.'

To Tahiti

Almost immediately upon his return to Paris from Le Pouldu at the start of 1891, Gauguin made concrete preparations to depart for Tahiti. He arranged a lucrative fundraising auction of his works, attended a benefit evening organized for him at the Théâtre des Arts and enjoyed a farewell banquet presided over by Mallarmé. After a two-month voyage, Gauguin arrived in Tahiti in June 1891. He hoped to find there a primitive Eden, unspoiled by the hypocrisy of Western civilization, in which he could indulge his longing to 'go back, far back … as far back as the dada from my childhood, the good old wooden horse'. To venture to an innocent society was thus also to regress and go back to the innocence of childhood.

However Tahiti, already subject to French colonization and an influx of Protestant missionaries, was not the virgin soil Gauguin hoped for; finding in the capital Papeete only a parody of France, Gauguin remained itinerant, travelling around the island, fleeing European influence as much as seeking primitive purity.

It was perhaps this sense of disappointment at Tahiti's Europeanization that inspired *Parau na te Varua ino* (*Words of the Devil*) (1892, *see page 156*). The painting depicts a nude Tahitian woman standing in a dense, tropical forest, the ground of which melts into a transcendent sea of pure, vibrant colour. As the nude modestly covers her right breast and pubis – her uncomfortable expression connoting fear and scepticism – behind her, a kneeling figure grimaces with a mask-like intensity directly at the viewer. Out of the foliage emerges a highly abstracted, but nevertheless recognizable, serpent. If it is this creature that utters the 'words of the devil', then we are surely located in a tropical Eden, and our modest nude must be Eve.

Just as he had in Brittany – where he was faced by a reality that did not live up to his expectations (the Breton women, for example, no longer wore the traditional costumes in which he insisted on depicting them) – Gauguin distorted reality to match his illusion, freely adulterating his partial understanding of Tahitian folklore with Western influences (the posture of the nude references the classical *Venus Pudica*) and Christian myths. In combination, these elements suggest original sin, lost virginity and temptations of the flesh.

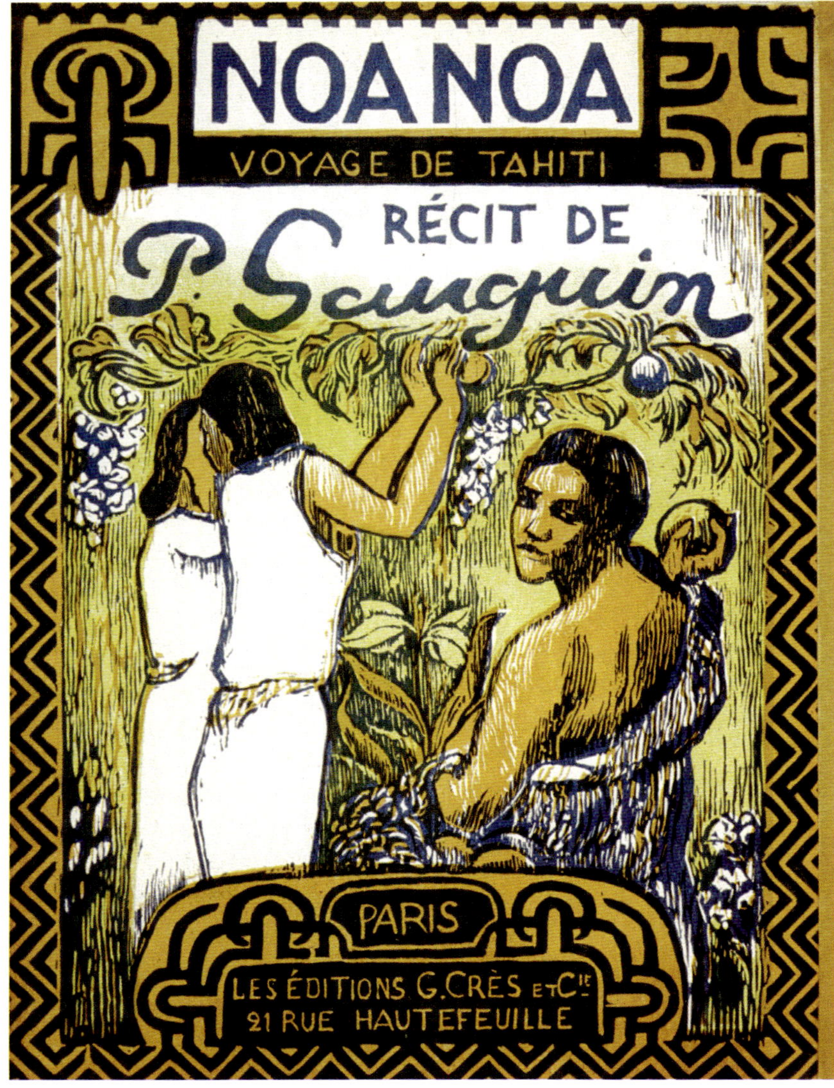

Above : Front cover of a 1924 edition of Gauguin's journal
Noa Noa, Voyage de Tahiti, first published 1893–94

Right : *Two Tahitian Women*, 1899, Paul Gauguin (1848–1903)

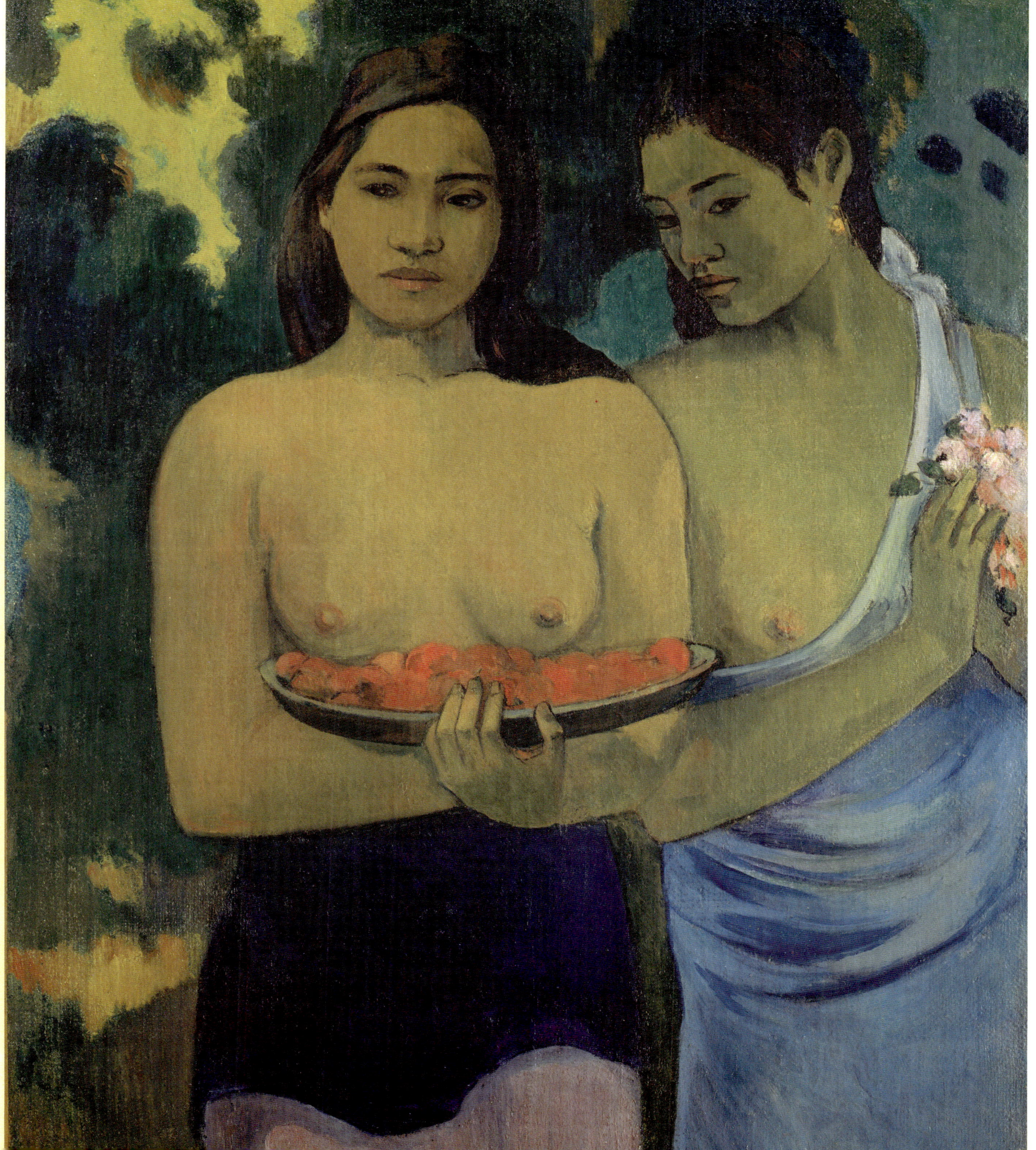

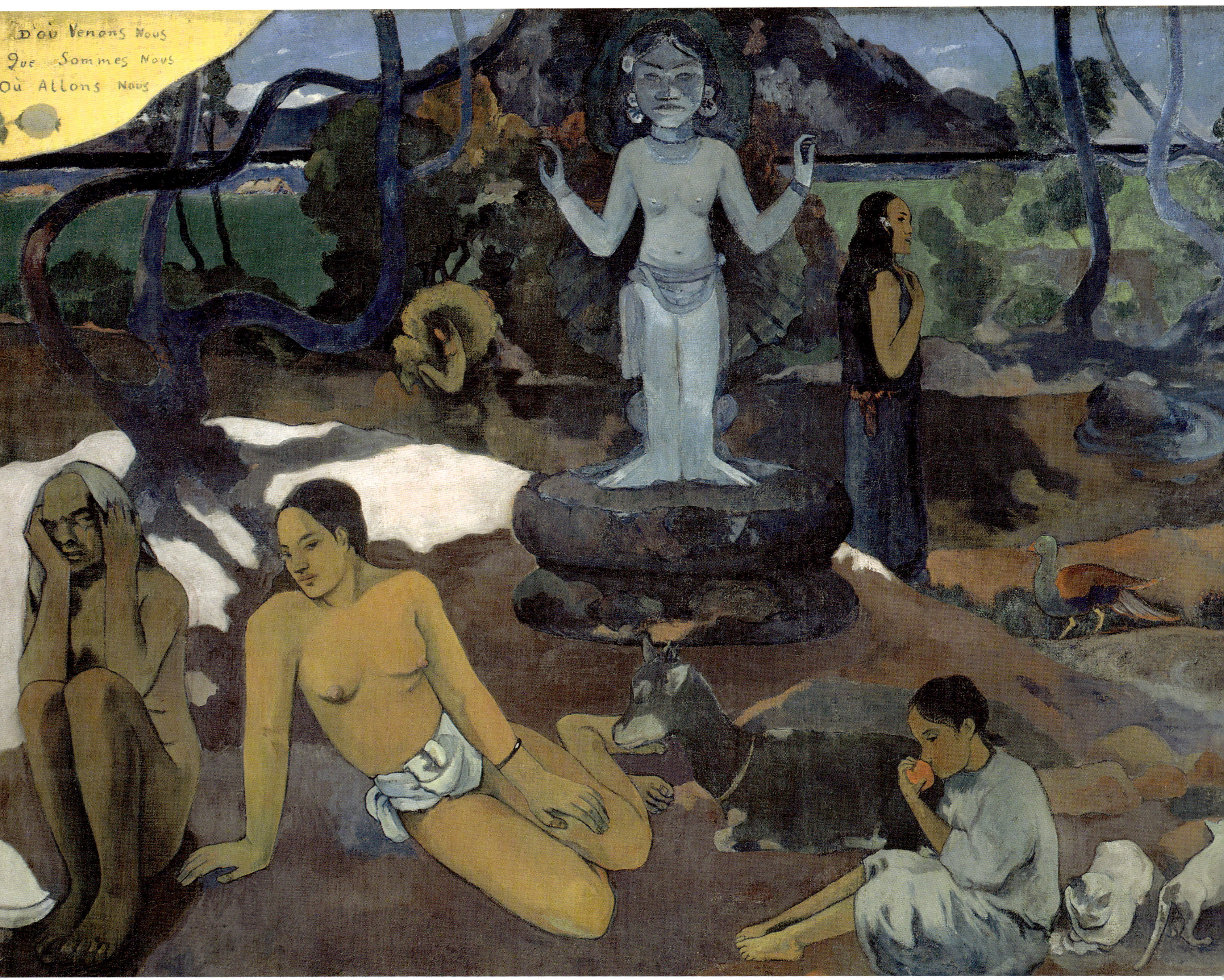

Detail above : *Where Do We Come From? What Are We? Where Are We Going?*, 1897–98, Paul Gauguin (1848–1903)

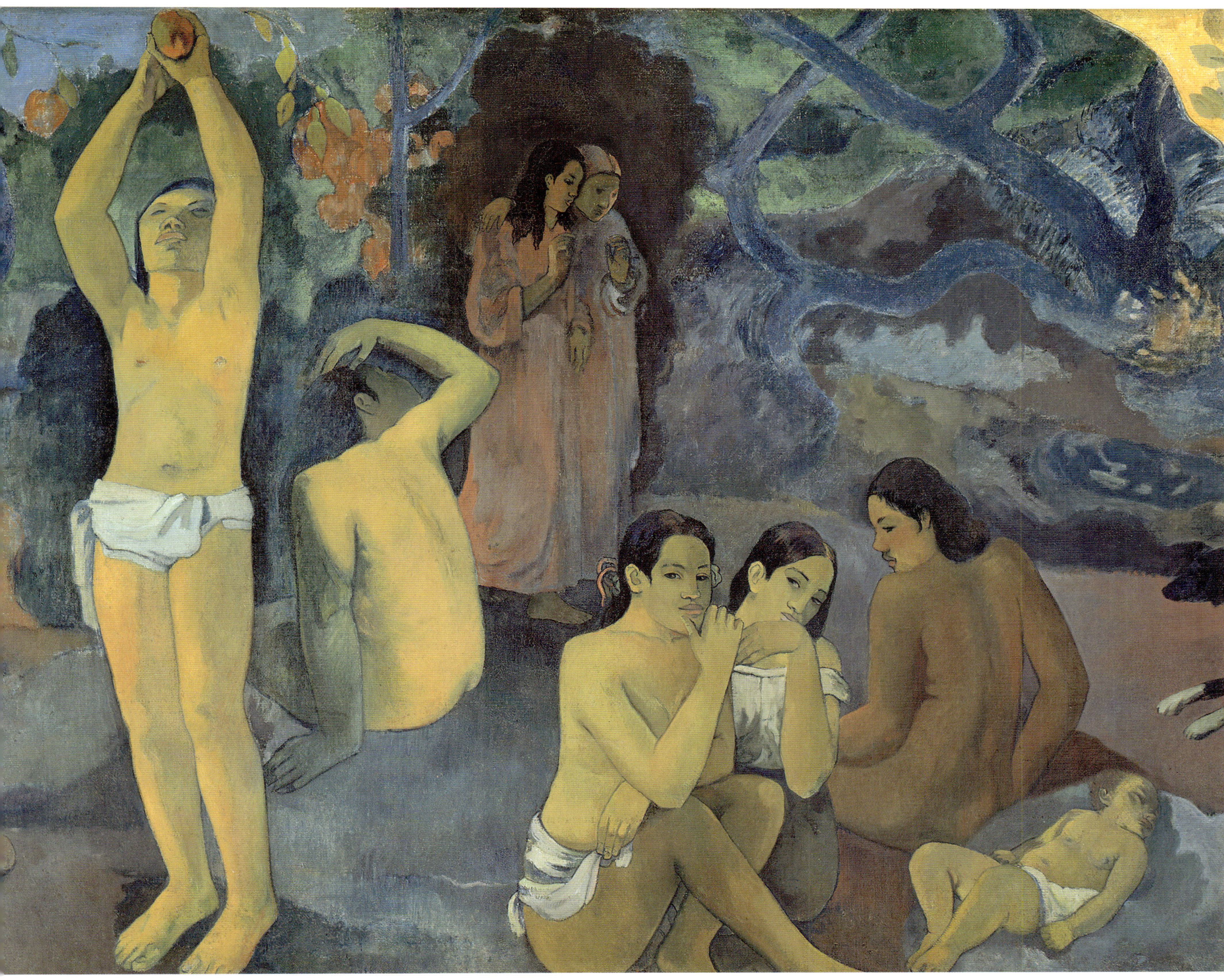

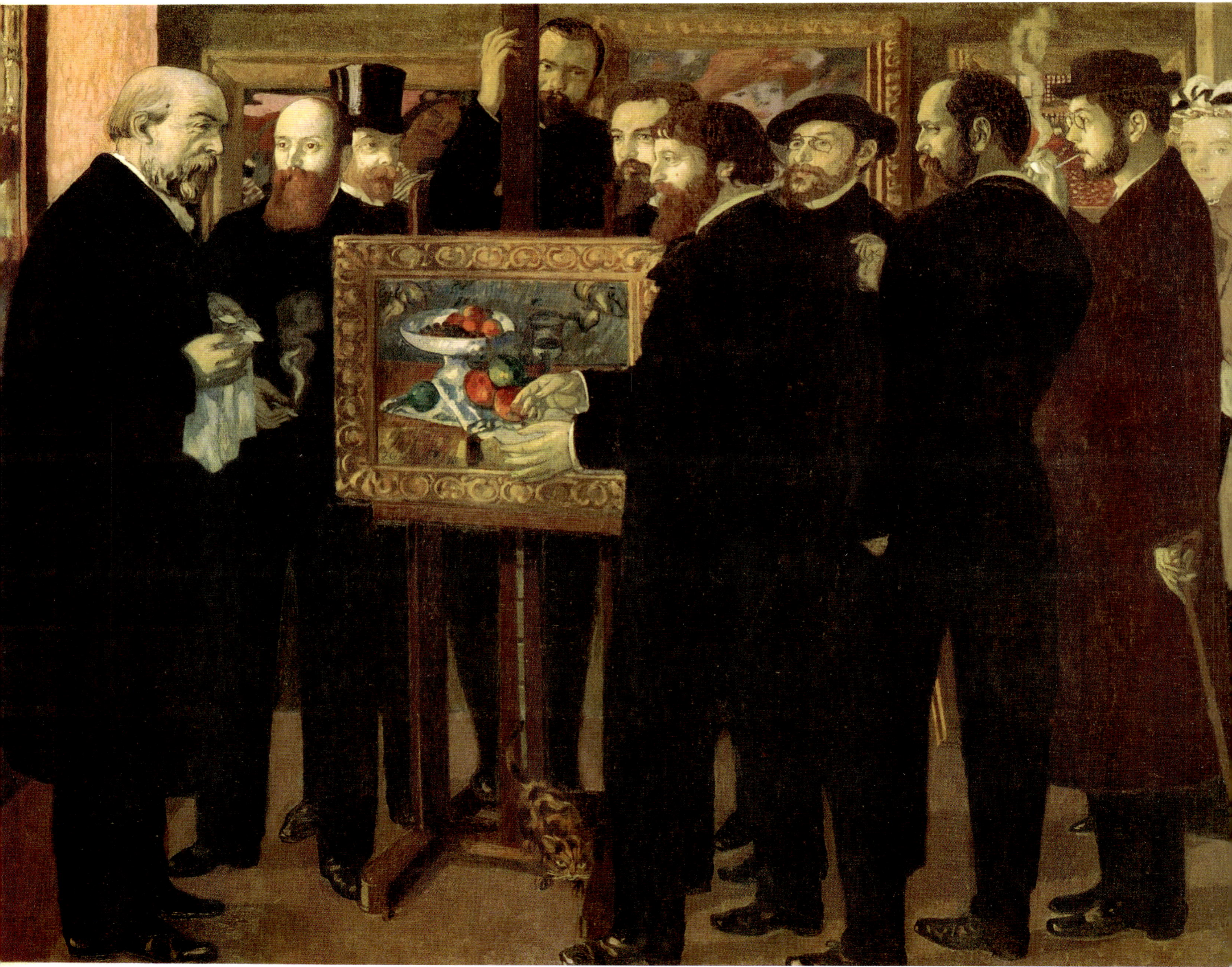

Above : *Homage to Cézanne*, 1900, Maurice Denis (1870–1943)

Femme Fatale

The sexual availability of Tahitian women was an abiding theme in Gauguin's painting during these years. French culture at the end of the nineteenth century was in the grip of a profound pessimism at its perceived loss of vitality. France was invaded by the Prussians. It was a particular trauma because it came to be understood not only as a political humiliation, but also evidence of a lack of virility and vitality, a bodily defect. The birth rate was declining precipitously; feminism, socialism and anarchism were infecting susceptible minds like pathogens. While men's sexual prowess faltered, women, more visible and forthright than ever before in public life, seemed to harbinger a unique threat. Panicked fantasies of their wives' adultery gripped the masculine imagination; female sexuality became entwined with the pervasive sense of cultural decay ('[t]he West is now in a state of decay') to the extent that they seemed synonymous. It was for this reason that the *femme fatale* was such an enduring theme for painters following Moreau and Puvis; Salomé's frank instrumentalization of her sexuality to exert control over the ostensibly powerful Herod offered the painting's viewers an allegory of what they saw as the cultural collapse going on around them.

Thus for colonialists who justified their endeavour by way of reference to theories of European racial superiority, the forcible acquisition of overseas territories offered a means of compensating for their perceived emasculation. Violently asserting their dominance over colonized bodies, European settlers conflated political authority and sexual prerogative; sublimating their Oedipal fear of the *femme fatale* in fantasies of unchallenged sexual mastery. Gauguin was keenly susceptible to such cultural neuroses. Having lost his job and his wife, having endured the ridicule of capricious critics and the incomprehension of the public, Gauguin was almost desperate in his search for foreign lands in which he could replenish his mastery, over self and others.

In *Manao tupapau* (*Spirit of the Dead Watching*) (1892, *see* page 21), Gauguin invites us to indulge in one such fantasy of sexual mastery. The painting depicts Tehura, a 13-year-old girl who Gauguin had taken as his *vahine* (native wife) and was, by the end of 1892, to impregnate. Gauguin described the genesis of the painting in his diary:

Tehura lay motionless, naked, belly down on the bed; she stared up at me, her eyes wild with fear, and she seemed not to know who I was. For a moment, I too felt a strange uncertainty. Tehura's dread was contagious: it seemed to me that a phosphorescent light poured from her staring eyes. I had never seen her so lovely; above all, I had never seen her beauty so moving.

Aroused by his child-bride's contagious dread, Gauguin goes on to transpose himself in the place of 'one of those legendary demons … of her people'. Women, Gauguin wrote elsewhere in his journal, 'long to be taken, violently'.

Detail above : *Still Life with Compotier, c. 1879–80, Paul Cézanne (1839–1906), see page 122*

Gauguin's fetishization of Tahitian purity thus went hand-in-hand with the colonial discourse that justified the subjugation of its people by way of reference to their primitivism (racial inferiority). His fantasy that such primitive people were, 'so to speak, obligatory' (the women willing and available), offers an indication of the indelible conflation of colonial and sexual oppression by Europeans in general, and Gauguin specifically, in the late nineteenth century.

Gauguin returned to France in 1893. During this sojourn, which was to last until 1895, he published his Tahitian journal (*see* page 158), accompanied by a series of woodcuts (including *Noa Noa (Fragrant Scent)*, 1893–94, and *Nave nave fenua (Delightful Land)*, 1893–94), and interspersed with poems by Charles Morice (1861–1919). Gauguin hoped that his travel-journal-cum-didactic-manual of Tahitian myth would provide his French audience with the key to understanding the complex symbolism of his paintings. However, his exhibitions in these years were unsuccessful; discouraged by failure, in 1894, Gauguin prepared to permanently quit France and abandon painting ('except as a distraction'). He returned to Tahiti in 1895; life there, however, was no less troubling than in Paris. Beset by ill health (he suffered from syphilis – with which he also infected his three *vahines*, all aged between 13 and 14), and in the midst of an existential crisis following a failed suicide attempt, in 1897, he set out on a painting that was to represent his last will and testament.

Where Do We Come From? What Are We? Where Are We Going? (1897–98, *see* pages 160–161) is a work of monumental scale. Painted on rough hessian sacking and hastily finished, it represents the zenith of Gauguin's primitive and savage style. Indeed, Gauguin reused a number of the figures from his earlier paintings, as if this work were a montage summary of his aesthetic achievements. In a letter to his friend Daniel de Monfried in 1898, Gauguin revealed that the figure groups, dispersed horizontally across the non-naturalistic landscape, are symbols that combined to form 'a philosophical work'. Reading from right to left, the sleeping infant describes where we come from, the central figures (in existential contemplation) where we are, and the old woman (crouching in grim acceptance of the inevitability of her death) where we are going. The blue idol symbolizes 'the Beyond'. In a letter to Maurice Denis, written in June 1899 as a response to Denis' attempt to solicit some works for a Nabis exhibition, Gauguin replied that 'I no longer paint except on Sundays and holidays.' In many of his late works, such as *Two Tahitian Women* (1899, *see* page 159), he retreated to the eroticism of the sexually pliant Tahitian nude. Gauguin left Tahiti for the island of Hiva Oa in the Marquesas at the end of 1901. He died there expecting that his paintings would never be appreciated.

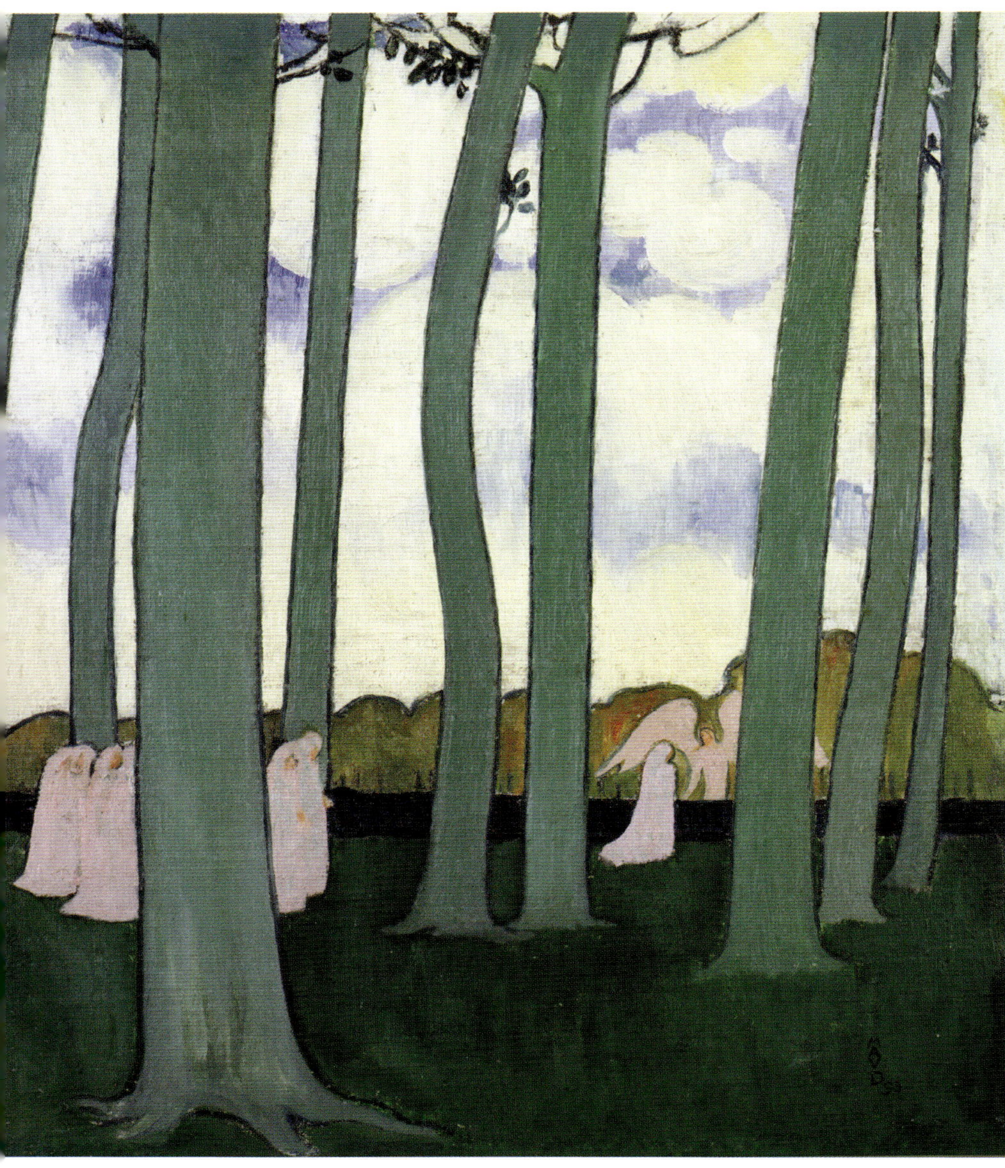

Above : *Landscape with Green Trees*, 1893, Maurice Denis (1870–1943)

Right : *Sunflowers*, 1888, Vincent van Gogh (1853–90)

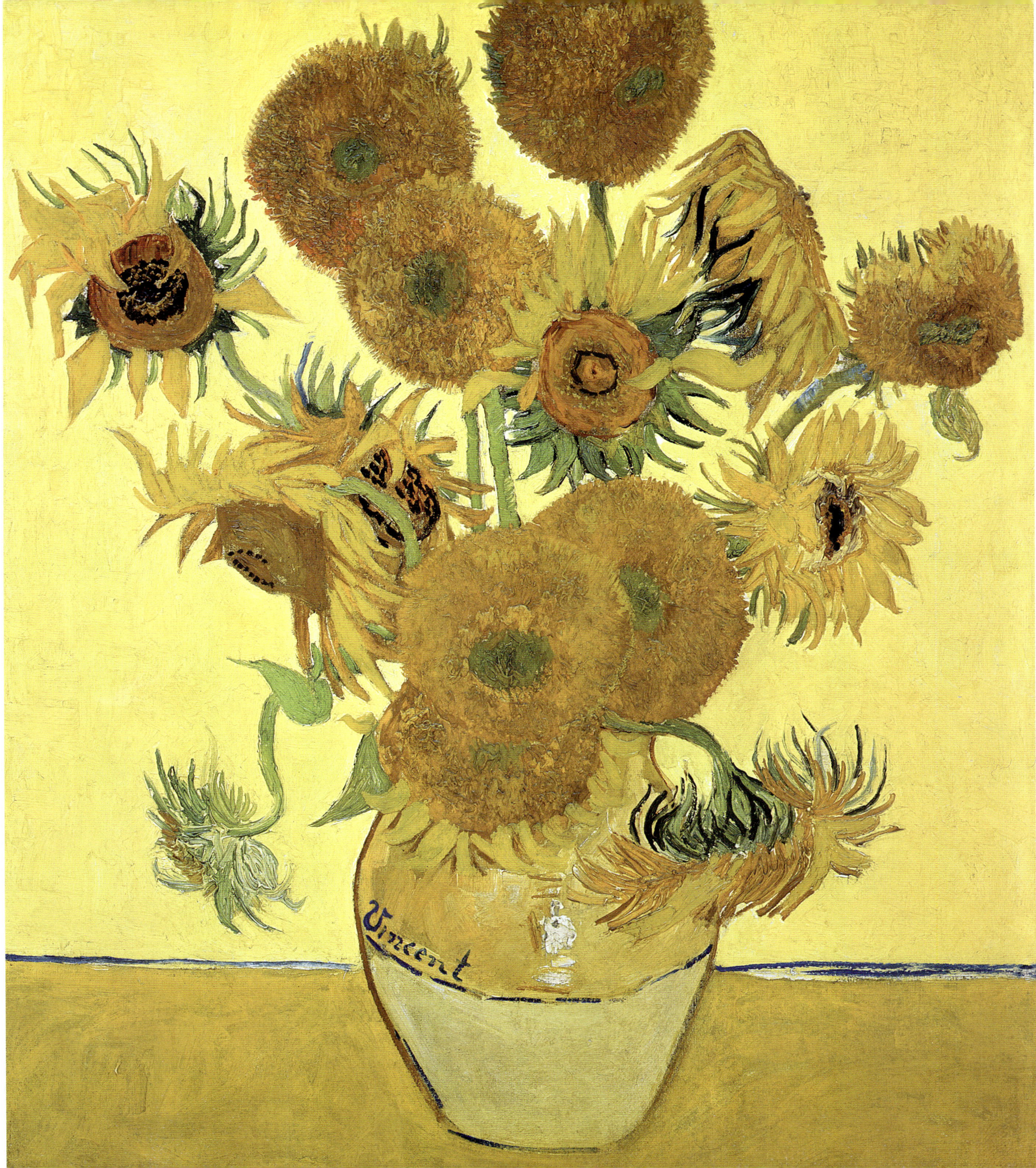

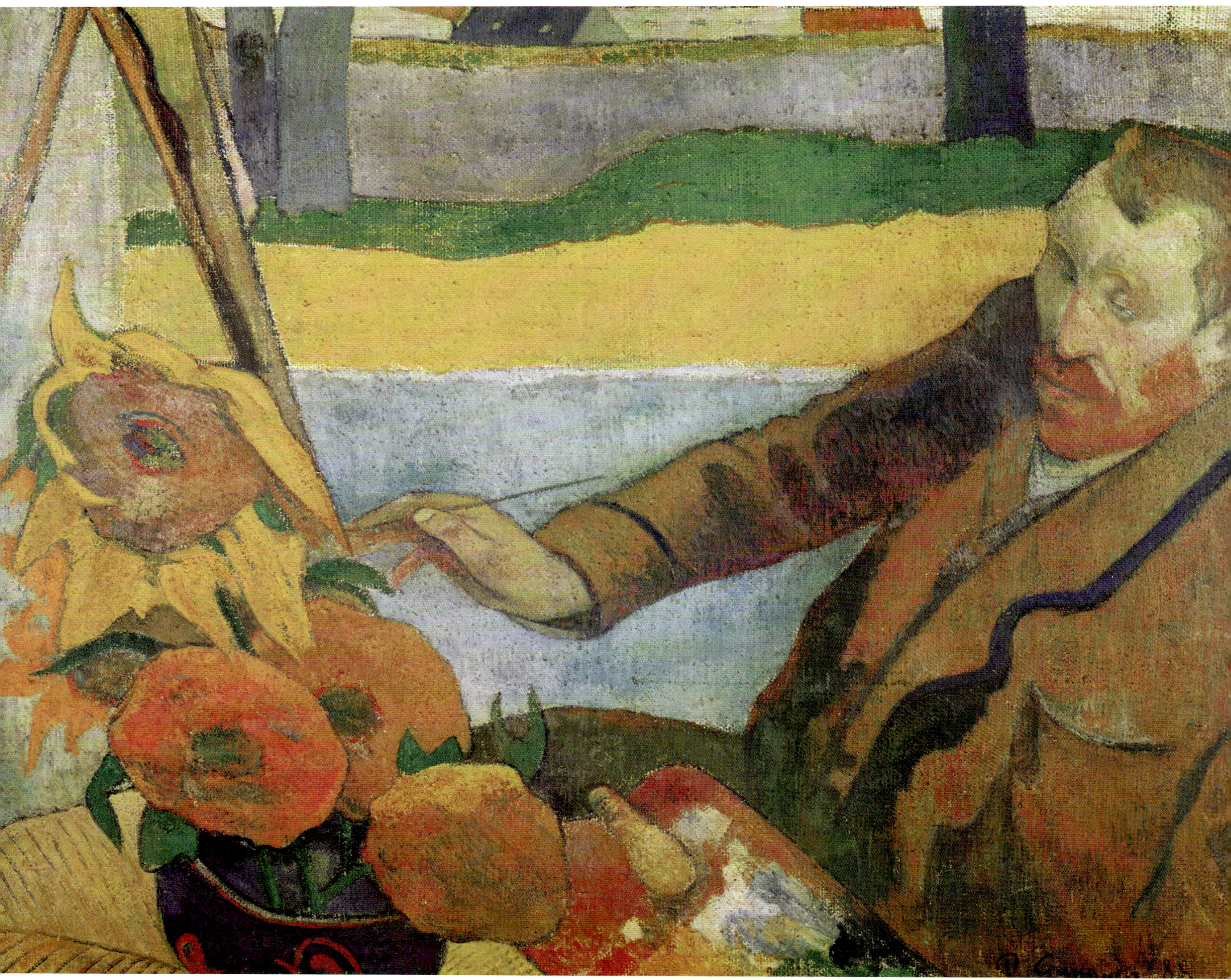

Above : *The Painter of Sunflowers: Portrait of Vincent van Gogh, 1888, Paul Gauguin (1848–1903)*

The End of the Nabis

The year in which Denis was soliciting Gauguin to exhibit with the Nabis, 1899, was to be the group's last. Denis' 1900 *Homage to Cézanne* (*see* page 162) was something of a nostalgic group portrait, commemorating a group unity that had already evaporated. It depicts the Nabis (Sérusier, Vuillard, Denis, Ranson, Roussel and Bonnard) with Redon, the dealer Vollard, and the critic André Mellerio (1862–1943) gathered around Cézanne's *Still Life with Compotier* (*c*. 1879–80) which Gauguin had owned. In the background, works by Gauguin and Renoir are visible.

In their heyday, under the guidance of their theoretician Denis, the Nabis had developed a decorative symbolism that perfectly matched the prevailing mood of the end of the century. In *Landscape with Green Trees* (1893, *see* page 164), Denis places us at the heart of Baudelaire's forest of symbols; highly abstracted and distorted, the flattened and unmodulated green trees partially disguise a procession of cloaked figures, one of whose number breaks away to meet an angel. Denis distorted nature to communicate a mystical and magical Idea of Nature. Despite their commitment to a shared Symbolist ethos and their group participation in cult-like rituals (of the kind captured by Sérusier in his *Portrait de Paul Ranson en tenue nabique*, 1890), the Nabis did not rally around a singular style or aesthetic. After the group disbanded this pluralism set some of the Nabis on sharply diverging trajectories. Denis, Sérusier and Ranson remained committed to religious mysticism and symbolism; whereas Bonnard and Vuillard evolved a more purely decorative idiom known as '*intimisme*', which they applied to everyday domestic interiors.

Sunflowers

Where Gauguin professedly addressed 'the Beyond', his one-time housemate Van Gogh instead developed a complex symbolism through which he hoped to communicate the vicissitudes of his troubled subjectivity and his insights about the human condition. In a rare period of excitable optimism, however, between 1888 and 1889, Van Gogh executed a series of sunflowers – including *Sunflowers* (1888, *see* page 165) – intended to decorate the Yellow House in which he lived with Gauguin. Painted in 'the three chrome yellows [orange, yellow and lemon], yellow ochre, and Veronese green and nothing else', these unconventional still lifes symbolized his happiness and 'gratitude'. Yellow flowers in a yellow jug against a yellow wall represented a bold pictorial choice; as Gauguin put it, 'completely Vincent'. The association was strong enough for Gauguin to have given Van Gogh the moniker of *The Painter of Sunflowers* (1888, *see* opposite). Finding the beauty in the overlooked and crude – as he had in his multiple still lifes of ordinary, workaday boots, for example *A Pair of Boots* (1887, *see* left) – Van Gogh imbued this simple motif with a profound emotional intensity and symbolic resonance.

Such halcyon days were not, however, destined to last. Van Gogh's worsening mental health led to the violent breakdown of his friendship with Gauguin in an episode that also led to his famous auto-mutilation. A bittersweet *Self-portrait with Bandaged Ear* (1889, *see* page 168) commemorates his return from the hospital, bandage in place. On the wall behind him is a Japanese print,

Above : *A Pair of Boots*, 1887, Vincent van Gogh (1853–90)

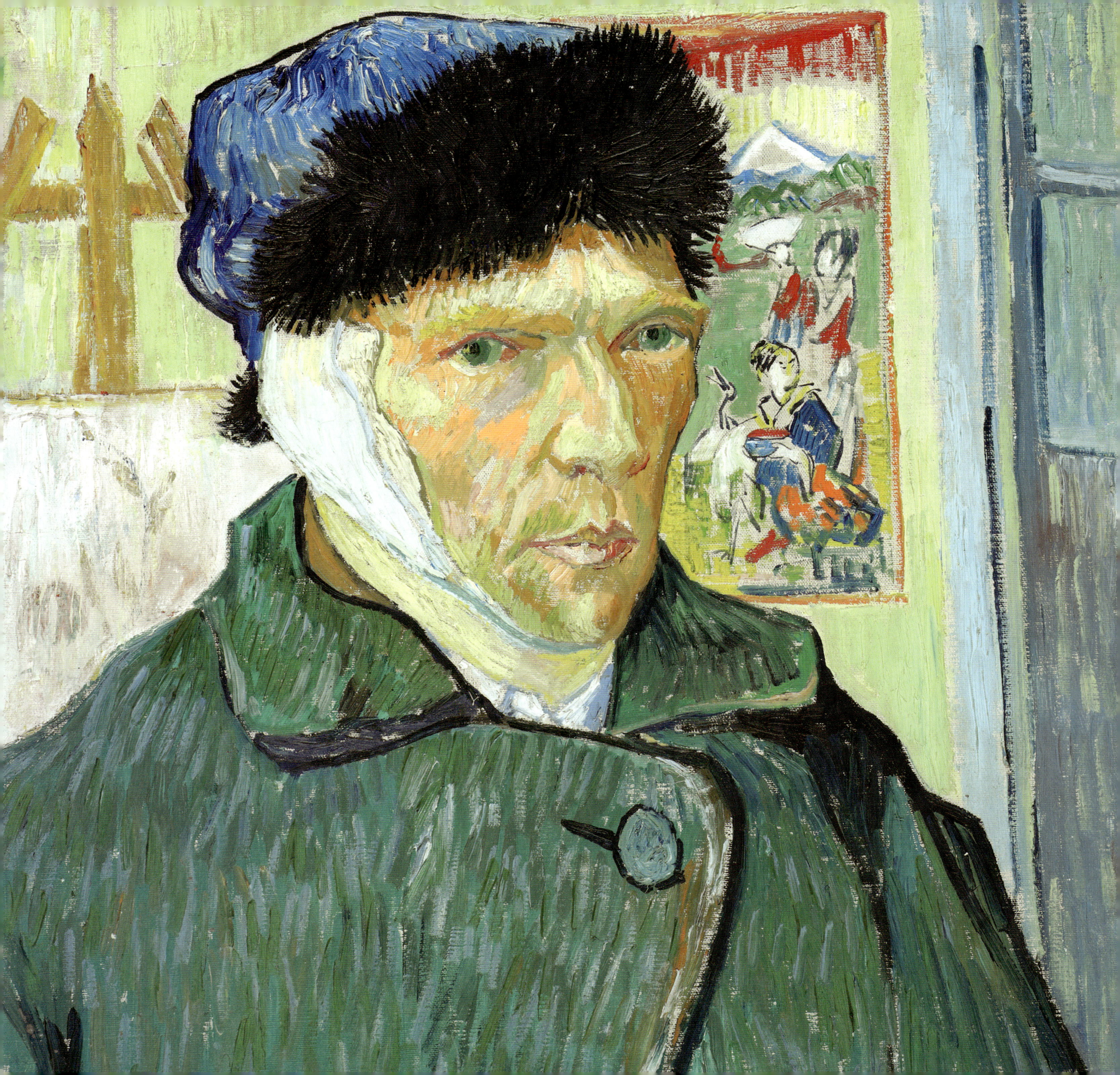

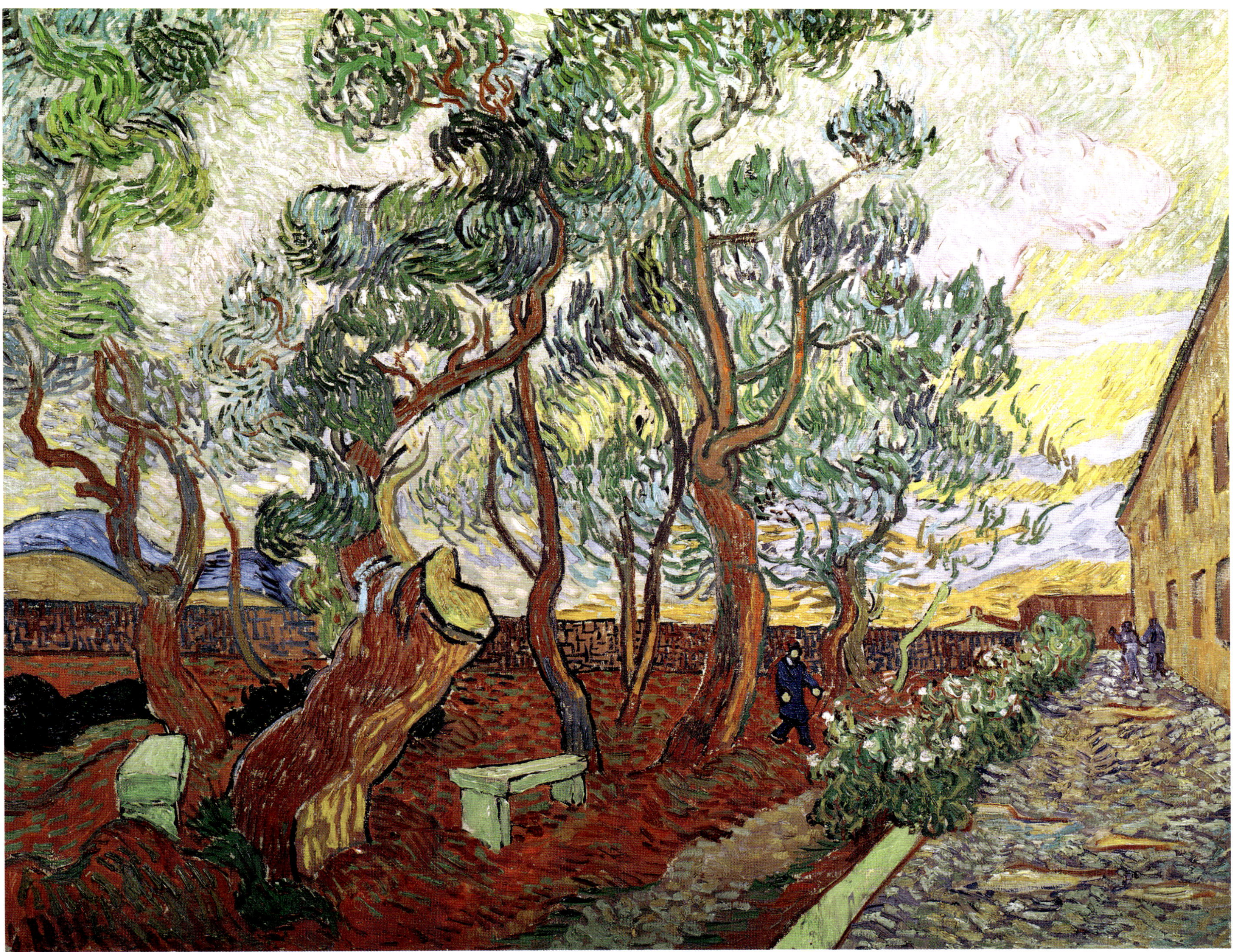

symbolizing the hopes for renewal he pinned on such artefacts; to his left, a blank canvas, symbolizing work yet do to. However, by May of that year, Van Gogh found himself confined in Saint-Rémy mental hospital, 15 miles outside Arles.

Van Gogh painted *The Garden of the Asylum* (1889, *see* above) in which he was being held; in the very background, one can discern the yellow strip of a wheatfield. Earlier, Van Gogh had painted the wheatfields around Arles to symbolize the eternal cycle of nature: a motif whereby his work as a painter

Left : *Self-portrait with Bandaged Ear, 1889,* Vincent van Gogh (1853–90)

Above : *The Garden of the Asylum, 1889,* Vincent van Gogh (1853–90)

evoked calm and pleasing emotions, but also connected him to the divine. Now, however, as Van Gogh described it in a letter to Émile Bernard, 'a grey terrace' and red ochre 'wall … blocks the view'. Thus barred from the symbol of his happiness, Van Gogh uses colour relations ('green saddened with grey') to encode a 'feeling of anxiety from which some of my companions in misfortune often suffer and which is called "seeing red". And what's more, the motif of the great tree struck by lightning, the sickly pink and green smile of the last flower of autumn, confirms this idea.'

Van Gogh was still confined to the asylum when he conceived of perhaps his most famous painting, *The Starry Night* (1889, *see* right). Writing to his brother, Van Gogh described his inspiration: '[t]his morning I saw the countryside from my window a long time before sunrise with nothing but the morning star, which looked very big'. Painted partly from nature, partly from imagination, the canvas depicts a swirling night sky above the sleeping village of Saint-Rémy. On the left, a cypress tree stretches almost to the very top edge of the canvas; its verticality echoed by the Dutch-style church steeple.

Nature held a special resonance for Van Gogh. His parents followed a non-dogmatic and mystical school of Protestantism, which imbued in the young Vincent a belief in God and in panentheism (the notion that because the divine penetrates every part of existence, the imminent glory of Nature reveals the presence of God – not to be confused with pantheism, a worship of Nature as God). The sun, moon and stars were potent symbols for Van Gogh of the heavens above ('*quelque chose là-haut*') and the world beyond. Sources of divine light, the luminous radiation of celestial bodies weaved together all those who laboured under it (from sowers and reapers to Van Gogh himself) into a fraternity powered by nature's infinite cycling. '[I]s life visible to us in its entirety, or before we die do we know of only one hemisphere?' he wrote to Theo, continuing:

the sight of the stars always makes me dream in as simple a way as the black spots on the map, representing towns and villages, make me dream. Why, I

Right : *The Starry Night*, 1889, Vincent van Gogh (1853–90)

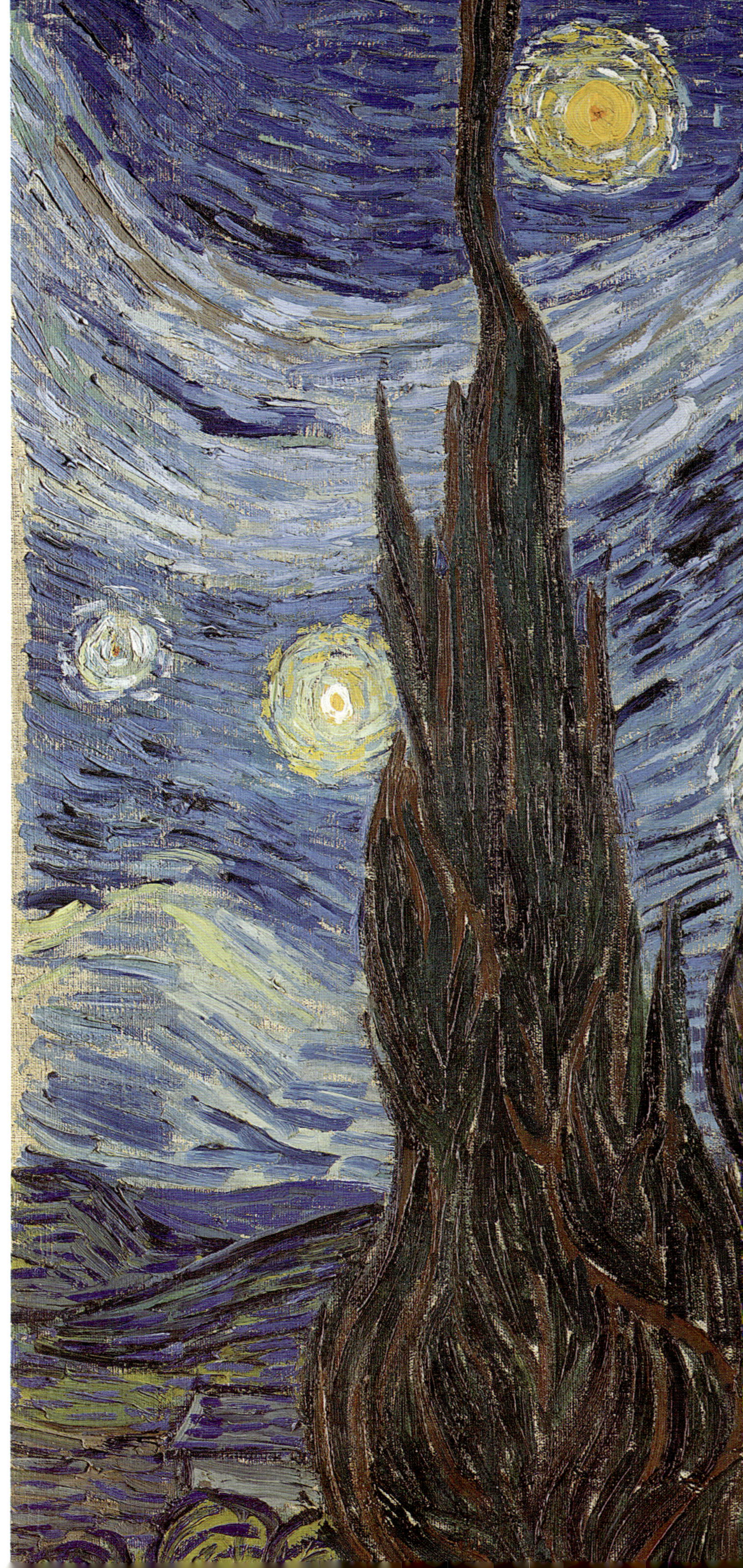

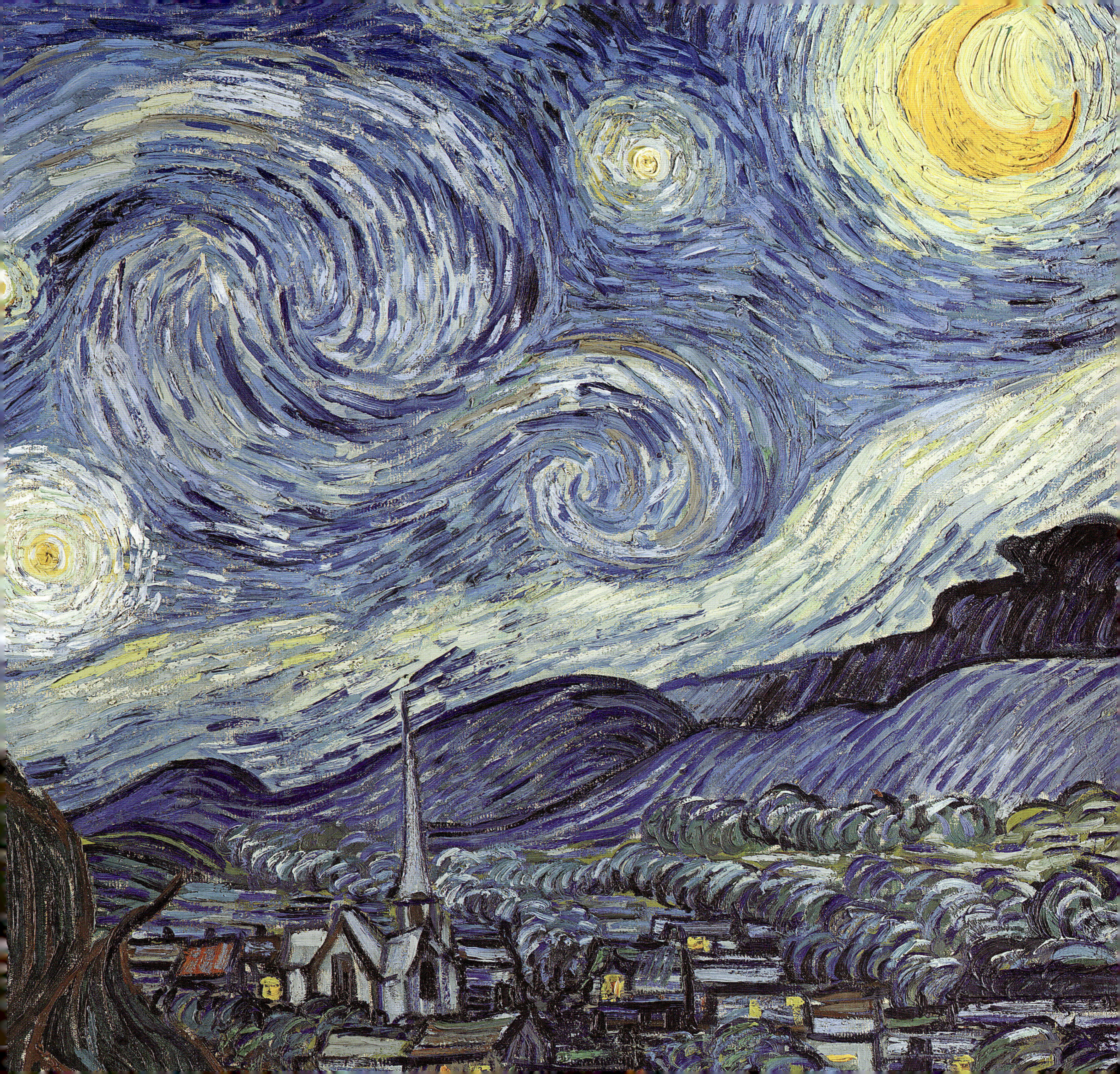

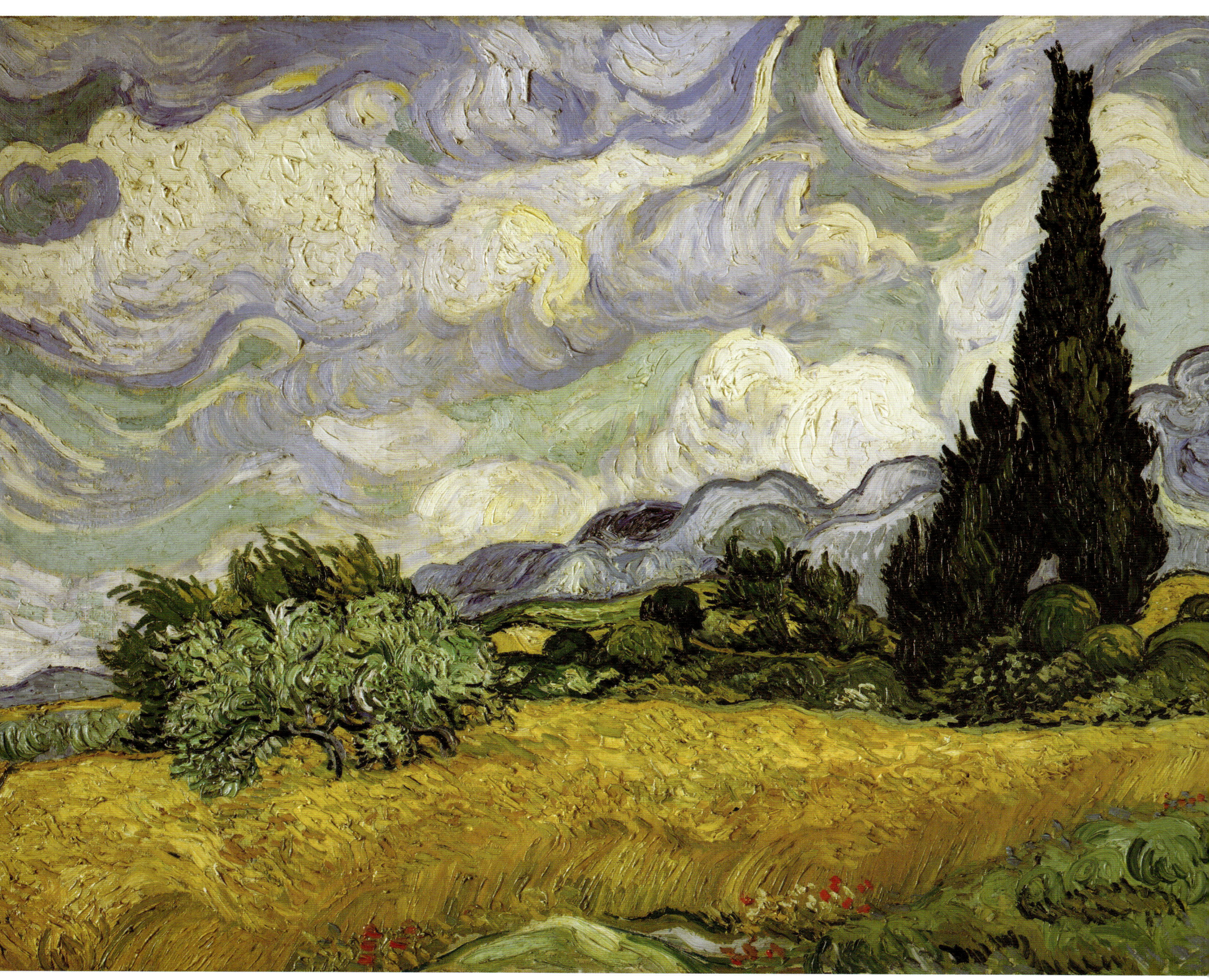

Above : *Wheatfield with Cypresses*, 1889, Vincent van Gogh (1853–90)

say to myself, should the spots of light in the firmament be less accessible to us than the black spots on the map of France. Just as we take the train to go to Tarascon or Rouen, we take death to go to a star.

Spiritual Hearing

In the early 1880s, Van Gogh was describing his experiences of 'spiritual hearing' and 'seeing musicality' in nature, a notion drawn from northern Romantics and related to Rosicrucianism and medieval mystic beliefs in 'cosmic harmony' (that celestial motion was like music). Thus, in a heightened state of sensation, the mystic could perceive the universal music resonating with God's immanence. Van Gogh wrote of one such experience, during a walk in the Dutch countryside, to Theo:

And then, when dusk fell – imagine the silence, the peace of that moment! [… I heard] in the dusk … the finale of the symphony that I heard yesterday. That day passed like a dream, I had been so immersed in that heart-rending music all day that I had literally forgotten even to eat and drink…. The day was over, and from dawn to dusk, or rather from one night to the other night, I had forgotten myself in that symphony.

The night sky of *The Starry Night*, then – its pulsating stars, vibrating crescent moon and quavering blues; the rhythmic movement of its billowing swirls – evokes a divine, astral symphony. The energy of the brushstrokes makes palpable Van Gogh's spiritual ecstasy. The cypress tree that stretches from earth to heaven in *The Starry Night* was another important symbol, one that Van Gogh was to explore in other paintings, including *Wheatfield with Cypresses* (1889, *see* left). On the one hand, the cypress tree, like the sunflower, was typical of Provençale flora; Van Gogh expressed his astonishment to Theo that nobody had yet mined such a rich symbol. The more time Van Gogh spent in the south of France, the more in tune he felt with its nature, and the stronger his resolution grew to capture it. Van Gogh's series of olive trees – at least 15 strong and including *Olive Trees with the Alpilles in the Background* (1889, *see* page 175) – were motivated by this drive to represent Provence. However, as with *The Starry Night* (to accompany which Van Gogh painted *Olive Trees with the Alpilles*), there was an additional, deeper symbolism:

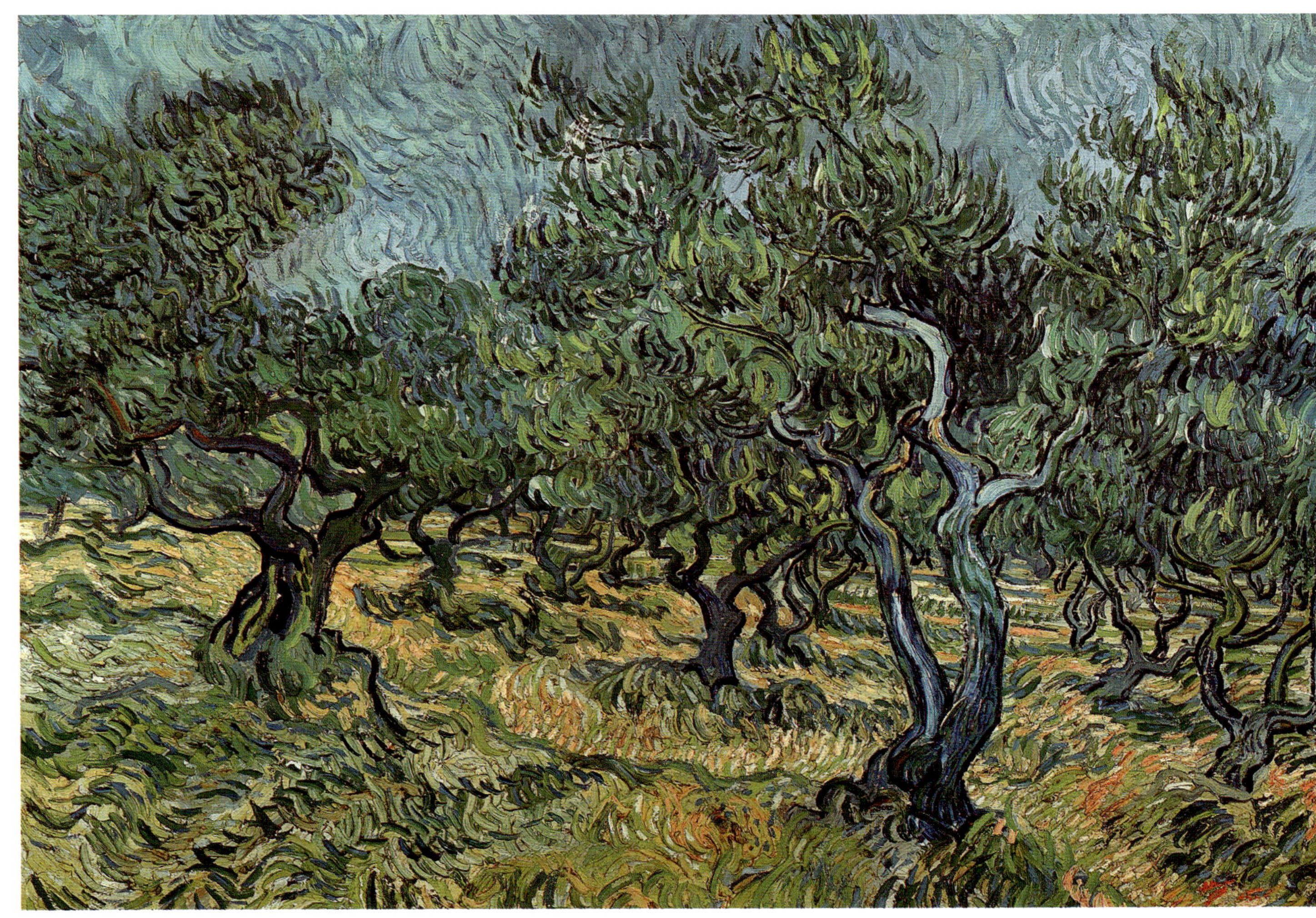

Above : *Olive Grove*, 1889, Vincent van Gogh (1853–90)

a reference to the betrayal of Christ by Judas in the olive grove of Gethsemane, a biblical episode that had similarly inspired Gauguin's *Christ in the Garden of Olives* (1889, *see* page 153). Going beyond 'the photographic and silly perfection of some painters', Van Gogh emphasized the expressive potential of his form and style, content that it should '[become] a little abstract'.

Cypresses also had a spiritual symbolism. In both *Wheatfield with Cypresses* and *The Starry Night*, Van Gogh emphasized the verticality of the tree, as it towers above the rest of the landscape, seemingly more at home in the sky than on the ground. The gestural churning with which Van Gogh applied the paint on both elements reinforces this affinity; deliberately juxtaposing green and blue hues. For Van Gogh, cypress trees symbolized mankind's desire for ascent to the divine, the yearning for traffic between the profane and the sacred – they were the axis by which the heavens above and the earth below were put in contact. The lively lines of the trees draw the eye and soul upwards, along the *axis mundi* (cosmic axis) to the great beyond.

Expressionism

Van Gogh's nuanced symbolism and his expressive intensity were important precursors for those artists grouped under the banner of 'Expressionism' in the twentieth century. As has already been mentioned, Roger Fry (1866–1934) 'suggested various terms such as "Expressionism"' as the title for the landmark 1910 exhibition by which England was introduced to Post-Impressionism. Fry sought to distinguish Gauguin, Van Gogh, Cézanne, Seurat, Picasso and Matisse from the Impressionists on the grounds that – to varying degrees and from varying positions – they each rebelled against the way in which Impressionism conceived of the relation between individuals and the world. Where the Impressionists sought to render nature as visible to the eye, Post-Impressionists and Expressionists sought to express, by way of abstract forms or abstruse symbols, the otherwise invisible.

Right : *Olive Trees with the Alpilles in the Background, 1889, Vincent van Gogh (1853–90)*

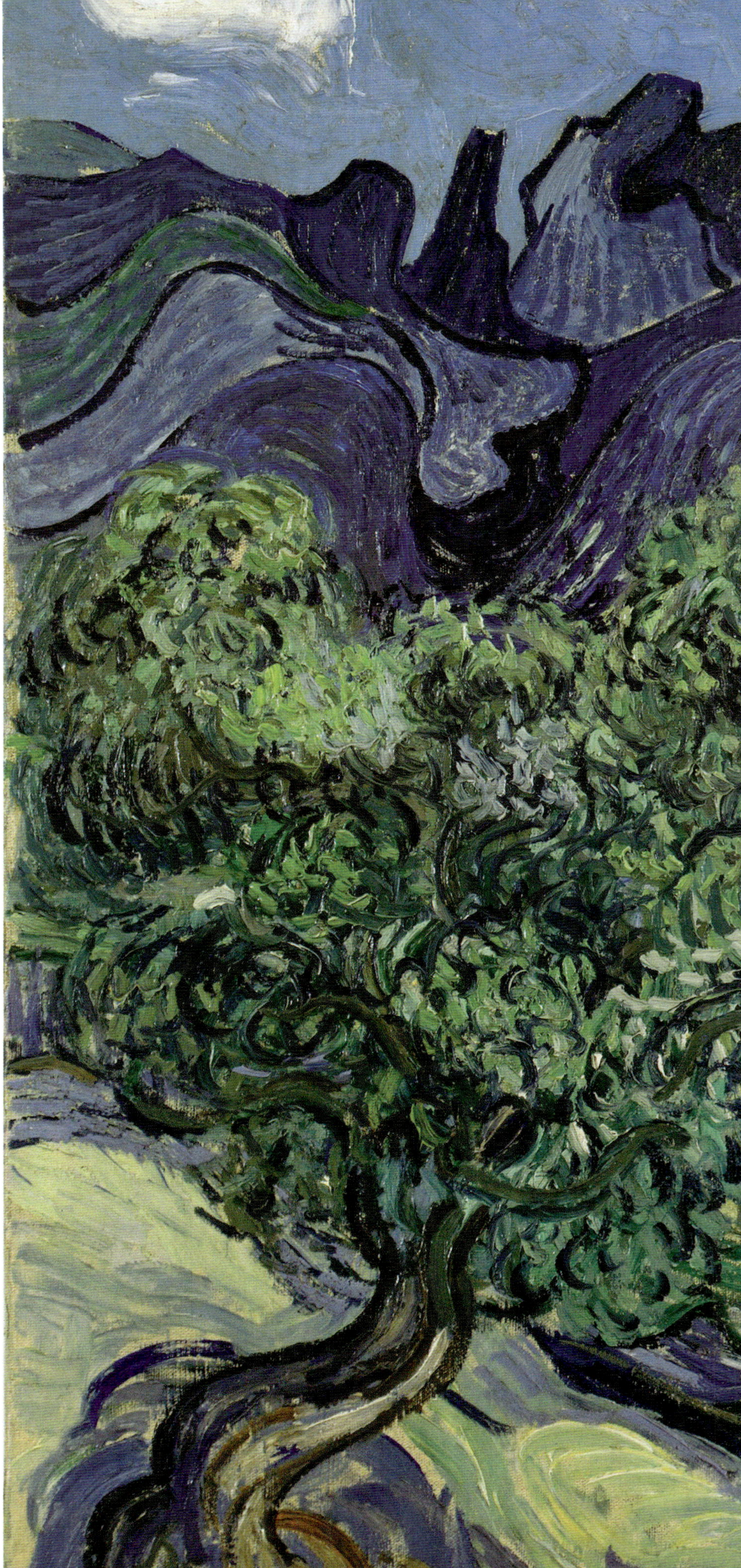

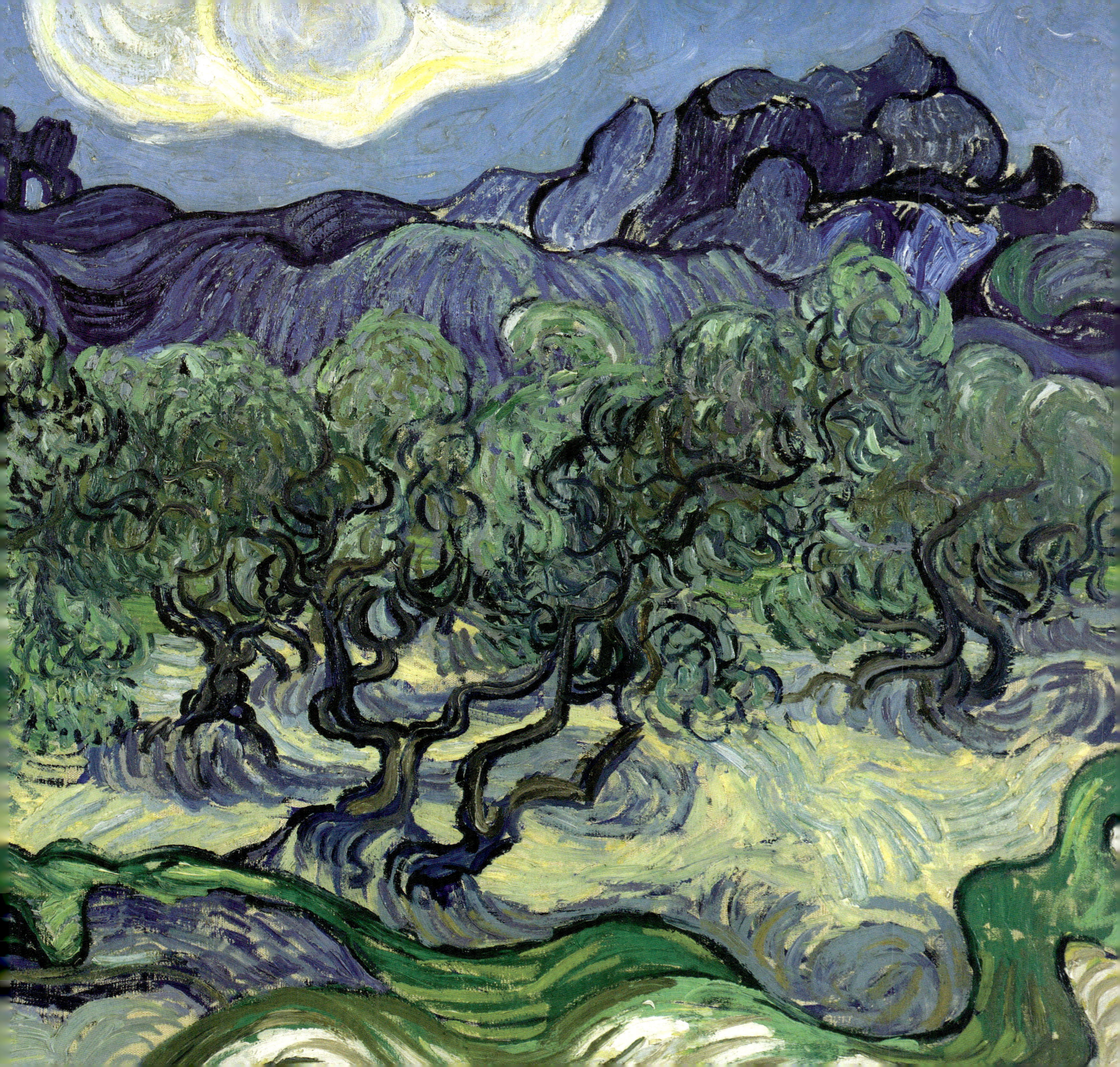

Munch

One such Expressionist was Edvard Munch (1863–1944). Although Van Gogh and he never met, they had much in common. Munch was born to an aristocratic but impoverished family who lived in the insanitary working-class suburbs of Christiania (later renamed Oslo). He was afflicted by bronchitis and tuberculosis, the latter of which claimed his mother in 1868 and older sister nine years later. Munch's father, an extreme Christian fundamentalist, suffered bouts of violent depression and believed that his son's illness was the product of divine retribution, to be cured only by puritanical repentance. 'I was born dying,' recalled Munch later in life, '[s]ickness, insanity and death were the dark angels standing guard at my cradle and they have followed me throughout my life.'

Themes of sickness, insanity and death traversed Munch's art. In works such as *The Scream* (1893, *see* right and page 178), Munch explored the extreme emotional states associated with his personal (alienated) experience of modern life. Describing the genesis of the painting, Munch recalled that:

I was walking along the road with two friends – the sun was setting – suddenly the sky turned blood red – I paused, feeling exhausted, and leaned on the fence – there was blood and tongues of fire above the blue-black fjord and the city – my friends walked on, and I stood there trembling with anxiety – and I sensed an infinite scream passing through nature.

The distorted forms, expressive colours and sinuous brushwork convey Munch's anguish and isolation; outer-nature and inner-self amalgamate through the agency of the infinite scream.

Picasso's Blue Period

Before his decisive encounter with Cézanne's analytical landscapes, Picasso was first drawn to the expressive intensity of Symbolism and Expressionism, tendencies he encountered in Barcelona and then Paris in the 1890s and 1900s. In February 1901, while in Madrid, Picasso learned that his best friend Carles Casagemas (1880–1901) had committed suicide. Casagemas was in love with a model called Germaine Pichot (1880–1948). However, she rejected his advances and in response, during a dinner with friends, Casagemas shot at Pichot and (erroneously) thinking her murdered, turned the gun on himself. Stricken by grief, Picasso embarked on a series of melancholic and intense portraits of Casagemas that stood as allegories for alienation and loss.

La Vie (1903, *see* right) offers perhaps the most complex and forceful artefact from this episode in Picasso's career, known as his Blue Period. A complex, Symbolist allegory, *La Vie* resists straightforward interpretation. A statuesque, if emaciated, nude couple stand in an ambiguous interior space before a berobed

Detail above : *The Scream*, 1893, Edvard Munch (1863–1944), *see page 178*

Right : *La Vie*, 1903, Pablo Picasso (1881–1943)

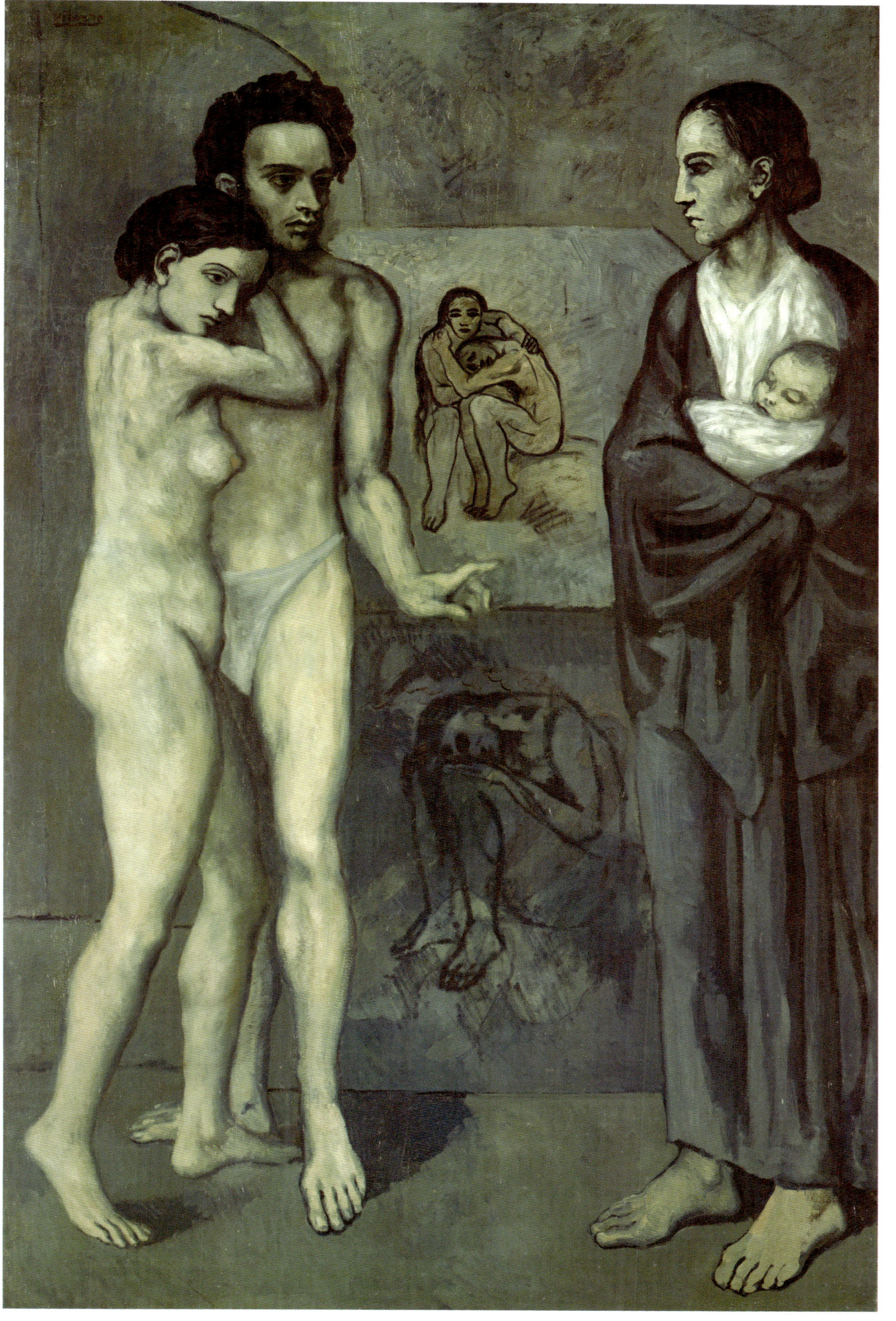

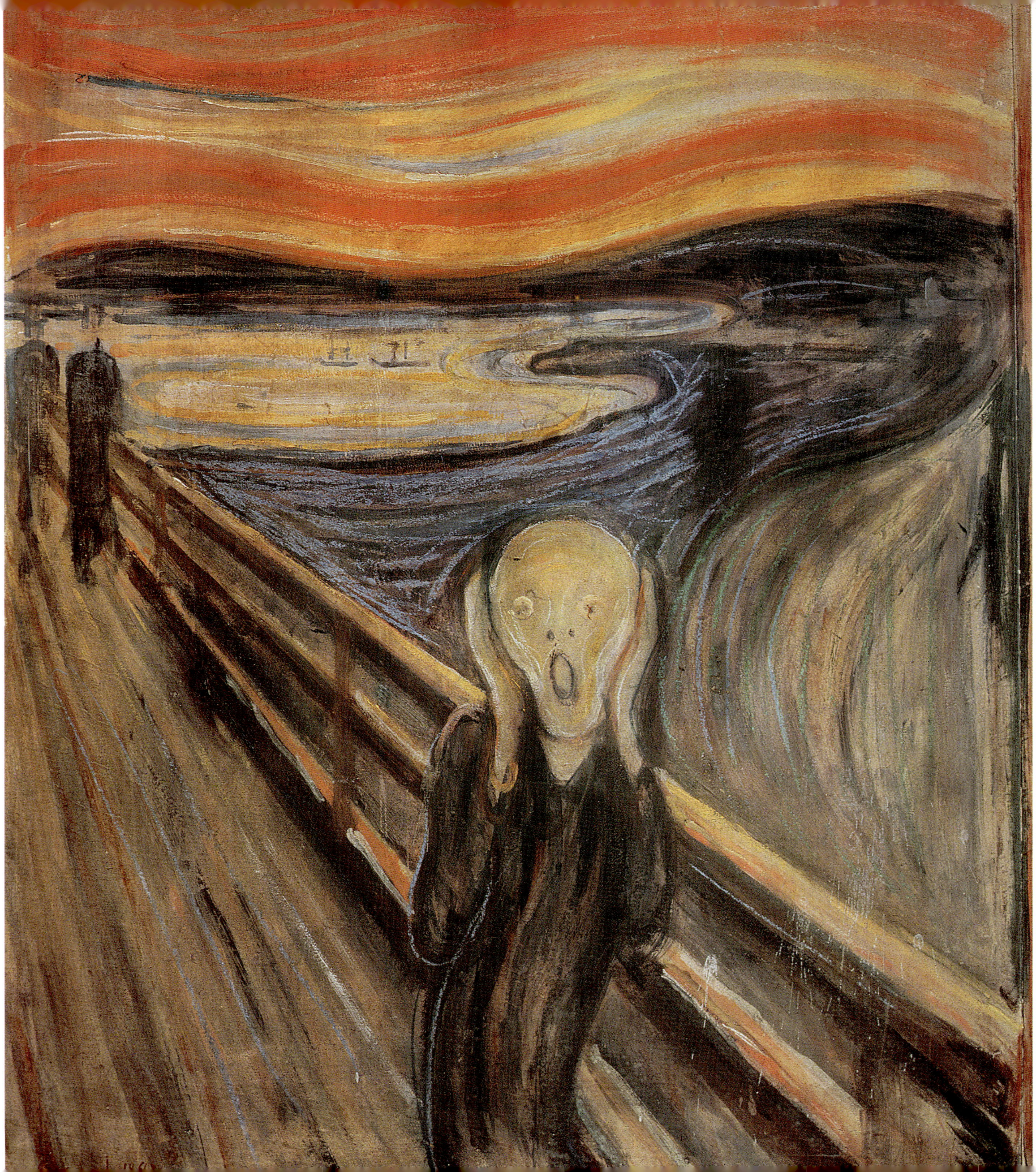

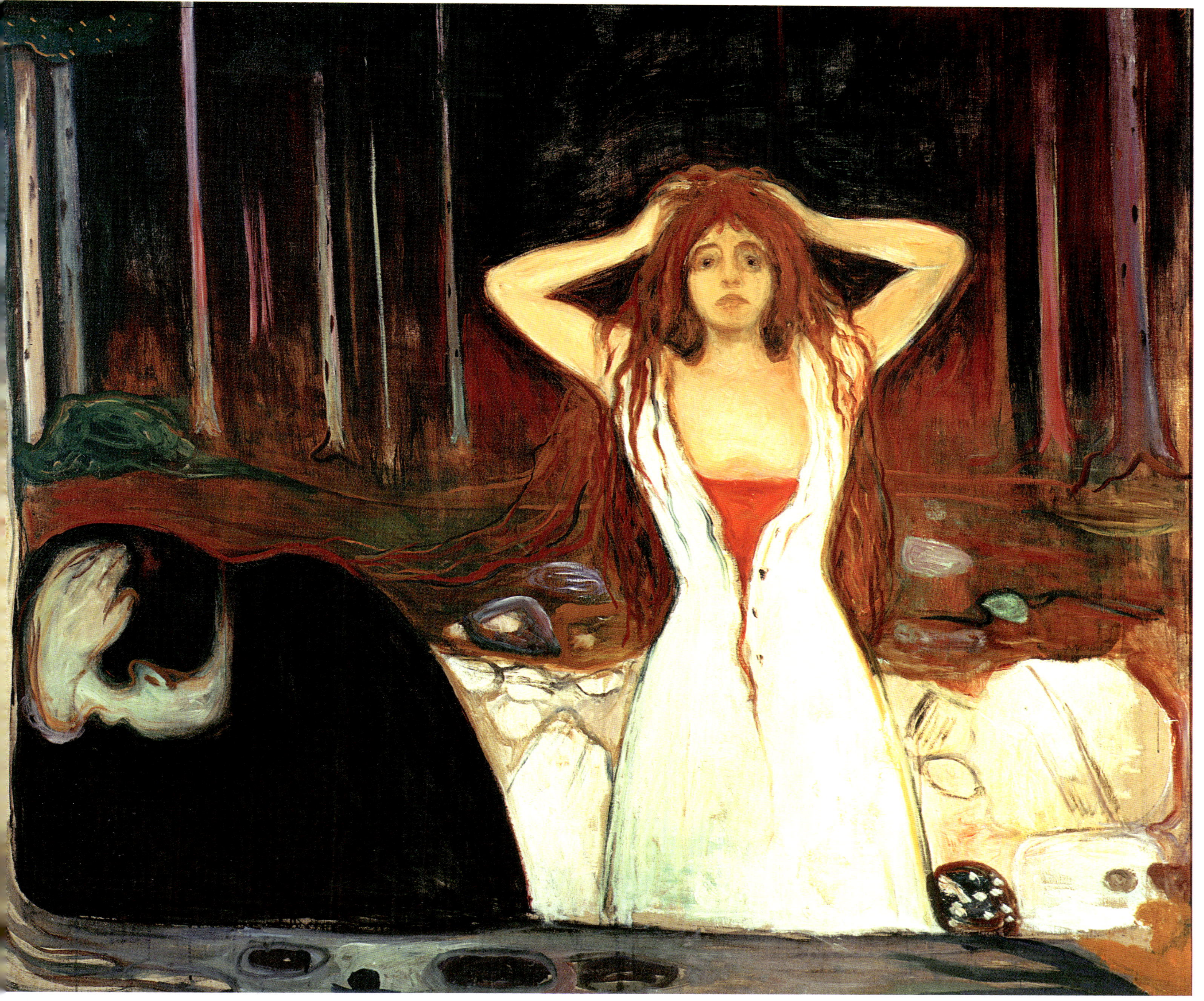

Left: *The Scream*, 1893, Edvard Munch (1863–1944)

Above: *Ashes*, 1894. Edvard Munch (1863–1944)

older woman holding a baby. On the background wall are affixed two images of crouching figures that have been identified as relating to an 1882 drawing by Van Gogh entitled *Sorrow*. The compressed space, stiff postures, narrative opacity and blue palette make the painting's tone one of deep anxiety. Beneath this general interpretation is an autobiographical one: the nude couple has been identified as resembling Casagemas and Pichot, and recent x-ray investigations have revealed that Casagemas was originally a self-portrait of Picasso himself. These complex layers of identity and emotion underscore the work's ambiguous significance and indebtedness to Post-Impressionists from Gauguin to Van Gogh.

Matisse

Matisse was another artist whose early works emerged from the cauldron of Post-Impressionist experimentation. Matisse had been trained in the studio of the Symbolist Gustave Moreau, yet it was the guiding influence of Pissarro that proved most decisive, since he introduced Matisse to the diversity of Impressionism, Post-Impressionism and Neo-Impressionism. Matisse distilled these influences and, in conjunction with some younger painters – André Derain (1880–1954) and Maurice de Vlaminck (1876–1958) – developed a new style that came to be known as Fauvism. Begun in the summer of 1904 in the presence of Signac, Matisse's *Luxe, Calme, et Voloupté* (1904–05) marries a divisionist technique (drawn from Neo-Impressionism) with a veritable explosion of bright, prismatic colour (justified by Van Gogh's and Gauguin's liberation of colour from its traditional descriptive function). This painting was exhibited at the 1905 Salon des Indépendants alongside *Woman with a Hat* (1905), in which Matisse moved away from divisionism and towards a more expressive and gestural brushwork closer to Expressionism. Reviewing the show, the art critic Louis Vauxcelles (1870–1943) remarked on the incongruity between Matisse's works and Albert Marque's traditional Italianate portrait bust with which they shared the room, noting that 'Donatello [had been placed] amongst the wild beasts', *parmi les fauves*.

Right : *Tiger in a Tropical Storm (Surprised!)*, 1891, Henri Rousseau (1844–1910)

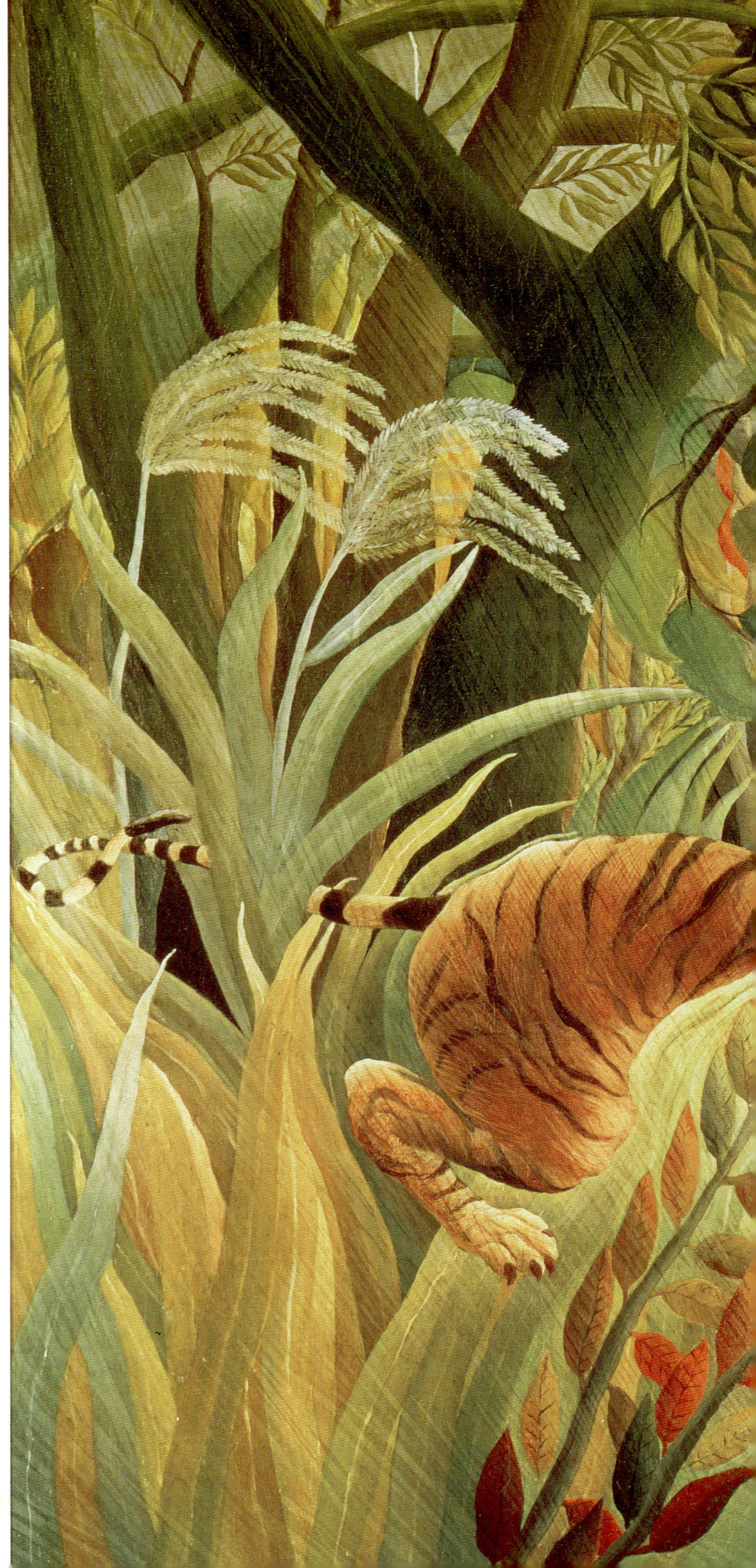

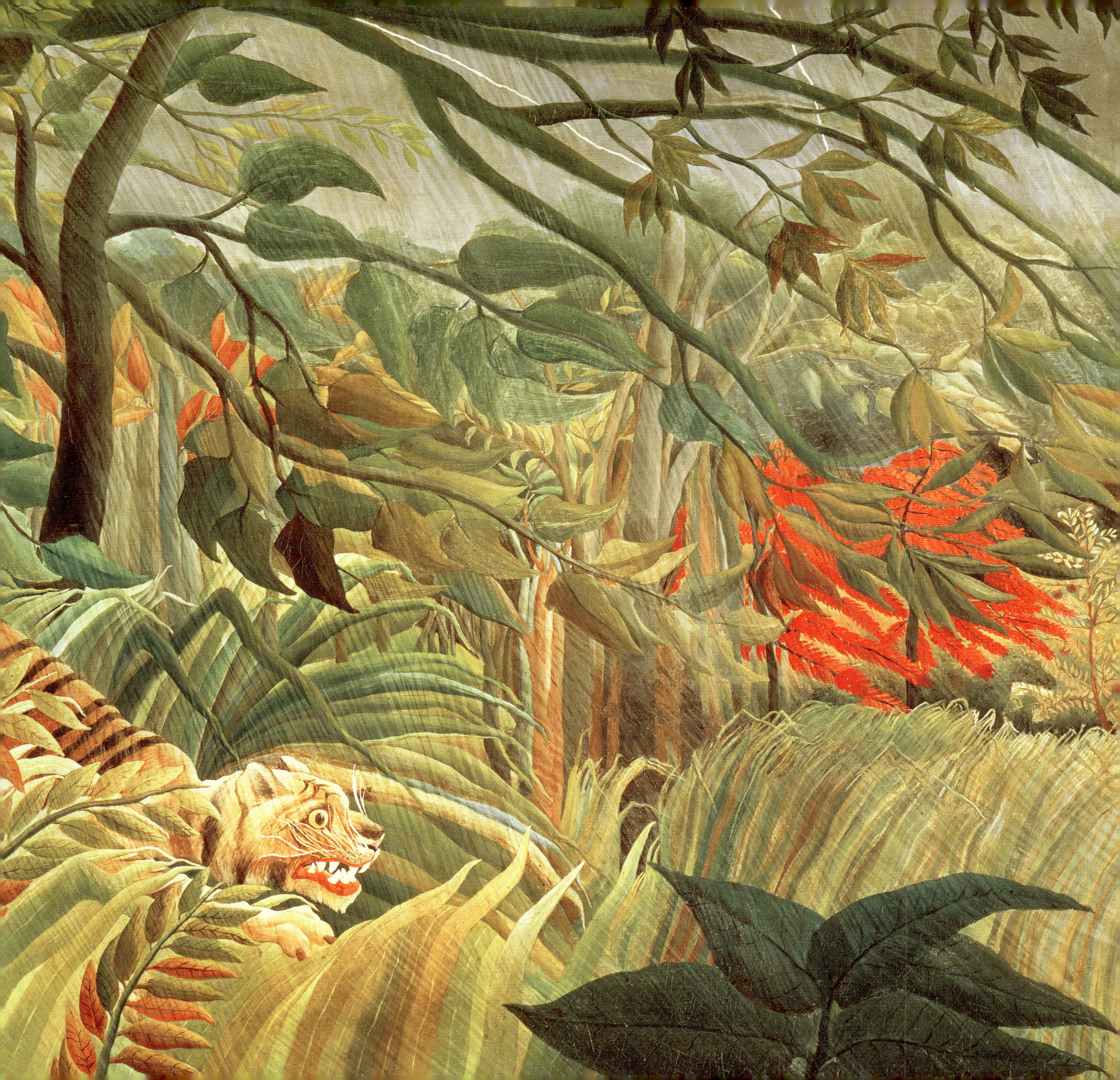

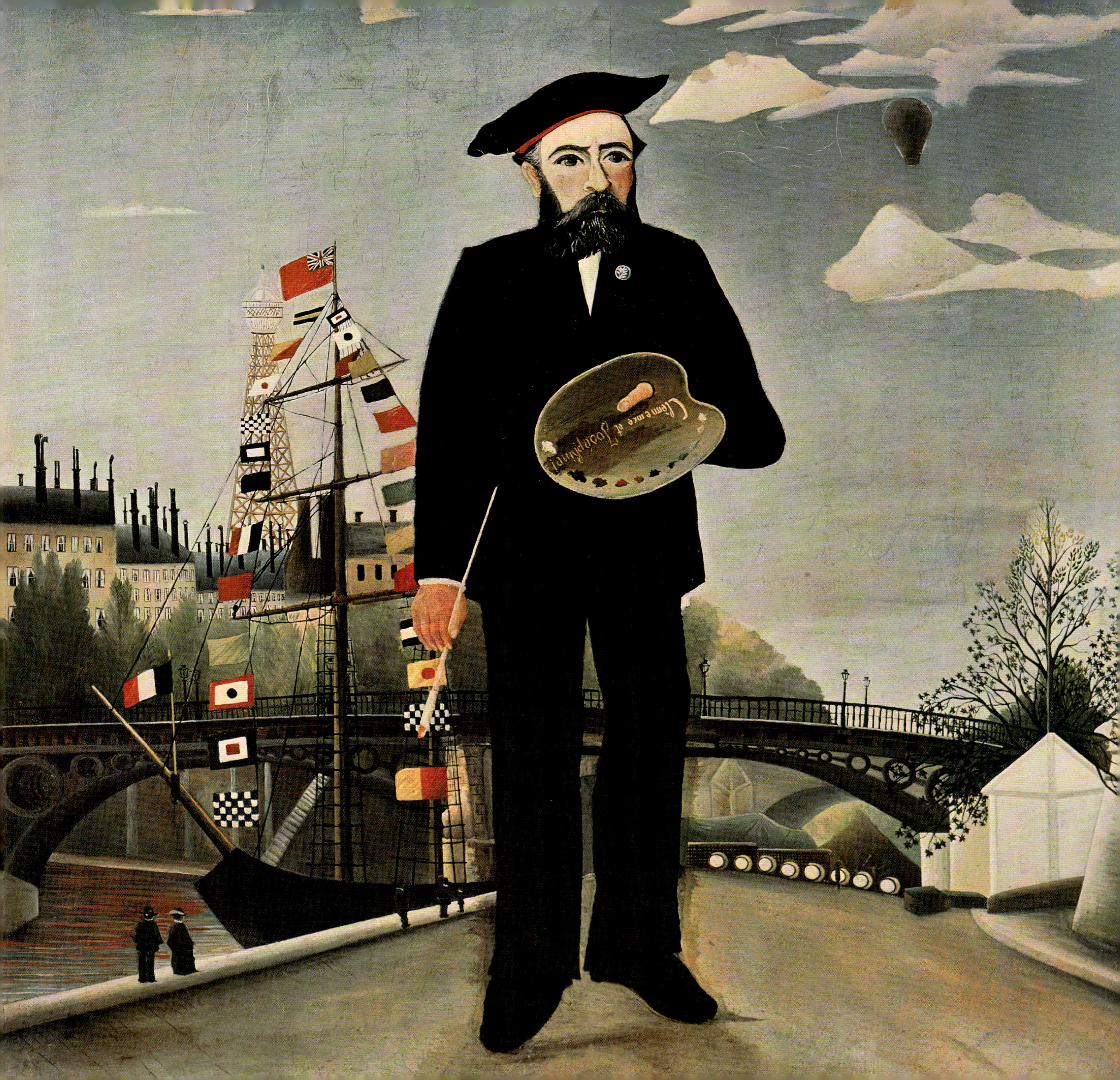
Clémence et Joséphine

Rousseau

Also exhibited alongside the Fauves at the 1905 Salon des Indépendants, the self-taught primitivist Henri Rousseau (1844–1910) testified to the enduring influence of the kind of primitivism popularized by Gauguin. Rousseau's early *Self Portrait* (1890, *see* left) is characteristic of his folk-art style (and indeed, his own conception of it). Juxtaposing himself with the icons of Parisian modernity – the Eiffel Tower and a hot-air balloon – Rousseau deliberately elides the sophisticated techniques of naturalist art in favour of a streamlined and simplified monumentality. *Tiger in a Tropical Storm (Surprised!)* (1891, *see* page 181) represents a tiger hunting explorers; its schematized flatness connotes not a real-life scene but theatrical decoration. Despite this seeming artificiality, Rousseau's deliberate naivety (bolstered by his autodidacticism) was celebrated by the avant-garde of the early twentieth century, including Picasso, Robert Delaunay (1885–1941), Constantin Brancusi (1876–1957) and Signac. In 1908, Picasso threw a banquet in Rousseau's honour at the Bateau-Lavoir in Paris, cementing his reputation among the post Post-Impressionist generation.

Post-Impressionist Impressionists

As paradoxical as it might seem, even the Impressionists were not impervious to the effects of the innovations perpetuated by artists coming in their wake.

In June 1883, Monet moved to the small village of Giverny where, after the dissipation of Impressionism as an exhibitionary force in 1886, he was to spend the majority of his time. Aided by the expert horticultural knowledge of his friend Gustave Caillebotte, Monet created a vibrant and imaginative flower garden, and in the early 1890s, a Japanese-inspired water garden. It took some time, however, before the flowers and the water lily pond came to feature in Monet's painting. Monet's work in the early 1890s was instead focused on the grainstacks that dotted the farmyards around his house. Works such as *Grainstacks (Snow Effect)* (1891, *see* page 184) reveal just how far Monet had progressed since the peak of Impressionist naturalism in the 1870s and 1880s. No longer as concerned with modern life, Monet's interest in the ephemerality and transitory nature of light and the unifying 'envelope' of air itself has become predominant and exaggerated. Across the series, Monet revelled in abstract colour harmonies that transcended pure observation, of the kind that had attracted the Fauves. The repetitive simplicity of the motif, in conjunction with the often evocative atmospheric effects, appealed to the Symbolists as offering a vision of 'what lies beyond progress itself', as the critic Octave Mirbeau put it.

The flattened, decorative character of the grainstacks was to reappear in Monet's final (and perhaps most famous) series: *The Water Lilies* (1915–26, *see* pages 186–87). Of these late works, Monet wrote that '[t]he water flowers are far from being the whole scene, really they are just the accompaniment. The

Left : *Self Portrait*, 1890, Henri Rousseau (1844–1910)

Detail above : *Self-Portrait*, 1889, Paul Gauguin (1848–1903), *see page 154*

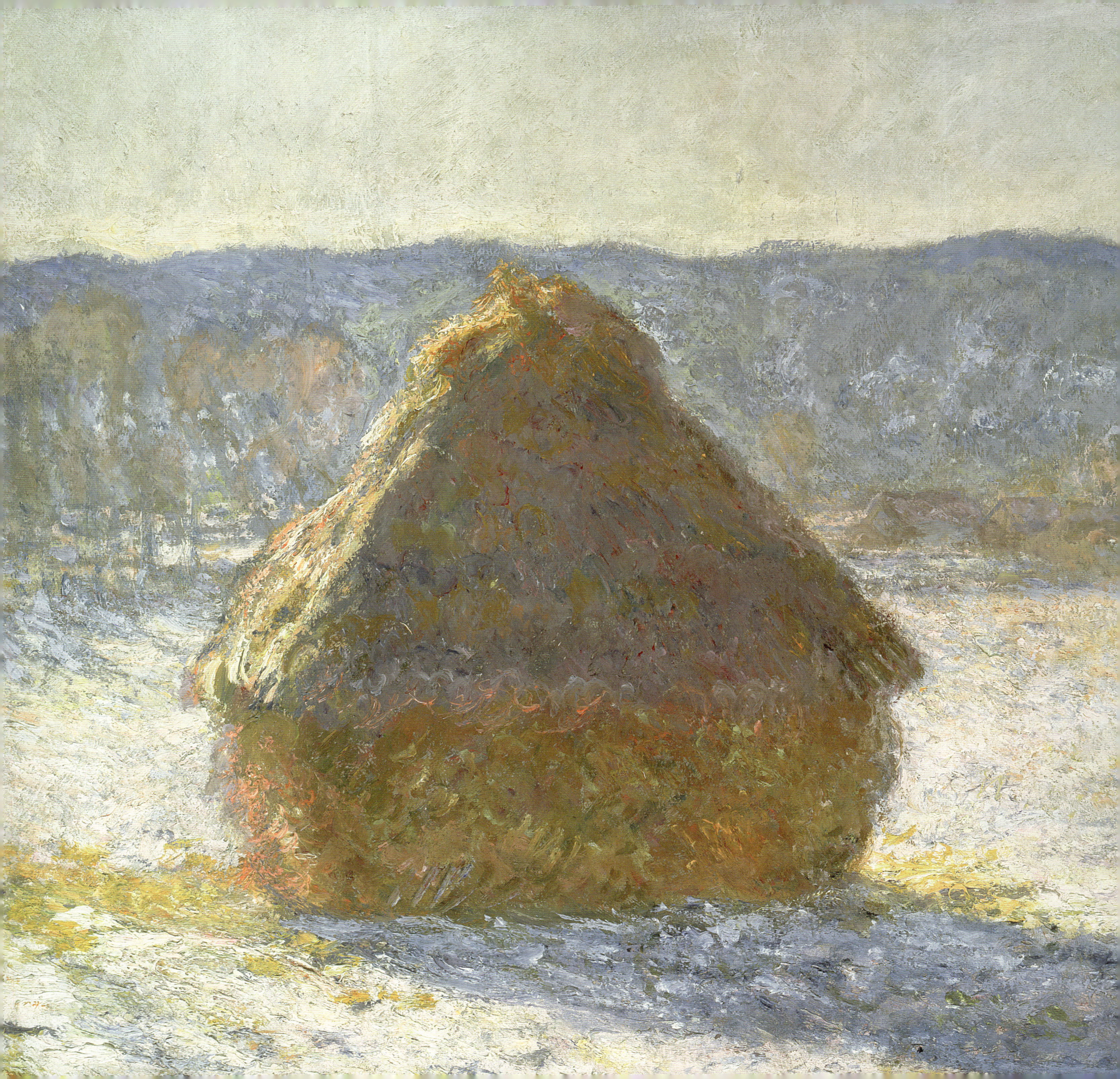

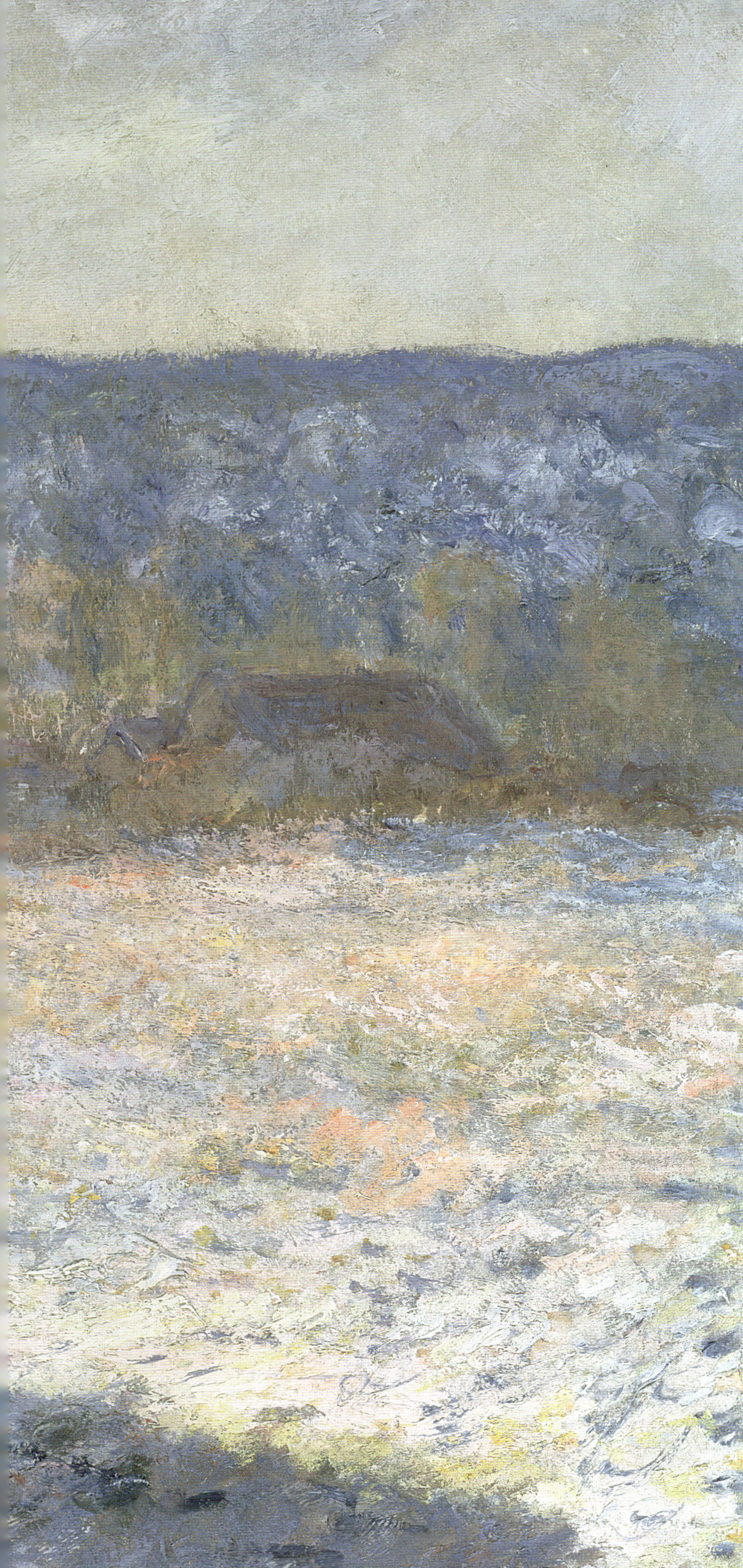

essence of the motif is the mirror of the water whose appearance alters at every moment, thanks to the patches of sky which are reflected in it, and which give it its light and movement.' Closely cropped to capture the light as it shimmered and shifted in the decontextualized mirror-surface of the pond, these canvases draw attention to their abstract and decorative flatness. Painted following the trauma of the First World War, this restorative cycle is Post-Impressionist not only in chronological terms, but also in its transcendence of description.

'The Impressionists focused their efforts around the eye, not in the mysterious centre of thought, and from there they slipped into scientific reasons... There is physics and metaphysics.'

Gauguin

Left : *Grainstacks (Snow Effect)*, 1891, Claude Monet (1840–1926)

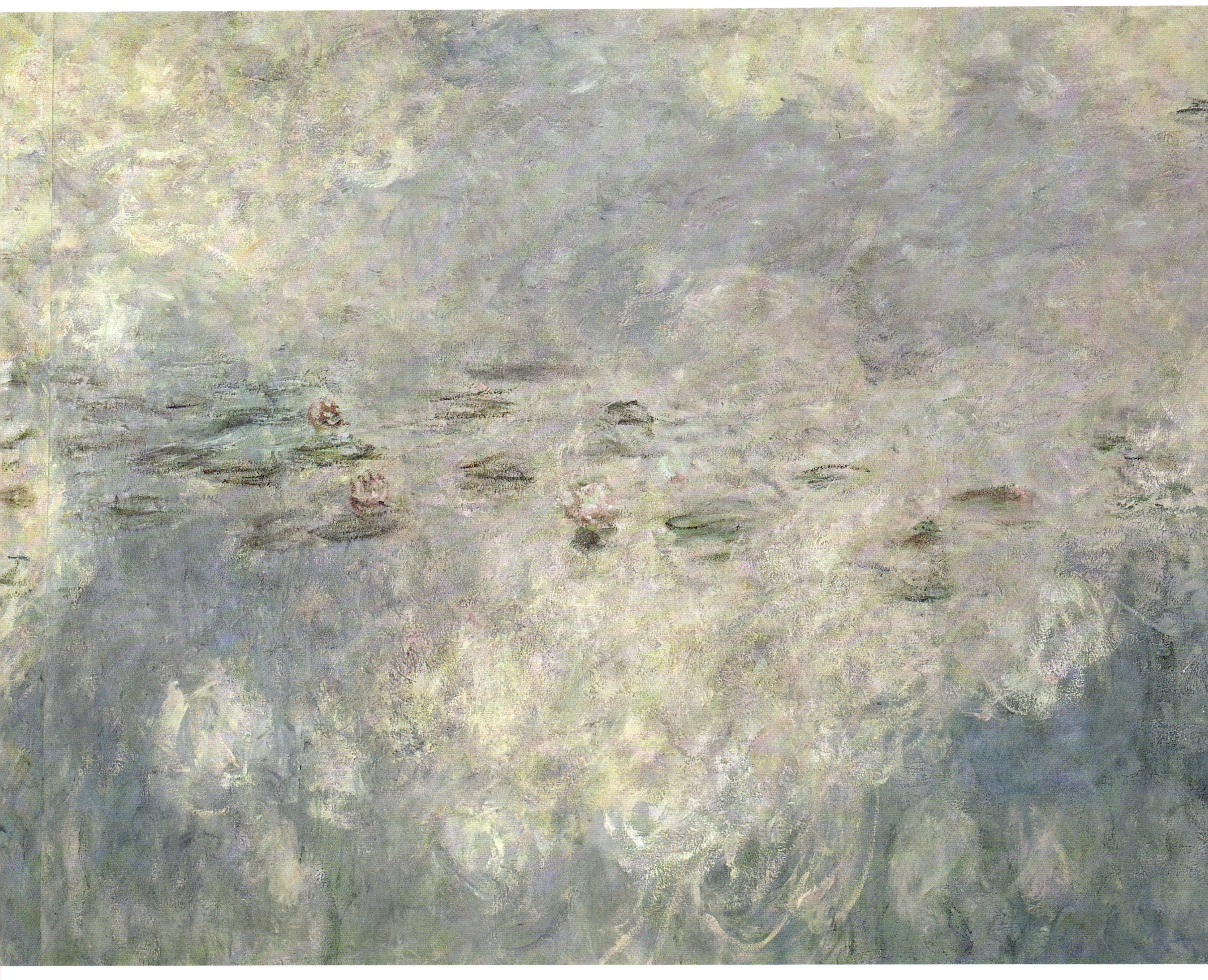

Above : *The Water Lilies – The Clouds* (central panel), 1915–26, Claude Monet (1840–1926)

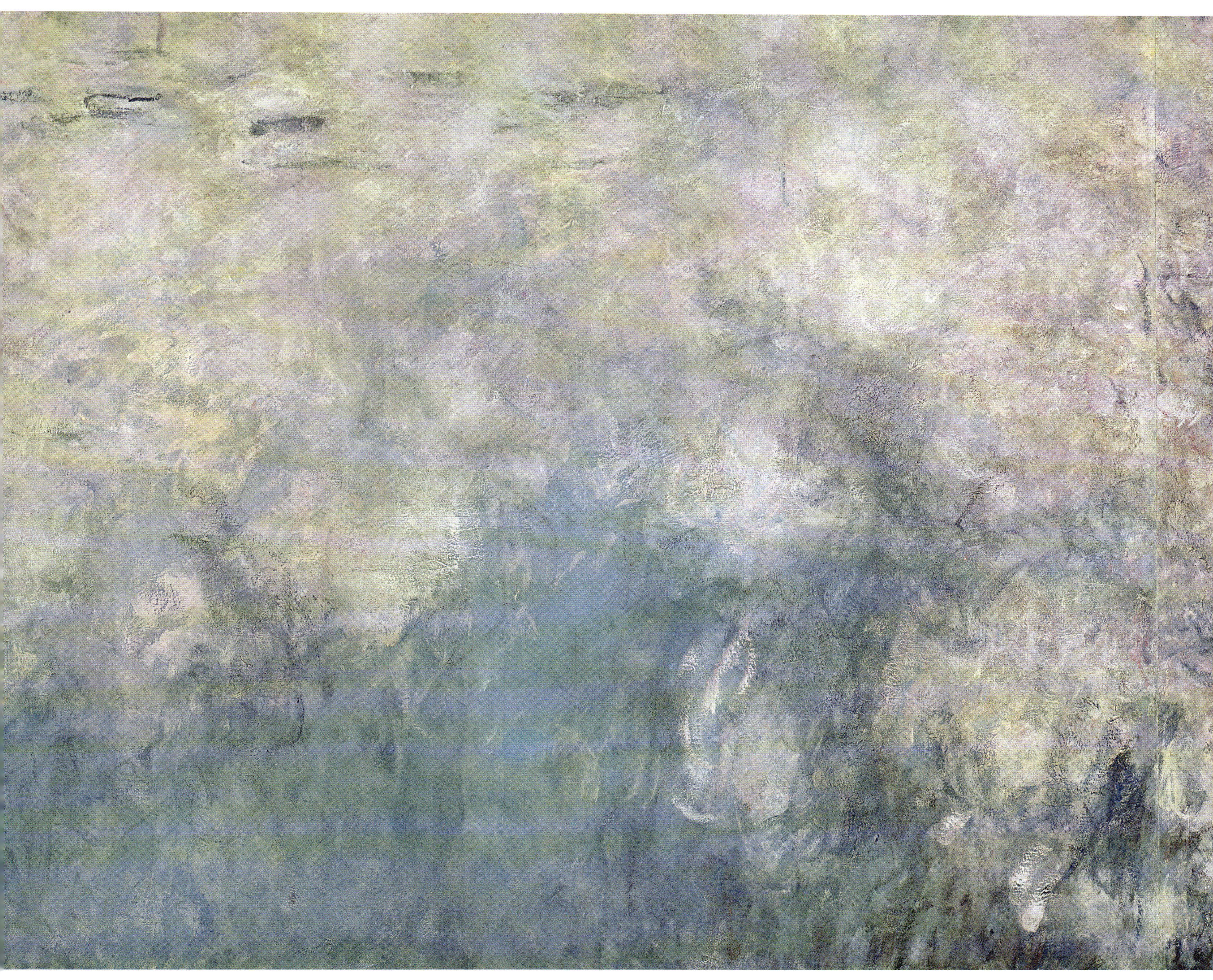

Further Reading

D'Souza, Aruna, *Cézanne's Bathers: Biography and the Erotics of Paint*, Pennsylvania: Penn State University Press, 2008

Danchev, Alex, *The Letters of Paul Cézanne*, London: Thames & Hudson, 2013

Dorra, Henri, *The Symbolism of Paul Gauguin: Erotica, Exotica, and the Great Dilemmas of Humanity*, Berkeley, Los Angeles, and London: University of California Press, 2007

Eisenman, Stephen, Thomas E. Crow, Brian Lukacher, Linda Nochlin, David L. Phillips and Frances K. Pohl, *Nineteenth Century Art: A Critical History*, 4th ed., London: Thames & Hudson, 2011

Foa, Michelle, *Georges Seurat: The Art of Vision*, New Haven and London: Yale University Press, 2015

Hutton, John, *Neo-Impressionism and the Search for Solid Ground: Art, Science and Anarchism in fin-de-siècle France*, Baton Rouge and London: Louisiana State University Press, 1994

Jansen, Leo, Hans Luijten and Nienke Bakker, 'Vincent van Gogh: The Letters': www.vangoghletters.org

Lucie-Smith, Edward, *Symbolist Art*, London: Thames & Hudson, 2001

Padiyar, Satish, ed., *Modernist Games: Cézanne and His Card Players*, London: Courtauld Books Online, 2013

Reff, Theodore, 'Cézanne's Constructive Stroke', *Art Quarterly* 25 (1962): pp214–227.

Rewald, John, *Post-Impressionism: from Van Gogh to Gauguin*. New York: Museum of Modern Art, 1978

Rubin, James Henry, *Impressionism*, London: Phaidon, 1999

Shiff, Richard, *Cézanne and the End of Impressionism: A Study of the Theory, Technique, and Critical Evaluation of Modern Art*, Chicago and London: University of Chicago Press, 1984

Silverman, Deborah, *Van Gogh and Gauguin: The Search for Sacred Art*, New York: Farrar, Straus and Giroux, 2000

Spretnak, Charlene, *The Spiritual Dynamism in Modern Art*, Palgrave MacMillan, 2014

Thomson, Belinda, *Post-Impressionism*, London: Tate Gallery Publishing, 1998

Thomson, Richard, *Seurat's Circus Sideshow*, New York: The Metropolitan Museum of Art, 2017

Acknowledgments

Samuel Raybone (author) read History at Durham University before completing an MA and PhD in the History of Art at the Courtauld Institute of Art. His doctoral research centred on Gustave Caillebotte in the context of late-nineteenth-century class and labour politics, bringing to light the artist's myriad labours and the complexities of his class-bound alienation. His wider research connects Impressionism, Naturalism, and Post-Impressionism to the broader sphere of visual culture. Samuel teaches at the Courtauld Institute and Oxford University.

Gavin Parkinson (foreword) was a BA student in Manchester, then completed his MA at The Courtauld in 1997, followed by a PhD in 2000. After lecturing at Birkbeck College and the University of Oxford, he joined The Courtauld teaching staff as a Lecturer in 2008 and became a Senior Lecturer in 2014. Gavin's teaching and writing are concerned with European art and visual culture of the nineteenth and twentieth centuries, with a special interest in French Surrealism. His books are: *Futures of Surrealism: Myth, Science Fiction and Fantastic Art in France 1936–69* (Yale University Press, 2015); *Surrealism, Art and Modern Science: Relativity, Quantum Mechanics, Epistemology* (Yale University Press, 2008); and *The Duchamp Book* (Tate Publishing, 2008). He is just completing a book on the Surrealist reception of late-nineteenth-century art, entitled *Enchanted Ground: Surrealist Appraisals of Fin de Siècle Painting*.

Picture Credits

Detail right : *A Studio in the Batignolles Quarter*, 1870, Henri Fantin-Latour (1836–1904), *see page 12*

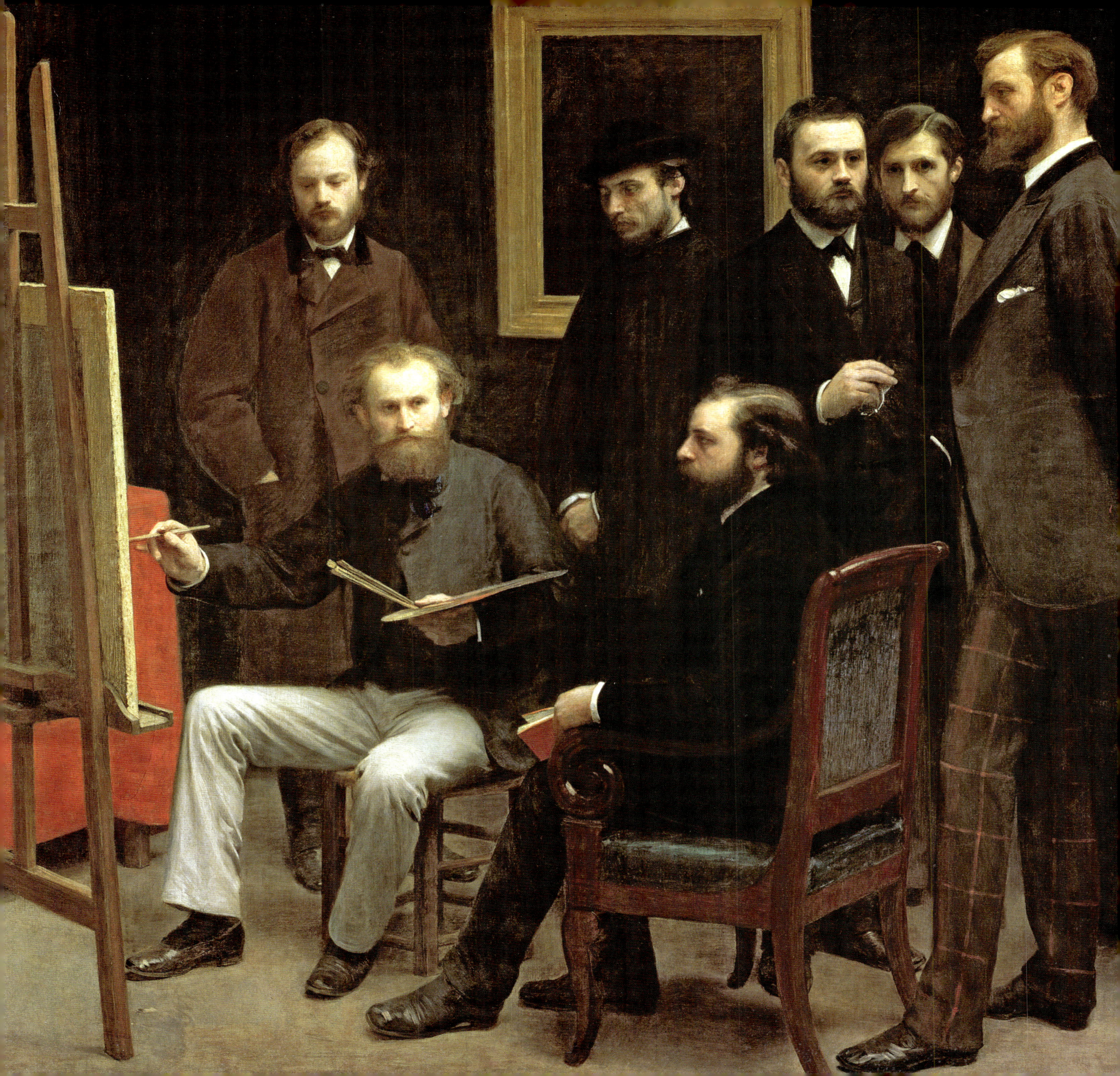

Index

Page numbers in *italics* refer to illustrations.

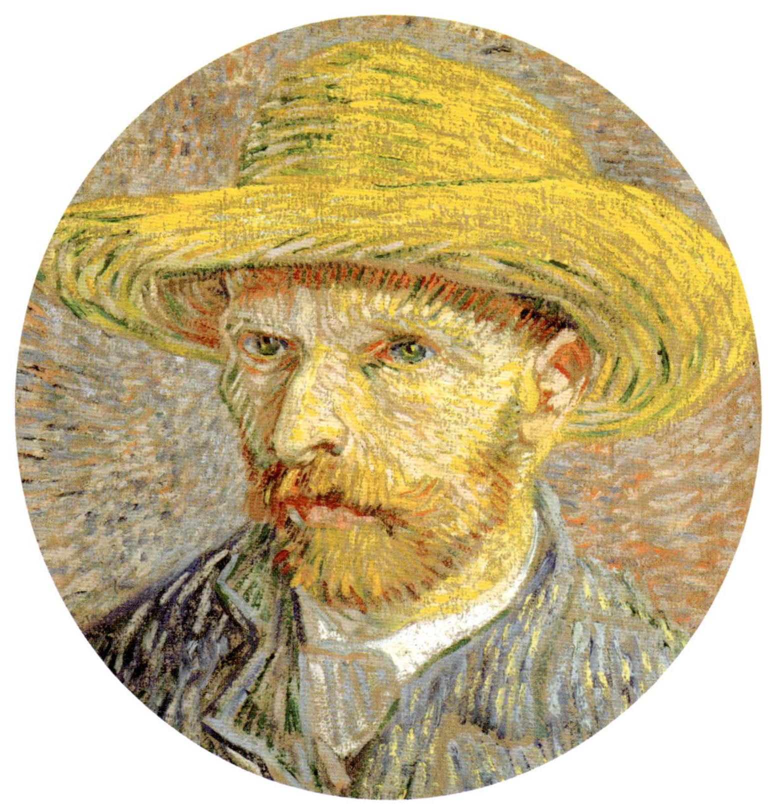

For further information about art, artists and art movements
please visit our blog where we have a wide range of articles:

blog.flametreepublishing.com

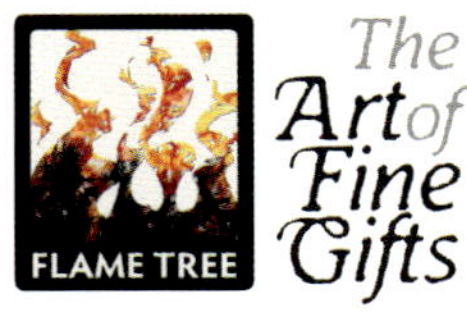